The Gnostic

A Journal of Gnosticism, Western Esotericism and Spirituality

Issue 4

Copyright Page and Acknowledgments

The Gnostic 4, Early 2011.

Editor: Andrew Phillip Smith

Published by Bardic Press
71 Kenilworth Park
Dublin 6W
Ireland.

ISBN: 978-1-906834-06-7

Thanks to the contributors and all others who have made this possible, including but not limited to: Tessa Finn, Lance Owens, Stephan Hoeller, Laurence Caruana, Sean Martin, Chris Staros, Alan Moore, Miguel Conner, Bill Darlison, Anthony Peake, Samer Muscati, Robert M. Price, Jeremy Puma, Mike Grenfell, Petra Mundik, Jorunn Buckley, W.W. Norton & Co., Quest Books, Watkins Books, Harvard University Press, Oxford University Press, The Grey House in the Woods, Hay House, Skylight Paths, Inner Traditions, Columbia Univesity Press, Mandrake Press, Harper Collins.

The Gnostic

A Journal of Gnosticism, Western Esotericism and Spirituality

Issue 4

Alan Moore, Laurence Caruana,
Stephan Hoeller, Anthony Peake, Rob-
ert M. Price, Miguel Conner, Sean
Martin, Bill Darlison, Jeremy Puma,
Mike Grenfell, Petra Mundik, Samer
Muscati, et al

Edited by Andrew Phillip Smith

Bardic Press
Dublin 2011

Contents

Editorial

From the Mouth of the Demiurge

After the doom and gloom of last issue's editorial I made a funeral pyre of my remaining copies of the first three issues of *The Gnostic* and lit it, determined to raze them from existence. Yet what should emerge but a flaming phoenix, burning with energy and renewal. Here then in May 2011 is issue 4, six months to the day after issue 3 (published July 2010.) Adorned with daffodils and other Spring flowers, surrounded by new-born lambs, which baa with joy, floppy-eared bunnies frolic through its pages, breathing the sweet air of— alas—the fallen material world.

This has turned out to be a very Gnostic issue of *The Gnostic*. We interview Stephan Hoeller, bishop of the Ecclesia Gnostica and perhaps the most influential figure in the revival of Gnosticism, and Miguel Conner, host of *Aeon Byte*, himself interviewer extraordinaire. (See his interviews with John Turner, April DeConick and Daniel Matt in issues 1,2 and 3 and the wealth of the interviews collected in *Voices of Gnosticism*.) Radical scholar Robert M. Price examines the Gospel of John. Anthony Peake's talent in drawing profound human meaning from the cutting edge of science results in the suggestion of a real pleroma just below the surface of the material universe. Petra Mundik's long article about Gnostic themes in Cormac McCarthy's *Blood Meridian* emphasises the harsh fallen world. Bill Darlison looks at the astrological hinterland of the Gospel of Mark, and Mike Grenfell looks at the author John Cowper Powys.

Laurence Caruana, also the author of the Gnostic-inspired novel *The Hidden Passion*, contributes his visionary art.

This has been a strange issue. Along with the usual delays and procrastination I discovered on one and the same day that Alan Moore had given permission for us to include his blistering critique of the occult scene, "Fossil Angels," and that one of our contributors had been sending his submissions from prison, enduring a 21 year sentence for sexual assault on a child.

Reginald Freeman, formerly a bishop in the Ecclesia Gnostics Catholica Hermetica, had submitted two articles and two reviews for this issue plus a long piece for issue 5 and had contributions published in issue 3. His biography only mentioned that he was "currently living a cloistered life in the U.S. Midwest." It emerged that Reggie had been giving his typewritten submissions, along with the text of his emails, to his mother, who was scanning them in and emailing them to me from Reggie's address. It should be noted that Reggie protests his innocence, and that I consider his sentence to be extreme. But, given the published information on the trial, something did happen and Reggie confessed to it. Thus I feel unable to include his well-researched and intelligent pieces. My concerns are not merely those of respectability but I felt that he was deceptive in concealing his situation and I was quite disturbed by the gulf between his possible sexual crime and his high-minded esoterica. I wish Reggie well but urge him to be honest about his situation, either to acknowledge his actions if he is guilty or otherwise work on clearing his name.

Andrew Phillip Smith

An Interview with Stephan Hoeller

Stephan Hoeller is probably the single most influential figure in modern Gnosticism. Born in Hungary, he attended university in Innsbruck, Austria after the communist takeover and moved to the United States, where he still resides, in 1952. A Theosophist and Freemason, he founded his Gnostic Church, eventually titled the Ecclesia Gnostica, in 1959. He is the author of several books, including *The Gnostic Jung and the Seven Sermons to the Dead* (1982), *Jung and the Lost Gospels* (1989) and *Gnosticism: New Light on the Ancient Tradition of Inner Knowing* (2002).

SH: If I may do so, I want to congratulate you on the magazine. It is a terrific idea and it is a terrific magazine. It was something that was so greatly needed and something that we haven't had around ever, so far as I'm aware of, so you're doing a wonderful thing with that as well as some of your other publications with Bardic Press—*Voices of Gnosticism* and things like that. It's very nice material.

APS: Thanks very much. Perhaps we could start with an overview of your life.

SH: Oh dear! Like most aged gentlemen I am working on my autobiography, so if I live long enough to complete it and if it ever gets published, he and others may have a more complete view of it. My life, especially as these matters are concerned, for some curious reasons, which are maybe a little too intricate to go into, I became really interested in Gnosticism at a very early age, in my teens, and I have been on the hunt for the Gnostics ever since. When you are that much interested in something and have such an intense interest, undoubtedly you

will find it. And I continued to seek and to find and eventually when I left my own country, which was Hungary and which came under communist rule after the war, when I left there I spent a little less than a year—this would be in 1947—in Belgium. And in Belgium by sheer accident, if there are any accidents, I actually met some people who considered themselves contemporary Gnostics, and who were connected with the French Gnostic Church. These folk then turned me on to quite a bit of literature and various sources of information on the subject. Although I did not stay in Belgium, they were very helpful to me in terms of guiding me along these lines subsequently.

APS: You mentioned that there were some intricate circumstances surrounding your earliest interest in Gnosticism. What were the very first writings that you read, and how did you discover the Gnostics?

SH: Well, I had some dreams quite early in life. As time went on, by happenstance I was reading an encyclopedia and the books in my parents' library I recognised that the themes of these dreams were of a Gnostic nature. Or at least that the Gnostics held views that seemed to be in accordance with these dreams, and that really fired me up on the search. So those were really the earliest circumstances. They were very personal, and really had to do with my own personal experiences rather than anything else. But then, of course, I was searching for the relevant and confirming material in objective sources.

APS: How did these first modern Gnostics that you met strike you?

SH: They were very urbane, very nice gentleman. They were all men, at least the ones I met, Belgians, who had worked with the French Gnostic Church—Belgium and France are very close together—and were really very sincerely interested in the tradition, and they weren't just flakey people who had appropriated the name Gnostic. They were very serious about their interest and their devotion to their tradition. So they were very nice honourable people. Members of society, professional people, business men, people like that.

APS: So you met them in Belgium, and then what was the next stage in your development?

SH: In the next stage, I lived for a number of years in Austria, and I completed much of my schooling there. And of course much of my interest in Gnosticism continued, but about the closest I could come to it in terms of books and things of that sort was Theosophy. So I contacted the Austrian Theosophists, and there were always some among them who were more interested in the western tradition and in Gnosticism, and they in turn supplied me with literature and things of that sort, and then in 1952 I came to the United States and here too I joined the Theosophical Society—I've been a member of the Theosophical Society about 58 years now—and there I found a good framework and surroundings where I could continue my interest in the Gnostic tradition and in the esoteric traditions that relate to it.

APS: What do you think now of Madame Blavatsky's contribution, and particularly G.R.S. Mead's contribution to the study of Gnosticism?

SH: I think that these people, Blavatsky and her disciple—he was her last personal secretary I believe—Mead, he had done a tremendous amount for the revival of the Gnostic tradition and it would seem really that for the most part Blavatsky, even though she had access to very little Gnostic material, had at an intuitive level caught the content and the meaning and the thrust of the Gnostic effort and the Gnostic tradition in a very, very splendid way. There was a book some years ago edited by a Dutch

Theosophist Spielenberg, on Blavatsky and the Gnostics which contains all the quotations from Blavatsky throughout her various works about Gnosticism. It's a large book and I would say for the most part very, very accurate. And of course Mead was inspired by, one might say, her Gnosis, and he devoted himself in a very scholarly way—I think he was an Oxford man to begin with—a very good Latin and Greek scholar, to the sources and has done a tremendous amount to produce readable and enjoyable material from Gnostic sources and about the Gnostics. I think that his books are still of extremely great value along these lines.

APS: His *Pistis Sophia* still seems to be the most popular translation.

SH: His *Pistis Sophia* still continues to be published. Everything that he did was really, really fine. There is a book of his, ten little books, called *Echoes from the Gnosis*, which has been republished recently, within the last few years, that has very, very fine material in it. And *Fragments of a Faith Forgotten*, which has not been republished, is also a wonderful collection of translations of the then available Gnostic scriptures and references to the Gnostics in patristic literature, and so forth.

APS: Quest did *Echoes From the Gnosis*, and you provided new introductions, didn't you? *Fragments* is actually in print in a dozen different, mostly poor-quality editions.

SH: Maybe eventually it will appear in a better edition also. But certainly, these people, the Theosophists, have done a great deal to call attention to the Gnostics and rehabilitate the Gnostics and the Gnostic tradition, which was very greatly needed—perhaps is still greatly needed now.

APS: And what was the next step in your Gnostic journey after going to the USA and being involved with the Theosophical Society?

SH: Well, I suppose the next step was that I was involved with the Theosophists, and to a lesser extent with the Liberal Catholic Church, and then I was advised that there was a Gnostic Bishop in England, Richard de Palatine, and

that he would be coming to the United States. Then I met him and we became quite friendly. And under his auspices, and with his guidance, I started the Gnostic Church, and a also a Gnostic educational forum called the Gnostic Society, which had actually existed before but had gone underground. And I've been working within that framework ever since.

APS: What was Richard de Palatine like as a man?

SH: Well, you know, like so many of these people he was an unusual person. He was certainly a person of great inspiration and great charisma. He also had some personal peculiarities that were maybe sometimes difficult to deal with, but on the whole I'm extremely grateful to him and for having met him, for he set me on a certain path and straightened out my ideas in certain ways which I feel were very helpful. He was a prophetic figure who had in his own way also done a great deal for the revival of the tradition in our days, and after all most of his work was done prior to the availability of the Nag Hammadi materials. So all of these people really needed a good deal of inspiration and intuition—Blavatsky, Mead, others—to really discern the core of the Gnostic tradition when there was really so little available literature of an authentic nature.

APS: Looking back at yourself at that time, as you said with very little reliable information in comparison to what we have today, how do you feel that the Nag Hammadi literature has affected your view of Gnosticism?

SH: Well, of course, by way of a somewhat trite contemporary metaphor, one could say that prior to the availability of the Nag Hammadi Library materials we were looking at looking at a small 12" television screen and then all of a sudden it opens up to cinemascope proportions. Which really means that in essence, in terms of the essential message of the gnostic tradition, we had the right idea, we had the right material to discern the essence if we were capable of doing so, if we were thus disposed, if we were sympathetic enough, but then the amplifying

source material became so much larger that we had a wonderful wealth of Gnostic materials available now, which also made the Gnostic tradition much more accessible and defused some of the severe and antagonistic criticism which had come of course originally from the heresiologist church fathers, and which had lingered on and still lingers on, although Nag Hammadi has to a very large extent defanged these attacks. I had a very interesting experience in that regard subsequently with Dr James Robinson who became really a friend. He's retired now and I don't see him as often, but he was initially of course quite influenced by the heresiologist material, and then as the Nag Hammadi material became available, which he had helped really, magnificently, to publish and to work with, then his attitude to Gnosticism became more and more mellow and more and more sympathetic. I think this was true of a lot of scholars and it was true of the general public as well.

APS: Do you remember the first time you came across the new Nag Hammadi discovery and the new materials?

SH: Well, of course I was here in America already. I can't be entirely certain, but it was in the fifties, and then the first publication appeared, which was the Gospel of Thomas, in the Harper edition which was translated by a whole number of people, Gilles Quispel being one, Puech, Till, and a Coptic man, and that was really the first Nag Hammadi scripture that became available to us. I heard of the discovery quite a bit earlier. Soon after I arrived here in the States, and then I heard that there was wrangling going on over who's going to translate, and who owns it, and that sort of thing. There was a certainly rivalry and conflict between the European scholars and the Americans But eventually, under Robinson's guidance, they managed to publish the entire material. It was published in a translation and in a format that became available to the general public, which was extremely important, because when these publications came out of Holland by E.J. Brill, the very cost, the very price that one had to pay for those books was prohibitive.

APS: When exactly did you establish your church?

SH: We began working in the church around 1958. We have been working with it ever since.

APS: Do you have any particular memories of those early years?

SH: Well, the early years were different. The interest was less. The number of people who would come to lectures and church services was smaller. And there were also aspects of the Gnostic materials, the Gnostic teachings, that were very difficult to communicate and that we sometimes just kept quiet about for a while until people were more used to it. Teachings about the demiurge, teachings about the corrupt and evil nature of the world, these were all rather unpopular teachings at the time. But somehow as time went on this has changed. Some of it I think had to do perhaps with the conditions in the world, and the conditions in society. It somehow seems much easier for people now to contemplate the possibility that this world was put together and is being managed by agencies that are not altogether nice and altogether wise. It seems that idea comes much more easily to people now, with much less resistance, than was the case, shall we say, in the 1950s, or even in the earlier part of the 1960s.

APS: In the sixties, with the counterculture and everything, I should think that there might well have been a surge of interest in Gnosticism, but at the same time it was such a naïve and optimistic period.

SH: The interest in matters of this sort, let's say of a very generalised Gnostic interest, definitely existed, but I think the difficulty then again was precisely this kind of naïve, starry-eyed optimism, the expectation of a marvellous new age that would come very, very quickly, and things of that description Also perhaps the somewhat competing teachings and ideologies of eastern origin, which did not harmonise entirely with gnostic ideas. A lot of interest in reincarnation and karma, which are not really Gnostic ideas. Professor Quispel, of blessed memory, said once to us, when questioned on that particular matter, said, "Reincarnation perhaps, karma no." A typical categorical Dutch answer. But I think he was right. So there are differences between much of the eastern and western presentation. The gurus were here in large numbers and attracting large crowds, but at the same time, in our own modest way we were also attracting people, so certainly the sixties phenomenon, which extended into the seventies, was to our advantage, there's no doubt about it.

APS: Were there any figures from the late sixties and the seventies who particularly impressed you, either way, either as fakes or as sincere people?

SH: You mean teachers and teachings?

APS: Yes.

SH: Well a number of schools of thought and inner activity that came into some degree of prominence at that time were related to Gnostic thought. The Gurdjieff Work, I think, is a form of Gnosis. The various spin-offs from the theosophical movement have a relationship. Krishnamurti was defined by a friend of mine as a protestant Gnostic, in the sense of being opposed to ritual and things of that sort, but having ideas that are at their core very Gnostic in nature. And it has been pointed out by various scholars, beginning with the late and great Edward Conze, Buddhism, especially Tibetan Buddhism, has very powerful similarities with Gnosticism. It has been called, I think justly, the Gnosis of Asia. Hinduism I think to a lesser degree, except for some teachings. So there were certainly kindred ideas and kindred movements floating around in the culture, and of course they are still there in various ways at the present time.

APS: The publication of Nag Hammadi led to a great deal of interest in Gnosticism. When did you notice that more people were being attracted to Gnosticism and having more knowledge of it?

SH: Well, the English popular translation was published, I think, around 1977. But reverberations of it were around earlier because people had access to portions of the material. So

I would say that Nag Hammadi did not really begin to impact the culture probably until the 1980s.

APS: Which was quite a materialistic time.

SH: In some ways, Yes. But one always has to realise that even in materialistic times there is always a stratum of people who are aspiring to higher and better things. And when there is a certain amount of material prosperity abroad in the land, people are making money, and when they are making money some of them will buy books as well with that money. They will go to lectures and classes and things of that sort. It's never entirely a bad situation.

APS: And then we have in the nineties we have the emergence of virtual reality as a very appropriate fictional tool for Gnostic themes.

SH: Yes, developments of that sort at the most subtle and psychological level have created an atmosphere of great receptivity to Gnostic ideas. And also by the later eighties and the nineties, the exegetical literature, the interpretations of Nag Hammadi started really appearing in print, and they have been a great help. Elaine Pagels' *The Gnostic Gospels* came out soon after the Nag Hammadi translation itself was published, and popularised the Nag Hammadi materials to a great extent. Then one by one the interpreters, the exegetes, came forward, and while some of that was strictly on an academic level, but not all. Certainly *The Gnostic Gospels* was a popular book.

APS: Looking back at your life, which people have influenced you the most, or impressed, you, of those who you have met personally?

SH: Oh dear, that's a difficult one . . .

APS: Well, you don't have to give a ranking! Just mention some.

SH: Certainly I regard Richard de Palatine as one of my primary teachers. But there were a number of very fine people that I met in the Theosophical Society who were greatly interested in these matters. A writer by the name of Alvin Boyd Kuhn, whom I knew quite well—of course, all of these people were vastly older than myself so

they passed out of my life fairly rapidly. Alvin Boyd Kuhn, Professor Ernest Wood, who was an expert on Eastern teachings but who also, let's say, knew what Gnosis was like. And a number of others. Then later on I met the great Gnostic scholar Quispel, who became a friend of ours in the Gnostic movement. Whenever he came to America he visited us and gave lectures to us. Without having had personal contact with him, to a monumental degree Carl Jung, whom I considered to be a Gnostic prophet from the time I first read some of his material, and I think my intuitions in that regard have been justified, especially recently by the publication of his Red Book.

APS: That's been attracting a lot of interest.

SH: Oh yes. I have been lecturing and writing about Jung in a Gnostic context for a long time. My book *The Gnostic Jung and the Seven Sermons to the Dead* appeared in 1983 and it became a kind of minor little classic, and it was quite well received by the Jungian community, which I did not expect. The Jungians were still quite reluctant at that time to own up to Jung's Gnostic interest, but certainly it was very well received, and then I followed it with *Jung and the Lost Gospels*. So my involvement with Jung in a Gnostic context has been a long one, and I have felt all along that Gnostic material just about dilated Jung's books, and practically every one of Jung's books is heavily saturated with Gnostic materials. But I think the full justification of that point of view only came about now with the publication of the Red Book.

APS: If you were to critique Jung's interpretation of Gnosticism, what would you say? For Jung everything is psychological.

SH: Of course, a lot of people have said that, but I don't think that his approach to Gnosticism was ever really guilty of what people call psychologisms. Psychology, so it would seem, was really mainly an avenue for him to express and to amplify certain insights which came out of his own Gnosis. He was a psychologist. He became known as that. He was the second most important advocate of the depth psychological movement after Freud, and this was a way for him to express what he had experienced. His experiences are catalogues in the Red Book. Now of course he was not the exact same kind of Gnostic as Valentinus or Basilides or Carpocrates or any of those old boys, but that's understandable because he lived in this particular time. He was a modern Gnostic. But I believe Gnostic he was, and the most essential core recognitions of the Gnostic tradition are all present within and very well represented by his writings.

APS: I've always been a little puzzled that he said that he detested metaphysics.

SH: Well, here again one has to see those things in context. He lived in an era—he was born in 1875, so in the last 25 years of the nineteenth century and in the early twentieth century when esoterica, let's say, were very heavily intellectual and speculative in nature. This is true of much of Theosophy, certainly of the anthroposophy of Rudolf Steiner and of many other schools. I think that this kind of speculative occult metaphysics was obnoxious to Jung. Primarily because it had no experiential basis. So he felt that this kind of speculative metaphysics acted as a kind of barrier to the kind of personal, individual experience that in ancient days was called Gnosis. One might say with some degree of justification that many of the Gnostic scriptures contain teachings which could be called metaphysical. This is true. But Jung, I believe, felt, and I certainly do that the teaching, the myths and other teachings in the Gnostic scriptures are the result of experience. So they are ways in which the Gnostic experiences were, if we can use that trite word, processed, were amplified and explained by the Gnostic seers and teachers, rather than the other way around. But your average Theosophist, Anthroposophist and others becomes infatuated with the intellectual metaphysics and does not go beyond it. Although I am sure that that was not the case with Blavatsky and a few others. I think that's where the great difference lies. When Jung took a look at the Gnostics—and this was documented by Quispel and others—

he in essence said, "This is not speculation. This is not philosophising. *Philosophoumena*, as the Church Fathers called it. These are the results of intensely felt inner experience. I can tell because I'm a psychologist." Of course, he could tell because he had experiences of an analogous nature himself. So he felt that really the Gnostic scriptures were really very different to metaphysical speculation as he encountered in the occult world in his time.

APS: An interesting comparison there. I would say that the Theosophical cosmology is obviously very static. It stayed as it was at the tie of Blavatsky, for the most part, whereas the Gnostic was continuously developing.

SH: It is a fairly common contention of scholarship that one must study these materials to a considerable extent within the context of their time. And so there has to be a historical and sociological and intellectual context, and one must realise that the nineteenth century when the Theosophical teachings were enunciated and formulated was an extremely intellectual era. Everything was concept, concept and precept, but very little experience. So one has to have some understanding of that in an historical sense. But at the same time, I think that in the present time a lot of, as you say, rigid and highly complicated cosmological material is somewhat irrelevant.

APS: Modern Theosophical societies are involved in all sorts of ideas and researches.

SH: There has been an opening to various contemporary ideas, and there are a lot of good people around, but that was really the difference between Jung and the occult scene of his time. Also I think he was particularly annoyed by a couple of occult schools, historically speaking. One of them being Alice Bailey, who established her school for a period of time in Switzerland, and who he felt was most particularly in this metaphysical, categorical mood. Then the other one was Rudolf Steiner. And Jung's wife Emma had actually a considerable interest in Steiner, who again was living and teaching in Switzerland. He was next door.

APS: Ah, I didn't realise that.

SH: Also, all of these people had a core of Gnosis, but what constellated itself around that Gnosis became a barrier to Gnosis rather than helpful material that would lead to Gnosis. This is always something that has to be watched.

APS: I don't think very highly of Steiner's cosmology and all that, but it obviously worked for him and enabled him to achieve so much in so many different areas.

SH: Oh yes, there's a lot of interesting material there. Obviously there would have been a considerable difference between Jung's experiential, psychological approach and Steiner's highly metaphysical and highly abstract approach. And also highly personalised, because Steiner was so much involved in the late-nineteenth-century, early-twentieth-century concepts of clairvoyance, that he was constantly reporting from the Akashic Records and no one can duplicate that, no one can say yes or no, because they don't have access to his sources of information, and that becomes a problem.

APS: It's a great tool for authority.

SH: The Anthroposophists have a joke about it: Der Doktor hat gesagt. "The doctor said so," which is the last word on everything.

APS: You mentioned Quispel as well. He was unusual in having a personal sympathy with the Gnostic teachings.

SH: Oh Yes. He was really sympathetic, and his sympathy became more and more evident after he retired from teaching, which is true of a lot of these professors, when they no longer jeopardise their standing. When he lectured for us, he always addressed us as "My fellow Gnostics." So he was definitely there, and one of the interesting things about him being there was he was very close to Jung. He was really Jung's principle advisor on matters Gnostic. He was the one who discovered the Jung Codex in an antiquary shop in Belgium, and then rushed to Switzerland to tell Jung, "We have the Gospel of Truth, the gospel of Valentinus." Because it had been mentioned in patristic literature as

being authored by Valentinus. So Jung made efforts with his contacts to purchase what became the Jung Codex, Codex I of the Nag Hammadi library which eventually, certainly to my great regret, they returned to Egypt, where the Egyptian government neglects the Coptic Museum where these things are. Why? Because it's Christian stuff. Even a taxi cab driver told some friends of mine who went there, "Why would you want to go to the Coptic Museum? That's not interesting. You should go to the Egyptian Museum where the pharoahs are."

At any rate, Quispel was very unique in one respect in that he was not a psychologist. He was not an analyst. He was not a Zurich school graduate. But he accepted Jung's quasi-psychological approach to Gnosticism. He was somewhat derogated because of that by his fellow scholars, but he stuck by his guns and he said that one experiences Gnosis through one's psyche. Therefore the psyche and the psyche's activities in connection with Gnosis are extremely important. And I think that is something that cannot be denied. He was an interesting gentleman.

APS: Do you remember any other particular insights from Quispel?

SH: He regarded—he and his wife, who also knew Jung—regarded Jung very, very highly and it was true of all the early associates of Jung, that even though they didn't know about the Red Book, or things of that sort, they intuitively sensed, having been exposed to Jung's presence, that they were in the presence of something very high and unusual. That they were dealing not just with a shrink, but that they were dealing with a very, very insightful, very profound and really prophetic figure. And Quispel definitely knew that, and he didn't mind saying it now and then either. So I think that he was a very important influence in the scholarly community. It worked both ways. He was able to convey to the scholarly community at least some measure of the validity of Jung's approach to Gnosis, and he was at the same time also able to convey the value of Gnosis and of Gnosticism to the Jungian community. So he was a mediator between the two.

APS: Which contemporary academics do you most admire?

SH: I think that the person in whom we Gnostics have the highest hopes—my kind of Gnostics—is Marvin Meyer, who of course teaches here in southern California at Chapman University in Orange County, and we have had some contact with him for a long time, because he was an assistant to Jim Robinson in Claremont years ago, around the time of the publication of Nag Hammadi, and all of that. And I think that Meyer is both an excellent scholar and a person of great intuitive sympathy for the Nag Hammadi material that he's studying. That kind of combination is not easily come by. I think Pagels had great merit with some of her publications, but I do have a little bit of a bone to pick with her. I met her long ago in Claremont when she was a young lady, but she and Karen King have gotten on the bandwagon of Professor Williams, who made a big case that the terms Gnostic and Gnosticism should not be used. Well, you know, if it walks like a Gnostic and talks like a Gnostic and quacks like a Gnostic it is a Gnostic. If it is justified to call members of the hundreds of Christian sects Christian, who differ from each other in so many things, then I think it is justified to call the people who share at least a core of basic recognition, it is justified to call them by a common name. And Meyer has pointed out on the basis of patristic literature, coming primarily from Irenaeus, that we have a record that there were people at that time, back in the second century who called themselves Gnostics. Marvin Meyer has pointed this out in several of his books and articles. So he stands on that side while Pagels and Karen King stand on the other side. It's not really that important, but it is still important to some extent. Because to say that this was just another alternative Christianity takes the energy, takes the guts out of the Gnostic tradition. It also minimises its uniqueness, which I think is really there. Now,

if it walks like a Gnostic and talks like a Gnostic and quacks like a Gnostic it is a Gnostic.

if I may say so, at the time that the Gnostics were around, when they were working in the second and third centuries, the fourth century maybe, they were not as unique as all that, because there were of course Hermetists, there were neoplatonists, there were probably some sorts of proto-Kabbalists around, and they al shared the same basic belief—more than belief, probably realisation—namely an emanationist view of reality, not creationist, but emanationist, and connected with that emanation view the presence in the depth of the human soul of a totally transcendent divine spark, the celestial twin, which if one managed to contact, one was actually in contact with the divine. So this kind of thing was around. You even find it in Mithraism. It was a particular orientation towards spirituality that was predominantly present it what is referred to as late antiquity. But then as time went on it was no longer there, and even today I think this point of view has a certain uniqueness of its own. Owing particularly to Nag Hammadi it's the Gnostic branch of this particular esoteric tradition that has come into prominence now. Just as the Hermetic came into prominence right around the time of the Renaissance as the result of the rediscovery of the Hermetic writings, and their translation in Italy by Ficino and people like that. So the Gnostic scriptures are doing now what the Hermetic scriptures did then. But then to reduce the uniqueness of the Gnostic tradition to just another alternative Christianity is inaccurate. I conclude my ranting on that subject.

APS: The deconstruction of Gnosticism was a question I had on my list anyway.

SH: Deconstruction. Well, from a personal point of view, as a student of philosophy and culture, I regard deconstructionism not very highly. It looks to me like an intellectual fad rather than anything else. Much of it is politically a kind of crypto-Marxist in its undertones. I have very little use for the deconstructionists. Let's say if you take the deconstructionism

Holy Sophia Chapel of the Ecclesia Gnostica, Los Angeles, California.

out of this contemporary faddish context then you might say that at least a certain aspect of the Gnostic tradition is a deconstruction of the monotheistic Jewish and Christian, even Islamic framework. The Gnostics are able, and have from time to time have deconstructed much of that framework and so that is perhaps a relationship. Somewhat like the relationship of Gnosticism to existentialism, which was recognised and extolled by various people. Hans Jonas studied with the existentialists, I think he was a student of Heidegger. Existentialism is a sort of halfway house to Gnosticism, because it doesn't go beyond the recognition of the inadequacy and the darkness of the world, but doesn't see any redemption anywhere. Similarly deconstructionism may have little elements that lead towards Gnosticism, but they're not really numerous. I may be wrong about that. But I am deriding Derrida.

APS: How do you see the relationship between the purely academic examination of these texts and their history, and our attempts to put them into practice and to use them as a worldview? It has to be a slightly uneasy relationship, I think, because there are different motives involved.

SH: Yes, it has been and still is an uneasy relationship, but if there is a certain kind of intelligent modesty present in both camps then I think that relationship doesn't have to be too dicey. Because if the scholar recognises that there are limits to his scholarship … the scholar deals with data that can be ascertained historically, linguistically, in comparative terms, and so forth, and that's really where the work of the scholar ends. On the other hand, the practising Gnostic looks at the entire framework from an experiential point of view and says that the issue of Gnosis, the experience of Gnosis, and all this material, these scriptures and so forth, grew from that experience. The experience is something that a scholar—with the exception perhaps of some more intuitive psychologists like Jung—a scholar cannot relate to it because it's not really a subject of scholarship, it's a subject of experience. If we recognise our limits, if the practising Gnostic recognises his limits and if the scholar recognises his own limits, then I think we can get on quite well. But if we don't then the relationship becomes ever more uneasy.

APS: Well put. In some ways, although it has some pernicious aspects, the postmodern environment is a little friendlier to spirituality than the previous intellectual environment.

SH: In what might be called the postmodern environment, it's certainly more permissive, and it has helped to dispel the shadow of the heresiologists, which has so heavily rested on scholarship owing to the fact that the majority of the material that was available on Gnosticism before Nag Hammadi came from antagonistic heresiological sources, Irenaeus and his cohorts. The antagonistic judgment of these heresiologists has also penetrated scholarship, particularly scholars who have gone, at least for a while, to seminary. And many of the biblical scholars have been originally ministers or priests of some Christian denomination or the other. And so they carry that heresiological bias with them. But fortunately the combination perhaps of Nag Hammadi and, as you say, the postmodern environment, this bias is no longer as prominent as it has been, and it seems to be dissipating.

APS: Have you read *The Gnostics* by David Brakke? He sees the Sethians as the Gnostics and, while he acknowledges that the Valentinians used the Gnostic myth, they didn't call themselves Gnostics and should be treated separately.

SH: Well, these are matters of nomenclature, but I would be interested in the book. There are certain core ideas there, such as salvation by Gnosis, rather than works or by faith. Cosmologically emanationism instead of creationism, the presence of some kind of demiurgic element. There are others. As long as these are present, I really don't see any reason why these various schools could not be called Gnostic. Because they are based on Gnosis, they come from Gnosis and they continue to adhere to the importance of Gnostic experience, which is Gnosis. So one can go around splitting hairs. Valentinus is certainly the most Christian.

APS: Would you say that you are more sympathetic to the Valentinians or to the Sethians or to some other variety of Gnosticism?

SH: It has been my endeavour—I don't know whether always successful or not—to devote my interest and devotion to the totality of the Gnostic tradition. No doubt there are some scriptures, and consequently some authors who are more compatible with my inclinations, but what I'm devoted to is the total Gnostic tradition. Maybe it's legitimate to talk about Sethians, I'm not even so sure about that. But certainly a lot of the other names, they all come patristic sources and they're all the result of name calling, not scholarship but antagonistic and pejorative name calling. If it's not justified to call all Gnostics Gnostics, it is perhaps even less justified to apply the names that the heresiologists have called various Gnostic groups.

APS: It's true. No Valentinian text ever uses the word "Valentinian" anywhere.

SH: They show the ideas and the influences of the great Valentinus. Scholars like to categorise and scholars like to dissect and scholars like to divide materials into various sects so that they can study them individually and look at their differences and make comparison. This is understandable, but it can be overdone.

APS: Now, Lance Owens told me that I should ask you about Gnostic tradition at the threshold of a new aeon. So that's what I'm going to do.

SH: Oh dear. Well, the notion of a new aeon is one that has appeared from time to time, and under a different name it certainly was present in the sixties, as the Age of Aquarius and so forth, which has really kind of fizzled out. Now we have a new slant on it, really from Jung's Red Book. Because Jung definitely propounds, along with many, many other things, the coming of a new aeon in the Red Book. But there are indications of that teaching on the part of Jung in some of his other books also. While I am generally very suspicious of prophecy, predictive prophecy, that is, some kinds of predictive prophecy have a little validity. So the notion of the precession of the equinoxes and the consequent coming of the passing of the world into the aegis of Aquarius from Pisces, this has some objective merit. The important thing is that the new aeon as predicted by Jung—and Jung was very careful, he didn't predict any exact dates, he was thinking in centuries and centuries, so it's a long term project—but as Jung saw it, the principle keynote of the new aeon will be the religion of the indwelling godhead, indwelling within us. So that, rather than envisioning the divine always outside of ourselves, whether in a personal or even in a impersonal fashion, the divinity shall be recognised within the human being and dealt with there. That seems to be the keynote of the new aeon as predicted by Jung. And this I think itself is a thoroughly Gnostic project because we certainly see that in the early Gnostic writings, we find it in the Poimandres of the Hermeticists, we find it everywhere because the Gnostic pneumatopsychology always declares that deeply within the human psyche there resides a point of transcendence which is connected with the ultimate reality and so if we have made contact with that then we have made contact with God, which incidentally is very much present in Hinduism wherein the atman, the spirit in the individual human, is identical with the Brahman, which is the spirit of God. And so if this is to be the keynote of the new aeon then I think the new aeon will be a return to at least some Gnostic recognitions, not just because they are Gnostic, but because they are true, and they have been true all along. Christianity especially has gone wrong in certain interpretations of its own faith, and among these was the lack of recognition being given to what St Paul calls "the Christ in us, the hope of glory."

some of the people who are running around calling themselves Gnostics are not really people whom you would want to invite for dinner.

Now, as to the details of the new religion, which according to Jung would be an outgrowth or modification of Christianity, we don't really know a great deal, but this seems to be the central emphasis, the central keynote. Jung even indicates that there will be three steps of that and they are called, War, Magic and Religion. Now how one interprets this is another matter. So really to say, as a lot of people do nowadays, that we live in a post-religious era, even a post-Christian era, would not be accurate according to Jung's statements about the new aeon. I somewhat agree with that, because a lot of people say, I'm not religious, I'm spiritual. So what does that mean? Well, I think to most people it means that they have no sympathy with the religious establishments, and they do like an American television said from a few years ago, that you are probably too young to remember, it said, Mother, I'd rather do it myself!" So people think that they should do their religion themselves. Up to a certain extent I think this is a valid idea, but on the other hand there is only so much that the individual can do by himself. There have to be practices, whether they are in the nature of meditations, prayers, rituals, there has to be a practical side to it, otherwise it remains very, very tenuous and even of limited value to the individual. So let's say the current fashionable point of view of religion: no, but spirituality: yes, would need to be amended. I fully recognise that, for instance, the ritual sacramental practices that I practise with my close group are not for everybody— of course not. But something has to be there. Religion without practice, and regular, intense, dedicated practice, doesn't go anywhere.

So if we really want to be serious about this, from the War, which is probably conflict, and the Magic, maybe we are in that phase now, we move into religion again. Religion will have to have some of the characteristics of religion, but we are probably not historically at that point yet. Yet all of this is very Gnostic, because the original, the valuable, the transformative part of Christianity was Gnosticism. When this essence, the deeper essence of the Christian tradition, is unearthed, what is being unearthed will be Gnostic. Whether it is called that or not. I accept the possibility of a new aeon because that seems to be the way history works. Certainly when Christianity came and then conquered the known world, there was a new aeon. Whether it was better than the ancient pagan world, that's a value judgement. But it was a new era. And then maybe when after the Renaissance when maybe the more secular impulses of science and all of that came, that was also a new era, or was another new age. Maybe not as big an aeon as Pisces or Aquarius but it was. So history seems to work in such divisions, so it stands to reason that maybe another division will come. How soon, and how it will dawn upon us, we are not prepared to say. And I don't think Jung was prepared to say it either.

APS: How about the modern Gnostic movement? How healthy do you feel it is? What new developments are pleasing you? What do you think needs to be fixed? In terms of the broader aspects of he movement. That could be divided into several segments again. There is on the one hand the movement of scholarship, which you mentioned, and which has been of immense value to all of us because without the scholars and their translations we would not have access to Nag Hammadi and things of that sort, which have been of immense benefit. So that's an important element there. But then there are those who, at least ostensibly, want to be Gnostics, want to be called that, and then inasmuch as we are dealing with a very diffuse, fledgling movement, we have all kinds of variations. And I think a good many variations, or the little movements within the movement, are not very effective, and not even very commendable, because many of them get very theoretical, and faddish, and since it's a completely open field, at least here in America, and I believe also in Britain, anybody can call himself a Gnostic and jump on the bandwagon, but it makes for very varied company. So some of the people who are running around calling

themselves Gnostics are not really people whom you would want to invite for dinner. Maybe that's an uncharitable remark, but I think it's true. There is a wide, wide variety. I would say that there are people who honestly and sincerely pursue Gnosis and recognise that this pursuit must include, in addition to theory, some valid and regular practice, there I think we may be coming up with something valuable and something important. There are various circles. The circle of the scholars, the circle of the general culture which becomes more sympathetic to Gnostic ideas, and then perhaps the inner circle of Gnostic practitioners. I don't want to make a blanket judgement about anybody, but there is a lot of fantasy, and lot of pretentiousness and things of this sort going on, but that is always going on, whether it is in connection with Gnosticism or anything else, and you have churches and archbishops and patriarchs on the Internet who have nothing but titles. It's all on an electronic spot. They have no followers, they are not doing anything, they are just trying to achieve some kind of prominence, largely by Internet means, but not backing it up with any actual work. That's unfortunate, but people like that don't have staying power, so these kinds of lightweight Gnostics are going to fall away. There will be those remaining who are doing something serious, who are both dedicated and informed about what they are doing, and I have every hope that that is going to happen, I think increasingly. Obviously because of the very nature of the subject there is not going to be a monolithic Gnostic movement that will be the same everywhere in the world. It wasn't that way the other time around either. So there will be individual schools with individual teachers, having their own particular approach, and maybe nomenclature, but as long as they have the basic Gnostic recognitions there will be something important happening.

APS: I think that's a good place to end, on a positive note.

SH: Well, thank you.

Anthony Peake

A Gnostic Model of Consciousness
The Zero-Point Field and the Pleroma

In the first of his Seven Sermons to the Dead, the Gnostic founding father of depth psychology Carl Gustav Jung, wrote the following

> I began with nothingness. Nothingness is the same as fullness. In infinity full is no better than empty. Nothingness is both empty and full.

adding

> This nothingness or fullness we name the PLEROMA. Therein both thinking and being cease, since the eternal and infinite possess no qualities. In it no being is, for he then would be distinct from the pleroma, and would possess qualities which would distinguish him as something distinct from the pleroma.

The belief that there is a reality behind the fabrication of the perceived universe is central to Gnosticism. The reality that is presented to us by our senses is a false one. Our true nature, our "Spirit", is trapped within what William Blake called the "Mind Forged Manacles" and modern Gnostic science fiction writer Philip K. Dick termed the "Black Iron Prison".

The word "Pleroma" is from the Greek πλήρωμα, means "fullness". This place is regularly referred to as the light existing outside of our phenomenal world, a place that is the true "ground-state" of reality.

This is theology. As we know the twenty-first century seems to have become a battleground between "irrational" theologies and "rational" science. However recent developments in the world of quantum physics suggest to me that Gnostic theology may be proven right. It seems that there is a "fullness" that exists within nothingness, and that light itself may be the facilitator by which we, within the "Black Iron Prison" may be able to access the riches of the Pleroma.

Most people who are given a basic education in the sciences are taught that space is exactly that, empty. Of course on Earth no space is ever really empty but Outer Space is a different concept altogether. By definition it is empty of anything. However in the nineteenth century the idea that Outer Space was really empty was a huge issue. The problem was a simple one—electromagnetic energy. As we have already discussed it was a known scientific "fact" that light was a wave and that it travelled through space as a sound wave travelled though air. However therein lay the problem. Sound in itself does not exist. It is simply a compression wave in the air. This wave travels like waves travel in the water (which again, if you think about it, would not exist if there was no water. No water to wave no wave!) But it was clear that light waves did travel through the vacuum of outer space. So how did light and heat get from the Sun to the Earth? In effect what was doing the "waving"?

Victorian scientists proposed that space was not empty and contained a substance that carried the electromagnetic waves through space. This substance was called the "luminiferous aether". Its role was made clear by the word "luminiferous" which means "light carrying". However there was no evidence that this invisible substance existed except as a tool for one scientific paradigm to remain unchallenged against all the counter-evidence. However, in 1887, two American researchers, Albert Michelson and Edward Morley proved, in a very ingenious experiment, that the luminiferous aether did not exist.

This was one of the first discoveries that contributed to the discovery of the present paradigm of science. If light was a wave, which experimentation clearly showed it was, then how could it travel through empty space?

In 1905 Albert Einstein proved that light was also particulate—it was made up of tiny individual particles called photons. The problem of light propagation was solved. Particles exist in their own right and do not need a medium in which to travel through. As such light particles could easily fly through space from the Sun to the Earth.

It is ironic that recent discoveries regarding the nature of space itself may suggest that we are in need of another paradigm change. In a curious echo from the past it seems that a substance similar to the aether may indeed fill up all of space. This is the zero point field, a field that fills all of space and is, in many ways, the backdrop to what we call "reality".

The zero point field is a consequence of something long known to particle physicists. Called the Heisenberg Uncertainty Principle this states that if we know the position of a sub-atomic particle we cannot know its speed and if we know its speed we cannot know its momentum. If a particle were at rest we would know both. Such particles can never be at rest, not even at absolute zero, the coldest state known to science. This is minus 273.15 degrees Celsius. This is three degrees below the temperature of the vacuum of space. Why this is of significance is that there should be no energy at absolute zero but there is. Lots of it. All space is filled with this quantum vacuum energy. It fills everything and in doing so changes what we think is a vacuum into a space absolutely full to the brim with energy.

A "field" is a medium by which information is transferred from one particle to another. Modern science also tells us that electromagnetic field exists everywhere. Well this is not quite true. At absolute zero all known forms of energy, including electromagnetic energy, vanish. This really is "empty space". This is a very strange place, in many ways linked to the quantum world simply by its very environment. At these super-low temperatures a fascinating new form of matter is created, something called a Bose-Einstein condensate.

This new form of matter was first predicted by Indian physicist Satyendra Nath Bose, a scientist brought up within the Eastern rather than the Western philosophical tradition. In a paper that he sent to Albert Einstein in 1924 he described how it may be the case that if particles were cooled to a few degrees above absolute zero they may change from being a single particle to a collection of particles that act as if they were one. Such a bizarre idea was proved when the first Bose-Einstein condensate was created in 1995 at the University of Colorado. Many years before, in 1938, a similar phenomenon was observed when a substance called helium 4 was found to have absolutely no viscosity. This meant that it could flow with absolutely no loss of energy.

In principle what is happening is that all the particles within the condensate have become one, a single particle spread out in space and time. These condensates pull their energy directly out of the zero point field in the form of zero point energy.

However what is more amazing is that these peculiar Bose-Einstein condensates have been found to exist within the human body. Indeed it has been discovered that much of all living things are liquid crystalline in structure. For example the collagen in bone is a semi-solid substance and is referred to as "liquid crystal." If you have ever used a pocket calculator you will have seen liquid crystals in action. However a liquid crystal is an extremely odd state of matter. They are neither liquid nor solid but a peculiar hybrid state. It is now known that information is transferred instantaneously within this state and is also totally non-local. Nearly all the connecting tissues and cell membranes contain this substance. Significantly, within all the cells of the body can be found tiny structures that are, in effect, biological Bose-Einstein condensates. Known as "microtubules" these intriguing structures can be found in all cells of the body that have a nucleus. They are responsible for communication across each cell and as such have been called the cell's "brain". As the name implies microtubules are both microscopic and tubular in shape. In some brain cells (neurons) they can be surprisingly long, some reaching nearly a metre in length, and bundled in arrangements consisting of hundreds or even thousands of individual structures. These bundled structures are reminiscent of fibre optics and indeed they have a great similarity with this man-made form

of communication because they function in a similar way in that they send information using a form of light propagation. However what is of significance is that it has been shown that the coherent single-photon micropulses of light that are sent along the length of each individual microtubule is generated from Bose-Einstein condensates. In other words the communication processes that the microtubules use is facilitated by quantum effects.

Indeed many of us use a Bose-Einstein condensate when we listen to music reproduced by a CD player. The information from the disc is read using a laser beam and a laser beam is technically coherent light—a beam in which all the light particles (photons) are all sharing a single "coherent" state. But there is another application of laser technology that has direct reference to the workings of the human brain, the hologram.

Holograms are three dimensional images created by using lasers to "photograph" an object and then reproducing the subsequent image by illuminating it with another set of lasers. This is again an application of coherent light in which a seemingly solid image can be reproduced from stored information. In 1986 two Japanese researchers, Isuki Hirano and Atsushi Hirai, suggested that coherent light is generated in vast quantities by tiny structures found deep within the neurons of the brain. Microtubules are so small that it is possible that the energy they use to generate the coherent light is Zero Point Energy drawn directly from the Zero Point Field. In other words they draw energy from what Gnostics call the Pleroma, Indian traditional philosophy called the Akashic Record and what Chang Tsai knew as the Ch'i.

Ch'i translates as "gas" or "ether" and is a tenuous and non-perceptible form of matter which is present throughout space and can condense into solid material objects.

The idea that matter somehow condenses out of the Ch'i is amazingly prescient and echoes the Gnostic belief that matter is a form of adulterated light. Indeed it may be recalled that the great Gnostic teacher Mani was once quoted as stating that matter was "bottled light"

Intriguingly it has recently been suggested that zero point energy provides the fuel to create the Bose-Einstein condensates. Could this be the unified model that we have been looking for? Remember, if this model is correct then the zero point field is the ultimate ground state of the universe, the "universe behind the universe. Something that Gnostics call "the Pleroma".

In my opinion it is reasonable to conclude that the microtubules of the brain could have a direct communication with the zero point field through a form of electromagnetic energy called "coherent light".

Hirano and Hirai argue in their paper that each micropulse of light generates single-photon holograms. Now there are literally trillions of microtubules in the human body. If each one can create single-photon holograms then the amount of information that the human body can store is effectively unlimited.

In another research paper Peter Marcer and Walter Schempp have shown that microtubule communication across the body works in a non-local fashion. In other words information was sent instantaneously between different locations within the body.

But the singularly most amazing fact about microtubules is that any two closely situated parallel microtubules would give off an intense beam of light of a single wavelength in the direction of its partner. If this is the case then an interference pattern identical to those used to create holographic images would be created with light and dark bands. Encoded within these bands will be huge amounts of information.

If this is correct then the human brain has direct access to the Pleroma and the virtually limitless information that it contains. It will be recalled that the Pleroma can be described as a huge digital database that stores the records of everything that has happened, and will happen, in the universe. In fact, if modern quantum physics is correct, then there are trillions of universes containing billions of copies of every human being that has ever lived and ever will live. Each one of these consciousnesses will download their life experiences into the "Fullness" via their microtubules and similarly they can upload limitless data from the Pleroma using the same process.

Similarly if Hirano and Hirai are correct then the "pleromic" data can be reassembled using the laser-like coherent light to create seemingly three dimensional holographic images of the stored information. This would create in the mind of the experiencer a three dimensional version of the recording that would be totally life-like in every way. It would be like the illusionary world of the *Matrix* movies. It would be indistinguishable from the "real" thing. I use the speech marks because such a model suggests that the "reality" we take for granted that is external to our bodies and supplied to us by our senses may not be as "real" as we believe. Indeed modern neurology tells us that what we take to be external reality is a construct of the brain modelled out of the electro-chemical information supplied to it from our senses.

In my books I call this internally generated model of reality the Bohmian IMAX or BIMAX. I call it Bohmian in honour of the late, and great, Professor David Bohm who first suggested the holographic nature of perception. The IMAX reference is to convey the "virtual-reality" feel of the BIMAX.

So is it possible that in the early years of the twenty-first century it may be discovered that it is the Gnostic model of the universe that is the correct one, a model that has been carried through the centuries within the esoteric groups of Christianity (the Gnostics), Islam (the Sufis) and Judaism (the Kabbalists)? Indeed this model can also be found in the great religious traditions of the East such as the Hindu concept of Maya and the Buddhist concept of Sunyata.

Science looks out and mysticism looks in, both are different routes but both may lead us to true Gnosis.

Robert M. Price

Is John's Gospel Gnostic?

WHO DARES?

As far back as the fourth-century faction of the Alogoi who wanted to bar the Fourth Gospel from the emerging New Testament canon,[1] the Gospel of John has now and again been suspected of being Gnostic in character. The greatest modern exponent of this view has been Rudolf Bultmann.[2] I will attempt to set forth the basic case for a Gnostic (or Gnostic-influenced) John, drawing largely on the work of Bultmann.

First, just what is Gnosticism? It is not a sharply defined set of doctrines, since there were so many Gnostic sects, schools, and gurus, but there are certain recurrent ideas that enable scholars to construct an ideal type.[3] Here it is in broad outline.[4] There is an anti-cosmic dualism. This world is considered as absolutely evil, irredeemable, and under the despotic control of evil powers and demons. Certain individuals may be saved from this vale of tears. They are the rare ones who harbor a true soul or spark of the divine light. To them God has sent a Redeemer or Revealer, who saves them by revealing to them the hitherto unsuspected fact of their heavenly identity. Knowing who they truly are, destined for better things, they will be able to slough off the gross body at death and ascend to heaven. This is basically the soteriology of Gnosticism. Conjoined with it was usually a set of doctrines seeking to explain how things had come to such a pass. This was the Gnostic theodicy. According to it, the world was evil because matter is inherently evil, and the material world could not have been created by a good God, and thus was the work of an insane and incompetent "demiurge," identified with the Old Testament YHWH.

Often Gnostics inferred from all this that when the Revealer appeared in the world, he must have only "seemed" to take on flesh; it was in fact an illusion (hence "docetism," which means "seem-ism"). I will suggest that the Gospel of John does contain Gnostic soteriology but lacks the attendant theodicy. This is a vital distinction to make. For failure to draw it, many scholars have rejected Bultmann's thesis, being unable to find enough Gnostic cosmology in the document. On the one hand, we will see that not all even of classic Gnostic writers employed all the items described above, so to lack them does not disqualify a text as Gnostic. On the other hand, we do not find even the Gnostic soteriology in the other New Testament Gospels. We can also see John's distinctiveness in, e.g., his pre-existence Christology, unique to the canonical gospels.

1. THE WORLD

The Johannine writings are apparently ambivalent about the world and whether or not it is properly an object of love by the righteous or by God. On the one hand, "God so loved the world that he gave his only son that whoever believed in him should not perish but have everlasting life" (John 3:16). On the other, the same writer exhorts his readers to "Love not the world nor the things in the world, for if anyone loves the world the love of the Father is not in him" (1 John 2:15), because "we know that the whole world lieth in the power of the Evil One" (1 John 5:19).

The world-God enmity, for John, is not the result of world-creation by an evil power. Rather, his demiurge, the Logos, is a part of the divine being, what later Gnostics would call one of the Aions (among whom, by the way, they, too, numbered the Logos). The trouble was that the world had perversely turned away from God to the Evil One, God's opposite number. He now rules the world as a usurper. The gospel calls him "the Prince of this World" (12:21). I see this as simply a variation on the typical theme of Gnosticism. Marcion's lack of a multiplicity of Aions in the Godhead is a comparable variation. John's implied otherworldliness and bitter sectarianism[5] seem to me typically Gnostic.

2. Anti-Judaism

One of the most uncomfortable aspects of the Gospel of John for modern readers is its attitude toward non-Christian Jews. For John, Jesus' enemies are simply "the Jews," while the occasional Jesus-friendly Jew is called an "Israelite"(1:47; 3:10). Similarly, we notice that Jesus' attitude toward the Old Testament is not unambiguously positive. He calls it "your Law" (8:17) and seems to argue from it in an *ad hominem* fashion, appealing to it as an authority his opponents will accept, not that he does, so as to beat them at their own game.

All this strikingly recalls the double-edged attitude taken toward Judaism and the Jewish scriptures in the Gnostic Nag Hammadi texts. It is clear that Gnostic mythology grows out of Old Testament exegesis (once A.D. Nock[6] said that all one would need to come up with Gnosticism is the early narratives of Genesis and a wild imagination!), yet Gnostics took a hostile, jeering attitude towards Jews and Judaism. One way to read this phenomenon is the theory of C.K. Barrett[7] that Gnosticism grew out of a disappointed apocalyptic Judaism. The focus would have shifted from oft-debunked hopes for external redemption to an unfalsifiable, inward-looking mysticism.

3. Realized Eschatology

Historically, when a religion has made the mistake of predicting the near end of the world, it has had to find some sort of face-saving rationalization, or else disintegrate. Usually the strategy is to claim that the End did in fact come but in a hidden, spiritual manner, accessible only to the eye of faith. Any subsequent visible coming of the apocalypse was deferred into the ever-receding future or simply dropped altogether. Whether because of disappointment or not, Gnosticism seems to have lacked a futuristic eschatology. The only resurrection was the one to be experienced here and now in mystical initiation or baptism. As Bultmann points out, in the New Testament Paul and John are both already beginning this process of realizing eschatology in the present. While Paul still also expected an external coming of the Christ, Bultmann reads John as dispensing with it entirely. Certain passages in John seem to imply not only that John had dropped the idea but that he meant to disabuse his readers of it. That is, he not only assumed a realized eschatology, but he sought to make it explicit. Such texts include John 5:24-25; 11:23-26; 14:22-23.

There are, as any reader knows, also various passages in the gospel which seem clearly to teach a futuristic eschatology. These include 5:28-29; 6:39, 54; 21:22. What are we to make of these? Bultmann suggests they are the work of an "ecclesiastical redactor," a later editor who sought to "rehabilitate" the gospel for more congenial use by the orthodox church. Such "correction" in the interests of orthodoxy is a well-attested phenomenon in the ancient church (cf., Rufinus' redaction of Origen, and 2 Peter's of Jude), and it is not arbitrary to suggest in the case of John since on entirely distinct grounds we have signs of redaction and reshuffling.

4. Predestinarianism

The Gnostic Revealer came into the world, much like the Christ of later Calvinism, to save only a select group. According to classical

Gnosticism the elect were those who possessed one of the fragments of the divine nature of the Primal Man, a heavenly being captured and devoured by the evil beings of the material world. John shows no knowledge of such a myth (unless John 1:9 is a vestige of it), but, again, this simply means that he lacked or rejected this particular set of inferences from the Gnostic soteriology. All he says is that the Revealer has appeared in the world on behalf of his own, not why they are his own and others are not. At any rate we do indeed find a textual basis for the idea of a predestined elect in John. Primarily we find this in the Good Shepherd discourse, where Jesus taunts the Jews thusly: "you do not believe because you do not belong to my sheep. My sheep hear my voice and I know them and they follow me, and I give them eternal life, etc."(John 10:26-27f). Note that he does not say they are not among his flock because they do not believe, but just the opposite. They lack the option to believe in the first place. And in view of all this, it comes as no surprise to learn that the Good Shepherd lays down his life for his sheep and for them only (10:11).

Bultmann himself seeks to distance Johannine predestinarianism from the Gnostic variety by characterizing the former as a "dualism of decision"[8] rather than as an unalterable metaphysical sentence. For John, as Bultmann reads him, it is one's decision for or against the Son of God that renders him destined to hear the truth or not. One is tempted to ask whether that is not rather just the *opposite* of predestinarian doctrine, whether John's, Gnostic, Calvin's, or any other kind. But the contrast is illusory: the truth is that *all* ostensible predestinarian language is a rhetorical strategy designed to affright the hearer and urge him to get on the right side *now!* In the Markan Parable of the Soils/Sower (Mark 4:2-9, 13-20) the point is obviously not to gloat over the destined salvation of the minority and the inescapable doom of the rest; no, the point is to make the hearers get busy becoming receptive soil! Ebenezer Scrooge got the point exactly right when he looked up from the gravestone, emblazoned with his name, to

the Spirit of Christmas Yet to Come, saying, "Why show me these things if I am past all hope?"

5. Docetism?

I have already observed that many Gnostics drew the inference from their dualistic cosmology that the Revealer could not have become truly incarnate, since the flesh was altogether corrupt, totally depraved. Some have ruled out any Gnostic character for John in view of John 1:14, "The Logos was made flesh and dwelt among us."

In the first place, we must note that not all Gnostic texts are thus docetic. The *Gospel of Truth* says the Risen Christ gladly "divested himself of these perishing rags"(20:30-31). Similarly, the *Hymn of the Pearl* has the reascending Christ declare, "I stripped off the filthy garment and left it in their land" (line 63). These statements do evidence an ascetic contempt for the flesh, but the sentiments are not so different from those of the Apostle Paul in 2 Corinthians 5:1-4. (In fact the disparaging reference to the fleshly body as a mere "tent"—cf. also 2 Peter 1:13-14—recalls the word used for the temporary incarnation of the Logos in John 1:14, "and tabernacled, pitched his tent, among us." Is the idea, then, that the fleshly covering of the Logos was a mere veil? At any rate, the references in the Gnostic texts make it sufficiently clear that Gnostic texts need not expound docetism (and conversely we could show that docetism could occur in otherwise orthodox, non-Gnostic texts, like the *Acts of John*).

Finally, we should note that the picture of John as non-docetic is not entirely unambiguous. Ernst Kasemann[9] has argued that John is in fact guilty of a "naive docetism" in that he doesn't seem to take the implications of a real incarnation very seriously. For example, those[10] who deny a Gnostic coloring to John are quick to point out the scene in John 4:7-8 where Jesus is thirsty and sends the disciples into the town to buy food. Ah! There is a truly human Jesus, we are told. Yet when we come to the end of the story, the disciples urge Jesus to eat, and he will not! "I have food to eat that you know not of. My food and drink is to do the will of him who sent me and to accomplish his work" (vv 32, 34). The crucified Jesus says, "I thirst," but he is only mouthing the lines prophecy has scripted for him (John 19:28). Thomas insists on touching Jesus' wounds and is invited to do so (John 20:25, 27), but apparently he doesn't.

6. THE REVELATION DISCOURSES

By far the most striking evidence for some kind of Johannine dependence on Gnostic sources is the parallels between the "I am" discourses (found only in John of the New Testament Gospels) and similar discourses attributed to other revealers in the scriptures of Mandaean Gnosticism. These texts must be used with some caution, as we have only medieval copies to work with,[11] but it seems to many scholars to be quite strong evidence just the same. Note the "Johannine" flavor of this self-revelation: "I am the Messenger of Light, whom the Great One sent into this world. The true messenger am I, in whom there is no falsehood... I am the Messenger of Light: whoever smells at his scent is quickened to life. Whoever receives his word, his eyes are filled with light." It is hard to miss the characteristic Johannine structure of an introductory "I am" followed by a declaration of the benefits accruing to the one who will accept and follow the Revealer. Note also the familiar phrases "sent into the world" (cf. John 3:16) and "in whom there is no falsehood" (1:47).

Even more startling are the parallels between the Mandaean writings and particular Johannine discourses. Compare John's True Vine discourse (15:1-11) with these words of the Mandaean Revealer: "A vine am I, a vine of life, a tree in which there is no falsehood. The tree of praise, from which everyone who smells of it becomes alive. Whoever hears his word, his eyes are filled with light... The vine which bears fruit ascends, the vine which bears nothing is cut off here from the light. Whoever is enlightened and instructed by me rises and beholds the place of light. Whoever is not enlightened and instructed by me is cut off from the light and falls into the great ocean of Suf."

With the Johannine discourse of the Good Shepherd (10:1-18) compare, "I am a shepherd who loves his sheep, I protect the sheep and the lambs. The sheep are upon my neck, and the sheep do not go away from the villages. I refresh them not on the sea shore, so that they do not see the whirlpool... I carry them and give them water to drink from the hollow of my hand, until they have drunk their fill." (All these texts come from the *Mandaean Book of John*, i.e., of John the Baptist, though he is not the speaker).[12]

The Johannine "I am" discourses are so unlike anything to be found in the Synoptic Gospels, and so much like what we find in the Mandaean texts, that Bultmann felt the author of the Gospel must have used as source material a collection of revelation discourses derived from a rival Gnostic sect. Specifically, Bultmann guessed that the Fourth Evangelist had been an adherent of a group which viewed John the Baptist as the Revealer. Converting to Christianity, the Evangelist took over some of the sacred traditions of the Sect of John, reapplying them to Jesus Christ. I do not believe we need to go the whole way with Bultmann in order to recognize the Gnostic sources and features of John, though neither is Bultmann's complete theory implausible.

NOTES

1 F.F. Bruce, *The New Testament Documents: Are they Reliable?* (Grand Rapids: Eerdmans, 1960), p. 51, referring to the fourth-century Epiphanius, Bishop of Salamis.

2 Rudolf Bultmann, *The Gospel of John: A Commentary*. Trans. G.R.Beasley-Murray, R.W.N. Hoare, and J..K. Riches. (Philadelphia: Westminster Press, 1971), "The Relation to Gnosticism," pp. 7-9. Cf. also Elaine H. Pagels, *The Johannine Gospel in Gnostic Exegesis: Heracleon's Commentary on John*. .Society of Biblical Literature Monograph Series 17 (Atlanta: Scholars Press, 1989).

3 Some recent scholars have sought to dismantle the category of "Gnosticism" simply because not all ostensible instances of it are exactly alike. They appear to have been absent on the day their professors explained what an ideal type is. One might as well argue there is no such thing as Protestantism, or Buddhism.

4 Rudolf Bultmann, *Theology of the New Testament*. Vol. 1. Trans. Kendrick Grobel (NY: Scribners, 1951), pp. 164-183.

5 J. L. Houlden, *Ethics and the New Testament* (Baltimore: Penguin Books, 1973), pp. 35-41, 68. "It is hard to believe that a work such as this is not to be rightly considered as Gnostic in tendency" (p. 35).

6 Oral tradition via Professor David M. Scholer, 1977 or 1978.

7 C.K. Barrett, *The Gospel of John and Judaism*. Franz Delitzsch Lectures, 1967 (Philadelphia: Westminster Press, 1975). A similar case is set forth in Hyam Maccoby, *Paul and Hellenism* (Philadelphia: Trinity Press International, 1991), Chapter 1, "Gnostic Anti-Semitism," pp. 1-35. Maccoby posits Gnosticism as a bitter parody of Philonic-type Judaism to which some Alexandrians were temporarily attracted, but thought better of it and, ashamed of their near conversion, belittled the Jewish scripture, especially Genesis.

8 Bultmann, *Gospel of John*, pp. 158-159, 316-317.

9 Ernst Käsemann, *The Testament of Jesus: A Study of the Gospel of John in the Light of Chapter 17*. Trans. Gerhard Krodel (Philadelphia: Fortress Press, 1978), p. 26.

10 Udo Schnelle, *Anti-Docetic Christology in the Gospel of John*. Trans. Linda M. Maloney (Minneapolis: Fortress Press. 1992).

11 Edwin Yamauchi, *Pre-Christian Gnosticism: A Survey of the Proposed Evidences* (Grand Rapids: Eerdmans, 1973), goes so far as to disqualify any and all Johannine use of the Mandaean materials on this basis. On the same basis should we refuse to date the canonical New Testament gospels before the earliest manuscripts of them we have?

12 This text is included in my *The Pre-Nicene New Testament: Fifty-Four Formative Texts* (Salt Lake City: Signature Books,

Andrew Phillip Smith

This Compost

They sat on shelves for century after century, tens, even hundreds, of thousands of them, their green eyes lifeless, their dry organless bodies wrapped in bandages. The mice played away happily watched by stiff sentinels, each of them looking like Tom after a bit of particularly vicious trickery by Jerry. They waited for resurrection.

Cats were sacred animals in Egypt and were mummified, as were crocodiles, hawks and ibises, jackals and baboons, bulls and cows, rams and lambs and mongooses. And people of the better, wealthier sort. Bast was an Egyptian cat goddess depicted as a woman with the head of a cat (or, depending on your point of view, a cat with the body of a woman.) Sekhmet ditto with a lion head, arguably one of the predecessors of the lion-headed Gnostic demiurge Yaldabaoth,or perhaps that was Bast's son Maahes. Mafdet was a cat goddess too.

The bandages were often made from recycled papyrus. The papyrus bandages found on crocodile mummies at Tebtunis contained fragments of lost works by Sappho and Sophocles, sliced into long strips, early versions of the cut-ups of William Burroughs, lyrics and tragedies winding their ways around the limbs and torsos of

desiccated reptiles.

There were millions of cat mummies altogether. They were preserved for millennia, less eroded than the Sphinx, arranged on shelves in cat cemeteries only to dug up by the Empire on which the sun would never (until the mid twentieth century) set. The dead saw light again. The papyrus fragments found in the rubbish heaps of Ocyrhynchus by Victorian double act Grenfell and Hunt, including the Greek fragments of the *Gospel of Thomas*, were taken to Oxford, to be preserved and published and pored over. Likewise 300,000 cat mummies, carefully bound in bandages for sacred preservation, were shipped off to England.

They could have adorned the mantlepieces of hundred of thousands of families. They could have sat next to models of the Blackpool tower, above china dogs, below seascapes and ornate mirrors. Instead they were pounded down and shipped to Liverpool to be sold as fertilizer. The auctioneer used one of the stiffer cats instead of a gavel. The price of these immortal moggies: less than £4 a ton.

Omar Khayyam wrote, "And look—a thousand Blossoms with the Day

Woke and a thousand scatter'd into Clay"

Ah, those cat-fed roses of Lancashire! The sacred flesh, nitrogen-rich and feline-fuelled mingles with the native soil in allotments and fields and back gardens. Perhaps John Lennon ran his youthful fingers through the dust of Sekhmet. Perhaps scouse pussies scratched and sniffed at their divine African cousins.

In his poem "This Compost" Walt Whitman contemplated the mystery of life emerging from corruption.

O how can it be that the ground itself does not sicken?

How can you be alive you growths of spring? How can you furnish health you blood of herbs, roots, orchards, grain?

Are they not continually putting distemper'd corpses within you?

Is not every continent work'd over and over with sour dead?

...

The summer growth is innocent and disdainful above all those strata of sour dead.

What chemistry!

This meditation on corruption and transformation in nature gave me the title for my own musings.

When I dug a little deeper I discovered that Walt Whitman himself viewed "mummied cats, lizards, ibises, and crocodiles" many times at Dr. Abbott's Museum of Egyptian Antiquities in New York in 1853.

Recently I found out that millions of dog mummies were discovered underground at Saqqara. I'll stop here.

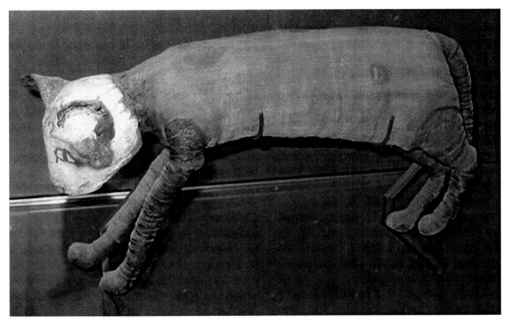

Petra Mundik

"Terra Damnata":

The Anticosmic Mysticism of Cormac McCarthy's *Blood Meridian, or the Evening Redness in the West*

Blood Meridian, Or the Evening Redness in the West, McCarthy's first western novel, follows the debaucheries of the historical Glanton gang as they murder, rape and scalp their way across the Wild West of the 1850's. McCarthy's graphic portrayals of violence, set within surreal, nightmarish landscapes, convey an unmistakably anticosmic attitude towards existence and creation. The marked absence of divine intervention in the face of such extravagant depravity suggests, at best, total divine indifference to human suffering, or, at worst, the presence of a malevolent entity that delights in blood. In *Blood Meridian*, McCarthy presents the reader with a vision of evil allowed to run rampant and unchecked; few novelists have attempted such a devastatingly honest portrayal of the depths of darkness to which human nature can sink.

Critical opinion concerning McCarthy's work tends to divide into two camps; namely, that of the nihilists, who agree with Vereen M. Bell's statement that McCarthy's novels "are as innocent of theme and ethical reference as they are of plot"[1]; and that of the moralists who, like Edwin T. Arnold, argue that the novels contain "moral parables" and "a conviction that is essentially religious"[2]. Some critics, like Dana Phillips, are positioned entirely in the nihilist camp and see nothing beyond the violent excesses of the novel. Phillips writes that: "McCarthy's fiction resembles [Flannery] O'Connor's in its violence, but he entirely lacks O'Connor's penchant for theology and the jury-rigged, symbolic plot resolutions that make theology seem plausible. In McCarthy's work, violence tends to be just that; it is not a sign

or symbol of something else"[3]. Shane Schimpf similarly concludes that "*Blood Meridian* is a profoundly nihilistic novel entirely devoid of optimism or hope"[4]. Others, like John Sepich, feel that there is more to *Blood Meridian* than initially meets the eye. As Edwin T. Arnold writes in the foreword to Sepich's meticulously researched *Notes on 'Blood Meridian'*: "For [Sepich], it seems to be a magical, revelatory text in the sense that it contains secrets…One gets the sense in reading *Notes on 'Blood Meridian'* that Sepich is searching for some urtext, a cabala hidden in the guise of this western novel. He may be right. Certainly the book has taken a mysterious grip on many of its readers"[5]. So is *Blood Meridian* a nihilistic portrayal of the human condition, or is meaning to be found among all that carnage and destruction?

Despite their varying positions on 'meaning', or lack thereof, in McCarthy's fiction, Both Vereen M. Bell and Edwin T. Arnold agree that McCarthy's writing exhibits strains of mysticism; Bell concedes that despite some nihilistic tendencies, "there can be no doubt that McCarthy is a genuine—if somehow secular—mystic"[6]; while Arnold suspects that although McCarthy "makes compelling use of western Christian symbology…his own belief system embraces a larger and more pantheistic view"[7]. In "Meeting McCarthy" Gary Wallace cites McCarthy's views on this very subject, recalling a conversation in which the reclusive novelist talks about his own experience of spiritual reality: "McCarthy commented that some cultures used drugs to enhance the spiritual experience, and that he had tried LSD before the drug was made illegal. He said that it had helped to open his eyes to these kinds of experiences". Wallace adds that McCarthy "said that he felt sorry for me because I was unable to grasp this concept of spiritual experience. He said that people all over the world, in every religion, were familiar with this experience". When Wallace admits to being "nonplussed" by these words, McCarthy tells him that he is simply talking about "Truth", which is what "writers must accomplish in their writing". When, in typical postmodern fashion, Wallace fails to understand what "Truth" is, McCarthy tells him that Truth is simply "Truth" and that "the mystical experience is a direct apprehension of reality" [8]. McCarthy's views on mysticism are in complete agreement with the major tenets of the Perennial Philosophy, whose subject matter "is the nature of eternal, spiritual Reality"[9].

McCarthy's mysticism is preoccupied with the question of evil and the examination of this question is, as William Spencer argues, not only "a pervasive theme" in McCarthy's novels, but "perhaps *the* issue of human existence that he is most interested in confronting in his fiction"[10]. Similarly, in a review of *Blood Meridian*, Tom Nolan writes that: "McCarthy's screed is a theological purgative, an allegory on the nature of evil as timeless as Goya's hallucinations on war, monomaniacal in its conception and execution, it seeks and achieves the vertigo of insanity, the mad internal logic of a noon-time nightmare that refuses to end"[11]. McCarthy's preoccupation with evil, coupled with the mystical quality of his writing and his anticosmic representation of the created world, has much in common with the ancient Gnostic heresy, which is similarly characterised by a deeply pessimistic world-view, a preoccupation with evil and a reliance on mystical insights.

Before we proceed any further, we ought to briefly consider the main tenets of the Gnostic belief system. According to Gnostic theology, the entire manifest cosmos was created by a hostile (or at best, ignorant) force of darkness and is thus a hideous aberration. This force of darkness usually takes the form of a creator-God known as the *demiurge* (William Blake's "Nobodaddy"),

identified as Yahweh of the Old Testament. The demiurge rules over all that he has created, sometimes with the assistance of evil angels known as *archons*, while the real or *alien* God remains wholly transcendent and removed from the created world. Some Gnostic texts claim that the demiurge is merely ignorant and genuinely believes that he is the only God, while other texts claim that he purposefully conceals the existence of the alien God in order to maintain his sole dominion over the manifest cosmos. Humanity has a divided nature, composed of a body and soul, which were created by and belong to the demiurge, but also a spirit, or *pneuma*, which belongs to the alien God. The pneuma is actually a fragment, or "spark", of the divine substance which has fallen into, or in some cases, been maliciously trapped in the evil manifest cosmos. Thus people are composed of both mundane and extra-mundane principles and carry within them the potential for immanence as soul and flesh, or transcendence as pure spirit.

Hans Jonas, in his seminal work, *The Gnostic Religion*, explains that: "In its unredeemed state the pneuma thus immersed in soul and flesh is unconscious of itself, benumbed, asleep, or intoxicated by the poison of the world: in brief, it is "ignorant." Its awakening and liberation is effected through 'knowledge.'"[12] Knowledge of the true state of the cosmos and of the nature of the alien God is referred to as *gnosis* and, as Elaine Pagels explains in *The Gnostic Gospels*, just as "those who claim to know nothing about ultimate reality are called agnostic (literally, 'not-knowing')", so "the person who does claim to know such things is called Gnostic ('knowing')"[13]. The possession of gnosis enables the spirit, or pneuma, to become aware of its divine origins, escape from the created world, and reunite with the transcendent God; much as the state of Enlightenment enables the attainment of *Nirvana* in Buddhist thought. Gnostics who have attained this perfected state of enlightenment by becoming aware of the *pneuma* within refer to themselves as *pneumatics*. Although a vision of the cosmos as a terrible aberration may at first glance appear nihilistic, Gnosticism's primary concern is soteriological; evil is perpetuated through ignorance, hence salvation can be attained through knowledge.

Leo Daugherty recognises this Gnostic vision in *Blood Meridian* in his perceptive essay "Gravers False and True: *Blood Meridian* as Gnostic Tragedy". Daugherty points out that while "most thoughtful people have looked at the world they lived in and asked, How did evil get into it?, the Gnostics have looked at the world and asked, How did *good* get into it?" He goes on to explain that for the Gnostics "evil was simply everything that *is*, with the exception of the bits of spirit emprisoned here," asserting that what the Gnostics saw is precisely "what we see in the world of *Blood Meridian*"[14]. Though Daugherty was the first to offer an in-depth Gnostic reading of *Blood Meridian*, other critics have made passing remarks on the Gnostic elements in McCarthy's fiction. Vereen Bell writes: "What with any other novelist would be a merely ornate style repeatedly seems to move us toward an epiphany, though only the kind that a seasoned Gnostic might construe"[15]. Similarly, Sven Birkerts notes that: "McCarthy has been, from the start, a writer with strong spiritual leanings. His orientation is Gnostic: he seems to view our endeavors here below as a violation of some original purity"[16]. More recently, in *Reading the World: Cormac McCarty's Tennessee Period*, Dianne Luce offers a Gnostic reading of McCarthy's earlier novel, *Outer Dark*. Luce argues that *Outer Dark* "reflects McCarthy's awareness of Gnostic symbols, character types, and anticosmic attitudes and his extensive borrowing from or alluding to them in creating his own parable of spiritual alienation in the cosmic realm"[17].

Even Harold Bloom identifies a Gnostic trend running through the masterpieces of American fiction in his influential *How to Read and Why*. Beginning with Melville's *Moby-Dick*, Bloom asks "just who is Melville's God, or the God of those who came after him: Faulkner, West, Pynchon, Cormac McCarthy?" Bloom's answer is that "Melville was not a Christian, and tended to identify with the ancient Gnostic heresy" and that "Faulkner is a kind of unknowing Gnostic", while "West, Pynchon, and McCarthy in their different ways are very knowing indeed"[18]. Bloom's insightful comments suggest that the Gnostic elements in McCarthy's fiction are not forced onto the novels by critics eager to superimpose their own reading on the narrative, nor do they slip into his work unconsciously as a result of some repressed grudge against fundamentalist Christian theology. Rather, McCarthy is a "very knowing" Gnostic indeed, and thus we can assume that he consciously draws inspiration from the symbols, allegories and belief systems of this ancient heresy.

McCarthy's *Blood Meridian* is replete with Gnostic symbols and concepts; the most immediately striking, however, is the novel's anticosmic depiction of hostile landscapes. According to Gnostic thought, "earthly material existence, like the world itself, is a product of the Demiurge and correspondingly is a sphere hostile to God, dominated by evil powers"[19]. The narrative voice within McCarthy's novel refers to the landscape as a "terra damnata of smoking slag" (61) , a "godless quadrant cold and sterile" (293), "a purgatorial waste" where "nothing" moves "save carnivorous birds" (63), "a country where the rocks would cook the flesh from your hands and where other than rock nothing was" (138). This nightmare vision offer no relief and no hope of escape; journeys only take the traveller "into a land more hostile yet" (152). The utter desolation through which McCarthy's characters wander often evokes the spiritual desolation of T.S. Eliot's *The Wasteland*. In particular, passages such as the following— "the rock trembled and sleared in the sun, rock and no water and the sandy trace and they kept watch for any green thing that might tell of water but there was not water" (62)—strongly recall Eliot's verse in "What the Thunder Said": "Here is no water but only rock / Rock and no water and the sandy road"[20].

Other critics have also noted the overwhelming hostility of the McCarthy's landscapes; for example, John Beck, writing about McCarthy's deserts, argues that: "One way or another, deserts signal and invite annihilation. The desert is evidence of cosmic indifference or, worse, of an actual hostility toward human life, a mineral disdain for the vulnerability of the organic"[21]. John Lewis Longley writes that the "landscape in *Blood Meridian* is like the landscape on the moon, or like the surface of the earth will be after a prolonged nuclear winter when everything is dead. On the prosaic level of factual realism, this landscape is simply the Great American Desert—desolate, arid, littered with the bones of animals and men….At a wider and deeper level, this landscape is the landscape of Hell—the inevitable configuration of a world without Grace"[22]. Such a vision of the created world as Hell predates even Gnostic thought. As Paul Oppenheimer explains in *Evil and the Demonic: A New Theory of Monstrous Behaviour*: "The view of nature, or *Natura*, as itself a *daemon* capable of gargantuan malevolence is at least as old as the Stoics (third century BC)"[23].

Oppenheimer's book includes a study of the most notorious villains of literature and cinema, and the ways in which these characters are projected upon the landscapes which house them strongly evoke *Blood Meridian* and its wandering band of scalp-hunters: "Once set free in a society, charismatic violence becomes a nomad. It wanders, heedless and thirsty, across a landscape that flattens before it into an emotional desert. Only the winds of hatred and revenge, if such hurling about of the brain can be called emotions, blow across it, and seldom others. That boneless and defleshed desert, somehow alive itself"[24]. Thus, in a sense, the landscape of *Blood Meridian* is one of the chief characters of the novel.

John Sepich points out that the "landscape of McCarthy's Southwest is composed not only of deserts and mirage effects, but also of heavenly phenomena"[25]. Indeed, one of the most obscure allusions to the hostility of the created world is evoked through such heavenly phenomena, in a passage which describes Glanton's gang sleeping "with their alien hearts beating in the sand like pilgrims exhausted upon the face of the planet Anareta, clutched to a nameless wheeling in the night" (46). Leo Daugherty, with the aid of the Oxford English Dictionary, interprets the reference to "Anareta" in the following way: "Anareta was believed in the Renaissance to be 'the planet which destroys life,' and 'violent deaths are caused' when the 'malifics' have agents in 'the anaretic place' (OED entry, 'anareta')…the implication is clearly that our own Earth is Anaretic"[26]. McCarthy's evocative descriptions of malevolent landscapes, in which "death seem[s] the most prevalent feature" (48) can thus be read as Gnostic portrayals of a nightmarish, Anaretic world.

Indeed, even the sun in *Blood Meridian* is brutal, malevolent and Anaretic, signifying death and violence, rather than traditional notions of renewal and illumination. McCarthy's trademark "bloodred" sunsets abound in *Blood Meridian*, establishing clear associations between the numerous scenes of bloodshed that occur throughout the novel. The most fascinating references to the sun, however, are those which defamiliarise the celestial sphere entirely. For example, the sun is described as "the color of steel" (15), immediately strengthening the association with weaponry, and hence violence, but also introducing an unexpected sensation of coldness. The revolting "urinecolored sun" which rises "blearily through panes of dust on a dim world" (47) is similarly unsettling.

But the most startling solar imagery consists of the following: "the top of the sun rose out of nothing like the head of a great red phallus until it cleared the unseen rim and sat squat and pulsing and malevolent behind them" (44-45). It is likely that McCarthy picked up this image from Jung[27], who, in one famous case, "tells of a schizophrenic patient who said 'he could see an erect phallus on the sun. When he moved his head from side to side, he said, the sun's phallus moved with it, *and that was where the wind came from.*' Jung found a remarkably similar image in a liturgy of the Mithraic religion, a mystery cult of late antiquity (which he had in a translation by Mead). The Mithraic text reads, 'And likewise the so-called tube, the origin of the ministering wind. For you will see hanging down from the disc of the sun something that looks like a tube"[28]. The likelihood of the Jungian influence is compounded by the fact that, later in the novel, the narrative voice described how "a wind was blowing out of the sun where it sat squat and pulsing at the eastern reaches of the earth" (227). The remarkable similarity between these passages of *Blood Meridian*'s and the Mithraic Phallus Solaris must be deliberate, for McCarthy's usage of the words "squat" and "pulsing" occurs in both instances, thus consciously linking the two passages together.

In *Blood Meridian*, McCarthy utilises the Mithraic image of the sun—worshipped by initiates as the visible manifestation of the divine principle of the Absolute[29]—and inverts it into a symbol of cosmic malevolence. It is noteworthy that in this inversion of a concept upheld by the philosophers of classical antiquity McCarthy is following in the subversive footsteps of the Gnostic heretics[30]. Hans Jonas explains that "Gnostic dualism comes as a new principle of meaning, appropriates the elements which it can use for its purposes, and subjects them to a radical reinterpretation". Whereas for the Classical mind, the seven "heavenly spheres"— namely the sun, the moon, Mercury, Venus, Mars, Jupiter and Saturn—"had represented the divinity of the cosmos at its purest, they now most effectively separated it from the divine. Enclosing the created world, they made it a prison for those particles of divinity which had become entrapped in this system"[31]. For the Gnostics, the heavenly spheres become a symbol of oppression, representing the barriers which surround the earth and keep man's divine spirit imprisoned within the manifest realm of evil matter.

Hans Jonas explains that even for nature-worshippers, the sun occupied many-faceted position, being at the same time "the god which dispenses light, warmth, life, growth...who victoriously rises out of night, puts to flight the winter, and renews nature" but who also brings "scorching, pestilence, and death"[32]. The sun in *Blood Meridian*, however, has been reduced to its wholly negative components. It

brings pestilence in the form of the "heliotropic plague" of gold seekers described as "itinerant degenerates bleeding westward" (78). According to the OED, the word "heliotropic" refers to a "bending or turning in a particular direction under the influence of light", thus the degenerate gold seekers who spread like a disease across the landscape seem to be under the maleficent influence of the sun. Pestilence is also evoked through the image of the Dieguenos, who "watched each day for that thing to gather itself out of its terrible incubation in the house of the sun...and whether it be armies or plague or pestilence or something altogether unspeakable they waited with a strange equanimity" (300-1). The concept of the sun bringing disease is emphasised not only through direct references to "plague or pestilence", but the oblique reference to "incubation", as though the sun were hatching a bacterial menace.

The idea that the sun may bring "something altogether unspeakable" is emphasised throughout the novel. When the Glanton gang abandon a murdered Apache in the desert, they leave him to "scrutinize with his dying eyes the calamitous advance of the sun" (110), as though the progression of the sun across the sky marked the progress of some terrible catastrophe. The imagery of disaster and chaos is further developed in a passage which describes the sunset as the "red demise of that day" and "the distant pandemonium of the sun" (185). The sun in *Blood Meridian* is portrayed as a merciless devourer. Wandering in the dessert, men with "burnedout eyes" grow "gaunted and lank under the white hot suns of those days" until they appear "like beings for whom the sun hungered" (248). Its indifference to human beings is made apparent in its ability to wipe out all trace of their violent deaths: "In the days to come the frail black rebuses of blood in those sands would crack and break and drift away so that in the circuit of few suns all trace of the destruction of these people would be erased... and there would be nothing, nor ghost nor scribe, to tell to any pilgrim in his passing how it was that people had lived in this place and in this place died" (174). The sun in *Blood Meridian* is a bringer of death, not life. Such a description of a celestial body usually associated with the life-giving properties of light and warmth, suggests that the horror of existence extends well beyond our planet.

Watching over the world like an indifferent god, the sun treats the impermanence and fragility of human lives with utter indifference and contempt. The Glanton gangs stumbles across the remains of a group of scalped travellers, again described as "right *pilgrims* nameless among the stones with their terrible wounds" [emphasis mine]. *Blood Meridian* is replete with "pilgrims" whose never find their way to any kind of god and whose journeys lead straight to death. The dead, in "their wigs of dried blood", lie "gazing up with ape's eyes at brother sun now rising in the east" (153). Here, the reference to "brother sun" is a chillingly sarcastic reference to Saint Francis of Assisi's (1182-1226) *Canticle of the Sun*, or *the Laudes Creaturarum* ("Praise of the Creatures"): "Be praised, my Lord, through all your creatures, / especially through my lord Brother Sun, / who brings the day; and you give light through him". The next two lines of the song are most telling: "And he is beautiful and radiant in all his splendor! / Of you, Most High, he bears the likeness." McCarthy's implications are clear; if the sun bears the likeness of the creator god, what terrible things can we deduce about this deity's nature by examining the malevolent sun of *Blood Meridian*? In keeping with the Gnostic penchant for theological subversion, McCarthy's portrayals of the sun utilise inversions not only of Classical philosophies, but also of Christian teachings.

In *Blood Meridian*, as in Gnostic thought, the evil inherent within the created world is not restricted to the earth and sun, but extends outwards to include the entire cosmos. Jonas explores this concept in great detail, stating that: "We can imagine with what feelings Gnostic men must have looked up to the starry sky. How evil its brilliance must have looked to them, how alarming its vastness and the rigid immutability of its courses, how cruel its muteness! The

music of the spheres was no longer heard, and the admiration for the perfect spherical form gave place to the terror of so much perfection directed at the enslavement of man. The pious wonderment with which earlier man had looked up to the higher regions of the universe became a feeling of oppression by the iron vault which keeps man exiled from his home beyond"[33].

Thus, for the Gnostics the night sky becomes a symbol of all that is terrifying and evil about creation. *Blood Meridian* features numerous references to the starry sky, all of which are marked with a sense of dismay, fear or loneliness. "The night sky lies so sprent with stars that there is scarcely space of black at all and they fall all night in bitter arcs and it is so that their numbers are no less" (15). Such descriptions evoke a sense of oppressive eternity, for no matter how many stars fall in their "bitter arcs", their numbers are never lessened. The oppressive quality of the cosmos is emphasised further when the kid watches the stars burn "with a lidless fixity" (213) as though they were unblinking eyes, fixed upon him in unceasing surveillance. The night sky is full of evil omens, such as the "pale green meteor" that "passed overhead and vanished silently in the void" (227). Even the "constellation of Cassiopeia" evokes a sense of cosmic malice, burning "like a witch's signature on the black face of the firmament" (256), as though the malevolent forces responsible for creation had signed their handiwork for all to see.

Much like the French mathematician and mystic, Blaise Pascal (1623-1662)[34], the Gnostics were dismayed by the spatial and temporal enormity of the cosmos, believing that "the vastness and multiplicity of the cosmic system expresses the degree to which man is removed from [the Absolute] God"[35]. Such an apprehension of the terrible vastness of the cosmos is a concept prevalent throughout McCarthy's work[36]. The narrative voice in *Blood Meridian* frequently evokes the enormity of the cosmos in passages such as the following: "the sun when it rose caught the moon in the west so that they lay opposed to each other across the earth, the sun whitehot and the moon a pale replica, as if they were the ends of a common bore beyond whose terminals burned worlds past all reckoning" (86). Not only does the universe extend forever outwards to infinite numbers of other worlds, but this terrible infinitude also extends forever downwards, albeit in more metaphysical sense, into "the awful darkness inside the world" (111).

German mystic and theologian, Jacob Boehme (1575-1624) also held such a view, admitting that he "fell into a state of deep melancholy and grief in beholding the great depth of this world, the sun and the stars, the clouds, rain and snow, and in fact the whole of creation. I compared all that with the little speck called 'man', and how insignificant he is before God, if compared with this great work of heaven and earth"[37]. Boehme's influence on McCarthy is made evident through one of *Blood Meridian*'s epigraphs—"It is not to be thought that the life of darkness is sunk in misery and lost as if in sorrowing. There is no sorrowing. For sorrow is a thing that is swallowed up in death, and death and dying are the very life of the darkness". Taken from Boehme's *Six Theosophic Points*, the quote describes the condition of the devils in hell, who have turned their back on the God's light so completely that they no longer even feel the pain of its absence; unlike man, who struggles between the two polarities of good and evil, heaven and hell. Boehme also describes the enormity of the cosmos in *Six Theosophic Points*, stating that the "hellish dominion" is "powerful in various places in the locus of this world" and that "the hellish quality" may be discerned "in the deep between the stars and the earth"[38].

Like Boehme's works, *Blood Meridian* abounds in passages preoccupied with the

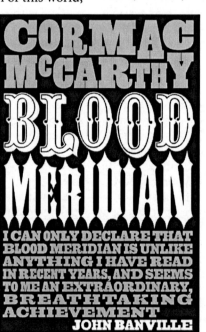

enormity of the cosmos, featuring descriptions of "the vast world of sand and scrub shearing upward into the shoreless void" and "to the uttermost rebate of space" (50), or "staccato mountains bespoken blue and barren out of the void" (175), or the "ribbed frames of dead cattle" which lie "like the ruins of primitive boats upturned upon that shoreless void" (247). Wandering lost through the wilderness, the kid contemplates a wounded companion named Sproule and sees that: "He was wounded in an enemy country far from home and although his eyes took in the alien stones about yet the greater void beyond seemed to swallow up his soul" (65)[39]. This passage evokes a Gnostic despair at the terrible vastness of creation, which "swallow[s] up" and imprisons the human spirit. It also emphasises the Gnostic motif of 'alienation', which teaches that the divine spirit within us feels estranged among the "alien stones" of the created world. In fact, the idea that man is imprisoned on earth is alluded to directly in *Blood Meridian* when the Glanton gang are referred to as "a patrol condemned to ride out some ancient curse" (151). Given the purgatorial wasteland which dominates the novel, this ancient curse seems to be manifest existence itself.

John Sepich counts over ninety direct and indirect references to a "hallucinatory void, adding that "the scale of the landscape often leads into passages in which a greater 'void,' beyond the earth, is the intended allusion"[40]. This void beyond the earth is both the void of outer space and the metaphysical void within. Paul Oppenheimer explains that the nihilistic 'void' is a concept closely allied with cinematic portrayals of evil, especially in situations depicting the aftermath of evil actions: "Past the disaster lies not a horror but a blank, a nothing, a zero, a black hole…The very physics of the universe, their natural laws, have devoured themselves, to leave a silent state of nil. The universe has performed itself into exhaustion, chaos, a word to that the Greeks who invented it meant not anarchy or disorder but a yawn, a gap, nothing". In *Blood Meridian*, the frenzied eruptions of violence leave only a "shoreless void" in their wake.

In what is perhaps the most interesting passage dealing with this recurring thematic trope, the narrative voice describes how the horses of the Glanton gang "trudged sullenly the alien ground and the round earth rolled beneath them silently milling the greater void wherein they were contained" (247). Here, the stress is once again placed on the alien nature of the created world, placed within the context of the enormity of the cosmos. The voice then goes on to evoke the metaphysically complexity of this vision: "In the neuter austerity of that terrain all phenomena were bequeathed a strange equality and no one thing nor spider nor stone nor blade of grass could put forth claim to precedence. The very clarity of these articles belied their familiarity, for the eye predicates the whole on some feature or part and here was nothing more luminous that another and nothing more enshadowed and in the optical democracy of such landscape all preference is made whimsical and a man and a rock become endowed with unguessed kinship" (247).

This "strange equality" is not to be mistaken for the transcended state of unity experienced by some mystics in altered states of consciousness, in which all phenomena appear equally "unreal", or as manifestations of *māyā* (illusion). Frithjof Schuon explains that "the metaphysical doctrine of illusion is not just a solution of convenience which justifies bringing everything on the plane of phenomena to a single level". He adds that "metaphysical synthesis is not a physical levelling out" because "there is no true synthesis without discernment"[41]. The description of

the "optical democracy" in *Blood Meridian* is concerned with just such a "physical levelling out". The reader is presented with a disturbingly reductionist vision, such as that celebrated by postmodernity, in which inherent value and meaning has been levelled out so that it is no longer possible to say that a man is better than an inanimate lump of dead minerals.

René Guénon also attacks this false concept of "levelling out" in *The Reign of Quantity*, a work which details the decline of the perennial philosophy in the modern world. Guénon writes that unity and uniformity are often mistaken for the same thing, but "the imposition of uniformity" actually leads "in a direction exactly opposite to that of true unity, since it tends to realize that which is most remote therefrom" and "takes shape as a sort of caricature of unity". Guénon explains that the "uniformity, in order that it may be possible, presupposes beings deprived of all qualities and reduced to nothing more that simple numerical 'units'". The "result of all efforts made to realize" such uniformity "can only be to rob beings more or less completely of their proper qualities". He concludes by stating that all efforts at "levelling"—such as we witness in *Blood Meridian*'s "optical democracy"—"always work downwards" being "only an expression of the tendency towards the lowest, that is, towards pure quantity, situated as it is at a level lower than that of all corporeal manifestation, not only below the degree occupied by the most rudimentary of living beings, but also below that occupied by what our contemporaries have a habit of calling 'lifeless matter'"[42]. Hence, what we witness in *Blood Meridian* is a caricature of true unity, in which man is not only reduced to the level of a spider, or a blade of grass, but in which all of these living things are placed on the same level as inanimate stones, thus completely obliterating the hierarchal chain of being.

Looking at this passage in the context of McCarthy's entire oeuvre, with its metaphysical overtones and theological preoccupations, it is unlikely that this vision of "optical democracy" constitutes McCarthy's understanding of the world, at least as it is presented in his novels. Rather, this is the vision that arises out of the perversities—both in thought and action—that constitute the depraved and parodic world of *Blood Meridian*. Though it is difficult to prove that at the time of writing *Blood Meridian* McCarthy disapproved of such a reductionist view of living beings, his latest work, *The Sunset Limited*, provides us with some deeper insights into McCarthy's view on the matter. In this "novel in dramatic form," the character "Black" puts forward a view of man that is completely in line with the teachings of the Perennial Philosophy. "I would say that the thing we are talkin about is Jesus", says "Black", "but it is Jesus understood as that gold at the bottom of the mine. He couldnt come down here and take the form of a man if that form was not done shaped to accommodate him" (95). The image of the "gold at the bottom of the mine" occurs in both Buddhist and Gnostic thought, referring to much the same concept in both traditions.

Writing about the parallels between Buddhism and Gnosticism, Edward Conze explains that: "There is a striking similarity between some of the similes used as well as the conclusions drawn from them". Conze compares the Gnostic parable of "gold sunk in filth" that "will not lose its beauty but preserve its own nature" with the Buddhist *Ratnagotravibhaga*, which states that even if "gold" falls into "a place full of stinking dirt, as it is indestructible by nature, it would stay there for many hundreds of years". Conze concludes that "in both cases this is a simile for the divine spark in man"[43]. The Gnostics stress the "metaphysical status of man in the order of existence". Their "doctrine of the God 'Man'", also known as the "Urmensch" or "Anthropos" myth, stresses the "close relationship or kinship of nature between the highest God and the inner core of man" [44]. The Buddha also taught that: "Rebirth as a *man* is…essential for the appreciation of the Dharma", because beings in the higher realms "are too happy to feel dislike for conditioned things, and they live too long to appreciate impermanence", while those in the lower realms "lack in clarity of mind"[45].

In the *Sunset Limited*, "Black" goes on to stress this divine essence within all men, even at the cost of sounding like a heretic: "And if I said that there aint no way for Jesus to be ever man without ever man bein Jesus then I believe that might be a pretty big heresy. But that's all right. It aint as big a heresy as sayin that a man aint all that much different from a rock. Which is how your view looks to me" (95). Here, man and rock do not share an "unguessed kinship". Even the character "White"—a suicidal rationalist whose argument runs counter to "Black's" throughout the play—has to concede that man is higher than a rock: "It's not my view", he retorts, "I believe in the primacy of the intellect" (96). Thus, the "optical democracy" passage in *Blood Meridian* puts forward a perverted view; one that keeps human beings from seeking their full potential. As the traditions of the perennial philosophy, as well as the metaphysics underlying McCarthy's fiction proclaim, man is capable of great evil, but also of great good. No matter how blackened his heart may be, a divine essence remains. Whether one considers man in spiritual or intellectual terms, the existence of the spirit, or, if you like, the mere presence of consciousness, necessarily separates man from the inanimate stones around him.

That is not to say that man is not capable of horrendous acts of evil. In *Cormac McCarthy's Western Novels*, Barcley Owens concedes that hostile landscapes, or indeed, skyscapes, are a "favourite motif" of McCarthy's writing, but points out that nature serves only as a mirror to man's depravity; because "man reflects the violent character of a brutal environment"[46]. Owens goes on to argue that: "As one of the most violent novels in contemporary American literature, *Blood Meridian* parallels its times. The mirror of art that McCarthy holds up to the nineteenth century reflects the ugliness of our time as well"[47]. Arguing along the same lines, Edwin Arnold, in "Go To Sleep: Dreams and Visions in the Border Trilogy," describes *Blood Meridian* as "an extended nightmare of history", adding that to "read it is to enter the darker places of the imagination, to witness the malignity of humankind at its worst".[48] John Cant, in *Cormac McCarthy and the Myth of American Exceptionalism*, writes that while "the postmodern critic…rejects the essentialist notion of a fixed human nature", "McCarthy's depiction of various of his protagonists 'in extremis' makes it clear that he believes in an all too powerful 'essential' human nature and that violence is inherent to that essence"[49]. *Blood Meridian* is a unique masterpiece of twentieth century literature, for few novels—save Vassily Grossman's own masterpiece, *Life and Fate*—have attempted such a devastatingly honest portrayal of the depths of depravity to which this "essential" human nature can sink.

Blood Meridian begins with the words: "See the child" (3), which effectively evoke an image of archetypal innocence through simple storybook language; however this effect is almost immediately subverted by the reminder that in this little child "broods already a taste for mindless violence" (3). Bloodlust lies at the very core of human nature; it is something that comes from within, not without. When the child grows into "the kid," he indulges his taste for violence in pub brawls with soldiers: "They fight with fists, with feet, with bottles or knives. All races, all breeds" (4). The narrative voice thus implicates the entire human race in this mad, violent struggle.

The trope of human depravity is voiced by a lone hermit that shelters the kid early in the novel. After showing the kid "[s]ome man's heart, dried and blackened", the hermit cradles "it in his palm as if he'd weigh it" (18). This strange action evokes an esoteric reference to the Egyptian Anubis, the jackal-headed god of dead, who weighs the hearts of men after death to determine which is righteous and which corrupt. Clearly, the human heart does not pass the test, for the hermit announces: "A man's at odds to know his mind cause his mind is aught he has to know it with. He can know his heart, but he don't want to. Rightly so. Best not to look in there. It ain't the heart of a creature that is bound in the way that God has set for it" (19). Traditionally the heart was

considered to be the seat of passions and desires and thus not equivalent with the spirit, but rather a barrier to the spiritual life, which must be overcome by the extinguishing of earthly desires. For example, Buddhist sutras describe the heart as "the poisonous serpent" coiled in our breast "which is always breathing out the fire of the three poisons, bringing us agonies and sufferings"[50]. Gnostic teachings also warn against the danger of letting oneself be ruled by one's heart, for the "evil powers" which rule the cosmos are "evident and active in [man's] passions and desires"[51]. Similarly, Manichean doctrines teach that: "Although man has Light within him, the Darkness made sure that he would perpetuate his enslavement by desire"[52].

These traditions, however, all stress the importance of self-knowledge; "Know Thyself" advised the Delphic Oracle, as did the Gnostic gospels: "Let every man be watchful of himself. Whosoever is watchful of himself shall be saved from the devouring fire"[53]. Thus, the hermit's "Rightly so" can be read sarcastically, for man would greatly benefit from knowing his own heart, if only he had the courage to examine what lies within. In fact, in *The Achievement of Cormac McCarthy* Vereen Bell argues that the hermit, with his pronouncements on man's wilful ignorance of his own depravity, "comes closer to speaking the paraphrased theme of the novel than any other spokesman"[54]. The narrative voice of *Blood Meridian* forces the reader to closely examine this blackened "heart of darkness," already weighed, and found wanting, by the hermit.

As mentioned earlier, the terrifying "void" that constitutes the cosmos is a central metaphor in *Blood Meridian*, but the horror applies not only to the macrocosm of the solar system, but to the microcosm of man's inner life. Brady Harrison argues that in *Blood Meridian*, the "void without speaks to the void said to lurk within the Western consciousness". He goes on to cite "Conrad's *Heart of Darkness* (1899) as the most famous example of the void within as the void without" because "the heart of darkness lurks as much in Kurtz, as Conrad presents it, as in the African jungle"[55]. Extrapolating this idea to *Blood Meridian*, we could argue that "the secret dark of the earth's heart" (195) mirrors the awful darkness inside the heart of man.

Similarly, in *Six Theosophic Points*—a work whose influence McCarthy acknowledges in an epigraph to *Blood Meridian*—Boehme writes: "External Reason supposed that hell is far from us. But it is near us. Every one carries it in himself"[56]. According to Boehme, an individual hell lies within every man's heart, waiting to swallow him up if he succumbs to the darkness within. The various atrocities described in vivid detail throughout the novel confirm this view. On one occasion, the Glanton gang—a band of scalp hunters—attack a village of peaceful elders, women, and children simply because their scalps are indistinguishable from those of the Apaches they were hired to kill. The men are depicted knee-deep in blood-red water, "hacking at the dying and decapitating those who knelt for mercy" (156), while others lie "coupled to the bludgeoned bodies of young women dead or dying on the beach" (157). Not content with the bounty collected for the scalps, the men also make belts and harnesses from the skins of the slain.

The Glanton gang is often depicted in ways which evoke the primitive hunting clans of prehistory. The narrative voice describes them as "a pack of viciouslooking humans…bearded, barbarous, clad in the skins of animals stitched up with thews and armed with weapons of every description…dangerous, filthy, brutal" (78). The gang immediately calls to mind a band of cannibals[57]; "the trappings of their horses" are "fashioned out of human skin and their bridles woven up from human hair and decorated with human teeth", the riders themselves wear "scapulars or necklaces of dried and blackened human ears" and the entire procession is "like a visitation from some heathen land where they and others like them fed on human flesh" (78). Being scalp-hunters, the members of Glanton's gang do in fact feed on human flesh, albeit in an indirect sense, for they exchange the scalps for goods and services and are therefore using human flesh as a form currency.

The atavistic theme is continued throughout the novel and the Glanton gang are often portrayed as having somehow regressed to man's early history; "there was nothing about these arrivals to suggest even the discovery of the wheel" (232). Or to suggest even the invention of fire, or speech, for that matter: "in darkness absolute the company sat among the rocks without fire or bread or camaraderie any more than banded apes. They crouched in silence eating raw meat…and they slept among the bones" (148). As they wander through the plains, they appear to predate speech itself: "Like beings provoked out of the absolute rock and set nameless and at no remove from their own loomings to wander ravenous and doomed and mute as gorgons shambling the brutal wastes of Gondwanaland in a time before nomenclature was and each was all" (172). The hyperbolic reference to Gondwanaland—one of the early Cambrian continents resulting from the break-up of Panterra—further emphasises the point that mankind has essentially not evolved since its relatively recent arrival on this planet.

Perhaps the most shocking aspect of *Blood Meridian* is that there is nothing unusual about the behaviour of the Glanton gang. Bill Baines notes that "McCarthy's book focuses on cruelty, perhaps man's most apparent quality in the world the author creates. The book's inhumanity is not—as is often the case in Westerns—the cruelty of white to Indian or Indian to white, but the cruelty of human to human perennial to literature and to other affairs of mankind"[58]. The novel is not solely preoccupied with the depravity of the Glanton gang, but also features a lengthy description of a horde of Comanches attacking Captain White's gang of Filibusters. Piping on "flutes made from human bones" (52), the Comanches are depicted as "a horde from a hell more horrible yet than the brimstone land of christian reckoning, screeching and yammering and clothed in smoke like those vaporous beings in regions beyond right knowing where the eye wanders and the lip jerks and drools" (53). The passage not only masterfully captures the hallucinogenic and nightmarish qualities of this vision, but also suggests that this world is already worse than any hell we could ever imagine, a belief held by the heretical Cathars of the twelfth and thirteenth century. After the slaughter, "some of the savages" were "so slathered up with gore they might have rolled in it like dogs" and others "fell upon the dying and sodomized them with loud cries to their fellows" (54). Clearly, this is no ordinary Western and there are no "good guys" among these cowboys and indians.

The world of *Blood Meridian* is one drenched in violence and bloodshed and the enigmatic Judge Holden takes every opportunity to remind the Glanton gang that human life has always been this way[59]. While the scalp-hunters sit amongst the ruins of a settlement of the Anasazi, the judge proclaims: "All progressions from a higher to a lower order are marked by ruins and mystery and a residue of nameless rage" (146). His words evoke W.B. Yeats' poem, "Meru", which describes how man "despite his terror, cannot cease / Ravening, raging, and uprooting that he may come / Into the desolation of reality"[60]. It is this "nameless rage" which shapes human history and the world of *Blood Meridian* is not some perversion of the normal state of things, but rather human nature allowed to run rampant and unchecked. Judge Holden's words serve as a reminder of the cyclical nature of history, doomed to repeat itself in the rise and fall of civilizations: "This you see here, these ruins wondered at by tribes of savages, do you think that this will be again? Aye. And again. With other people, with other sons" (147). Barcley Owens argues that: "When Judge Holden gestures toward the Anasazi ruins and describes them as the end result of empire building, he prophesises America's future"[61]. Indeed, this is the future of the entire human race, which we will later see depicted in McCarthy's apocalyptic novel, *The Road*.

This remarkable penchant for brutality and mayhem has characterised the human race since the beginning of our history, as McCarthy's epigraphic reference to the 300,000-year-old skull which "shows evidence of having been scalped" demonstrates. The reference, taken from a June 13, 1982 article in *The Yuman Daily Sun*, also serves as a reminder that the violence of *Blood Meridian* is not the work of outlandish fiction, but historical reality. Harold Bloom makes this point in *How to Read and Why* when he writes: "None of [*Blood Meridian*'s] carnage is gratuitous or redundant; it belonged to the Mexico-Texas borderlands in 1849-50, which is where and when most of the novel is set"[62]. Sadly, one does not need to look far to find other instances of carnage in the annals of human history.

The novel continually highlights man's inherent savagery by developing a running theme of the kinship between human beings and wolves. "Wolves cull themselves, man" announces the judge. "What other creature could? And is the race of man not more predacious yet?" (147). After reading through *Blood Meridian*'s catalogue of massacres, depravities and atrocities, one must surely answer this question in the affirmative. After all, "the hunters [smile] among themselves" after hearing "the howling of a wolf" (117), the ex-priest-cum-scalphunter Tobin announces that he "would never shoot a wolf" and knows "other men of the same sentiments" (129), and at "night the wolves in the dark forests called to [the scalp-hunters] as if they were friends to man" (188). Evolving in a harsh, brutal environment where the rule was "kill, or be killed," human beings had to compete with each other as well as with wild predators in order to survive as a species, and, as a result, no animal is as efficient a killer as man. The Glanton gang functions like a wolf pack: "although each man among them was discrete unto himself, conjoined they made a thing that had not been before and in that communal soul were wastes hardly reckonable more than those whited regions on old maps where monsters do live" (152). The collective sum of their brutality is greater than its individual components. Their "communal soul" becomes a magnified version of the darkness inside each man's heart, where man feels it is "best not to look" (19) for fear of what "monsters" one may find[63].

Precisely because the suffering and cruelty inflicted by human beings against one another is so ubiquitous in *Blood Meridian*, it is quite easy to overlook the fact that nature itself is cruel. The narrative voice reminds the reader than animals also injure and devour each other with a grotesque description of a "snakebit" horse, "with its head enormously swollen and grotesque….It had been bitten on the nose and its eyes bulged out of the shapeless head in a horror of agony and it tottered moaning toward the clustered horses of the company with its long misshapen muzzle swinging and drooling and its breath wheezing in the throttled pipes of its throat. The skin had split open along the bride of its nose and the bone shone through pinkish white" (115). The other horses show no compassion for the crazed animal, instead it frightens and infuriates them and it is clear that they would like to kill it: "A small mottled stallion…struck at the thing twice and then turned and buried its teeth in its neck. Out of the mad horse's throat came a sound that brought the men to the door" (115). The suffering of the horse is as senseless as the suffering of the victims of Glanton's gang, and yet it is entirely natural. *Blood Meridian* establishes no dichotomous opposition between the natural and moral evil, suggesting that the condition of all life on earth is one of violence, suffering and brutality.

Blood Meridian presents the reader with a world in which everything devours everything else64. The novel is filled with such sights as a "howling wilderness", where "coyotes had dug up the dead and scattered their bones" (42), "three buzzards hobbl[ing] about on the picked bone carcass of some animal" (26), the stone floor of a church "heaped with the scalped and naked and partly eaten bodies of some forty souls" (60), a village where "the dead were still in the streets and buzzards and pigs were feeding on them" (181). Men, too, partake in this devouring: "One of the mares had foaled in the desert and this frail form soon hung skewered on a paloverde pole over the raked coals while the Delawares passed among themselves a gourd containing

the curdled milk taken from its stomach" (161). Towards the end of the novel, the kid encounters a field of slain buffalo with "the meat rotting on the ground and the air whining with flies and the buzzards and ravens and the night a horror of snarling and feeding with the wolves half crazed and wallowing in the carrion" (317). The latter feeding frenzy strongly recalls a scene from McCarthy's favourite novel65, Herman Melville's *Moby-Dick*, where "thousands on thousands of sharks, swarming round the dead Leviathan, smackingly feasted on its fatness" (286). Melville's words—"Consider, once more, the universal cannibalism of the sea; all whose creatures prey upon each other, carrying on eternal war since the world began" (270)—may well be extended to cover the wastelands of *Blood Meridian*, and indeed the entire planet.

The horror felt at the sight of this frenzied feasting—evoked both by *Blood Meridian* and *Moby-Dick*—is also a strikingly Gnostic sentiment. As a Manichean text demonstrates, it is the fate of all living creatures to be "cast into all things, to the teeth of panthers and elephants, devoured by them that devour, consumed by them that consume, eaten by the dogs, mingled and bound in all that is, imprisoned in the stench of darkness"[66]. Jacob Boehme was also dismayed by this brutal aspect of existence and lamented that: "Within all nature there is a continual wrestling, battling, and devouring, so that this world may truly be called a valley of sorrow, full of trouble, persecution, suffering, and labour"[67]. Boehme also dealt with this theme in his *Six Theosophic Points*, writing that the essence of the "life of darkness"—mentioned in the epigraph to *Blood Meridian*—is "a perpetual stinging and breaking, each form being enemy to the other" and that this behaviour is also "seen among men and beasts" where "there is a biting, hating and striking, and an arrogant self-will, each wishing to rule over the other, to kill and devour the other, and elevate itself alone; also to trample upon everything with guile, wrath, malice and falsehood, and make itself lord"68. Boehme's description of the "life of darkness" reads like a summary of the narrative action within *Blood*

Meridian.

Whether for the Manicheans, for Boehme, or for McCarthy, an anticosmic stance emerges organically from a vision of "nature, red in tooth and claw"[69]. Not only are the living organisms on this planet subject to an endless cycle of devouring, but they are also threatened by the hostile forces of nature, as is made apparent when the men ride past "parched beasts" that "had died with their necks stretched in agony in the sand and now upright and blind and lurching askew with scraps of blackened leather hanging from the fretwork of their ribs they leaned with their long mouths howling after the endless tandem suns that passed above them" (247). It is as though the very earth demands the blood of creatures; "This is a thirsty country", an old Mennonite announces early in the novel. A country that has soaked up the "blood of a thousand Christs" and still "Nothing" has changed, or will every change. (102). The world is a "great stained altarstone" (102), demanding constant blood sacrifice. As Vasily Grossman asks in *Life and Fate*, "Is it that life itself is evil?"[70] According to the Gnostics, who "saw evil as something inherent in the material creation itself"[71]—the answer to the above question is a resounding "Yes!" And it is difficult to draw any other conclusion after reading through McCarthy's historically accurate world of *Blood Meridian.*

After establishing that creation was evil, the Gnostics asked another question: "Who is to blame?" The answer they gave was that "the created order cannot be the product of the transcendent God[head] but must have been created by a lower divine being"[72]. In most Gnostic myths, the demiurge, with the assistance of a host of evil angels knows as archons, created the cosmos after seeing a reflected image of the divine light of the true Godhead. Hans Jonas writes that "it is with the help of the projected *image* of the divine *form* that the lower forces make the world or man, i.e., as an *imitation* of the divine original"[73]. Jonas explains that this concept arises out of the "mythic idea of the substantiality of an image, reflection, or shadow

as representing a real part of the original entity from which it has become detached"[74]. Hence, the Gnostics believed that a fragment of the divine—essentially, the spirit or *pneuma* within all living things—had become trapped in the mire of created matter, simply through this act of reflection, or mirroring of the light in the darkness.

Of course, the idea of the original Absolute, or the Ideal Forms can be traced back to the creation myth in Plato's *Timaeus*, who, in his famous Parable of the Cave, saw "the entire manifest world as a pale image of a Reality and Light beyond the Cave of Shadows, the Cave in which the troglodytes are chained. No matter how much 'beauty' or 'joy' or 'wonderment' we might find in the manifest realm, it remains only a shadow...of the Beauty beyond, which is revealed in direct contemplative experience and confirmed by all who have the eyes to see"[75]. The troglodytes, here, are the ordinary, unenlightened human beings who mistake the "shadow' for the 'thing itself", or, in other words, mistake the illusory nature of the manifest world for the reality of the Absolute Godhead. In *Blood Meridian*, the Glanton gang, representative of the human race at its worst, can only see the shadows. As they descend the mountain—in itself a movement evoking devolution rather than progress—the men walk "with their hands outheld before them and their shadows contorted on the broken terrain like creatures seeking their own forms" (65). Seeking after their shadows in the mistaken belief that these are the Ideal Forms themselves, the Glanton gang strongly resemble "the troglodytes who worship the Shadows without seeing the Light"[76]. As previously mentioned, the Glanton gang is often described in atavistic terms, descriptions which strengthen the connection with Plato's cave dwelling troglodytes.

Though both the Gnostics and the Platonists (and Neoplatonists) spoke of the created world as a mere shadow of an Ideal Absolute, Jonas explains that the crucial difference between these traditions "is that the former deplore the 'descent' by image-reflection as the cause of divine tragedy", while the latter "affirm it as the necessary and positive self-expression of the efficacy of the first source"[77]. The Gnostics go as far as to describe the process of creation as an "imitation, illicite and blundering, of the divine by the lower powers"[78]. Both traditions, however, stress the "vertical structure of this scale of unfolding, that is, the *downward* direction of all metaphysical generation which therefore cannot be but deterioration"[79]. In other words, according to both the Gnostics and Plato, created things are only an inferior imitation of a perfected original source. This idea is hinted at during a strange scene in *Blood Meridian*, where the "lifeforms"—prisoners, guards, dogs, mules, and a fat priest—"all lightly shimmering in the heat", appear "like wonders much reduced. Rough likeness thrown up at hearsay after the things themselves had faded" (75). Here, the narrative voice offers a perspective on reality in which all "lifeforms" appear as mere shadows of the "things themselves", or as inferior imitations of the original divine source.

Shadows—along with their metaphysical and theological connotations—feature prominently in *Blood Meridian*. Not only are the shadows symbols of the inferior quality of created things, but they also represent the obscuration of light. Light has long been associated with divine illumination, while darkness has stood for the ignorance of evil, as in St John's pronouncement: "And the light shineth in darkness; and the darkness comprehended it not" (John 1:5). Similarly, in Gnostic thought the alien God is known as "the "King of Light," whose world is "a world of splendour and of light without darkness", while the manifest cosmos of the demiurge is "the world of darkness, utterly full of evil"[80]. Even Boehme associated the material world with darkness and evil, writing: "The realm of matter and darkness is the realm of anguish, contention, and suffering; the realm of the Spirit is the kingdom of light, joy, peace, and happiness"[81]. Similarly, in his *Six Theosophic Points*, which also include the passage McCarthy used as an epigraph to *Blood Meridian*, Boehme writes that the "life of darkness is repugnant

to all life of light"[82]. Thus, shadows are often representative of evil forces, both within and without man.

In *Blood Meridian*, the shadows "of the men and their mounts advanced elongate before them like strands of the night from which they'd ridden, like tentacles to bind them to the darkness yet to come"(45). Here, the shadows seem to be residues of the night itself, binding the men to both literal and metaphorical darkness. Later, "horse and rider" appear "spanceled to their shadows on the snowblue ground" (152). According to the *Oxford English Dictionary*, to spancel is to "fetter or hobble" with "a short noosed rope", thus repeating the motif of man's imprisonment in fetters of darkness. Such imprisonment seems to be the fate of all created things; even the stones of the desert" like "in dark tethers of shadow" (227). In this anticosmic vision of the world, all things are tainted by the very corporeality of their manifest existence.

The evil forces seem to possess an autonomous existence of their own; the shadows appear "austere and implacable like shapes capable of violation their covenant with the flesh that authored them and continuing autonomous across the naked rock without reference to sun or man or god" (139). So strong are these ties to they darkness, that when "White" John Jackson rides in "Black" John Jackson's shadow, the "black would check or start his horse to shake him off. As if the white man were in violation of his person" (81). The shadow, here, is not just "the shape he stood from the sun", but it seems as though it "bore something of the man himself and in so doing lay imperilled" (81). The depraved men of Glanton's gang, utterly devoid of spiritual or even moral values, seem to embrace such evil as their natural element. They ride, "treading their thin and flaring shadows" until they cross "altogether into the darkness which so well became them" (163). The passage strongly evokes the description of the supernatural "grim triune" (129) in *Outer Dark*. The three mysterious figures walk at sunset, "until they had gone on for such a time as saw the sun down altogether and they moved in shadow altogether which suited them very well" (3). In both instances, the characters feel at home surrounded by darkness and all its evil connotations.

The Gnostic idea that creation is flawed, or at least not as perfect as it ought to be, is discussed in *Blood Meridian* through the words of the hermit. "God made this world", he announces "but he didnt make it to suit everybody, did he?" (19). The kid agrees, that he "can think of better places and better ways" (19). Man, as voiced by the kid, knows instinctively that there must be better worlds than this one, if not actually than certainly potentially. But the hermit deflates this argument when he asks: "Can ye make it be?" to which the kid naturally replies "No" (19). The hermit, here, seems to be arguing along the lines of Gottfried Wilhelm Leibniz's (1646-1716) "Best Possible World Theodicy," which "seeks to demonstrate that God cannot be blamed for the existence of evil in the world, since this world is the best of all possible worlds"[83]. Leibniz envisioned "God actualizing that possible world that contains the amount of evil necessary to make the world the best one on the whole" even if that entailed "bringing about a world that has a great many evils in it but evils of such kinds and arranged in such ways that they contribute to the world being the very best one possible"[84]. According to Leibniz, God is perfectly omnipotent, omniscient and benevolent, thus whatever world exists must logically be the best possible world.

The hermit's argument, however, would not meet the standards of David Hume (1711-1176), who argued that: "If you find inconveniences and deformities in [a] building, you will always, without entering into any detail, condemn the architect". Even if the "architect would in vain display his subtilty, and prove to you, that if this door or that window were altered, greater ills would ensue….still you would assert in general, that, if the architect had had skill and good intentions, he might have formed such a plan of the whole, and might have adjusted the parts in such a manner, as would have remedied all

or most of these inconveniences. His ignorance, or even your own ignorance of such a plan, will never convince you of the impossibility of it"[85]. In other words, one need not posses the knowledge, the skills, or the means to create a better world to realise, as the kid does, that there is something horribly wrong with this one. Thus, like the kid, the Gnostics could envision "better places and better ways" and, like Hume, they blamed an inept architect for the existence of this abortive creation.

According to Gnostic beliefs, not only is the demiurge inept as a creator, incapable of creating a perfect world, but he is also totally indifferent to human suffering. According to the Gnostics, the demiurge revealed his true nature when he rejected the sacrifice of Cain, "whereas he accepted the bloody sacrifice of Abel: for the lord of this world delights in blood"[86]. McCarthy's preoccupation with God's refusal to intercede in the proliferation of evil is thoroughly Gnostic. As the judge asks: "If God meant to interfere in the degeneracy of mankind would he not have done so by now?" (146). The judge's words echo those of the Marquis de Sade's (1740-1814), who argued that "true crimes against nature are impossible" because "the impulse to crime is natural". Hence, if "even evil has its own purpose" then "every crime you commit is a brick in the wall of providential design"[87]. In one of Sade's novels, God speaks and asks: "Did not the perpetual miseries with which I inundate the universe convince you that I love only disorder, and that to please me one must emulate me?"[88]. This idea has also been put forward by Christopher Douglas, who argues that McCarthy's fiction explores the notion that "the silence of God in the face of human misery" is "characterised by a certain malice"[89]. The demiurge has no desire to alleviate human suffering, or to intervene in humanity's slow self-destruction, as he is a malevolent, bloodthirsty deity, and the manifest world is his sadistic playground.

McCarthy's novels often call into doubt the nature of the creator of this world. In *Suttree*, for example, the protagonist doubts the nature of the creator, asking: "What deity in the realms of dementia, what rabid god decocted out of the smoking lobes of hydrophobia could have devised a keeping place for souls so poor as is this flesh. This mawky worm-bent tabernacle" (130). Later, as Suttree contemplates the death of his young son, he asks, "what could a child know of the darkness of God's plan?" (154). Perhaps the ragpicker says it best, telling Suttree, "I always figured they was a God…I just never did like him" (147). In *All the Pretty Horses*, Alfonsa refuses to "believe in a God who could permit such injustice…in a world of his own making" (232). John Grady feels that he has "no reason to be afraid of God", adding that he even has "a bone or two to pick with Him" (272). In *The Crossing*, an ex-priest recalls how he was "seeking evidence for the hand of God in the world" and that he had "come to believe that hand a wrathful one" (142). Similarly, recounting the tale of a heretic, he states: "It was never that this man ceased to believe in God. No. It was rather that he came to believe terrible things of Him" (148). Finally, in *The Road,* the "man" cannot bring himself to believe that the world he finds himself in could be the will of a benevolent God: "He raised his face to the paling day. Are you there? he whispered. Will I see you at the last? Have you a neck by which to throttle you? Have you a heart? Damn you eternally have you a soul? Oh God, he whispered. Oh God" (11-12). Such quintessentially Gnostic attacks on the creator of this world constitute a running theme throughout McCarthy's fiction.

The character of the creator can be gauged by the nature of his creation, whether we examine the nature of human beings, or of the created world. The idea that there is something awry in creation is first put forward by the hermit, who announces that: "You can find meanness in the least of creatures, but when God made man the devil was at his elbow" (19). Though the hermit does not blame the creator directly, his words imply that the creation of man was influenced by the forces of evil. The desolate and hostile landscapes which abound in *Blood Meridian* also point to a supremely indifferent, if not downright malevolent, creator. Douglas writes

that: "As with earlier Christian theologians, McCarthy believes that the details of creation can tell us something interesting about the character of the creator; but unlike them, McCarthy is not comforted by the evidence of design that he discerns in the universe. For McCarthy, that design is evidence of a no-longer benign creator whose dark purposes can be discerned in the awful silence of an empty landscape"[90]. In other words, divine silence does not necessarily signify the non-existence of a creator-god.

A particular telling in the novel explores these concepts of divine intervention, or lack thereof, via a description of the senseless deaths of travelers in the dessert: "Far out on the desert to the north dustspouts rose wobbling and augured the earth and some said they'd heard of pilgrims borne aloft like dervishes in those mindless coils to be dropped broken and bleeding upon the desert again and there perhaps to watch the thing that had destroyed them lurch onward like some drunken djinn and resolve itself once more into the elements from which it sprang" (111). The reference to "pilgrims" immediately places this passage in a religious context, suggesting a search for spiritual development. This religious context is emphasised by the addition of "dervishes"; a dervish being "a Muslim friar, who has taken vows of poverty and austere life. Of these there are various orders, some of whom are known from their fantastic practices as *dancing* or *whirling*" (OED). Both "pilgrim" and "dervish" signify those who have set out in search of God, either through spatial or spiritual journeys, yet these seekers in the wilderness encounter only a senselessly maleficent force in the mindless dustspout.

The dustspout, however, evokes a sense of hostile agency despite its apparent "mindlessness", for it lurches away like one of the "djinn", which, according to "Muslim demonology", is "an order of spirits lower than the angels, said to have the power of appearing in human and animal forms, and to exercise supernatural influence over men" (OED). It is noteworthy that in *Blood Meridian*, the supernaturally evil Judge

Holden is also described as "a great ponderous djinn" (96). The dustspouts may be "mindless", but the "mindlessness" of evil does not detract from its destructive efficacy, for the dustspout moves with a certain sinister deliberation, lurching onward and then resolving itself into the elements. Though the dustspouts may be described as mindless, in the sense that they do not consciously orchestrate the evil they cause, their very existence points to some terrible flaw in the scheme of things.

McCarthy later raises the same idea in *All the Pretty Horses*; where John Grady imagines "the pain of the world to be like some formless parasitic being seeking out the warmth of human souls wherein to incubate" and comes to the realisation "that it was mindless and so had no way to know the limits of those souls and what he feared was that there might be no limits" (256-7). Again, the mindlessness here is that of a creature, and does not suggest a lack of agency, for this parasitic being actively seeks out "the warmth of human souls" like a larvae burrowing into its host. The concept of an evil as having a parasitic nature is emphasised within *Blood Meridian* itself, in the image of a dead babies hung from the "broken stobs of mesquite". Their bodies are described as: "Bald and pale and bloated, larval to some unreckonable being" (57). The horror of this image does not rely solely on the portrayal of the slaughter of innocence; the babies themselves are hideous and "larval," as though they were waiting to hatch and spawn more evil still.

Apart from the dual reference to the Muslim faith in the usage of "dervish" and "djinn", the passage also evokes the Biblical Book of Job, strengthening the connections to the Semitic religions which worship a lone creator god. Unlike the voice of God which speaks to Job out of the whirlwind, McCarthy's narrator reminds us that: "Out of that whirlwind no voice spoke and the pilgrim lying in his broken bones may cry out and in his anguish he may rage, but rage at what?" (111). This terrible silence does not necessarily point to the non-existence of a creator-deity, but might rather be read as an indication of his malevolent nature. Christopher

Douglas also puts forward this argument, stating that *Blood Meridian*'s "reverse-agnosticism, that perhaps God *does* exist, is not a cause for hope for McCarthy, but a cause for terror. There are patterns of evil in our world. God's silence is no longer seen as indifference, but as the possibility of his malice"[91]. Or, as the Marquis de Sade pointed out: "the alternative to God's absence is His presence. If He should be known by His works, what must we infer about His nature?"[92] What can we infer about the nature of a deity that leaves his pilgrims lying in their broken bones?

Blood Meridian very subtly questions that nature of the relationship between the god of the Semitic religions and his people. Although the novel is set in the nineteenth century, McCarthy is a twenty-first century writer writing for a contemporary audience. Thus, the description of the "sun to the west" which "lay in a holocaust" (105) cannot fail to evoke the remembrance of the atrocities committed against the Jewish people in Nazi concentration camps, even though the original meaning of the word "holocaust" is "a burnt offering". The following lines—"where there rose a steady column" (105), leads the reader to anticipate the rising of a column of smoke, such as that seen over the crematoriums, or, perhaps, the pillar of smoke which the Lord used to guide the children of Israel through the desert (Exodus 13:21). The steady column, however, is composed of "small desert bats", but smoke is evoked nevertheless through the "dust" that "was blowing down the void like the smoke of distant armies" (105); an image that also reminds the reader of the violent struggles in human history, whether in the Old Testament or in our own time. Only a few lines down, McCarthy strengthens this reading with the words: "Here beyond men's judgements all covenants were brittle" (106). It is impossible to ignore the close proximity of the words "holocaust" and "covenant"; the covenant being the agreement between Yahweh and the children of Israel, whereby they would be protected in exchange for their obedience and worship.

The Holocaust of the twentieth century was viewed by some Jewish scholars as a breaking of this Covenant; a betrayal which gave rise to that perennially insoluble question of theodicy: "Why would a benevolent god allow such senseless suffering?" In *Holocaust: Religious and Philosophical Implications*, David Weiss and Michael Berenbaum discuss this problem in a chapter entitled "The Holocaust and the Covenant", arguing that: "The classic Judaic delineation of the relationship between God and the House of Israel is no longer tenable" because the "covenant that was, or the illusion of this covenant, has been abrogated in the German death camps". They argue that the survivors of the Holocaust must form "a new covenant, a unilateral, voluntary assertion by the House of Israel of the will to continue Jewish existence in the face of an indifferent, changeable, or non-existent deity"[93]. Weiss and Berenbaum add that this is not just a problem for the Jewish people, but for all individuals, because "the question to God, Why? is the same for the first child struck down in human history and for the last to perish in Auschwitz. That is the eternal confrontation of all men with God"[94]. McCarthy alludes to these problems in *Blood Meridian* precisely because the question of how one must live in the face of an indifferent, non-existent, or, worst of all, malevolent deity extends to innocent people everywhere who have suffered, continue to suffer, and helplessly watch while evildoers flourish under the terrible silence of an indifferent cosmos.

Both the Gnostics and the Buddhists taught that suffering lies at the very core of existence, but, being soteriologically focused, both systems offered a way out. Edward Conze explains that "salvation takes place through *gnosis*" in Gnostic terms, "or *jñāna*" for the Buddhists; both words approximating "spiritual insight". Conze adds that in "both cases" such "insight into the origination and nature of the world liberates us from it"[95]. Both the Buddhists and the Gnostics arrived at strikingly similar conclusions as to what the nature of this world may be. The "Buddhist idea of *samsara*… teaches that the world in which we live our daily lives is illusory"[96], in the sense that "it is

deceptive, because, one mistakes it for what it is not"[97]. While the Gnostic *Gospel of Truth* states that "those who live in [the world] experience 'terror and confusion and instability and doubt and division', being caught in 'many illusions'"[98]. The Buddha taught his followers that "All conditioned things are impermanent"; that everything in the manifest cosmos is "everchanging, doomed to destruction, quite unreliable, crumbling away however much we try to hold it"[99]. Similarly, Gnostic also texts stress the impermanent aspects of creation, reminding their readers that the world "is a thing wholly without substance…in which thou must place no trust" because "all works pass away, take their end and are as if they had never been"[100]. In both traditions, these insights into the nature of the world reveal that all created things are ultimately illusory and impermanent.

Impermanence and illusion also constitute the true nature of the manifest world as revealed in *Blood Meridian*. For example, the violent lightning storms which persists throughout the novel, illuminate "the mountains on the sudden skyline stark and black and livid like a land of some other order out there whose true geology was not stone but fear" (47). The concept of fear being more real than stone evokes a Gnostic vision of a world that, though frightening and hostile, is ultimately impermanent and illusory. Lightning also lights up the "blue and barren" desert, revealing a "demon kingdom summoned up or changeling land that come the day would leave neither trace nor smoke nor ruin more than any troubling dream" (47). This "demon kingdom" or "changeling land" is exactly how the Gnostics or the Buddhist perceived consensus reality; a collective nightmare born of ignorance and spiritual blindness. The Buddhist *Hridaya Prajñāpāramitā* ("Heart Sutra" of the "Perfection of Wisdom") teaches that once Enlightenment has been attained "everything that we can see around us" is revealed in its essential "emptiness" and disappears "like an insignificant dream"[101]. Similarly, the Gnostic *Gospel of Truth* teaches that the *pneumatics* (enlightened Gnostics) have "cast ignorance aside from them like sleep, not esteeming it as anything, nor do they esteem its works as solid things either, but they leave them behind like a dream in the night"[102]. As Jonas explains, the "metaphor of sleep" serves "to discount the sensations of 'life here' as mere illusions and dreams, though nightmarish ones, which we are powerless to control"[103]. In *Blood Meridian*, metaphors of nightmarish sleep, or hallucination, continue in descriptions such as that of the rising sun, in whose "eastern light the fires on the plain faded like an evil dream and the country lay bare and sparkling in the pure air" (205), or that of "the secular aloes blooming like phantasmagoria in a fever land" (163). The feverish quality of these visions and evil dreams not only highlights the fundamental "unreality" of the manifest world, but also it's profoundly sinister nature.

In *Blood Meridian*, Judge Holden seems to possess preternatural insights into this illusory, evanescent and sinister nature of the manifest world. "The truth about the world," he tells the men "is that anything is possible. Had you not seen it all from birth and thereby bled it of its strangeness it would appear to you for what it is, a hat trick in a medicine show, a fevered dream, a trance bepopulate with chimeras having neither analogue nor precedent, an itinerant carnival, a migratory tentshow whose ultimate destination after many a pitch in many a mudded field is unspeakable and calamitous beyond reckoning" (245). These words could have been taken right out of the Buddhist *Vajracchedikā Prajñāpāramitā* ("Diamond Sutra" of the "Perfection of Wisdom"): "As stars, a fault of vision, as a lamp, / A mock show, dew drops, or a bubble, / A dream, a lightning flash, or cloud, / So should one view what is conditioned"[104]. Precisely like the judge's description of the world as a "medicine show" or "carnival", the "Diamond Sutra" describes the world as a "mock show", because "like a magical show it deceives, deludes and defrauds us" and "is false when compared with ultimate reality"[105], or Nirvana.

The trope of the world as a "medicine show" or an "itinerant carnival" is repeated throughout

Blood Meridian. For example, a travelling troupe of "itinerant magicians" is described as "a set of right wanderfolk cast on this evil terrain" (89). The tribe of Yuma that massacre the Glanton gang watch the fire "as might some painted troupe of mimefolk recruiting themselves in such a wayplace far from the towns and the rabble hooting at them across the smoking footlamps" (276). Even the Judge Holden, leading a naked "idiot" on a lead through the wilderness, seems like "some degenerate entrepreneur fleeing from a medicine show and the outrage of the citizens who'd sacked it" (298). According to both Buddhist and Gnostic doctrines of transmigration, all living things are itinerant travellers, cast out into the "evil terrain" that is the manifest world and forced to wander from one life to another, like the participants in Judge Holden's "migratory tentshow".

The judge's sermon about the true nature of the created world seems to draw upon other similes from the "Diamond Sutra". For example, his description of the world as "a fevered dream" echoes the Sutra's teachings that the world is like "a dream", because "only the enlightened are awake to reality" and "compared with their vision of true reality, our normal experience is that of a dream, unreal and not to be taken seriously"[106]. Even the judge's description of the world as a hallucinatory "trance bepopulate with chimeras"—one of the definitions of "chimera" being a "horrible and fear-inspiring phantasm" (OED)—evokes the Sutra's reference to "a fault of vision" because "the world as it appears to the ignorant is like a hallucination which springs from an eye-disease"[107]. The judge's description of the world as "itinerant" and "migratory", places emphasis on its lack of stability, impermanence and transience. The "Diamond Sutra" also emphasises the impermanent nature of existence; comparing the world to a "dew-drop" because of its evanescence, and "a bubble" because "it can be enjoyed only for a moment"[108] before bursting and revealing its inherent emptiness.

Finally, the judge predicts an "unspeakable and calamitous" end for the world, views also upheld by both Buddhist and Gnostic texts. The *Buddhacarita* ("The Acts of the Buddha"), describes how the "world is carried away in distress on the flooded river of suffering, which the foam of disease oversprays, which has old age for its surge and rushes along with the violent rush of death"109. The Buddhists also believe that the cosmos undergoes regular cycles, or *kalpas*, of creation and annihilation: "During the course of one kalpa, a world system completes its evolution, from its initial condensation to the final conflagration. One world system follows the other, without beginning and end, quite interminable"110. Gnostic texts such as the *Tripartite Tractate*, also predict an apocalyptic end to creation, in which "the fire that is hidden in the world will blaze forth and burn" and "when it has consumed all matter it will be consumed with it and pass into non-existence"111. The Gnostic texts differ from the Buddhist in that the "termination (or oblivion) which the cosmos meets at the end of time is irreversible and does not allow for a fresh start in the cosmic process"112. Since the judge claims that the world has "neither analogue nor precedent", his description of the calamitous ending seems to support the Gnostic view in which creation is a singular aberration, never to be repeated; rather than the Buddhist view in which the world systems appear and disappear in endless cycles of creation and destruction.

Though Judge Holden's discourse on the hallucinatory nature of the world is, in itself, a nihilistic denial of reality, his words point to a more authentic state of being beyond the absurdities and delusions of manifest existence. Dreams and hallucinations only lack reality in comparison to the full consciousness with experience in waking life. In other words, there would be no point in talking about the unreality of dreams if there were no waking life; dreams, in that case, would be our *only* reality. By this same logic, it makes no sense to talk about the unreality of manifest existence unless we are prepared to admit the existence of a higher level of reality. The Buddhists teach that the "world is like a dream" because "just as one perceives

the lack of objectivity in the dream pictures after one has woken up, so the lack of objectivity in the perceptions of waking life is perceived by those who have been awakened by the knowledge of true reality"113. For the Gnostics and Buddhist—and indeed for all traditions that adhere to the Perennial Philosophy—"the crown of all…endeavour" is "an attempt to penetrate to the actual reality of things as they are in themselves"114. As McCarthy himself puts it: "the mystical experience is a direct apprehension of reality" 115. This ultimate Reality "is defined as that which stands completely outside the sensory world of illusions and ignorance"116. The "mystic is a realist"117, because a mystic's sole purpose is to strip away all the veils of illusion which obscure the absolute reality of the Godhead. Thus, by comparing the world to a "fevered dream", the judge is inadvertently pointing to the existence of an Absolute which transcends the illusions and deceptions of the manifest cosmos—the very essence of the "Truth", which McCarthy believes "writers must accomplish in their writing"118.

NOTES

1 Vereen M. Bell, *The Achievement of Cormac McCarthy* (Baton Rouge: Louisiana State University Press, 1988), 31.

2 Edwin T. Arnold, "Naming, Knowing, Nothingness: McCarthy's Moral Parables", in Edwin T. Arnold and Dianne C. Luce (eds) *Perspectives on Cormac McCarthy,* rev. ed. (Jackson: Mississippi University Press, 1999), 46.

3 Dana Phillips, "History and the Ugly Facts of *Blood Meridian*" in James D. Lilley (ed). *Cormac McCarthy: New Directions* (Albuquerque: University of New Mexico Press, 2002), 19.

4 Shane Schimpf. *A Reader's Guide to Blood Meridian* (USA: Bon Mot Publishing, 2006), 49.

5 Edwin T. Arnold, "Foreword," in John Sepich, *Notes on 'Blood Meridian'* (Austin: Texas University Press, 2008), xiv.

6 Bell, "Between the Wish and the Thing, the World Lies Waiting," *Southern Review* 28.4 (1992), 926

7 Arnold, "The Mosaic of McCarthy's Fiction", in Wade Hall and Rick Wallach (eds), *Sacred Violence: A Reader's Companion to Cormac McCarthy* (El Paso: Texas University Press, 1995), 22.

8 Gary Wallace, "Meeting McCarthy", *Southern Quarterly* 30.4 (1992), 138.

9 Aldous Huxley, *The Perennial Philosophy* (New York: Harper & Row Huxley 1945), vii.

10 William C. Spencer, "Cormac McCarthy's Unholy Trinity: Biblical Parody in *Outer Dark*", in Wade Hall and Rick Wallach (eds), *Sacred Violence: A Reader's Companion to Cormac McCarthy* (El Paso: Texas University Press, 1995), 69.

11 Tom Nolan, "A Review of *Blood Meridian, or the Evening Redness in the West*," *Los Angeles Times Book Review*, (9 June 1985).

12 Hans Jonas, *The Gnostic Religion: The Message of the Alien God and the Beginnings of Christianity* (Boston: Beacon, 1958), 44.

13 Elaine Pagels, *The Gnostic Gospels* (London: Weidenfeld and Nicolson, 1979), xix.

14 Leo Daugherty, "Gravers False and True: *Blood Meridian* as Gnostic Tragedy," in Edwin T. Arnold and Dianne C. Luce (eds), *Perspectives on Cormac McCarthy* rev. ed. (Jackson: Mississippi University Press, 1999), 162.

15 Bell, *The Achievement of Cormac McCarthy*, 132.

16 Sven Birkerts, "The Lone Soul State," *New Republic* (11 July 1994), 38-41.

17 Dianne C. Luce, *Reading the World: Cormac McCarthy's Tennessee Period* (South Carolina: The University of South Carolina Press, 2009), 68.

18 Harold Bloom, *How to Read and Why* (New York: Scribner, 2000), 237.

19 Kurt Rudolph, *Gnosis: The Nature & History of Gnosticism*. Robert McLachlan Wilson (trans), (New York: Harper Collins, 1987), 88.

20 T.S. Eliot, "The Wasteland: V. What the Thunder Said", lines 331-2.

21 John Beck, "'A Certain but Fugitive Testimony': Witnessing the Light of Time in Cormac McCarthy's Southwestern Fiction" in Rick Wallach (ed), *Myth, Legend, Dust: Critical Responses to Cormac McCarthy* (New York: Manchester University Press, 2000), 210.

22 John Lewis Longley Jr. "The Nuclear Winter of Cormac McCarthy", *The Virginia Quarterly Review* 62:4 (1986). 748.

23 Paul Oppenheimer, *Evil and the Demonic: A New Theory of Monstrous Behaviour* (New York: New York University Press, 1996), 37.

24 ibid., 77.

25 Sepich, *Notes*, 160.

26 Daugherty, *Perspectives*, 163.

27 Edwin Arnold comments on Jung's influence on McCarthy, writing that: "McCarthy's use of dreams seems closer to the Jungian concept than to the Freudian, for they are often 'mystical' in their manner" ("Go To Sleep: Dreams and Visions in the Border Trilogy", in Edwin T. Arnold and Dianne C. Luce [eds.], *A Cormac McCarthy Companion: The Border Trilogy* [Jackson: Mississippi University Press, 2001], 40).

28 Richard Smoley, *Forbidden Faith: The Secret History of Gnosticism* (New York: Harper Collins, 2007), 161.

29 The last pagan Emperor of Rome, Julian II (AD 331/2-363), who valiantly tried to save his empire from the corrosive influences of the barbaric "Galileans" (Christians), was also a devout Mithraist. In his philosophically and spiritually subtle oration, "Hymn to King Helios", Julian describes how the visible sun is a symbolic manifestation of 'Helios', that is, of the Absolute Godhead (Wilmer Cave Wright (trans), *The Works*

of the Emperor Julian Vol I [Cambridge, Mass: Harvard UP, 1913], 348-435).

30 Dianne Luce identifies Gnostic solar imagery in McCarthy's *Outer Dark* and adds that "these Gnostic associations of the sun with a malevolent cosmic force dominate the solar imagery of McCarthy's desert novel, *Blood Meridian*, as well" (*Reading the World*, 78).

31 Jonas, *The Gnostic Religion*, 260-1.

32 ibid., 257.

33 ibid., 261.

34 Blaise Pascal, Christian mystic and mathematician, also felt this terror. In *Penseés*, he writes: "I see the terrifying immensity of the universe which surrounds me" (John Warrington [trans.], *Pensées: Notes on Religion and Other Subjects* [London: Dent, 1973], 6).

35 Jonas, *The Gnostic Religion*, 43, 53.

36 The vast, indifferent, and often downright malevolent universe is a frequent topic of contemplation in McCarthy's novels. In *Child of God*: "He [Lester Ballard] cast about among the stars for some kind of guidance but the heavens wore a different look that Ballard did not trust" (1973; reprint, New York: Vintage Books, 1993), 190. In *Suttree,* we find descriptions of the "cold indifferent dark, the blind stars beaded on their tracks and mitered satellites and geared and pinioned planets all reeling through the black of space" (1979; reprint, New York: Vintage Books, 1993), 284. The "enormity of the universe" fills Suttree "with a strange sweet woe" (353). In *All the Pretty Horses*, John Grady feels that this is a world that seems "to care nothing for the old or the young or rich or dark or pale or he or she. Nothing for their struggles, nothing for their names. Nothing for the living or the dead" (1992; reprint, London: Picador, 1993), 301. In *The Crossing*, perhaps McCarthy's most mystical novel, Billy Parham looks into the eyes of the she-wolf and sees a "world burning on the shore of an unknowable void. A world construed out of blood and blood's alcahest and blood in its core and in its integument because it was that nothing save blood had power to resonate against the void which threatened hourly to devour it" (1994, reprint., New York: Vintage Books, 1995), 73-4. *The Road* continues in this Gnostic vein of thought: "He walked out in the gray light and stood and he saw for a brief moment the absolute truth of the world. The cold relentless circling of the intestate earth. Darkness implacable. The blind dogs of the sun in their running. The crushing black vacuum of the universe" (2006; reprint, New York: Vintage Books, 2006), 130.). In fact, it seems that the true nature of the world is finally revealed in *The Road*, for all to see: "Out on the roads the pilgrims sank down and fell over and died and the bleak and shrouded earth went trundling past the sun and returned again as trackless and as unremarked as the path of any nameless sisterworld in the ancient dark beyond" (181).

37 Franz Hartmann, *Jacob Boehme: Life and Doctrines* (New York: Steiner Books, 1977), 47.

38 Jacob Boehme, *Six Theosophic Points: An Open Gate of all the Secrets of Life Wherein the Causes of all Beings Become Known; Six Mystical Points; On the Earthly and Heavenly Mystery; On the Divine Intuition*. John R. Earle (trans.) (Montana: Kessinger Publishing, 1992), 108.

39 Sproule's predicament echoes Keats's "Ode to a Nightingale": "Through the sad heart of Ruth, when, sick for home, / She stood in tears amid the alien corn" (lines 66-7).

40 Sepich, *Notes*, 160.

41 Frithjof Schuon, *Gnosis: Divine Wisdom* (Middlesex: Perennial Books Ltd, 1959), 67-8.

42 René Guénon, *The Reign of Quantity and the Signs of the Times*, Lord Northbourne (trans), (Baltimore: Penguin Books, 1972), 65-67.

43 Edward Conze, *Further Buddhist Studies: Selected Essays by Edward Conze*, (Oxford: Bruno Cassirer, 1975), 29.

44 Rudolph, *Gnosis*, 92-3.

45 Edward Conze, *Buddhism: Its Essence and Development* (New York: Harper Torchbooks, 1959), 51.

46 Barcley Owens, *Cormac McCarthy's Western Novels* (Tucson: Arizona University Press, 2000), 5, 7.

47 ibid., 20.

48 Arnold, "Go To Sleep: Dreams and Visions in the Border Trilogy", 44.

49 John Cant, *Cormac McCarthy and the Myth of American Exceptionalism* (New York: Routledge, 2008), 5.

50 Edward Conze, *Buddhist Scriptures* (Maryland:

Penguin Books, 1973), 142.
51 Rudolph, *Gnosis*, 88.
52 Smoley, *Forbidden Faith*, 57.
53 Jonas, *The Gnostic Religion*, 84.
54 Bell, *The Achievement of Cormac McCarthy*, 127.
55 Brady Harrison, "'That Immense and Bloodslaked Waste': Negation in *Blood Meridian*', *Southwestern American Literature* 25:1 (Fall 1999), 35.
56 Boehme, *Six Theosophic Points*, 108.
57 McCarthy will later develop these ideas in *The Road*, where bands of cannibals roam the apocalyptic wasteland; their "gray and rotting teeth" claggy "with human flesh" (75).
58 Bill Baines, "A Review of *Blood Meridian*," *Western American Literature,* 21:1 (1986): 59.
59 The idea that the world has always been an evil place is another of McCarthy's favourite themes. In *Outer Dark*, the tinker tells Rinthy: "I've seen the meanness of humans till I don't know why God ain't put out the sun and gone away" (1986; reprint, New York: Vintage Books, 1993], 192). In *Child of God*, the deputy asks an old man if he thinks "people was meaner then than they are now." The old man replies, "No [. . .] I don't. I think people are the same from the day God first made one" (168). In *Suttree*, the derelict railroader complains that he "never knowed such a place for meanness" as this world, but when Suttree asks if it was "ever any different?," he replies "No. I reckon not" (180). In *All the Pretty Horses*, Alfonsa proclaims: "What is constant in history is greed and foolishness and a love of blood" (239). However, McCarthy subverts this idea in *No Country for Old Men*, making Sheriff Bell wonder if perhaps there is a new breed of evil among men: "I thought I'd never seen a person like that and it got me to wonderin if maybe he was some new kind" ([2005; reprint, New York: Vintage Books, 2007], 5). Or, as he tells Torbert: "I aint sure we've seen these people before. Their kind. I dont know what to do about em even. If you killed em all they'd have to build an annex on to hell" (79).
60 W.B. Yeats, 'Supernatural Songs: XII Meru', lines 4-7.
61 Owens, *Western Novels*, 119.
62 Bloom, *How to Read and Why*, 255.
63 This passage echoes a similar theme in McCarthy's *Suttree*, where the protagonist wonders "Am I a monster, are there monsters in me?" (366). *Blood Meridian*'s reference to the "whited regions of maps where monsters do live" also seems to echo the question put forward by the narrative voice in *Suttree*: "Are there dragons in the wings of the world?" (29). Comparing these two passages, Christopher Campbell argues that: "There *are* dragons in the wings of the world, and in *Blood Meridian* they ride upon horses" ("Walter De Maria's *Lightning Field* and McCarthy's Enigmatic Epilogue: 'Y qué clase de lugar es éste?'", *The Cormac Journal 2* [Spring 2002], 47).
64 A sentiment beautifully expressed by Ernest Becker in his brilliant work, *The Denial of Death* (New York: Macmillan Publishing Co., 1973): "What are we to make of creation in which the routine activity is for organisms to be tearing others apart with teeth of all types—biting, grinding flesh, plant stalks, bones between molars, pushing the pulp greedily down the gullet with delight, incorporating its essence into one's own organisations, and then excreting with foul stench and gasses the residue. Everyone reaching out to incorporate others who are edible to him... Creation is a nightmare spectacular taking place on a planet that has been soaked for hundreds of millions of years in the blood of its creatures. The soberest conclusion that we could make about what has actually been taking place on the planet for about three billion years is that it is being turned into a vast pit of fertilizer" (282-3).
65 After an interview with the novelist, David Kushner writes that: "While [McCarthy] reserves high praises for a few contemporary narratives ("*Fear and Loathing in Las Vegas* is a classic of our time"), his list of great novels stops at four: *Ulysses*, *The Brothers Karamazov*, *The Sound and The Fury* and his favourite, *Moby-Dick*. Like his own work, they explore themes of life and death with both philosophical and artful precision" ('Cormac McCarthy's Apocalypse', *Rolling Stone* Issue: 1042/1043 [New York: Dec 27, 2007—Jan 10, 2008], 44).
66 Jonas, *The Gnostic Religion*, 86-7.
67 Hartmann, *Jacob Boehme: Life and Doctrines*, 166-7.
68 Boehme, *Six Theosophic Points*, 99, 104.
69 A.H.H. Tennyson, 'In Memoriam: LVI', line 15.

70 "Once, when I lived in the Northern forests, I thought that good was to be found neither in man, nor in the predatory world of animals and insects, but in the silent kingdom of the trees. Far from it! I saw the forest's slow movement, the treacherous way it battled against grass and bushes for each inch of soil… This is the life of the forest—a constant struggle of everything against everything. Only the blind conceive of the kingdom of the trees and grass as the world of good… Is it that life itself is evil?" (Vasily Grossman. *Life and Fate*. Robert Chandler (trans) [New York: New York Review Books, 1985], 407).

71 Birger A. Pearson, *Ancient Gnosticism: Traditions and Literature* (Minneapolis: Fortress Press, 2007), 106.

72 ibid.

73 Jonas, *The Gnostic Religion*, 163.

74 ibid., 162.

75 Ken Wilber, *Sex, Ecology, Spirituality: The Spirit of Evolution* (Boston: Shambhala, 1995), 323.

76 ibid., 366.

77 Jonas, *The Gnostic Religion*, 164.

78 ibid., 202.

79 ibid., 164.

80 ibid., 57.

81 Hartmann, *Jacob Boehme: Life and Doctrines*, 18.

82 Boehme, *Six Theosophic Points*, 99.

83 Michael L. Peterson, *God and Evil: An Introduction to the Issues* (Oxford: Westview Press, 1998) 92.

84 ibid., 93.

85 David Hume, "Dialogues Concerning Natural Religion", in Joel Feinberg and Russ Shafer-Landau (eds). *Reason and Responsibility: Readings in Some Basic Problems of Philosophy* (California: Cengage Learning, 2008), 67-8.

86 Jonas, *The Gnostic Religion*, 94.

87 Susan Neiman, *Evil In Modern Thought: An Alternative History of Philosophy* (Princeton and Oxford: Princeton University Press Evil, 2002), 170, 181.

88 Neiman, *Evil In Modern Thought*, 190.

89 Christopher Douglas, "The Flawed Design: American Imperialism in N. Scott Momaday's *House Made of Dawn* and Cormac McCarthy's *Blood Meridian*", *Critique* 45:1 (Fall 2003), 12.

90 ibid., 11.

91 ibid., 12.

92 Neiman, *Evil In Modern Thought*, 188.

93 David W. Weiss and Michael Berenbaum, "The Holocaust and the Covenant" in Roth, John K. and Berenbaum, Michael (eds), *Holocaust: Religious and Philosophical Implications* (New York: Paragon House 1989), 71.

94 ibid., 75.

95 Conze, *Further Buddhist Studies*, 16-17.

96 Rachel Wagner and Frances Flannery-Dailey. "Wake Up! Worlds of Illusion in Gnosticism, Buddhism, and *The Matrix* Project", in Christopher Grau (ed.), *Philosophers Explore 'The Matrix'* (Oxford: Oxford UP, 2005), 272.

97 Conze, *Buddhism: Its Essence and Development*, 173.

98 Pagels, *The Gnostic Gospels*, 125.

99 Conze, *Buddhism: Its Essence and Development*, 16, 113.

100 Jonas, *The Gnostic Religion*, 84.

101 Conze, *Buddhism: Its Essence and Development*, 84-5.

102 Wagner, *Philosophers Explore 'The Matrix'*, 268.

103 Jonas, *The Gnostic Religion*, 70.

104 Edward Conze, *Buddhist Wisdom Books: The Diamond Sutra and the Heart Sutra* (London: George Allen & Unwin, 1975), 67.

105 ibid., 69.

106 ibid., 70.

107 ibid., 69.

108 ibid., 70.

109 Conze, *Buddhist Scriptures*, 36.

110 Conze, *Buddhism: Its Essence and Development*, 49, 50.

111 Rudolph, *Gnosis*, 196.

112 ibid., 195.

113 Conze, *Buddhism: Its Essence and Development*, 168.

114 Conze, *Buddhist Scriptures*, 145.

115 Wallace, "Meeting McCarthy", 138.

116 Conze, *Buddhism: Its Essence and Development*, 110.

117 Evelyn Underhill, *Mysticism* (New York: E.P. Dutton, 1961), 93.

118 Wallace, "Meeting McCarthy", 138.

Andrew Phillip Smith

The Plight of the Mandaeans

The Mandaeans are the last Gnostics, venerating John the Baptist as a great prophet who established their rituals for them, but claiming to go still further back in time. Their language is a variety of Eastern Aramaic, their theology dualistic with variations on a typically complex Gnostic cosmological mythology.[1] They survived in the Muslim world in small numbers, tolerated as a people of the book, associated with the mysterious Sabians mentioned in the Qur'an. But they are suffering ongoing persecution in Iraq and Iran and Mandaean refugees are creating a widespread recent diaspora in the western world.

As research for this article I interviewed Jorunn Jacobsen Buckley, author of *The Mandaeans: Ancient Texts and Modern People*, by email. One of the world's leading scholars on the Mandaeans, she has also been privileged to have had personal contact with them in Iraq, Iran and the USA. She is involved in humanitarian work on behalf of the Mandaean people with Amnesty International and in obtaining special refugee status for them.

Buckley believes that the Mandaeans do indeed go back to the first century, partly from her work in tracing the long lineages of scribes detailed in Mandaean manuscripts (described in her book *The Great Stem of Souls: Reconstructing Mandaean History* (Gorgias Press, 2005)) and she accepts that they are the last surviving Gnostic group. The contemporary academic deconstruction of the category of Gnosticism has had no impact on how she perceives and classifies Mandaean religion. She believes that they were never part of Christianity but came

from Judaism and emigrated from Palestine to their present-day locations in Iraq and Iran, probably in the first century. They see John the Baptist "not as the founder of their religion but as their renewer, as their main prophet."

Even the information on Mandaeans in the western world is very confidential and sensitive. Buckley said that, "You can be in touch with Mandaeans directly, if they trust you. " It took her twenty years to track down Mandaeans in the United States. They don't have a public profile, are pacifist, and have no national or political ambitions beyond the desire to avoid persecution and maintain their traditions. Buckley herself is now trusted and even considered, as a scholar, an honorary male in certain circumstances!

The persecution of Mandaeans came to a head in the aftermath of the 2003 western invasion of Iraq. Their situation in Saddam Hussein's regime had been slightly better as they had an official status as people of the book but "of course they were 'tolerated' only to a very limited extent under Saddam Hussein only for complex reasons," said Buckley.

Mandaeans growing up in Iraq in recent decades were often told little about their religion so they would not draw attention to themselves. Mandaeans in Iraq are often perceived as being unclean which limits their ability to take part in public life. Sam, a Mandaean now in Australia, described what it was like to grow up in the Iraq of Saddam Hussein:

"Living in Iraq as a Mandaean boy, you first grow up feeling normal. And then somewhere in your classes you'd find that a religion class,

the Islamic religion class, would come up. And you would be asked to stand up, and then they'd either make you stand in the corner where all the students will look at you, as you being different. But at that age you don't understand the difference—but you feel it. Or you get told that you are a sinner and an infidel, and you must leave this class, because you are making this class religiously dirty. Also, then you would go back home, and you would find that your grandmother had gone to the vegetable shop, or to buy some fruit, where they were not allowed to touch the basket or the selection of vegetables, because you have made the whole thing religiously dirty—therefore all of it has to be destroyed. And usually you get told off in front of the whole market, or the street, or the supermarket, and that would be done on the spot, the destroying of the vegetables. It gives you the psychology that you have something wrong with you, a kind of religious leprosy."[2]

Mandaeans in Iran have not had an easy time either, particularly since the 1979 Islamic revolution "but the situation there is entirely different, politically. Nobody dares to reveal much public information on this." When Ayatollah Khomeini came to power he removed the officially protected status that Mandaeans had as Sabians and extended it instead to the Zoroastrians. Attempts to have their status restored have so far proved fruitless. In Iran they are concentrated in the South West, far from Tehran, and are little known to the Islamic theological authorities. Mandaeans in Iran have to give their children legally approved Muslim or Persian names, cannot opt out of Qur'an lessons as can Jews and, unlike Zoroastrians, Jews, and Christians have no representation in parliament.[3] They are not allowed to attend university.[4]

Both in Iran and Iraq Mandaean children have been spied on in schools are pressured into converting to Islam. Knowledge of the Mandaic language is also relatively rare, with most Mandaeans speaking Arabic or Farsi and now the languages of their new host countries.

Buckley was very cagey in giving specific

details of the current situation of Mandaeans. "Of course this is very sensitive—and too complicated to answer, and dangerous. Many [in Iraq] are dead, forcibly converted, tortured, have fled."[5] Since the fall of Baghdad there have been murders, rapes and kidnappings of Mandaeans, estimated by some as at over 80 murders just in the few months following the western victory.

The 2009 Mandaean Human Rights Annual report lists 63 reported murders and 271 reported kidnappings plus reports of rape (many rapes are never reported), assault, forced conversion to Islam, and forced displacements.[6] For instance, in 2009 three Mandaean jewellers were massacred in Baghdad.[7]

Samer Muscati, who was in Iraq observing the current conditions for Human Rights Watch wrote a report *At a Crossroads: Human Rights in Iraq Eight Years* after the US-Led Invasion. He also took beautiful photographs of various Iraqi minorities, two of which, depicting Mandaean baptisms, adorn this article.[8]

At the only Sabian Mandaean temple in Basra, community leader Naiel Thejel Ganeen told Human Rights Watch about the evening in 2006 that became the start of his enduring trauma.285 Masked assailants carrying AK47s and pistols pulled over Ganeen, 55, while he was driving in Basra with his son. They forced his son to leave the car at gunpoint and abducted Ganeen in his own vehicle. He said his kidnappers kept referring to him as "negis" (impure) and said he had to pay them "jizya."[9] His captors tortured him for nine days while keeping him blindfolded and bound in a dark cellar. His right arm is scarred from shrapnel from live rounds of ammunition shot by his kidnappers during a mock execution. Humiliated by what his kidnappers subjected him to, Ganeen refused to further discuss all the things they did to him over the nine days. On the last day, he said, after his kidnappers received a ransom of $40,000, they threw him, blindfolded, in a trash heap. "The extremists considered us as part of the occupation though we've been in Iraq since before it was a country," Ganeen said. "Most of our community has fled Iraq and will never return."

Several Sabian Mandaean elders who listened as Ganeen told his story said they consider him lucky since he made it out alive, even though Ganeen says he is still haunted by the ordeal and continues to see a psychological counselor."[10]

Muscati was able to view a Mandaean purification ritual in April 2010 but only a dozen Mandaeans were in attendance. Their baptism is a repeated ritual, not an initiation, performed every Sunday and at religious festivals by a priest. Photographs and film footage of Mandaean baptisms are now available online (search on Youtube for examples, there's even a recipe for Mandaean spiced duck.) In the aftermath of the Iraq war Mandaeans have been scattered around the world in a diaspora. In his BBC television series *Around the World in 80 Faiths* first broadcast on 2 January 2009 is a Peter Owen-Jones, an Anglican vicar travelled around the world researching a wide variety of ancient and modern faiths and taking part where possible in their ceremonies. Episode 1, shot in Australia, featured a small Mandaean community in Sydney who perform their weekly baptisms in a river in a public park.[11] The priest explained to Owen-Jones, whom he couldn't touch because he had already undergone ritual purification, "Water represents light and radiance and it's the womb from which everything manifests. Anyone who is baptised becomes like an angel in the kingdom of light. All the initiation is to prepare that person to be a spiritual king."

There are relatively high numbers of Mandaeans in Sweden, Holland, Australia,

Canada, Syria and Jordan, plus some in other countries such as the UK, "and what's left in the old countries [Iraq and Iran.]." Buckley estimates that there are around 80,000 surviving Mandaeans world-wide. According to some sources, out of the former population of 30,000 in Iraq only 5,000 or fewer are thought to be left.[12] The number of priests has been diminishing for some time and isolated Mandaeans are unable to take part in the weekly baptism or in other rituals such as ritual meals or sacraments for the dead.

Mandaean religious practice has no provision for adopting new members, and the numbers are likely to diminish. This is issue is discussed privately by Mandaeans, but any suggested changes to this are mere speculation. "The conversion issue is not something to be dealt with in public, at all, if you are an outsider." Traditional Mandaeans are even reluctant to talk about people who have married outside of the religion, who may be considered apostate. Young members of the new diaspora tend to be integrated in their new societies to the same extent as other Iraqis. Mandaean refugees have suffered internment at various times, along with refugees of other ethnic groups and from other countries, in Indonesia and Australia.

Few diaspora communities are large enough to truly preserve their traditions or have a priest to maintain full religious observance and even those that do have problems with finding unpolluted flowing water. Mandaeans in New York and New Jersey rely on occasional visiting priests and have been able to take advantage of a state park in New Jersey which allows them to use a clean river which has also been used by Christian Baptist groups.

Yahya Sam, a Mandaean electrical engineer in Sweden, is trying to grow myrtle, essential to Mandaean ritual. It grows wild in Iraq but is not native to Sweden. Sweden's cold climate means that outdoor baptism in running water is near impossible for half the year. Salam Gaiad Katia, a Mandaean priest in a rundown housing project in a Swedish industrial town, Sodertalje, which has taken in more Mandaean refugees than the whole of the USA and Canada, has adapted the rituals and conditions to his urban environment, borrowing the use of a public swimming pool and performing his ritual cleansing under a running tap rather than in a flowing river.[13] Mandaean tradition states that a deceased person should be buried on the day of death or the following day, but Western laws do not permit this. Nor is it easy to dress the corpse in the required Mandaean manner, which involves washing the body in running water, dressing the deceased in the white baptismal robe and tying a belt around the shirt.[14]

Jorunn Buckley has been an expert witness for Mandaeans in immigration courts since the 1990s.

"It's very hard to convince American legal authorities and the INS that there are credible reasons for fearing persecution, torture, jailing, etc. when you are sent back to your own country," Buckley said. She was first called on as an expert witness for the US Department of Justice in an immigration court in San Diego in 1995. There are particular difficulties in representing such little-known people. "You need to educate the judge. You need to be on very good terms with your own lawyer. Your own lawyer may not know anything about this unless he's worked with Mandaeans before." She found that US officials had trouble understanding the nature of Islamic law and the lack of representation for Mandaeans in Iraq and Iran because the separation of church and state in America.

The diaspora of the Mandaeans has resulted in a little more attention being given to the Mandaic language and literature in academia. A project to establish a text for the *Mandaean Book of John* and translate it into English has recently received funding.[15] A lexicon of Mandaic is now available online[16], plus material for the study of the *Ginza Rba*.[17]

Items on the Mandaeans appear in the news only occasionally. Buckley's advice for those concerned about the plight of the Mandaeans is to contact the normal channels of human rights organisations such as Amnesty International, Washington's IRF reports, and the site http://www.gfbv.de (Society for Threatened Peoples, German: Gesellschaft für bedrohte Völker, GfbV))The central website for the Mandaean community is The Mandaean Associations Union http://www.mandaeanunion.org/

NOTES

1 For a somewhat opinionated take on the Gnosticism of the Mandaeans by Brian Mubaraki, an ethnic Mandaean scholar see http://yardna. wordpress.com/

2 *The Religion Report*, "Mandaeans in Australia," 11 June 2003, http://www.abc.net.au/rn/talks/8.30/ relrpt/stories/s877145.htm

3 http://iwpr.net/report-news/mandaean-faith-lives-iranian-south

4 http://www.abc.net.au/rn/talks/8.30/relrpt/stories/ s877145.htm

5 Quotations from Jorunn Buckley are from my email interview on 27 Jan 2011. Additional quotations are taken from her podcast interview available at http://www.bowdoin.edu/podcasts/

6 The MHR 2009 annual report can be downloaded from http://www.mandaeanunion. org/ . The annual report lists the names of all the murdered and kidnapped Mandaeans. The abuses are summarised in the article "Who Cares for the Mandaeans?" http://www. islammonitor.org/index.php?option=com_ content&view=article&id=3198:who-cares-for-the-mandaeans&catid=190&Itemid=59

7 http://www.humanrightsdefence.org/save-the-mandaeans-of-iraq.html

8 See http://www.hrw.org/en/reports/2011/02/21/ crossroads where a PDF of his extensive report can be downloaded. More of his photographs can be seen on Flickr http://www.flickr.com/photos/sultan/ sets/72157623907031141/with/4622605961/

9 "a head tax that early Islamic rulers demanded from their non-Muslim subjects in return for communal autonomy and military protection."

10 His description of the Mandaeans is found in ibid. p.65-68.

11 The two and a half minute section on the Mandaeans in Sydney begins around 33:30 in the first episode.

12 http://www.gfbv.de/pressemit.php?id=1420 Other estimates place the figure as low as 3,500.

13 http://www.nytimes.com/2007/04/09/world/ europe/09iht-mandeans.4.5202220.html

14 See the video interview "Iraqi Refugees in Sweden: A Mandaean Priest Speaks" at http:// www.minorityvoices.org/news.php/en/281/iraqi-refugees-in-sweden-a-mandaean-priest-speaks

15 http://mandaeanbookofjohn.blogspot.com/

16 http://www.mandaic.org/Mandaic/lexicon/main. htm

17 https://sites.google.com/site/ginzarba/ginza-rba-download

Bill Darlison

Rethinking the Gospels

A NEW LOOK AT THE GOSPELS

In the summer of 1989 I made a discovery which changed the way I look at the Gospels. I had been teaching the New Testament to 'A' Level students for about ten years, and I had been dutifully imparting all the accepted ideas about Gospel origins. For example, the conclusion of the form critics, that the synoptic Gospels were composed of *pericopae*, small units of oral tradition which had been worn into patterns by constant retelling, and then strung together like beads on a string, I considered almost as an axiom. The miracle stories, so troublesome to religious liberals were, I taught my students, simple exaggerations of ordinary events, produced by a combination of missionary zeal and pious imagination.

One or two gospel incidents remained enigmatic, principally the account of the man carrying the jar of water, whom the apostles were sent to meet before the last supper (Mark 14:14). Who on earth could he be? He plays no part in the story before this time, and disappears from the scene immediately afterwards. The idea that he should occupy himself with women's work in order that the apostles might easily find him made little sense to me. How did Jesus know he would be there? We hear nothing about him setting up this curious meeting in advance. Was there a need for secrecy? If so, it was a strange way to ensure it: the man would be highly conspicuous, just like someone dressed like a harlequin would be today.

I knew that the man carrying a jar of water was the pictogram of the zodiacal sign Aquarius, and I had even seen this referred to, obliquely,

in conventional gospel commentaries, but why should he appear at this point in the narrative? It perplexed me, on and off, for a decade.

Then, on that sunny afternoon in June 1989, as I was invigilating a Spanish examination, I began to flick idly through a Bible which happened to be sitting on the desk in front of me, when the idea suddenly struck me (goodness knows why!) that if the image of Aquarius appears in the Gospel, perhaps the other signs of the zodiac are there, too, but that their presence may not be announced quite so dramatically. I looked closely at the text of Mark, forgetting all about the examination I was supposed to be invigilating, and my suspicions were immediately confirmed. Why had I never seen it before? Why had *nobody* ever seen it before? The signs of the zodiac appear in perfect order, from Aries to Pisces; not the pictograms, as with Aquarius (although Jesus riding into Jerusalem on a horse is a perfect representation of the Sagittarian centaur), but with the *psychological* meaning of each sign outlined and explored. Here are the zodiacal sections with a few words on each one:

Aries: Mark 1:1-3:35

Aries is the sign of the spring equinox, when the year begins in the northern hemisphere. It is associated with all beginnings, with newness, daring, controversy, confrontation. In Babylon it was called Lu Hunga, *The Hired Man*, which helps to explain the detail in Mark 1:20.

Taurus: 4:1-34

Taurus is the first Earth sign, associated with agriculture, growth, abundance, and because it is a particularly beautiful and bright constellation, it was also associated with light. The parables of the kingdom in this section all use agricultural metaphors, with the exception of the parable of the lamp on the stand.

Gemini 4:35-6:30

The Geminian twins, Castor and Pollux, were the patrons of seafarers, and sailors in distress would call upon them for assistance. Read Mark's account of the calming of the storm at the beginning of the Gemini section. The story of Jairus' daughter and the woman with the blood flow is the only miracle story in any of the Gospels told in *two* interweaving sections; later, the apostles are sent out *in twos*; Herod is in *two* minds; John the Baptist ends up in *two* parts! Sodom and Gomorrah, *the twin cities*, are mentioned only in this section of the Gospel.

Cancer 6:31-8:26

Cancer is the sign of the summer solstice. Its symbol is the hard-shelled crab. In the ancient world it was associated with clannishness, protectiveness, tradition, and in the 'zodiacal man' it represented the stomach. Here we find the two feeding stories and the dispute with the Pharisees over clean and unclean food. And Jesus utters the memorable word 'Ephphatha'— *Be open!*—an instruction to us all to break through our self-constructed carapace.

Leo 8:27-9:32

Leo, the sign of the summer time, has been called the Sign of Divine Splendour. This whole section concerns identity, and it culminates in the Transfiguration, in which the divine splendour of Jesus is shown to the apostles. The Catholic Church, which has incorporated a great deal of celestial symbolism in its calendar and in its liturgy, celebrates the Feast of the Transfiguration on 6th August, when the sun is in Leo.

Virgo 9:33-9:50

Virgo was associated with service, purity, modesty. Its symbol is the Maiden with the Sheaf of Wheat, although in some ancient zodiacs it is depicted as a Woman carrying a child. In this section of the Gospel, Jesus takes a child in his arms and teaches about the virtue of service to others. The birthday of the Virgin Mary is celebrated by Catholics on 8th September, when the sun is in Virgo.

Libra 10:1-10:34

Libra is the sign of the autumn equinox, the 'balance' point of the year. Its symbol is, in fact, a balance. It was associated with marriage, relationships, judgement, the very themes dealt with in this section of the Gospel. In Egypt, Libra was Maat, the goddess of judgement, who weighed the hearts of the dead in the balance. Those who failed her test were 'heavy hearted', exactly the term used of the rich young man who cannot bring himself to dispense with his possessions (Mark 10:22).

Scorpio 10:35-45

Scorpio is associated with hidden power and with sexuality. Its ruler was Mars, the god of war. In this section of Mark, James and John— the 'sons of thunder'—ask Jesus for power in the kingdom. This is the shortest zodiacal section, and something is obviously missing. Anyone who has read Morton Smith's book, *The Secret Gospel*,[1] will know of a recently discovered 'secret' passage of Mark, which belongs in this section and which contains some hint of sexual activity.

Sagittarius 10:46-11-26

The symbol of Sagittarius is the Centaur, half man, half horse. Here Jesus rides into Jerusalem on a colt, *a young horse*—not a donkey. The donkey comes from Matthew's Gospel, not from Mark's.

Capricorn 11:27-12-44

Capricorn, the sign of the winter solstice, was associated with authority, social structure, legalism. In this section of the Gospel, Jesus is shown in argument with all the various authority figures in Judaism—Pharisees, Herodians, Sadducees.

Aquarius 13:1-14-16

Aquarius is 'The Man Carrying a Jar of Water', who appears in this section, but it is also associated with social upheaval and anarchy which will be announced by signs in the heavens.

Pisces 14:17-16:8

The final part of the drama. Pisces was associated with suffering, betrayal, self-sacrifice, the very themes of this section of the Gospel. It is also the sign of the Fish, the sign of the new age which Jesus was to inaugurate, and so fish symbolism and references pervade the whole Gospel (and, indeed, the other three Gospels). The first Christian creed was based on an acrostic formed from the letters of the Greek word for Fish *ichthus*.

Iesus—Jesus
Christos Christ
Theou—of God
uios—son
soter—saviour

Catholics ate fish on Fridays as a kind of communion with Christ. Friday was chosen because it is the day of Venus, the planet 'exalted' in the sign of Pisces. The fish symbol worn by many Christians is just a version of the Pisces hieroglyph (if they only knew!).

The above outline just gives a few of the zodiacal correspondences; and finding these was only the beginning. Over the next few years I was to discover that Mark not only weaves the zodiacal signs into his narrative, he also alludes cryptically to the non-zodiacal constellations—the so-called 'decans'—which surround the constellations of the zodiac. So, for example, the constellation Cassiopeia, which is close to Aries, makes an appearance as Peter's mother-in-law (for reasons which are far too complicated to explain here!) in the Aries section of Mark's Gospel. The constellation Ara, which means *Altar* in Latin but *curse* in Greek appears in the strange story of the cursing of the fig tree in the Sagittarius section. Andromeda, one of the constellations associated with Pisces, is reflected in the story of the crucifixion of Jesus. (Read an account of the myth of Andromeda and you'll see what I mean.)

In addition to all this, I discovered that some of the gospel incidents reflect the ancient names of the stars in the various constellations. In the Cancer section of the Gospel, for example, we find the Feeding of the Five Thousand and the Feeding of the Four Thousand—and there is a star in the constellation Cancer called Ma'alaph, which means *numbered thousands*.

Mark has given us an account of the sun's journey in the sky, from its 'birth' in Aries in the spring, to its 'death' in Pisces twelve months later. This makes sense of the controversy which raged in the early church about the duration of Jesus' ministry. Irenaeus, orthodoxy's first champion (writing c.185 C.E), stated categorically that Jesus' ministry lasted for a number of years in order to counter the claims of the Gnostic Valentinus, who said that the career of Jesus lasted for *one year only*, and that Jesus suffered in the twelfth month (i.e. March, the month of Pisces). Anglican archbishop Philip Carrington, who proposed a calendrical theory of the structure of Mark,[2] says that Valentinus was actually claiming that the career of Jesus corresponded with the signs of the zodiac. My theory is not new, then: it's just been forgotten about (or deliberately buried) for eighteen centuries!

But why would Mark structure his story on the zodiac? In a way this is a question that only a modern can ask. We, who barely know the shape of the moon in the sky, forget that the ancient world was steeped in astrology. To begin with, our ancestors could actually see the sky at night, and before television and light pollution people would know their way around the constellation patterns. Such forgetfulness may not be too detrimental to our contemporary scientific endeavours, but it can only give us a distorted view of the cultural products of the past. The celebrated historian of religion, Franz Cumont, for whom astrology was 'nothing but the most monstrous of all the chimeras begotten of superstition' admitted that it was 'indissolubly linked not only with astronomy and meteorology, but also with medicine, botany, ethnography, and physics. If we go back to the earliest stages of every kind of learning, as far as the Alexandrine and even the Babylonian period, we shall find almost everywhere the disturbing influence of these astral 'mathematics'. He goes on to tell us that 'this hallucination, the most persistent which has ever haunted the human brain' left its mark on the religious life of past generations, dominating the religion of Babylon, informing the highest phases of ancient paganism, and 'by changing the character of ancient idolatry, it was to prepare in many respects the coming of Christianity'.[3]

Given the widespread influence of astrology on virtually every aspect of life in the ancient world, it is strange that most orthodox Jewish and Christian commentators, failing to find any examples of a narrowly defined system of stellar divination in its pages, seem to assume that the Bible is uniquely free of astrology's influence. This leads to the curious irony of Christian fundamentalists sporting the Piscean fish logo on their lapels and on their cars, while loudly proclaiming that astrology is a tool of Satan.

Mark's Gospel is not a rudimentary biography of Jesus, nor is it a collection of historical reminiscences exaggerated by constant retelling. Its stories are not arranged arbitrarily as the form critics would have it. The Gospel is, in fact, a series of dramatic 'parables' setting forth a version of the perennial philosophy, designed to accompany the spiritual seeker on the journey towards enlightenment or self-transformation. As Aldous Huxley says, such texts have nothing to do with history, but describe 'a process for ever unfolded within the heart of man',[4] i.e. they don't describe the public life of one individual, they describe the inner life of every human being. Mark's Gospel has its origin in an esoteric tradition which owes as much to the mystery schools of paganism as it does to Judaism. *It is a textbook of the spiritual life written in an astrological code which, when deciphered, completely transforms our understanding of its original nature and purpose.*

The implications of this theory for our understanding of Gospel origins and hermeneutics are profound. In the spring of 2007 I began a year-long series of sermons on the Gospel of Mark, devoting (at least) two sermons to each of the zodiacal sections. In each of these sermons I tried to tease out the meaning of the individual passages in the Gospel based on their location in the text. Here is the first of these, preached on Sunday 25th March 2007. It deals with a couple of passages in the Aries section of the Gospel—the call of the first apostles and the cure of the paralytic. It will give you some idea of the new dimensions opened up by an understanding of the zodiacal schema.

PICK UP YOUR BED AND WALK!

Last Wednesday was the first day of spring. It wasn't such a pleasant day in England; it was windy and cold, with the odd flurry of snow and sleet, but despite the inclement weather the evidence of new growth was everywhere, as it has been for a few weeks: the daffodils are blooming, the trees budding, the days lengthening. This is the season of new life, celebrated throughout human history with great rejoicing; the long sleep of winter is over, the sap is rising; it's when 'a young man's fancy turns to thoughts of love' (and 'an old man's stomach turns!') It is an optimistic time, when, according to Chaucer, 'folk long to go on pilgrimages'; it's when we start to make our plans, change our jobs, sell our houses. Forget January 1st, with its dreary darkness and its forced bonhomie; this is the real 'new year' and has been acknowledged as such in the northern hemisphere since human beings appeared on earth. The ancients believed that the creation of the world took place at this time of the year (as well they might), and the Jewish people said that the Exodus occurred in springtime; the waking of the earth from its winter sleep providing a powerful metaphor for casting off the shackles of slavery in Egypt and moving on to freedom in the promised land.

The sun has entered the zodiac sign of Aries, the sign of the Ram or Lamb, and it is this sign that is reflected in the first three chapters of Mark's Gospel. Aries is the sign of the springtime, the sign of new beginnings, vigour, activity, and impetuosity. People who born under Aries are often confrontational, somewhat aggressive, fiery, individualistic—like the ram itself, attacking head first, butting all those who would oppose it out of the way. One of the most characteristically Aries people of the modern world is Ian Paisley (born on April 6th 1926). He is fiercely individualistic, apparently incapable of negotiation or compromise, an initiator *par excellence*, who is prepared to take on all comers. Life for Ian Paisley is a battle. This is how he expressed his disapproval of the pope's visit to the European Parliament in Strasbourg in 1988:

This is the battle of the Ages which we are engaged in. This is no Sunday school picnic; this is a battle for truth against the lie, the battle of Heaven against hell, the battle of Christ against the Antichrist!'

Richard Dawkins—born on 26th March 1941—is another Aries. He is Darwin's champion, fearlessly challenging religion, even resurrecting the old idea of 'warfare' between religion and science. His equally disputatious colleague, Daniel Dennett, who is beating the rationalist,

antireligious drum in America, was born just a year and two days after Dawkins, on 28th March 1942. Archetypal Aries, Christopher Hitchens (born April 13th 1949) has entered the fray with his book *God is not Great,* along with the atheist philosopher A.C. Grayling (born 3rd April, 1949) author of *Against all Gods.* Aries people certainly relish a fight!

Of the great spiritual figures born under Aries, none is more typical or more appealing than the wonderful Teresa of Avila, who was born on 28th March 1515. She's one of my very favourite saints. There's nothing wishy-washy about Teresa. Her earliest desire was to become a martyr, and when she was a little girl she ran away from home just so that she could be captured and executed by the Moors! Fortunately, her uncle saw her trying to escape and brought her back. She'd only gone down the road. Her love for God was passionate, described by her in unambiguously erotic terms, and the famous Bernini statue of Teresa shows her lost in almost orgasmic rapture. Although she was a nun, and although at times she was said to levitate when lost in ecstasy at mass, she was certainly no recluse: she founded and ran a religious order, travelling by cart in Spain's scorching heat to the various convents under her jurisdiction, suggesting improvements, disciplining backsliders, dealing with finances, all the while writing the most startling religious prose. She deliberately avoided marriage, which she considered a kind of slavery, making her into one of the great feminist figures of the past, and one of a number of Aries women who have fought the battle for female rights down the ages (the other sign with more than its fair share of feminists is Aquarius). They are a force to be reckoned with!

Among the most Arien figures in the Bible is John the Baptist, the very first character we are introduced to in the Gospel of Mark. Mark doesn't tell us very much about him, except to say that he was dressed in no-nonsense Aries style—a garment made from camel's hair—and his diet didn't have too many frills either; he existed on locusts and wild honey! In the

Gospels of Matthew and Luke he lambastes the religious people of his day, calling them 'a brood of vipers' and threatening them with all manner of calamities if they don't mend their ways. His plain speaking eventually brings about his downfall. His fearless but rather foolhardy rebuke of King Herod for marrying his sister-in-law, Herodias, gets him beheaded—a most Arien death, since Aries was said to govern the head and was even called 'The Lord of the Head' by the Egyptians.

The figure of Jesus that we meet in these early chapters of Mark is equally confrontational. He goes into battle against his religious opponents with breath-taking fervour and more than a dash of rashness. He takes on the Pharisees and the Scribes, and even tackles good old Satan himself, casting the devil out of various disturbed people, and claiming that the kingdom of Satan has been brought to an end. Maya Angelou, a great contemporary Arien figure (born 4th April 1928), says, 'I love to see a young girl go out and grab the world by the lapels; life's a bitch; you've got to go out and kick ass,' which is exactly what Jesus is shown to be doing. 'Gentle Jesus meek and mild'? Forget it! That's just religious sentimentality. This is Jesus kicking ass, and his ass kicking provokes the religious authorities so much that even sworn enemies, the patriotic Pharisees and the collaborative Herodians, are prepared to join forces to plot his death.

So, what are the spiritual lessons of Aries? There are a number of them, but, unfortunately, (or maybe fortunately!) we can't deal with them all. Today I want to look briefly at two.

The first is found in those passages where Jesus calls his first disciples. They read very strangely as history. Jesus simply says 'Follow me!' to James and John, and later to Levi, the tax collector, and, without further ado, they all leave everything behind and impetuously follow him. No lengthy conversations, you notice; no police checks on his background; no, 'Give us a little time to think about it Jesus'. None of this; just, up and off. (Incidentally, James and John leave their father Zebedee in the boat 'along with the hired men'. 'The Hired Man' was the name of the

constellation Aries in ancient Babylon, a fact I discovered long after I'd developed my theory of Mark, but which made the hairs stand up on the back of my head when I discovered it!)

These passages teach us that procrastination has no part to play in the spiritual life. If we dither around telling ourselves that we will begin our journey of self-transformation—which is what 'living a spiritual life' means—when circumstances are favourable, when we've found a congenial path, when we have more time, when the kids are grown, when we retire, then we might as well forget it. The Hindu sage, Sri Ramakrishna, tells the following story which illustrates this very point:

> A wife once spoke to her husband, saying, 'My dear, I am very anxious about my brother. For the last few days he has been thinking of renouncing the world and of becoming a Sannyasin, and has begun preparations for it. He has been trying gradually to curb his desires and reduce his wants.' The husband replied, 'You need not be anxious about your brother. He will never become a Sannyasin. No one has ever renounced the world by making long preparations.' The wife asked, 'How then does one become a Sannyasin?' The husband answered, 'Do you wish to see how one renounces the world? Let me show you.' Saying this, instantly he tore his flowing dress into pieces, tied one piece round his loins, told his wife that she and all women were henceforth his mother, and left the house never to return.[5]

That's the way to do it! As St. Paul says, 'Now is the acceptable time; now is the day of salvation!'[6] That's lesson one: stop wasting time; stop kidding yourself that once you've sorted out the historical problems of Christianity to your own satisfaction, and come to satisfactory conclusions about the existence of God and the nature of Jesus, you'll start the process. Because you won't. The path beckons. Get on it.

Lesson two deals with another important aspect of the same procrastinating syndrome, and is brought out in the story of the paralysed man. You remember what happens: Jesus is teaching in somebody's house, but the place is crowded; even the doorway is packed with people. Four men carrying a paralysed man on a stretcher find that their way to Jesus is barred, so they go up on the roof, make a hole in the thatching, and lower the man down to Jesus. (Remember: Aries represents the head—or the roof!) Jesus is amazed by the faith of all concerned, and he tells the man that his sins are forgiven, but this so incenses the Pharisees ('How dare he presume to forgive sins!' they say), that Jesus changes his tactics. 'Okay,' he says, 'I won't say "Your sins are forgiven", I'll say "Pick up your stretcher and walk!"' which the man proceeds to do.

When we stop bothering ourselves about the theological implications of the expression 'Your sins are forgiven', we can make some sense of this lovely story. It simply means, stop letting the past paralyse you. The man on the stretcher is you and I. We are all paralysed by the past, or, in the words of Aries writer Ram Dass (born April 6th 1931), "we are too busy holding on to our unworthiness." We like the past, sins and all, because we are safe there. We know where we are with our habits and traditions. We may be, in fact we probably are, like Nasrudin in our children's story, chewing ferociously on hot peppers, simply because that's what we've always done.[7] "Habit is a great deadener" says Arien Samuel Beckett in *Waiting for Godot*. But now is the time to stop, to let the past go, to break with the comforting habits of thought and action we've allowed to cripple us for so long.

Pick up that stretcher and walk!

And do it today!

These are two important lessons of Aries.

NOTES

Another Aries sermon, and sermons on the other eleven signs can be found on Bill Darlison's website—billdarlison.com. A comprehensive account of the zodiacal theory is in *The Gospel and the Zodiac: The Secret Truth about Jesus*, published by Duckworth/Overlook and available in Amazon, and all good bookshops.

1 Smith, M. (1973) *The Secret Gospel*, The Dawn Press, Clearlake, California.
2 Carrington, P. ,(1952) *The Primitive Christian Calendar: A Study in the Making of the Marcan Gospel Volume 1: Introduction and Text*. C.U.P., England.
3 Cumont, F., *Astrology and Religion Among the Greeks and Romans*. First Published in 1912. Reprinted by Kessinger Publishing, Montana, USA (no date).
4 Huxley, A., (1994) *The Perennial Philosophy*, Flamingo, London.
5 Ballou, R.O., (1959) The Pocket World Bible, Readers Union, Routledge and Kegan Paul, London.
6 2 Corinthians 6:2

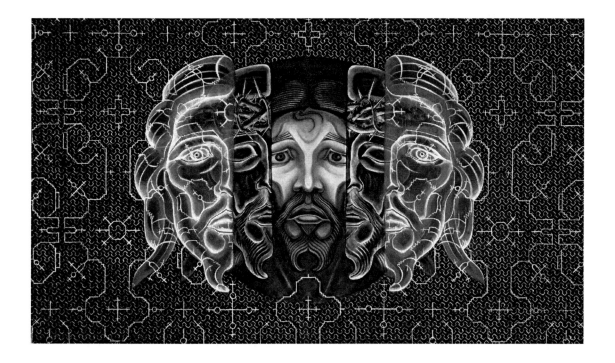

Sean Martin

Deep Field

I: A Discourse on the Eighth and Ninth

I was in the front room of Prolands in Hampstead. St Andrew's abided under an imminent dusk; dark birds circled its spire. Beyond the church, I could see a stand of beech trees gently shed their golden leaves onto the banks of the bathing pond. Governesses hurried children homeward for tea and cake. And then came that unmistakable hum. I searched the massing clouds and then saw them: a wave of zeppelins coming in from the south. I reached for the opium.

Captain Dudley came into the room. 'James, we're under attack. We must start the Ritual now,' he said, and then nodded toward the opium pipe. 'Do you mind?'

'Not at all,' I said. I handed him the opium pipe and he inhaled. He handed it back to me. I got a good lung full. The room was becoming vague, although the prospect of imminent bombardment kept me lucid. Dudley went to the gramophone and put on a recording of Hans Richter conducting Bruckner's Eighth Symphony. I squinted through the brass telescope that sat on a tripod near the window. The zeppelins loomed nearer as the first scratchy bars of the Bruckner made themselves present in the room. I could make out markings on their sides, numbers and black crosses.

'The *Apocalyptic* symphony,' Dudley said. 'I think it's appropriate, given our situation.' I looked at him and nodded. 'Are you ready?'

'I think so,' I replied, feeling uncomfortably amorphous from the drug. The opium helped in the Rituals, especially at times of emergency,

like this, when we had had no time to get into the right mindset through meditation and breathing exercises. Drugs were the necessary short cut. Dudley handed me a jewelled circlet of battered, dull gold. We nicknamed it the Crown of Lights, a slightly sinister thing of unknown provenance. Stories varied as to who had originally acquired it: looted from a monastery in Tibet by Younghusband, or found in a fleamarket in Cairo by Aleister Crowley and then accorded high ritual status. It didn't matter; it's what we've always used, and it had acquired its own mystique over the years. I placed it on my head and got down on my knees before Dudley. 'My Father, yesterday you promised that you would bring my mind into the Eighth and afterwards into the Ninth. You said that this is the way of tradition.'

'My Son, this is indeed true,' Dudley intoned. 'For when I conceived from the fountain that flowed to me, I gave birth.'

'Then, my Father, I have many brothers and sisters, if I am to be numbered among the offspring. Your word is true, Father; it has no refutation. My Father, begin the discourse on the Eighth and the Ninth, and include me also with my brothers and sisters.'

The Bruckner was slowly building. In all my years of training, this was the most difficult movement to get over, especially in Richter's version. I had heard legends of him conducting at the Royal Albert Hall where people were so overcome by the music they were weeping and staggered out into Kensington's night air, their very selves annihilated. I wanted that. I wanted annihilation, anything to get me out of this world. Out of existence.

Dudley put his hand on my head. 'Let us pray, my Son, to the Father of the universe, with your brothers and sisters who are my offspring, that he may give the spirit of—'

Dudley was cut short by an explosion. It shook the room, and we were flung across the floor like dolls. The cabin pressure alarm started to wail. Another bell rang from somewhere in the corridor outside. Looking up, I could see the windows flickering like a silent movie screen. Hampstead's green and pleasant land and the zeppelins were replaced by an intense whiteout, from which emerged the image of a silver and black ship, a lean intergalactic sprinter.

'Fuck!' I whispered. It was the *Dominica*: our doppelgänger, our dark, obsessive twin. She had caught up with us at last, and was greeting us with cannon fire. There was a pressure blast. The noise went to the inside of my brain. I covered my ears. Blood flowed from my eyes and my head felt like it was compressing under Jupiter's gravity.

In that split second afterwards, all I could hear was breathing, but I was not sure whose it was.

I heard Dudley whisper, 'Eloquence'. It was word he was trying to say when we were attacked. It was the last word he ever spoke.

II: Strange Days

The Hampstead I noted in my diary, this diary of our last days I've left for posterity, was an illusion. A Lord Kitchener-wants-you, cricket-on-the-green, *Dad's Army* England; a HoloDeck game. We liked games. Helped pass the time when you're in deep space, especially the distances we've come. No one had ever travelled further, using wormholes for our crazy, epic zigzagging away from the *Dominica* and her taskmasters. Sometimes I preferred the HoloDeck games to reality; sometimes I had trouble telling them apart. Sometimes I just forgot about it all, and just enjoyed the ride. As

a song in one of my playlists had it, *This is the strangest life I've ever known.*

We were the last of a kind, and we'd been running for hundreds of years. Or what seemed like hundreds of years: using wormholes the way we did threw your sense of time completely. Roma had put a bounty on our heads, and we had the high and mighty of every galaxy after us. Or, more often than not, bounty hunters who were just as desperate and mad as we were. But we had the last Krasnikov hybrid sprinter of her class, the *Theia*, whom we liberated from the test fields on Voss Eigen back when I was still just a rookie, learning about why we were all, as a community, heading towards the Eighth and the Ninth. She was hybrid as in part machine, part sentient. As with much else, I never did figure it out. I've felt like I've always been on *Theia*. I received a new education aboard her, a new life. I love her, and I love how she reacts, to me, to each of us, like a lover. We named her after the Titan Theia, from the Greek myths. She was the lover and sister of Hyperion, God of Light. Her name meant *the far-shining one*, and she was said to have given birth to the Sun. We thought the name apt, given our beliefs, and she seemed to like it.

III: Damage Report

McNamara paced on the bridge. She was a big woman, and her flight suit made her seem all the more solid and powerful. She reminded me of prize fighters I'd seen on the moons of Antares, in those hellish shanty towns set up for the miners, where all you did was dig and drink, and then try and fight your way out. McNamara gave us all sombre looks. Me, our pilots Krishna and Mouse, systems admin Nix and the Count, our chief engineer. 'I have to inform you that we've lost Captain Dudley. I shall now be assuming command on this trip. Or what's left of it.'

We nodded.

'Dudley's body is in cryo, but I doubt if there's anything that can be done to bring him back. Unless where we're going has some surprises in store for us.'

'Was it the *Dominica*?' I asked.

'Yes, it was the *Dominica*,' McNamara said. 'She must have calculated our position from entropic algorithms. Or just gotten very lucky.'

'I thought it was her,' I said. The *Dominica* was the very last ship still on our tail, Roma's very own hit squad.

'I thought we'd shaken them off in the D80s,' Nix said.

'Scariest ride in the funfair,' Krish said, trying to lighten the mood. He'd taken us through the D80s, quasars dotted with nova clusters—remnants of four galaxies that were being torn apart by gravity storms—and it had been hell to get out in one piece.

'You didn't do all the driving,' Mouse said. 'I was there for some of it.' She poked her tongue out at Krish. Typical Mouse: petite (hence the name), crazy; every day was April Fool's for her. She had *Reality Sucks* written on her helmet.

'Their pilots must be as good as you two,' McNamara said. 'And got them through those clusters. They're still on our tail and, as we now know, still want our blood. How are the systems?'

Nix checked her screens. 'We've lost some of the external cloaking. So we're visible. And vulnerable.'

'The Dorms?'

Nix pulled up more data. 'They're OK. Everyone's sleeping like babes.'

McNamara turned to the Count and arched a questioning brow.

'It's going to take a few days,' the Count said, chewing gum thoughtfully. 'Unless we can give the old girl some TLC.'

McNamara looked at me. I was still in my HoloDeck gear—plus-fours and tweed, although my decorum was sadly depleted by blood, dust and scorch marks. I looked like I'd wandered into the wrong party. 'Can you render your services, James?'

I nodded. 'I'll go see the Elect.'

'Good. Get to work everyone. We're going to be passing the last known solar system out here, G32W, in 16 hours, and after that, we'll be near our Novikov co-ordinates. We need to be ready by then.'

'Yellow Brick Road, here we come,' said Krish and Mouse gave him a high five. It was time to go to work.

IV: The Elect

We like to work to music. Our people have always valued creativity in all its forms. We believe, unlike the *Dominica* and Roma, that it is the way to the divine. Or, I could also say that the divine is more fully present in us when we are creative. And all art, as they say, aspires to the condition of music, which is nothing other than the condition of the divine, our God of Light. So we are all writers, singers, musicians, actors, jugglers, clowns, jongleurs, minstrels, bards and troubadours. Some nights, when we know we're safely on our own in the void of deep space, we let our hair down. Song, dance, colour: our very own renaissance fair. Roma stood opposed to all this; it was the black iron prison of the closed, fearful mind. And there were few things they hated more than people who did not obey them.

Work music tended to be loud: guitar-driven or industrial, something to get the blood up. The Count had a fondness for The Who; for Mouse, Nurse With Wound did the trick. Nix and McNamara claimed to like everything, as long as the job in hand got done. Music for the Rituals, on the contrary, was quiet: plainchant, polyphony, whatever the inductee liked best. With Dudley it was Beethoven; for me, Bruckner did the job. The Elect, who nourished the ship with intimate care, preferred drones or sitars. Something Indian, repetitive.

The Elect were just that: above us in terms of our religion. Our priests and leaders. We were the Listeners. We listen to the teaching of the Elect. We were soldiers of the soul, soldiers of *gnosis*; in our dreams, we sailed on Lightships of the Pure. I'm a Sethian, who trace their lineage back to the children of Adam and Eve; Seth was the brother Cain didn't kill. We were the visionaries, the mystics, halfway to being Elect. I was the only Sethian on *Theia*, which means I had certain duties that the others didn't.

The Elect stayed mainly in their small suite of rooms a few floors down and back from the bridge. For a long time they had been in the ship's Attic, their chambers glass-roofed so they could meditate on what we were fleeing fast away from: galaxies, nebulae, clusters, countless worlds. But a few close run-ins with the *Dominica* had made the Attic an untenable place for such valuable people, so we suggested that they moved to reinforced rooms near the heart of the ship. Without them, we'd be like children without parents.

Anna answered the door. She was in her usual lilac toga, head shaved, eyes piercing. I've never been able to figure out how old she is—sometimes she's like a teenager, other times a crone. I don't know how much regen she or Anders have done. I'm only on my second, but some of the others are older. Dudley was nearly 500 (and used to joke he didn't look a day over 350), so he must've been through 7 or 8 regens by the time the *Dominica*'s cannons did for him.

'James James,' she said. 'Come in.'

Their rooms were lilac, too, and low-lit. You couldn't read in that light, but it was good for meditation. Or sleep. Anna turned to me. 'And what can we do for you, my dear Listener?'

'TLC,' I said. 'To help speed the repairs.'

Anna nodded. She knew I was—unlike the others—of the Race of Seth. Pure blood. Pure everything. (Except my personal history, which was a little chequered. I'll come to that in a moment.) 'She needs love. Anders is with her now.' Anna nodded toward a door, the inner sanctum of the Seeding Room.

I frowned. Surely the Elect, unlike the Listeners and Sethians, were not allowed physical relationships?

Anna read my thoughts. 'He talks to her. He's

a good comforter.'

The Seeding Room door opened, and Anders walked out. He was almost identical to Anna, the shaved head, the piercing eyes, but taller. Anna explained my presence. Anders looked at me and nodded.

'She needs you, James. She has been asking for you. She even sang a song for you.'

V: SEEDING

The Seeding Room was a small steel chamber with a small fountain trickling water down out of one wall. There was also a chaise longue and a fruit bowl. I'd often thought it was an attempt at an ancient Roman townhouse, some sort of Villa of the Mysteries for the intergalactic refugee. Rubbery tendrils with gaping mouths snaked out of the fountain. They reminded me of seaweed. I put on the preprogrammed blastgoggles and earbuds. Bruckner's Eighth greeted me again. But apart from that, I had no opium, or any other enhancer.

So. In this most desperate of escapes, I now had to show my love in the most obvious way. Such is the nature of *Theia* that she could transform human body fluids into the fuel she needed to keep speeding us on our way, further towards the deep field. She knew about Mouse and I, so the goggles and headset showed me virtual Mouses. Sometimes, when I've had to do this before, I've had images come up from the past. E in particular. We met in 1967, when I was working at the British Library. I was 24, she was 16. Well, nearly 16. She had run away from the family home in Cambridge and was in the big city big time, discovering all life had to offer. She discovered me and soon we were offering each other all we had. Her laugh was infectious. Her tits were amazing. And she introduced me to Pink Floyd. We went to the 14 Hour Technicolour Dream at Ally Pally. Things were never quite the same again; reality had shifted. In retrospect, this was good grounding for my later training with Sethian mystics and teachers. After all, E had given me plenty of experience when it came to altered states of consciousness.

You might say it's become my one true calling.

But now, in my goggles, it was Mouse. There she was, in all her shaven, pierced and tattooed glory. The blastgoggles beamed into me the feelings I needed to give *Theia* what she wanted. I eased myself into one of her tendrilly mouths, and she had all of me. I'm sure at that moment, I could hear a woman singing somewhere, softly.

VI: A HOLIDAY CAMP WITH A DIFFERENCE

I came out of the Seeding Room and the Elect's quarters to the unmistakable strains of The Who's *Tommy*. Work mode was still in full force. The Count nearly ran into me.

'Good morning, Campers!', he said, mimicking the Who song. '*Hard* work, was it?'

'Very funny,' I said. He disappeared down the corridor smirking. He liked wordplay. His ship title, Chief Engineer, didn't last long before he changed it to Chief Buccaneer, which he felt to be more fitting a man of his piratical proclivities. His real name was Eric Geiger, hence Geiger Counter, and finally Count, or the Count, as if he were an aristo. But he's not. Like the rest of us, he's a fugitive. An outcast with an attitude.

Nix came up from the Dorms. 'How are they?' I asked. We had fifty fellow travellers with us in suspended animation, fellow dissenters who were dreaming the trip away.

'Good. All soundly asleep. You look like you could do with a kip yourself,' she smiled. 'We all know what you've been up to.'

She was right. I was tired after my encounter with *Theia*, and made my way back to my room. I recalled my former life, centuries ago, before we slipped down the rabbit holes of time, and what it was like to be with someone. E. And then these bastards on *Theia* introduced themselves to me, telling me I was a chosen one, of the Great Race of Seth. I had been helping organise a conference on the Dead Sea Scrolls and heretical religions at the British Library in 1968 when the very people we were talking about showed up in a spaceship. I seriously thought Syd Barrett was probably saner than I was at that point. Was

there something in the water? Or something in me? And that was the last I saw of London. To be honest, I was glad to be out of the place, although I did miss E. Christ almighty. I told them I needed her, ranted and raved about love and sex and drugs. They told me I had religious potential, and put me in one of their sleep pods. I spent months (or was it only days?) in a weird country house in Sussex. Runhill Court. They trained me there. I met Dudley and forgot, for the time being, about E.

I slept and dreamed of the crazy times. There were times we weren't travelling, making necessary pit stops to overhaul *Theia*, or raising funds to carry on. This was where the Count came into his own as a buccaneer, swindling and defrauding as he went, cutting a lucrative swathe across fifty galaxies. In my dream, he had a peg leg and eye-patch, just like a real pirate on the Spanish Main. Mouse, our other loosest cannon, had spent time running an Ice Bar on Andromeda for Offworld entrepreneurs; in reality it was a high-class clip joint, making a million clicks a month from her girls. The dream showed her working shows on feelgood ships running high-pressure booze cruises through Jupiter's atmos, 1000 miles down. I saw her ship heading through the Great Red Spot; Mouse was wearing a party hat, loving the maelstrom outside as if it were nothing more than a high tide in autumn. And then she turned into E, peachy, free in a Cambridge April, smiling with those big dark eyes. And all around us the doll's house darkness of Syd Barrett, and he's whispering to us, *Set the controls for the heart of the sun.*

I was woken by a thudding on my door. 'Come in,' I said, not knowing where I was.

It was Nix. The work rota had made her ebony skin glisten. 'Red giant outside! And it's fucking huge!'

I was on my feet and following her down the corridor before I knew anything else. My god, the things we've seen.

The bridge was bathed in the red glow of an evening unlike others. The Count had Ray-

Bans and a cowboy hat on. Mouse sported pink tail-fin sunglasses, a leftover from her Jupiter days. They went well with her Mohican haircut. Everyone looked at the main screen, marvelling at a star that would make Antares look small. The opening bars of Bruckner's Ninth kicked in. I smiled. Someone had left my playlist running. It went well with the view: nuclear reactions, hundreds of millions of miles of them. Ironic, really, given that we got into the deep field via the constellation of Fornax, which means 'furnace'. (Or, I should say, the ultra deep field, where we now were, amongst the oldest, remotest stars from earth. Stars that were formed when the universe was very young, the first travellers away from the centre of all things out toward the great unknown.) The star was a beauty. Even the Count seemed impressed, chewing his gum more thoughtfully than usual. In a million years or less, this big old girl would be a white dwarf twenty thousand times smaller than she was now, her fires dulled forever. But by then, we'll all be long gone.

Mouse stepped up and put her arm around me. 'She's dying,' she said quietly, looking at the star as if it were a family pet.

McNamara turned to me and smiled. She had a good smile, which belied her size. 'James, you need to do the Ritual.'

'What do you mean?' I asked.

'If you can reach the Eighth, we can relay it via the Crown of Lights to the HoloDeck and the screen in here. Should help everyone prepare themselves for when we reach the beginnings of the Ninth. You are Sethian, after all. The seers.'

'Any news on the *Dominica*?' I asked, glancing nervously at *Theia*'s screens.

'She's offline,' Nix said. 'Probably behind a nova cloud. MKV 347's close. Pretty much the only place to hide out here. But they won't hide for long.'

I nodded. 'So its back to Hampstead?'

McNamara nodded. 'Fraid so. You'll have to have a woman as your Father. We're a bit short of available men.'

Krish and the Count gave me looks. I shrugged.

'No problem,' I said. 'As long as they can put up with Bruckner.'

VII: A BRIEF HISTORY OF THE MANICHAEAN HERESY

I must leave a record of this before I do the Ritual for what will probably be the last time. I want you to know what the Eighth and the Ninth are, and what we have been running from for these last hundreds of centuries. We had been in existence long before they came for me in 1967, when E and I were entwined to the sounds of *The Piper at the Gates of Dawn*. We were in existence before the Victorians said that there would be no more inventions after 1900 because, by then, they would have everything they would ever need. Bless their little cotton child-and-country-abusing socks. They had not intuited that they, as human beings, were on the edge of eternity. Instead they ignored the best that was in them, the shard of divine light, and fed their young men to the mud of the Somme and Passchendaele.

Yes, the edge of eternity, which is the same as saying the edge of death. What we've been running from. And it's not the Kaiser this time. Come on, what century are you reading this in? Surely you must know, now, who we are? No? I will tell you, one last note before we are lost forever. Or, if we are not lost, we will begin again, new Columbuses in a new universe.

We came into the world in the third century CE. Our leader, Mani, the Blessed One, had a great vision of us all moving closer together, all humans as one family on our little blue planet. He came from a sect called the Cathars, the Pure Ones. He knew the words of Jesus, and how the Church Fathers had corrupted them. He knew the words of the Buddha, and how all life is suffering, but we all possess the means of escape. A means within us. He knew the words of Zarathustra, of how the Light and the Dark are in continual conflict. He knew how we leave this world—whatever world we are on at the time—he knew of the Soulships and their flight to the moon, that Ship of Death, and how they head then towards the Light along rivers dug in the cosmos. That was how he described them in the year 260, before the rich and powerful silenced him. Christ was only on the cross for 6 hours, tops; Mani had 26 days of it in that prison cell in Babylon. That's how powerful his message was. They feared him much more than Jesus. And when the blessed Mani was in the Light, our People had a thousand years on Earth of persecution. We fled east, to China, and then north, into the Mongol steppe. Our greatest teacher in the west, St Augustine, betrayed us after going mad in a garden in Milan. Evil children whispered to him from beyond the wall, tempting him over to Roma's way of thinking. We made sure our children kept their silence when playing outdoors, and taught them to stop their ears lest whispering voices summon them to the other side of that wall, and we lost them.

Rivers in the Cosmos, Mani called them. We know them as wormholes, Einstein-Rosen bridges, white holes. That's how we've escaped, hop-scotching across time and space into the ultra deep field, thirteen billion light years from Earth. Thirteen billion light years away from Roma and all she represents. Now we are finally at the Edge, the Fulcrum, and the bastards are still with us. But the *Theia* is faster than the *Dominica*; as soon as the co-ordinates are right, we'll hit our Novikov coordinates and be gone. They will never follow; they're scared of what's out there. We know: it's the Ninth sphere, spoken of so long ago by our forebears. And the Ninth is the edge of Heaven.

VIII: LATE HEAVY BOMBARDMENT

I was in my room, changing from my flight suit into a new set of tweeds. You couldn't do the Ritual without dressing up, it was all part of the game. And then the lights went out. Or at least, that was my memory of it. First the dark, then the explosions. The *Dominica* was back. I held onto a hand rail on the wall, bracing myself for more. Nothing. Not even music. Just the hum of

the *Theia*, her heartbeat. I scrabbled around in the dark for a helmet. Putting it on, I activated its light. I'd have to take it off for the Ritual, but it might help keep me alive until then. *Theia* occasionally needed my seed, but the Ritual needed my head.

The Crown of Lights, as we dubbed our antique tiara, had had its jewels replaced with small diamond transmitters. Sensors on the inside of the crown touched my head, and what was in my head would end up on the screen, via the diamonds: the state of my soul, the soul of the universe, or a glimpse of the World of Light. It all depended on the Ritual. We had many rituals, most written down centuries ago. I was both the conduit for higher worlds, higher spheres, and a lucky mascot. And the Elect's pupil. I wondered whether Anna and Anders were OK when further cannon fire rocked the room, propelling me towards the wall at speed.

I don't know how long I was out for, but the helmet had saved my life. The next thing I knew, I could hear machine gun fire coming from the corridor. I had the sudden feeling that we had ghosts aboard. I grabbed the nearest weapon, which turned out to be a rusty Mauser from the HoloDeck, and ran out.

The Count was out there, decked in body armour, with one of the big assault weapons mounted on a tripod. Nix had a gun in each hand.

'They're trying to gatecrash via teleport,' the Count said. 'Last ditch attempt. They must be getting desperate. Unless they want to read us the Last Rites. When they come through, we blast them to fuck.'

I nodded. We always liked a good shootout. It was another game to us by now. We'd almost forgotten we could get killed at any moment. We watched the corridor as its empty space grew fuzzy. Two armed men appeared. They flickered on and off, coming into reality and then out of it again like the image on a badly tuned monitor. The Count and Nix donned infrared goggles. The commandos came in again, and the Count either screamed or said something. I couldn't hear over the volley of gunfire that had turned the corridor into a meltchamber of white light and white noise. My Mauser was useless, no better than a cap gun. Smoke was everywhere, the heat from the guns tangible.

They stopped firing. The Count scanned the smoke.

The atmosphere in the corridor began to clear, and I could see two bodies lying at odd angles. Odd because pieces of them had been blown off by the cannon.

The Count stepped forward, inspecting the *Dominica*'s hitmen. 'They're cat food,' he said.

IX: TALES FROM TURFAN

As you might have guessed, we're the crazies. The lunatic fringe of the Manichaean faith. The rest of them are back there, somewhere, making their homes on obscure, peaceful worlds untouched by the taint of intergalactic, inter-species politics. Stay out of trouble could be their motto. But it was never Mani's. You couldn't keep the man down.

He told a story once, found by some German archaeologists when they were digging at a ruined monastery in a Chinese backwater called Turfan around 1900. These were the Manichaean Dead Sea Scrolls, the Master's works, all of them mildewed and moth-eaten. But they could reconstruct this:

In the beginning, there was Light and Dark. The Dark attacked the Light because it was jealous. Ambitious, greedy, insecure, *agitated*: the way politicos and businessmen are. The God of Light emanated the Primal Man, the ultimate superhero, to defend the Light; but instead, he committed the world's first act of military incompetence, being defeated by the Arch-Devil with fog and scorching heat (think surface of Venus, or any given Gulf War). The Primal Man prayed for release, and the Friends of Light and the Messenger, created to rescue the Primal Man's soul, swung into action. The Messenger distracted the Dark Lord's minions, the Archons, by splitting himself into many

different men and women, who proceeded to seduce the Archons. (Kinky stuff for a creation myth, huh? That's probably why I'm a born Manichaean, given my relationship with E and *Theia*.) The Archons got so aroused they accidentally let some of the Primal Man's soul go, enabling the Messenger to take it back to the world of Light. Some of the women Archons, however, got so hot and bothered they gave give birth to abortions, which become the material world. Our Earth. A mish-mash of Light and Dark, hopelessly intermingled. It is the lowest sphere of creation, while the Eighth and Ninth are the highest.

The Arch-Devil feared losing the remaining soul-portions, and embedded them in two mockeries of the God of Light, Adam and Eve. When they had children, Cain, Abel, Seth and the rest of the human race, those Light particles got further dissipated, making the Messenger's job of retrieval all the harder. All of nature, although the work of the Dark Lord, has the Light, or soul, within it. Mani predicted an apocalypse: the Hunter of Light, the final emanation, would appear at the end of time to rescue the final pieces of Light, and imprison forever the last shards of Dark. Eternity will begin then, but we hoped to get there sooner.

Our logic was simple: the material universe is inescapably evil. Therefore, as good Manichaeans, we had to get out of it. Hence our lengthy hop-scotch into the ultra-deep field. We know more about wormholes than anyone else, and put that to good use, *Theia* becoming the needle in the quantum haystack (her class of ship's nicknamed a corkscrew, and for good reason). Once we're beyond the earliest known galaxy, G32W, we are out of the known universe. Or well on the way to the big bang, depending on how you look at it. Either way, we're out of the clutches of the *Dominica*, and Roma. As another song from my druggy London days put it, *Time we left this world today.*

X: GRANTCHESTER MEADOWS

Nix and I were back at Prolands. Hampstead lay under a blanket of snow.

'Someone's feeling chilly,' I said, putting on the Crown.

'Maybe *Theia* is,' Nix replied. 'It's almost absolute zero outside, after all.'

She was right. The only sources of heat out here were from the occasional red giant, whose heat was beginning to fail them, despite their size. I brought up the actual view from the HoloDeck. The screen showed us the saddest of sights: a binary star, white dwarfs both. They were the first stars ever to have flared in this part of space, amongst the earliest nuclear reactions in the universe, when created matter first began to play. I shook the sentiment out of my head and brought the view of Hampstead back.

Nix consulted her notes. She did not know the Ritual by heart, but it wouldn't matter. The words, the play, were what mattered. She would assume the role of the Father, and we could summon up the Messenger and the Friends of Light to help us onto the Yellow Brick Road and into the Ninth sphere.

'The Bruckner record's broken, sir.' She said, holding up one half of the record. 'Looks like your opium pipe fell on it during the last attack.'

'Is the Beethoven there? The *Ode to Joy*?'

She flicked through the record rack and nodded.

'You know it's actually not about joy, but about freedom? Might be better than Bruckner's *Apocalyptic*. It'll do us. Let's get started,' I said, and lit the opium pipe.

* * *

On the bridge, everyone was strapped in, helmeted up. Strains of Beethoven filtered through from the HoloDeck. Everyone was at their stations, expectant.

'G32W passing,' Mouse said. 'Last house on the left. Looks like the lights are out, and no-

one's home. Goodbye cruel universe.'

'Anyone picking up the *Dominica*?', McNamara asked, scanning her own screen for our nemesis.

'I think *Dominica*'s fallen back,' said Nix.

'We're clear here,' Mouse said.

The Count squinted at his screen. McNamara held her breath. And then he said, 'Empty sky.'

'Finally,' McNamara said. 'Finally gone.'

'Yellow Brick Road's coming up, boss,' said Krish.

'Move up to three-quarters light speed,' McNamara said.

Krish and Mouse saluted, increasing the ship's speed. Krish turned to Mouse and said, 'We ain't going to be in Kansas anymore.'

She smiled.

* * *

I was on my knees in front of Nix with my eyes closed, the Crown of Lights on my turned head, my cheek pressed against her belly. The pungent smell of opium lay heavy in the room. On the record, the singers of the Berlin Philharmonic belted out Schiller's lines:

Brothers, above the starry firmament

A loving Father must surely dwell.

Do you fall down, O millions?

Are you aware of your Creator, world?

Seek Him above the starry firmament!

For above the stars He must dwell.

Nix and I chanted, our voices an odd unison:

'Lord, grant us wisdom from your power that reaches us, so that we may describe to ourselves the vision of the Eighth and the Ninth. We have already advanced to the Seventh, since we are pious and walk in your law. And your will we fulfil always. For we have walked in your way, and we have renounced evil, so that your vision may come. Lord, grant us the truth in the image.

Allow us through the spirit to see the form of the image that has no Deficiency, and receive the reflection of the Pleroma from us through our praise. Acknowledge the spirit that is in us. For from you the universe received soul—'

Nix stopped. I wasn't aware something was wrong at first. 'James,' she said. I opened my eyes and noticed that the view of Hampstead was fading out. I could feel the crown humming on my head, its dusty jewels sparking into strange life.

'Is it the *Dominica* coming back? I thought we'd lost them.'

We watched as the familiar faded from view.

And then E appeared on the screen. Or it appeared to be E. It was Cambridge, 1969. She was in Grantchester Meadows, wearing a white dress with red flowers on it. She knew she was being filmed, and smiled coyly for the camera; it looked like one of our old Super-8 home movies. For one terrible moment, I thought she might slip out of her dress, and the whole crew would see her naked.

'Who is she?'

'A Friend of the Light,' I said, banishing thoughts of a naked E from my mind. And then E changed, or Cambridge changed, fading like Edwardian Hampstead. I knew what this was. All was now white, E changing into a serene, noble being. Someone who looked like Anna, or Anders, I couldn't quite tell. They seemed to be both male and female, alive and dead at the same time. Was it a Friend of the Light, or even the Messenger himself? We all watched, Nix and I on the HoloDeck, the others on the bridge, as we passed the Fulcrum that marked the edge of the universe. Before us, all was white. Was it the light of the Big Bang? Or Mani's world, the Light world of the Ninth and higher spheres, that had been waiting patiently for us since the beginning of time? Whose game was this? Whose dream? I could no longer tell as we headed into it at near light speed, and the face on the screen once more became E, and she waved goodbye.

Alan Moore

Fossil Angels

Regard the world of magic. A scattering of occult orders which, when not attempting to disprove each other's provenance, are either cryogenically suspended in their ritual rut, their game of Aiwaz Says, or else seem lost in some Dungeons & Dragons sprawl of channelled spam, off mapping some unfalsifiable and thus completely valueless new universe before they've demonstrated that they have so much as a black-lacquered fingernail's grip on the old one. Self-consciously weird transmissions from Tourette's-afflicted entities, from glossolalic Hammer horrors. Fritzed-out scrying bowls somehow receiving trailers from the Sci-Fi Channel. Far too many secret chiefs, and, for that matter, far too many secret indians.

Beyond this, past the creaking gates of the illustrious societies, dilapidated fifty-year-old follies where they start out with the plans for a celestial palace but inevitably end up with the Bates Motel, outside this there extends the mob. The psyche pikeys. Incoherent roar of our hermetic home-crowd, the Akashic anoraks, the would-be wiccans and Temple uv Psychic Forty-Somethings queuing up with pre-teens for the latest franchised fairyland, realm of the irretrievably hobbituated. Pottersville.

Exactly how does this confirm an aeon of Horus, aeon of anything except more Skinner-box consumerism, gangster statecraft, mind-to-the-grindstone materialism? Is what seems almost universal knee-jerk acquiescence to conservative ideals truly a sign of rampant Theleme? Is Cthulhu coming back, like, anytime soon, or are the barbarous curses from the outer dark those of Illuminists trying to find

their arses with a flashlight? Has contemporary western occultism accomplished anything that is measurable outside the séance parlour? Is magic of any definable use to the human race other than offering an opportunity for dressing up? Tantric tarts and vicars at Thelemic theme nights. *Pentagrams In Their Eyes.* "Tonight, Matthew, I will be the Logos of the Aeon." Has magic demonstrated a purpose, justified its existence in the way that art or science or agriculture justify their own? In short, does anyone have the first clue what we are doing, or precisely why we're doing it?

Certainly, magic has not always been so seemingly divorced from all immediate human function. Its Palaeolithic origins in shamanism surely represented, at that time, the only human means of mediation with a largely hostile universe upon which we as yet exerted very little understanding or control. Within such circumstances it is easy to conceive of magic as originally representing a one-stop reality, a worldview in which all the other strands of our existence...hunting, procreation, dealing with the elements or cave-wall painting...were subsumed. A science of everything, its relevance to ordinary mammalian concerns both obvious and undeniable.

This role, that of an all-inclusive "natural philosophy", obtained throughout the rise of classical civilization and could still be seen, albeit in more furtive fashion, as late as the 16th century, when the occult and mundane sciences were not yet so distinguishable as they are today. It would be surprising, for example, if John Dee did not allow his knowledge of astrology to colour his invaluable contributions to the art of navigation, or vice-versa. Not until the Age of Reason gradually prevented our belief in and thus contact with the gods that had sustained our predecessors did our fledgling sense of rationality identify the supernatural as a mere vestigial organ in the human corpus, obsolete and possibly diseased, best excised quickly.

Science, grown out of magic, magic's gifted, pushy offspring, its most practical and thus materially profitable application, very soon decided that the ritual and symbolic lumber of its alchemic parent-culture was redundant, an encumbrance and an embarrassment. Puffed up in its new white lab coat, ballpoints worn like medals at the breast, science came to be ashamed in case its mates (history, geography, P.E) caught it out shopping with its mum, with all her mumbling and chanting. Her third nipple. Best that she be nutted off to some secure facility, some Fraggle Rock for elderly and distressed paradigms.

The rift this caused within the human family of ideas seemed irrevocable, with two parts of what had once been one organism sundered by reductionism, one inclusive "science of everything" become two separate ways of seeing, each apparently in bitter, vicious opposition to the other. Science, in the process of this acrimonious divorce, might possibly be said to have lost contact with its ethical component, with the moral basis necessary to prevent it breeding monsters. Magic, on the other hand, lost all demonstrable utility and purpose, as with many parents once the kid's grown up and gone. How do you fill the void? The answer, whether we are talking about magic or of mundane, moping mums and dads with empty nests, is, in all likelihood, "with ritual and nostalgia".

The magical resurgence of the nineteenth century, with its retrospective and essentially romantic nature, would seem to have been blessed with both these factors in abundance. Whilst it's difficult to overstate the contributions made to magic as a field by, say, Eliphas Levi or the various magicians of the Golden Dawn, it's just as hard to argue that these contributions were not overwhelmingly synthetic, in that they aspired to craft a synthesis of previously existing lore, to formalise the variegated wisdoms of the ancients.

It does not belittle this considerable accomplishment if we observe that magic, during those decades, was lacking in the purposeful immediacy, the pioneering rush characterising, for example, Dee and Kelly's work. In their development of the Enochian system, late Renaissance magic would seem typified as urgently creative and experimental, forward-looking. In comparison, the nineteenth century occultists seem almost to have shifted magic into a revered past tense, made it a rope-railed museum exhibit, an archive, with themselves as sole curators.

All the robes and the regalia, with their whiff of the historical re-enactment crowd, a seraphic Sealed Knot Society, only with fractionally less silly-looking gear. The worryingly right-wing consensus values and the number of concussed and stumbling casualties, upon the other hand, would probably have been identical. The rites of the exalted magic orders and the homicidal beered-up maulings of the Cromwell tribute-bands are also similar in that both gain in poignancy by being juxtaposed against the grim, relentless forward trundle of industrial reality. Beautifully painted wands, obsessively authentic pikes, held up against the bleak advance of chimney-stacks. How much of this might be most accurately described as compensatory fantasies of the machine age? Role-playing games which only serve to underline the brutal fact that these activities no longer have contemporary human relevance. A wistful recreation of long-gone erotic moments by the impotent.

Another clear distinction between the magicians of the sixteenth and the nineteenth centuries lies in their relation to the fiction of their day. The brethren of the early Golden Dawn would seem to be inspired more by the sheer romance of magic than by any other aspect, with S.L McGregor Mathers lured into the craft by his desire to live out Bulwer-Lytton's fantasy *Zanoni*. Encouraged Moina to refer to him as "Zan", allegedly. Woodford and Westcott, on the other hand, anxious to be within an order that had even more paraphernalia than Rosicrucian Masonry, somehow acquire a contact in the fabled (literally) ranks of the *Geltische Dammerung*, which means something like "golden tea-time". They are handed their diplomas from Narnia, straight out the back of the wardrobe. Or there's Alex Crowley, tiresomely attempting to persuade his school-chums to refer to him as Shelley's Alastor, like some self-conscious Goth from Nottingham called Dave insisting that his vampire name is Armand. Or, a short while later, there's all of the ancient witch-cults, all the blood-line covens springing up like children of the dragon's teeth wherever Gerald Gardner's writings were available. The occultists of the nineteenth and early twentieth centuries all seemed to want to be Aladdin's uncle in some never-ending pantomime. To live the dream.

John Dee, conversely, was perhaps more wilfully awake than any other person of his day. More focussed and more purposeful. He did not need to search for antecedents in the fictions and mythologies available to him, because John Dee was in no sense pretending, was not playing games. He inspired, rather than was inspired by, the great magic fictions of his times. Shakespeare's Prospero. Marlow's *Faust*. Ben Johnson's piss-taking *The Alchemist*. Dee's magic was a living and progressive force, entirely of its moment, rather than some stuffed and extinct specimen, no longer extant save in histories or fairytales. His was a fresh, rip-roaring chapter, written entirely in the present tense, of the ongoing magical adventure. By comparison, the occultists that followed some three centuries down the line were an elaborate appendix, or perhaps a bibliography, after the fact. A preservation league, lip-synching dead men's rituals. Cover versions. Sorcerous karaoke. Magic, having given up or had usurped its social function, having lost its *raison d'etre*, its crowd-pulling star turn, found itself with just the empty theatre, the mysterious curtains. Dusty

hampers of forgotten frocks, unfathomable props from cancelled dramas. Lacking a defined role, grown uncertain of its motivations, magic seems to have had no recourse save sticking doggedly to the established script, enshrining each last cough and gesture, the by-now hollow performance freeze-dried, shrink-wrapped; artfully repackaging itself for English Heritage.

How unfortunate, then, that it was this moment in the history of magic, with content and function lost beneath an over-detailed ritual veneer, all mouth and trousers, which the later orders chose to crystallize about. Without a readily apparent aim or mission, no marketable commodity, the nineteenth century occultist would seem instead to lavish an inordinate amount of his attention on the fancy wrapping paper. Possibly unable to conceive of any group not structured in the hierarchical manner of the lodges that they were accustomed to, Mathers and Westcott dutifully imported all the old Masonic heirlooms when it came to furnishing their fledgling order. All the outfits, grades and implements. The mindset of a secret and elite society. Crowley, of course, took all this heavy and expensive-looking luggage with him when he jumped ship to create his O.T.O, and all orders since then, even purportedly iconoclastic enterprises such as, say, the I.O.T, would seem to have eventually adopted the same High Victorian template. Trappings of sufficient drama, theories intricate enough to draw attention from what the uncharitable might perceive as lack of any practical result, any effect upon the human situation.

The fourteenth (and perhaps final?) issue of the estimable Joel Biroco's *KAOS* magazine featured a reproduction of a painting, a surprisingly affecting and hauntingly beautiful work from the brush of Marjorie Cameron, scary redhead, Dennis Hopper and Dean Stockwell's housemate, putative Scarlet Woman, top Thelemic totty. Almost as intriguing as the work itself, however, is the title: *Fossil Angel*, with its contradictory conjurings of something marvellous, ineffable and transitory combined with that which is by definition dead, inert and petrified. Is there a metaphor available to us in this, both sobering and instructive? Could not all magical orders, with their doctrines and their dogmas, be interpreted as the unmoving calcified remains of something once intangible and full of grace, alive and mutable? As energies, as inspirations and ideas that danced from mind to mind, evolving as they went until at last the limestone drip of ritual and repetition froze them in their tracks, stopped them forever halfway through some reaching, uncompleted gesture? Trilobite illuminations. Fossil angels.

Something inchoate and ethereal once alighted briefly, skipping like a stone across the surface of our culture, leaving its faint, tenuous impression in the human clay, a footprint that we cast in concrete and apparently remain content to genuflect before for decades, centuries, millennia. Recite the soothing and familiar lullabies or incantations word for word, then carefully restage the old, beloved dramas, and perhaps something will happen, like it did before. Stick cotton-reels and tinfoil on that cardboard box, make it look vaguely like a radio and then maybe John Frumm, he come, bring helicopters back? The occult order, having made a fetish out of pageants that passed by or were rained off some half-a-century ago, sits like Miss Haversham and wonders if the beetles in the wedding cake in any way confirm *Liber Al vel Legis*.

Once again, none of this is intended to deny the contribution that the various orders and their works have made to magic as a field, but merely to observe that this admittedly considerable contribution is of, largely, a custodial nature in its preservation of past lore and ritual, or else that its elegant synthesis of disparate teachings is its principal (perhaps only) achievement. Beyond such accomplishments, however, the abiding legacy of nineteenth century occult culture would seem mostly antithetical to the continued health, proliferation and ongoing viability of magic, which, as a technology, has surely long outgrown its ornate late-Victorian vase and is in dire need of transplanting. All of the faux-Masonic furniture and scaffolding imported

by Westcott and Mathers, basically for want of being able to imagine any other valid structure, is, by our own period, become a limitation and impediment to magic's furtherance. Leftover hoodwinks, too-tight ceremonial sashes that constrain all growth, restrict all thought, limit the ways in which we conceive of or can conceive of magic. Mimicking the constructs of the past, thinking in terms that are today not necessarily applicable—perhaps they never really were—seems to have rendered modern occultism utterly incapable of visualizing any different method by which it might organise itself; unable to imagine any progress, any evolution, any *future*, which is probably a sure-fire means of guaranteeing that it doesn't have one.

If the Golden Dawn is often held up as a paragon, a radiant exemplar of the perfect and successful order, this is almost certainly because its ranks included many well-known writers of proven ability and worth whose membership loaned the society more credibility than it would ever, by return, afford to them. The luminous John Coulthart has suggested that the Golden Dawn might be most charitably regarded as a literary society, where slumming scribes searched for a magic that they might have found demonstrable and evident, already there alive and functioning in their own work, were they not blinded by the glare of all that ceremony, all of that fantastic kit. One author who quite clearly contributed more that was of real magical value to the world through his own fiction than through any operations at the lodge was Arthur Machen. While admitting to his great delight at all the mystery and marvel of the order's secret ceremonies, Machen felt compelled to add when writing of the Golden Dawn in his autobiography, *Things Near and Far*, that "as for anything vital in the secret order, for anything that mattered two straws to any reasonable being, there was nothing in it, and less than nothing...the society as a society was pure foolishness concerned with impotent and imbecile Abracadabras. It knew nothing whatever about anything and concealed the fact under an impressive ritual and a sonorous phraseology." Astutely, Machen notes the seemingly inverse relationship between genuine content and baroque, elaborate form characterizing orders of this nature, a critique as relevant today as it was then, in 1923.

The territory of magic, largely abandoned as too hazardous since Dee and Kelly's period, was staked out and reclaimed (when that was safe to do) by nineteenth century occult enthusiasts, by middle-class suburbanites who turned the sere, neglected turf into a series of exquisitely appointed ornamental gardens. Decorative features, statues and pagodas of great intricacy, were contrived in imitation of some over-actively imagined priesthood past. Terminal gods among the neat beds of azaleas.

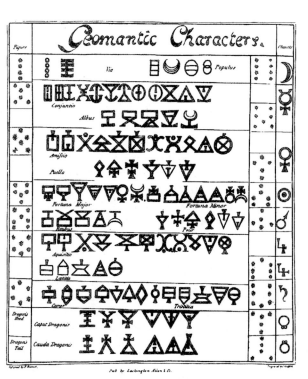

The problem is that gardeners sometimes quarrel. Boundary disputes. Tenant vendettas and evictions, moonlight flits. Once-enviable properties are boarded up, are often squatted by new problem families, new cabals. Hang on to the old nameplate, keep the same address but let the place go, and allow its grounds to fall into a state of disrepair. Slugs in the moly, bindweed spreading out amongst twenty-two-petal roses. By the nineteen-nineties, magic's landscape garden was a poorly maintained sprawl of tired, low-yield allotments with bad drainage, paintwork peeling on the cod-Egyptian summer houses, now become mere sheds where paranoid Home Counties vigilantes sat awake all night, nursing their shotguns and expecting teenage vandals. There's no produce that's worth mentioning. The flowers are without perfume and no longer manage to enchant. Y'know, it were all fancy lamens and Enochian chess round here once, and now look at it. The straggly hedgerows with their Goetic topiary as parched as tinder, dry rot in that Rosicrucian-look gazebo's listing timbers. What this place could do with is a good insurance fire.

No, seriously. Scorched earth. It has a lot to recommend it. Think how it would look when all the robes and banners caught. Might even take out that whole *Mind, Body, and Spirit* eyesore if the wind were in the right direction. Loss of life and livelihood would of course be inevitable, some collateral damage in the business sector, but it sure would be real pretty. Temple beams collapsing in a gout of sparks. "Forget me! Save the cipher manuscripts!" Amongst the countless Gnostic Masses, oaths and calls and banishings, whatever caused them to forget one lousy fire drill? Nobody's quite certain how they should evacuate the inner plane, don't even know how many might still be in there. Finally there emerge heart-wrenching tales of individual bravery. "H-He went back in to rescue the LAM drawing, and we couldn't stop him." Afterwards, a time for tears, for counselling. Bury the dead, appoint successors. Crack open the seal on Hymenaeus Gamma.

Cast a rueful eye across our blackened acres. Take it one day at a time, sweet Jesus. Blow our noses, pull ourselves together. Somehow we'll get through.

What then? Scorched earth, of course, is rich in nitrates and provides a basis for slash-and-burn agriculture. In charred dirt, the green shoots of recovery. Life boils up indiscriminately, churning from black soil. We could give all of these once-stately lawns and terraces back to the wilderness. Why not? Think of it as astral environmentalism, the reclaiming of a psychic greenbelt from beneath the cracked Victorian occult paving-slabs, as an encouragement to increased metaphysical biodiversity. Considered as an organizing principle for magic work, the complex and self-generating fractal structure of a jungle would seem every bit as viable as all the spurious imposed chessboard order of a tiled lodge floor; would seem, in fact, considerably more natural and vital. After all, the traffic of ideas that is the essence and lifeblood of magic is more usually transacted these days by bush telegraph of one kind or another, rather than as ritual secrets solemnly attained after long years of cramming, Hogwarts' CSEs. Hasn't this rainforest mode of interacting been, in fact, the default setting of practical western occultism for some time now? Why not come out and admit it, bulldoze all these lean-to clubhouses that are no longer any use nor ornament, embrace the logic of lianas? Dynamite the dams, ride out the flood, allow new life to flourish in the previously moribund endangered habitats.

In occult culture's terms, new life equates to new ideas. Fresh-hatched and wriggling, possibly poisonous conceptual pollywogs, these brightly-coloured pests must be coaxed into our new immaterial eco-system if it is to flourish and remain in health. Let us attract the small ideas that flutter, neon-bright but frail, and the much tougher, more resilient big ideas that eat them. If we're fortunate, the feeding frenzy might draw the attention of huge raptor paradigms that trample everything and shake the earth. Ferocious notions, from the most bacterially tiny to the staggeringly big and

ugly, all locked into an unsupervised glorious and bloody struggle for survival, a spectacular Darwinian clusterfuck.

Lame doctrines find themselves unable to outrun the sleek and toothy killer argument. Mastodon dogmas, elderly and slipping down the food-chain, buckling and collapsing under their own weight to make a meal for carrion memorabilia salesmen, somewhere for that droning buzz of chat-room flies to lay their eggs. Memetic truffles grown up from a mulch of decomposing Aeons. Vivid revelations sprung like London Rocket from the wild, untended bombsite sprawl. Panic Arcadia, horny, murderous and teeming. Supernatural selection. The strongest, best-adapted theorems are allowed to thrive and propagate, the weak are sushi. Surely this is hardcore Theleme in action, as well as representing a productive and authentic old-skool Chaos that should warm the heart of any Thanateroid. From such vigorous application of the evolutionary process, it is difficult to see how magic as a field of knowledge could do otherwise than benefit.

For one thing, by accepting a less cultivated, less refined milieu where competition might be fierce and noisy, magic would be doing no more than exposing itself to the same conditions that pertain to its more socially-accepted kinfolk, science and art. Put forward a new theory to explain the universe's missing mass, submit some difficult conceptual installation for the Turner Prize and be in no doubt that your offering will be subjected to the most intensive scrutiny, much of it hostile and originating from some rival camp. Each particle of thought that played a role in the construction of your statement will be disassembled and examined. Only if no flaw is found will your work be received into the cultural canon. In all likelihood, sooner or later your pet project, your pet theory will end up as scattered down and claret decorating the stained walls of these old, merciless public arenas. This is how it should be. Your ideas are possibly turned into road-kill but the field itself is strengthened and improved by this incessant testing. It progresses and mutates.

If our objective truly is advancement of the magic worldview (rather than advancement of ourselves as its instructors), how could anyone object to such a process?

Unless, of course, advancement of this nature is not truly our objective, which returns us to our opening questions: what exactly are we doing and why are we doing it? No doubt some of us are engaged in the legitimate pursuit of understanding, but this begs the question as to why. Do we intend to use this information in some manner, or was it accumulated solely for its own sake, for our private satisfaction? Did we wish, perhaps, to be thought wise, or to enhance lacklustre personalities with hints of secret knowledge? Was it rank we sought, some standing that might be achieved more readily by a pursuit like occultism where there are, conveniently, no measurable standards that we might be judged by? Or did we align ourselves with Crowley's definition of the magic arts as bringing about change according to one's will, which is to say achieving some measure of power over reality?

This last would, at a guess, provide the motive that is currently most popular. The rise of Chaos magic in the 1980s centred on a raft of campaign promises, most notable amongst these the delivery of a results-based magic system that was practical and user-friendly. Austin Spare's unique and highly personal development of sigil magic, we were told, could be adapted to near-universal application, would provide a simple, sure-fire means by which the heart's desire of anyone could be both easily and instantly accomplished. Putting to one side the question "Is this true?" (and the attendant query "If it is, then why are all its advocates still holding down a day-job, in a world grown surely further from the heart's desire of *anyone* with every passing week?"), we should perhaps ask whether the pursuit of this pragmatic, causal attitude to occult work is actually a worthy use of magic.

If we're honest, most of causal sorcery as it is practiced probably is done so in the hope of realizing some desired change in our gross, material circumstances. In real terms, this probably involves requests for money (even Dee and Kelly weren't above tapping the angels for a fiver every now and then), requests for some form of emotional or sexual gratification, or perhaps on some occasions a request that those we feel have slighted or offended us be punished. In these instances, even in a less cynical scenario where the purpose of the magic is to, say, assist a friend in their recovery from illness, might we not accomplish our objectives far more certainly and honestly by simply taking care of these things on a non-divine material plane?

If, for instance, it is money we require then why not emulate the true example set by Austin Spare (almost unique amongst magicians in that he apparently saw using magic to attract mere wealth as an anathema) regarding such concerns? If we want money, then why don't we magically get off of our fat arses, magically perform some work for once in our sedentary magic lives, and see if the requested coins don't magically turn up some time thereafter in our bank accounts? If it's the affections of some unrequited love-object that we are seeking, the solution is more simple still: slip roofies in her Babycham, then rape her. After all, the moral wretchedness of what you've done will be no worse, and at the very least you won't have dragged the transcendental into things by asking that the spirits hold her down for you. Or if there's someone whom you genuinely feel to be deserving of some awful retribution then put down that lesser clavicle of Solomon and get straight on the dog and bone to Frankie Razors or Big Stan. The hired goon represents the ethical decision of choice when compared with using fallen angels for one's dirty work (this is assuming that just going round to the guy's house oneself, or maybe even, you know, getting over it and moving on, are not viable options). Even the sick friend example cited earlier: just go and visit them. Support them with your time, your love, your money or your conversation. Christ, send them a card with a sad-looking cartoon bunny on the front. You'll both feel better for it. Purposive and causal magic would too often seem to be about achieving some quite ordinary end without doing the ordinary work associated with it. We might well do better to affirm, with Crowley, that our best and purest actions are those carried out "without lust of result".

Perhaps his other famous maxim, where he advocates that we seek "the aim of religion" utilising "the method of science", however well intentioned, might have led the magical community (such as it is) into these fundamental errors. After all, religion's aim, if we examine the word's Latin origins in *religare* (a root shared with other words like "ligament" and "ligature"), would seem to imply that it's best if everyone is "bound in one belief". This impulse to evangelism and conversion must, in any real-world application, reach a point where those bound by one ligament come up against those tied together by another. At this point, inevitably and historically, both factions will pursue their programmed urge to bind the other in their one and only true belief. So then we massacre the taigs, the prods, the goys, the yids, the kuffirs and the ragheads. And when this historically and inevitably doesn't work, we sit and think about things for a century or two, we leave a decent interval, and then we do it all again, same as before. The aim of religion, while clearly benign, would seem to be off by a mile or two, thrown by the recoil. The target, the thing they were aiming for, stands there unscathed, and the only things hit are Omagh or Kabul, Hebron, Gaza, Manhattan, Baghdad, Kashmir, Deansgate, and so on, and so on, and so on, forever.

The notion of binding together that lies at the etymological root of religion is also, revealingly, found in the symbolic cluster of bound sticks, the fasces, that gives us the later term fascism. Fascism, based upon mystical concepts such as blood and "volk", is more properly seen as religion than as a political stance, politics being based upon some form of reason, however misguided and brutal. The shared idea of being bound in one faith, one belief; that in unity (thus, unavoidably, in uniformity) there lies strength, would seem antithetical to magic, which, if anything, is surely personal, subjective and pertaining to the individual, to the responsibility for every sentient creature to reach its own understanding of and thus make its own peace with God, the universe and everything. So, if religion can be said to find a close political equivalent in fascism, might magic not be said to have more natural sympathy with anarchy, fascism's opposite (deriving from *an-archon* or "no leader")? Which of course returns us to the burned-down temples, dispossessed and homeless order heads, the scorched earth and the naturally anarchic wilderness approach to magic, as suggested earlier.

The other half of Crowley's maxim, wherein he promotes the methodology of science would also seem to have its flaws, again, however well intentioned. Being based upon material results, science is perhaps the model that has led the magic arts into their causal cul-de-sac, described above. Further to this, if we accept the ways of science as a procedural ideal to which our magic workings might aspire, aren't we in danger of also adopting a materialist and scientific mindset with regard to the quite different forces that preoccupy the occultist? A scientist who works with electricity, as an example, will quite justifiably regard the energy as value-neutral, mindless power that can as easily be used to run a hospital, or warm a lava-lamp, or fry a black guy with a mental age of nine in Texas. Magic on the other hand, from personal experience, does not seem to be neutral in its moral nature, nor does it seem mindless. On the contrary, it would seem, as a medium, to be aware and actively intelligent, alive rather than live in the third rail sense. Unlike electricity, there is the intimation of a complex personality with almost-human traits, such as, for instance, an apparent sense of humour. Just as well, perhaps, when one considers the parade of prancing ninnies that the field has entertained and tolerated down the centuries. Magic, in short, does not seem to be there merely to power up sigils that are astral versions of the labour saving gadget or appliance. Unlike electricity, it might be thought to have its own agenda.

Quite apart from all this, there are other sound, compelling reasons why it limits us to think of magic as a science. Firstly and most glaringly, it isn't. Magic, after it relinquished any and all practical or worldly application following the twilight of the alchemists, can no more be considered as a true science than can, say, psychoanalysis. However much Freud might have wished it otherwise, however he deplored Jung dragging his purported scientific method down into the black and squirming mud of occultism, magic and psychoanalysis cannot, by definition, ever be allowed a place amongst the sciences. Both deal almost entirely with phenomena of consciousness, phenomena that cannot be repeated in laboratory conditions and which thus exist outside the reach of science, concerned only with things that may be measured and observed, proven empirically. Since consciousness itself cannot be shown to provably exist in scientific terms, then our assertions that said consciousness is plagued either by penis envy or by demons of the Qlippoth must remain forever past the boundary limits of what may be ascertained by rational scrutiny. Frankly, it must be said that magic, when considered as a science, rates somewhere just above that of selecting numbers for the lottery by using loved ones' birthdays.

This would seem to be the crux: magic, if it is a science, clearly isn't a particularly well-developed one. Where, for example, are the magical equivalents of Einstein's General or even Special theories of Relativity, let alone that of Bohr's Copenhagen Interpretation? Come to that, where are our analogues for laws of gravity, thermodynamics and the rest? Eratosthenes once measured the circumference of the Earth using geometry and shadows. When did we last manage anything as useful or as neat as that? Has there been anything even resembling a general theory since the Emerald Tablet? Once again, perhaps magic's preoccupation with cause and effect has played a part in this. Our axioms seem mostly on the level of "if we do A then B will happen". If we say these words or call these names then certain visions will appear to us. As

to *how* they do so, well, who cares? As long as we get a result, the thinking seems to run, why does it matter how this outcome was obtained? If we bang these two flints together for a while they'll make a spark and set all that dry grass on fire. And have you ever noticed how if you make sure to sacrifice a pig during eclipses, then the sun always returns? Magic is, at best, Palaeolithic science. It really had best put aside that Nobel Prize acceptance speech until it's shaved its forehead.

Where exactly, one might reasonably enquire, does all this leave us? Having recklessly discarded our time-honoured orders or traditions and torn up our statement of intent; having said that magic *should* not be Religion and *can* not be Science, have we taken this Year-Zero Khmer Rouge approach too far, cut our own jugulars with Occam's razor? Now we've pulled down the landmarks and reduced our territory to an undifferentiated wilderness, was this the best time to suggest we also throw away our compass? Now, as night falls on the jungle, we've decided we are neither missionaries nor botanists, but what, then, are we? Prey? Brief squeals in pitch dark? If the aims and methods of science or religion are inevitably futile, ultimately mere dead ends, what other role for magic could conceivably exist? And please don't say it's anything too difficult, because for all the black robes and the spooky oaths, we tend to frighten easily.

If what we do cannot be properly considered as science or religion, would it be provocative to tender the suggestion that we think of magic as an art? Or even The Art, if you like? It's not as if the notion were entirely without precedent. It might even be seen as a return to our shamanic origins, when magic was expressed in masques and mimes and marks on walls, the pictograms that gave us written language so that language could in turn allow us consciousness. Music, performance, painting, song, dance, poetry and pantomime could all be easily imagined as having originated in the shaman's repertoire of mind-transforming magic tricks. Sculpture evolving out of fetish dolls, Willendorf Venus morphing into Henry Moore. Costume design and catwalk fashion, Erte and Yves St. Laurent, arising out of firelit stomps in furs and beads and antlers, throwing shapes designed to startle and arouse. Baroness Thatcher, in her baby-eating prime, suggested that society once more embrace "Victorian values", an idea that certainly would seem to have caught on within the magical fraternity. This clearly goes nowhere near far enough, however. Let us call instead for a return towards Cro-Magnon values: more creative and robust, with better hair.

Of course, we need not journey so far back into admittedly speculative antiquity for evidence of the uniquely close relationship enjoyed by art and magic. From the cave-wall paintings at Lascaux, on through Greek statuary and friezes to the Flemish masters, on to William Blake, to the Pre-Raphaelites, the Symbolists and the Surrealists, it is only with increasing rarity that we encounter artists of real stature, be they painter, writer or musician, who have not at some point had recourse to occult thinking, whether that be through the agency of their alleged involvement with some occult or Masonic order, as with Mozart, or through some personally cultivated vision, as with Elgar. Opera has its origins, apparently, in alchemy, originated by its early pioneers like Monteverdi as an art-form that included all the other arts within it (music, words, performance, costumes, painted sets) with the intent of passing on alchemical ideas in their most comprehensively artistic and thus most celestial form. Likewise, with the visual arts we need not invoke obvious examples of an occult influence such as Duchamp, Max Ernst or Dali, when there are more surprising names such as Picasso (with his youth spent saturated in hashish and mysticism, with his later work preoccupied with then-occult ideas pertaining to the fourth dimension), or the measured squares and rectangles of Mondrian, created to express the notions woken in him by his study of Theosophy. In fact, the greater part of abstract painting can be traced to famed Blavatsky-booster Annie Besant, and the publication of her theory that the rarefied essential energies of Theosophy's rays and currents and vibrations could be represented by intuited and formless swirls of colour, an idea that many artists of a fashionably mystic inclination seized on eagerly.

Literature, meanwhile, is so intrinsically involved with magic's very substance that the two may be effectively considered as the same thing. Spells and spelling, Bardic incantations, grimoires, grammars, magic a "disease of language" as Aleister Crowley so insightfully described it. Odin, Thoth and Hermes, magic-gods and scribe-gods. Magic's terminology, its symbolism, conjuring and evocation, near-identical to that of poetry. In the beginning was the Word. With magic almost wholly a linguistic construct, it would seem unnecessary to recite a role-call of the occult's many literary practitioners. In writing, as in painting or in music, an intense and intimate connection to the world of magic is both evident and obvious, appears entirely natural. Certainly, the arts have always treated magic with more sympathy and more respect than science (which, historically, has always sought to prove that occultists are fraudulent or else deluded) and religion (which, historically, has always sought to prove that occultists are flammable). While it shares the social standing and widespread respect afforded to the church or the laboratory, art as a field does not seek to exclude, nor is it governed by a doctrine that's inimical to magic, such as might be said of its two fellow indicators of humanity's cultural progress. After all, while magic has, in relatively recent times, produced few mighty theologians of much note and even fewer scientists, it has produced a wealth of inspired and inspiring painters, poets and musicians. Maybe we should stick with what we know we're good at?

The advantages of treating magic as an art seem at first glance to be considerable. For one thing, there are no entrenched and vested interests capable of mounting an objection to magic's inclusion in the canon, even if they entertained objections in the first place, which is hardly likely. This is patently far from the case with either science or religion, which are by their very natures almost honour-bound to see that magic is reviled and ridiculed, marginalized and left to rust there on history's scrap-heap with the Flat Earth, water-memory and phlogiston. Art, as a category, represents a fertile and hospitable environment where magic's energy could be directed to its growth and progress as a field, rather than channelled into futile struggles for acceptance, or burned uselessly away by marking time to the repeated rituals of a previous century. Another benefit, of course, lies in art's numinosity, its very lack of hard-edged definition and therefore its flexibility. The questions "what exactly are we doing and why are doing it", questions of "method" and of "aim' take on a different light when asked in terms of art. Art's only aim can be to lucidly express the human mind and heart and soul in all their countless variations, thus to further human culture's artful understanding of the universe and of itself, its growth towards the light. Art's method is whatever can be even distantly imagined. These parameters of purpose and procedure are sufficiently elastic, surely, to allow inclusion of magic's most radical or most conservative agendas? Vital and progressive occultism, beautifully expressed, that has no obligation to explain or justify itself. Each thought, each line, each image made exquisite for no other purpose than that they be offerings worthy of the gods, of art, of magic itself. The Art for The Art's sake.

Paradoxically, even those occultists enamoured of a scientific view of magic would have cause for celebration at this shift in emphasis. As argued above, magic can never be a science as science is currently defined, which is to say as being wholly based upon repeatable results within the measurable and material world. However, by confining its pursuits entirely to the world of the material, science automatically disqualifies itself from speaking of the inner, immaterial world that is in fact the greater part of our human experience. Science is perhaps the most effective tool that human consciousness has yet developed with which to explore the outer universe, and yet this polished and sophisticated instrument of scrutiny is hindered by one glaring blind-spot in that it cannot examine consciousness itself. Since the late 1990s the most rapidly expanding field of scientific interest is apparently consciousness studies, with two major schools of thought-on-thought thus far emerging, each contending with the other. One maintains that consciousness is an illusion of biology, mere automatic and behaviourist cerebral processes that are dependent on the squirt of glands, the seep of enzymes. While this does not seem an adequate description of the many wonders to be found within the human mind, its advocates are almost certainly backing a winner, having realised that their blunt, materialistic theory is the only one that stands a chance of proving itself in the terms of blunt material science. In the other camp, described as more transpersonal in their approach, the current reigning theorem is that consciousness is some peculiar "stuff" pervading the known universe, of which each sentient being is a tiny, temporary reservoir. This viewpoint, while it probably elicits greater sympathy from those of occult inclinations, is quite clearly doomed in terms of garnering eventual scientific credibility. Science cannot even properly discuss the personal, so the transpersonal has no chance. These are matters of the inner world, and science cannot go there. This is why it wisely leaves the exploration of mankind's interior to a sophisticated tool that is specifically developed for that usage, namely art.

If magic were regarded as an art it would have culturally valid access to the infrascape, the endless immaterial territories that are ignored by and invisible to Science, that are to scientific reason inaccessible, and thus comprise magic's most natural terrain. Turning its efforts to creative exploration of humanity's interior space might also be of massive human use, might possibly restore to magic all the relevance and purpose, the demonstrable utility that it has lacked so woefully, and for so long. Seen as an art, the field could still produce the reams of speculative theory that it is so fond of (after all, philosophy and rhetoric may be as easily considered arts as sciences), just so long as it were written beautifully or interestingly. While, for example, *The Book of the Law* may be debatable in value when considered purely as prophetic text describing actual occurrences or states of mind to come, it cannot be denied that it's a shit-hot piece of writing, which deserves to be revered as such. The point is that if magic were to drop its unfulfilable pretensions as a science and come out of the closet as an art, it would ironically enough obtain the freedom to pursue its scientific aspirations, maybe even sneak up on some unified field theorem of the supernatural, all in terms acceptable to modern culture. Marcel Duchamp's magnum opus, *The Bride Stripped Bare by Her Bachelors*, is more likely to be thought of seriously as genuine alchemy than is the work of whichever poor bastard last suggested that there might be something to cold fusion. Art is clearly a more comfortable environment for magic thinking than is science, with a more relaxing decor, and much better-looking furniture.

Even those damaged souls so institutionalised by membership of magic orders that they can't imagine any kind of lifestyle that does not involve belonging to some secretive, elite cabal need not despair at finding themselves homeless and alone in our proposed new wilderness. Art has no orders, but it does have movements, schools and cliques with all the furtiveness, the snottyness and the elitism that anyone could wish for. Better yet, since differing schools of art are not so energetically competing with each other for the same ground as are magic orders (how can William Holman Hunt, for instance, be said to compete with Miro, or Vermeer?), this should obviate the need for differing schools of occult thought to feud, or snipe, or generally go on like a bunch of sorry Criswell-out-of-*Plan 9*-looking bitches.

Just as there is no need to entirely do without fraternities, then similarly there is no necessity for those who've grown attached to such things to discard their ritual trappings or, indeed, their rituals. The sole requirement is that they approach these matters with a greater creativity,

and with a more discerning eye and ear for that which is profound; that which is beautiful, original or powerful. Make wands and seals and lamens fit to stand in exhibitions of outsider art (How hard can that be? Even mental patients qualify), make every ritual a piece of stunning and intense theatre. Whether one considers magic to be art or not, these things should surely scarcely need be said. Who are our private rituals and adornments meant to please, if not the gods? When did they ever give us the impression they'd be pleased by that which was not suitably exquisite or original? Gods, if they're anything at all, are known to be notoriously partial to creation, and may therefore be presumed to be appreciative of human creativity, the closest thing that we've developed to a god-game and our most sublime achievement. To be once more thought of as an art would allow magic to retain all that is best about the field it was, while at the same time offering the opportunity for it to flourish and progress into a future where it might accomplish so much more.

How would this mooted change of premise impact, then, upon our methodology? What shifts of emphasis might be entailed, and could such changes be to the advantage of both magic as a field and us as individuals? If we seriously mean to reinvent the occult as The Art, one basic alteration to our working methods that might yield considerable benefit would be if we resolved to crystallise whatever insights, truths or visions our magical sorties had afforded us into some artefact, something that everybody else could see as well, just for a change. The nature of the artefact, be it a film, a haiku, an expressive pencil-drawing or a lush theatrical extravaganza, is completely unimportant. All that matters is that it be art, and that it remain true to its inspiration. Were it adopted, at a stroke, a relatively minor tweak of process such as this might utterly transform the world of magic. Rather than be personally-motivated, crudely causal workings of both dubious intent and doubtful outcome, hand-job magic ended usually in scant gratification, our transactions with the hidden world would be made procreative, generating issue in the form of tangible results that everyone might judge the worth of for themselves. In purely evangelic terms, as propaganda for a more enlightened magic worldview, art must surely represent our most compelling "evidence" of other states and planes of being. While the thoughts of Austin Spare are undeniably of interest when expressed in written form as theory, it is without doubt his talents as an artist that provide the sense of entities and other worlds actually witnessed and recorded, the immediate authenticity which has bestowed on Spare much of his reputation as a great magician. More importantly, work such as Spare's provides a window on the occult world, allowing those outside a clearer and perhaps more eloquent expression of what magic is about than any arcane tract, offering them a worthwhile reason to approach the occult in the first place.

In our wilderness scenario for magic, with the fierce and fair Darwinian competition between ideas that's implied, treating the occult as an art would also lend a means of dealing with (or carrying out) any disputes that might arise. Art has a way of sorting out such squabbles for itself, inarguably, without resorting to lame processes like, for example, violent conflict resolution, litigation, or, much worse, girly democracy. With art, the strongest vision will prevail, even if it takes decades, centuries to do so, as with William Blake. There is no need to even take a vote upon which is the strongest vision: that would be the one just sitting quietly in its undisputed corner of our culture, nonchalantly picking its teeth with the sternums of its rivals. Mozart brings down Salieri, sleeps for two days after feasting, during which time the savannah can relax. Lunging out suddenly from tower-block shadows, J.G. Ballard takes out Kingsley Amis, while Jean Cocteau be all over D.W. Griffiths' scrawny Imperial Cyclops ass like a motherfucker. An artistic natural selection, bloody-minded but balanced, seems a far more even-handed way of settling affairs than arbitrary and unanswerable rulings handed down by heads of orders, such as Moina Mathers telling Violet Firth her aura lacked the proper symbols.

Also, if the vicious struggle for survival is enacted purely in the terms of whose idea is the most potent and most beautiful in its expression, then bystanders at the cockfight are more likely to end up spattered with gorgeous metaphors than with dripping, still-warm innards. Even our most pointless and incestuous feuds might thereby have a product that enriched the world in some small measure, rather than no outcome save that magic seem still more a bickering and inane children's playground than everyone thought it was already. Judged on its merits, such a jungle-logic attitude to magic, with its predatory aesthetics and ideas competing in a wilderness that's fertilised by their exquisite cultural droppings, would appear to offer the occult a win-win situation. How could anyone object, except for those whose ideas might be seen as plump, slow-moving, flightless and a handy source of protein; those well-qualified as primary prey who are perhaps beginning to suspect that this is all a tiger's argument for open-plan safari parks?

Upon consideration, these last-mentioned doubts and fears, while surely trivial within a context of magic's well-being as a field, are likely to be the most serious obstacles to any wide acceptance of a primal swampland ethic such as is proposed. However, if we accept that the sole alternatives to jungle are a circus or a zoo, the notion is perhaps more thinkable. And if our precious ideas should be clawed to pieces when they're scarcely out the nest, then while this is of course distressing, it's no more of an ordeal than that endured by any spotty schoolboy poet or Sunday painter who exposes their perhaps ungainly effort to another's scrutiny. Why should fear of ridicule or criticism, fear that the most lowly karaoke drunk is seemingly quite capable of overcoming, trouble occultists who've vowed to stand unflinching at the gates of Hell itself? In fact, shouldn't the overcoming of such simple phobias be a prerequisite for anyone who wants to style his or her self as a magician? If we regarded magic as an art and art as magic, if like ancient shamans we perceived a gift for poetry as magic power, magically bestowed, wouldn't we finally have some comeback when the ordinary person in the street asked us, quite reasonably, to demonstrate some magic, then, if we think we're so thaumaturgical?

How empowering it would be for occultists to steadily accumulate, through sheer hard work, genuine magical abilities that can be provably displayed. Talents the ordinarily intelligent and rational person can quite readily accept as being truly magical in origin; readily engage with in a way that current occultism, with its often wilful and unnecessary obscurantism, cannot manage. Urgently expressed and heartfelt though most modern grimoires most assuredly may be, a skim through Borges' *Fictions* or a glimpse of Escher or a side or two of Captain Beefheart would be much more likely to persuade the ordinary reader to a magically receptive point of view. If consciousness itself,

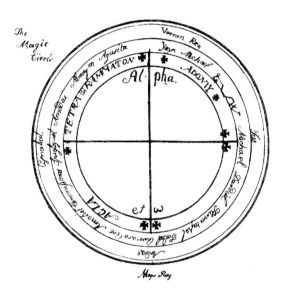

with its existence in the natural world being beyond the power of science to confirm, is therefore super-natural and occult, surely art is one of the most obvious and spectacular means by which that supernatural realm of mind and soul reveals itself, makes itself manifest upon a gross material plane.

Art's power is immediate and irrefutable, immense. It shifts the consciousness, noticeably, of both the artist and her audience. It can change men's lives and thence change history, society itself. It can inspire us unto wonders or else horrors. It can offer supple, young, expanding minds new spaces to inhabit or can offer comfort to the dying. It can make you fall in love, or cut some idol's reputation into ribbons at a glance and leave them maimed before their worshippers, dead to posterity. It conjures Goya devils and Rosetti angels into visible appearance. It is both the bane and most beloved tool of tyrants. It transforms the world which we inhabit, changes how we see the universe, or those about us, or ourselves. What has been claimed of sorcery that art has not already undeniably achieved? It's led a billion into light and slain a billion more. If the accretion of occult ability and power is our objective, we could have no more productive, potent means or medium than art whereby this is to be accomplished. Art may not make that whisk-broom come to life and multiply and strut round cleaning up your crib...but nor does magic, for that matter...yet simply dreaming up the image must have surely earned Walt Disney enough money so he could pay somebody to come by and take care of that stuff *for* him. And still have enough change to get his head put in this massive hieroglyphic-chiselled ice cube somewhere underneath the Magic Kingdom. There, surely to God, is all of the implacable Satanic influence that anybody, sane or otherwise, could ever ask for.

In reclaiming magic as The Art, amok and naked in a Rousseau wilderness devoid of lodges, it is probable that those made most uneasy by the proposition would be those who felt themselves unprivileged by such a move, those who suspected that they had no art to offer which might be sufficient to its task. Such trepidations, while they may be understandable, surely cannot sit well with the heroic, fearless image one imagines many occultists to have confected for themselves; seem somehow craven. Is there truly nothing, neither craft nor art, which they can fashion to an implement of magic? Do they have no talent that may be employed creatively and magically, be it for mathematics, dancing, dreaming, drumming, stand-up comedy, striptease, graffiti, handling snakes, scientific demonstration, cutting perfectly good cows in half or sculpting scarily realistic busts of European monarchy from their own faeces? Or, like, anything? Even if such abilities are not at present plentiful or evident, cannot these timorous souls imagine that by application and some honest labour talents may be first acquired then honed down to a useful edge? Hard work should not be a completely foreign concept to the Magus. This is not even The Great Work that we're necessarily discussing here, it's just the Good-But-Not-Great Work. Much more achievable. If that still sounds too difficult and time-consuming, you could always make the acquisition of profound artistic talent and success your heart's desire and simply spadge over a sigil. Never fails, apparently. So what excuse could anybody have for not embracing art as magic, magic as The Art? If you are truly, for whatever reason, now and for all time incapable of any creativity, then are you sure that magic is the field to which you are most eminently suited? After all, the fast-food chains are always hiring. Ten years and you could be a branch manager.

By understanding art as magic, by conceiving pen or brush as wand, we thus return to the magician his or her original shamanic powers and social import, give back to the occult both a product and a purpose. Who knows? It might turn out that by implementing such a shift we have removed the need for all our personally-motivated causal charms and curses, our hedge-magic. If we were accomplished and prolific in our art, perhaps the gods might be prepared to send substantial weekly postal orders, all without us even asking. In the sex and romance stakes, as artists we'd all make out like Picasso. Women,

men and animals would offer themselves naked at our feet, even in Woolworth's. As for the destruction of our enemies, we simply wouldn't bother to invite them to our launch-parties and openings, and they'd just *die*.

This re-imagining of magic as The Art could clearly benefit the occult world in general and the individual magician in particular, but let's not overlook the fact that it might also benefit the arts. It must be said that modern mainstream culture, for the greater part and from most civilised perspectives, is a Tupperware container full of sick. The artists of the age (admittedly, with a few notable exceptions) seem intent upon reflecting the balloon-like hollowness and consequent obsession with mere surface that we find amongst our era's governments and leaders. Just a year or two ago, the old Tate Gallery's Blake retrospective drew from critics sharp comparisons with the Brit-artists currently inhabiting Blake's Soho stamping ground, observing that the modern crop of tunnel-visionaries pale when held up to Blake's Lambeth light. The studied and self-conscious "craziness" of Tracey Emin is made tame beside his holy tyger madness, all accomplished within howling-range of Bedlam. Damien Hirst is shocking in a superficial manner, but not shocking to the point where he has loyalty oaths, vigilante lynch-mobs and sedition trials to deal with. Jake and Dinos Chapman's contributions to *Apocalypse* (the exhibition, not the situation with Iraq) are not in any sense a revelation. William Blake could pull a far superior apocalypse from *The Red Dragon*'s sculpted crimson butt without a second thought. The modern art world deals now in high-concept items, much like the related (through Charles Saatchi) field of advertising. It appears to be bereft of vision, or indeed of the capacity for such, and offers little in the way of nourishment to its surrounding culture, which could use a decent and sustaining meal right about now. Couldn't a reaffirmation of the magical as art provide the inspiration, lend the vision and the substance that are all so manifestly lacking in the world of art today? Wouldn't such a soul-infusion allow art to live up to its purpose, to its mission, to insist that the interior and subjective human voice be heard in culture, heard in government, heard on the stained Grand Guignol stages of the world? Or should we just sit back and wait for praeter-human intellects from Sirius or Disney's walking whisk-brooms or the Aeon of Horus to arrive and sort this mess out for us?

A productive union, a synthesis of art and magic propagated in a culture, an environment, a magic landscape lacking temple walls and heirloom furnishings that everyone tripped over anyway. Staged amidst the gemming ferns and purpled steam-heat of a re-established occult biosphere, this passionate conjunction of two human faculties would surely constitute a Chemic Wedding which, if we were lucky and things got completely out of hand at the Chemic Reception, might precipitate a Chemic Orgy, an indecent, riotous explosion of suppressed creative urges, astral couplings of ideas resulting in multiple births of chimerae and radiant monsters. Fierce conceptual centaurs with their legs of perfume and their heads of music. Mermaid notions, flickering silent movies that are architecture from the waist down. Genre sphinxes and style manticores. Unheard of and undreamed mutations, novel art-forms breeding and adapting fast enough to keep up with the world and its momentum, acting more like life-forms, more like fauna, more like flora to proliferate in our projected magic wilderness. The possible release of fusion energy made suddenly available when these two heavy cultural elements, magic and art, are brought into dynamic close proximity might fairy-light our jungle, might even help to illuminate the mainstream social mulch that it, and we, are rooted in.

Nothing prevents us throwing off the callipers and the restraints, the training wheels that have retarded magic's forward progress for so long that moss obliterates its railway tracks and branch-line sidings both. Nothing can stop us, if we have the will, from redefining magic as an art, as something vital and progressive. Something which in its ability to deal with the interior human world has a demonstrable utility, can be of actual use to ordinary people, with their inner worlds increasingly encroached upon by a tyrannical, colonialist exterior that's intent on strip-mining them of any dreams or joy or self-determination. If we so resolved we could restore to magic a potential and a potency, a purpose it has barely caught a glimpse of in the last four hundred years. Were we prepared to take on the responsibility for this endeavour then the world might see again the grand and terrible magicians that, outside of bland and inoffensive children's books or big-screen and obscenely-budgeted extravagances, it has all but managed to forget. It might be argued that at this nerve-wracking juncture of our human situation, magical perspectives are not merely relevant but are an indispensable necessity if we are to survive with minds and personalities intact. By redefining the term magic we could once again confront the world's iniquities and murk in our preferred, time-honoured method: with a word.

Make the word magic mean something again, something worthy of the name, something which, as a definition of the magical, would have delighted you when you were six; when you were seventy. If we accomplish this, if we can reinvent our scary, wild and fabulous art for these scary, wild and fabulous new times that we are moving through, then we could offer the occult a future far more glorious and brimming with adventure than we ever thought or wished its fabled past had been. Humanity, locked in this penitentiary of a material world that we have been constructing for ourselves for centuries now, has perhaps never needed more the key, the cake-with-file-in, the last-minute pardon from the governor that magic represents. With its nonce-case religions and their jaw-droppingly demented fundamentalists, with its bedroom-farce royalties, and with its demagogues more casually shameless in their vile ambitions than they've been in living memory, society at present, whether in the east or west, would seem to lack a spiritual and moral centre, would indeed appear to lack even the flimsiest pretence at such a thing.

The science which sustains society, increasingly, at its most far-flung quantum edges finds it must resort to terminology from the kabbala or from Sufi literature to adequately state what it now knows about our cosmic origins. In all its many areas and compartments, all its scattered fields, the world would seem to be practically crying out for the numinous to come and rescue it from this berserk material culture that has all but eaten it entire and shat it through a colander. And where is magic, while all this is going on?

It's trying to force our boyfriend to come back to us. It's scraping cash together to fend off the black hole in our plastic, trying to give that prick that our ex-wife ran off with something terminal. It's making sure that Teen Witch slumber parties go successfully. It's putting wispy New Age people into contact with their wispy New Age angels, and they're all, like, "No way", and the angels are all, like, "Whatever". It's attending all of our repeated rituals with the enthusiasm of a patron come to see *The Mouse Trap* for the seven hundredth time. It spends its weekends trying to read our crappy sigils under their obscuring glaze of jiz, and in retaliation only puts us into contact with outpatient entities, community-care Elohim that rant like wino scientologists and never make a lick of sense. It's at the trademarks office, registering magic seals. It's handling an introductions agency that represents our only chance of ever meeting any strange Goth pussy. It's off getting us a better deal on that new Renault, helping to prolong the wretched life of our incontinent and blind pet spaniel Gandalf, networking like crazy to secure those Harry Potter Hogwart's Tarot rights. It's still attempting to sort out the traffic jam resulting from the Aeon of Horus having jack-knifed through the central reservation and into the southbound carriageway, hit head-on by the Aeon of Maat, which spilled its cargo of black feathers onto the hard shoulder. It's not sure the ketamine was such a good idea. It's sitting looking nervous on a thousand bookshelves between lifestyle interviews with necrophiles and fashion retrospectives on the Manson family. It's hanging out at neo-nazi jamborees near Dusseldorf. It's wondering if it should introduce a "Don't Ask, Don't Tell" policy regarding the 11th Degree. It's advising Cherie Blair on acupuncture studs, the whole of Islington upon Feng Sui. It's pierced its cock in an attempt to shock its middle-class Home Counties parents, who've been dead for ten years, anyway. It wishes it were David Blaine. It wishes it were Buffy. Or, quite frankly, anyone.

We could, if we desired it, have things otherwise. Rather than magic that's in thrall to a fondly imagined golden past, or else to some luridly-fantasized Elder God theme-park affair of a future, we could try instead a magic adequate and relevant to its own extraordinary times. We could, were we to so decide, ensure that current occultism be remembered in the history of magic as a fanfare peak rather than as a fading sigh; as an embarrassed, dying mumble; not even a whimper. We could make this parched terrain a teeming paradise, a tropic where each thought might blossom into art. Under the altar lies the studio, the beach. We could insist upon it, were we truly what we say we are. We could achieve it not by scrawling sigils but by crafting stories, paintings, symphonies. We could allow our art to spread its holy psychedelic scarab wings across society once more, perhaps in doing so allow some light or grace to fall upon that pained, benighted organism. We could be made afresh in our fresh undergrowth, stand reinvented at a true dawn of our Craft within a morning world, our paint still wet, just-hatched and gummy-eyed in Eden. Newborn in Creation.

Andrew Phillip Smith

The Gospel of Thomas:
A Fourth Way Interpretation

1 These are the esoteric sayings that the living Jesus spoke and Judas Thomas the twin wrote down. And he said, "Whoever finds the inner meaning of these sayings shall not taste death."

2.

Jesus said, "The seeker should not stop searching until he finds, and when he finds he will suffer, and when he suffers he will be astonished and will be king over everything, and having become king he will find rest."

3.

Jesus said, "If those who lead you should say to you, 'Look, the kingdom is in the air,' then the birds of the air will be first, coming before you. If they say to you, 'It is in the sea,' then the fish of the sea will be first, coming before you. But the kingdom is within you and outside of you. When you know yourselves then you will be known and will find it, and you will discover that you are sons of the living father. But if you do not know yourselves then you are impoverished and you are poverty.".

4.

Jesus said, "The old man should not delay in asking a little seven days child about the place of Life, and then that man will be alive. For the many who are first shall be last, and the last first, and they shall become a unity."

5.

Jesus said, Recognise what is in front of your face, and what is hidden will be revealed to you. For there is nothing hidden that shall not be revealed, [and nothing buried that shall not be raised up.]

6

His students questioned him, they said to him, "Do you want us to fast? How should we pray? Should we give to the poor? What foods should we eat?"

Jesus said, Do not lie and do not do what you hate, for in the presence of truth all outward things are revealed. For there is nothing hidden that shall not be revealed, and nothing covered can continue unless it is exposed.

7.

Jesus said, "Blessed is the lion that the man consumes, and the lion becomes man. And cursed is the man that the lion consumes, and the lion becomes man."

8.

And he said, "The man is like a wise fisherman who cast his net into the sea; then he drew it up from the sea, full of little fish from below. Among them he found one good large fish. So he threw all of the little fish back down into the sea without regret. Whoever has ears to listen, let him listen."

9.

Jesus said, "Look, the sower came out, filled his hand and cast the seed. Some seed fell against the road; the birds came and gathered them. Others fell onto rock, and did not send roots down to earth or ears rising up to heaven. And others fell on thorns that choked the seed, and worms ate them. And some others fell upon good earth and gave good grain up to heaven; it came up sixty and one hundred and twenty per measure."

10.

Jesus said, "I have set fire to the earth and, look, I am watching it until it burns."

11.

Jesus said, "This heaven will pass away and the one above it will pass away. Those who are dead do not live and those who are living will not die. When you consumed what is dead you made it alive. When you are in the light, what will you do? When you were a unity, you split into two; now you are two, what will you do?"

12.

His students said to Jesus, "We know that you will leave us. Which of us will become great?"

Jesus said to them, "Wherever you have come from, go to James the Righteous, for whom heaven and earth came to be."

13.

Jesus said, "Compare me to someone, and tell me who I am like."

Simon Peter said to him, "You are a righteous angel."

Matthew said to him, "You are a wise philosopher."

Thomas said to him, "Master, my mouth will not allow me to say what you are."

Jesus said, "I am not your master; because you drank from the bubbling spring that I have poured out, you have become intoxicated."

And he took him, withdrew, and spoke three things to him. When Thomas came back to his companions they asked him, "What did Jesus say to you?"

He said to them, "If I tell you one of the things he told me, you will take up stones and throw them at me, and fire will come out of the stones and burn you."

14.

Jesus said to them, "If you fast, you will bring sin on yourselves, and if you pray you will be condemned, and if you give to the poor you will injure your spirits When you go into a country and walk in its lands, if you are received, then eat whatever they put before you. Heal those among them who are sick. For what goes into your mouth will not corrupt you, but what comes out of your mouth will corrupt you."

15.

Jesus said, "When you look upon the one who was not born of woman, throw yourself on your face and worship him, for he is your father."

16.

Jesus said, "Perhaps people think that I have come to bring peace to the world, and they do not know that I have come to bring division to the earth - fire, a sword, war. For there will be five in a house; three will be against two and two against three, the father against the son and the son against the father. And the unified ones will rise up."

17.

Jesus said, "I shall give you what no eye has looked upon and no ear has listened to, what no hand has touched, and what has not been revealed to the heart of man.".

18.

His students said to Jesus, "Tell us of our end, how will it be?"

Jesus said, "Have you found the beginning so that you are searching for the end? For the end will be in the same place as the beginning. Blessed is he who will rise up in the beginning, and he will know the end, and he will not taste death."

19.

Jesus said, "Blessed is he who exists from the beginning before he comes to be. If you are my students and listen to my words, these stones will become your servants. For you have five trees in Paradise, which do not move in summer or in winter, and their leaves do not fall down. Whoever knows them will not taste death."

20.

His students said to Jesus, "Tell us what the kingdom of Heaven is like."

He said to them, "It is like a mustard seed, which is smaller than all other seeds; but when it falls on earth that has been worked on, it sends out a great branch which becomes a shelter for the birds of the air."

21.

Mary said to Jesus, "What do your students resemble?"

He said, "They are like little children staying in a field which is not theirs. When the lords of the field come back, they will say, "Give our field back to us." So they will strip naked in their presence, and they will give the field back to them. Therefore I say, if the Lord of the house realises that the thief is coming, he will keep watch before he comes, and not allow him to dig from beneath into the house, which is his kingdom, so that he take his goods. So you must keep watch from the Beginning of the world. Prepare yourself with great strength, so that the thieves do not discover a way to get to you. For if you look outwards for help they will discover it. Let a man of understanding be within you. When the grain split open, he came in a hurry, his sickle in his hand, and reaped it. Whoever has an ear to listen, let him listen.

22.

Jesus looked at some little ones taking milk. He said to his students, "These little ones taking milk are like those who go in to the kingdom."

They said to him, "Then will we, as little ones, go into the kingdom?"

Jesus said to them, "When you make the two into one, and when you make the inside like the outside, and the outside like the inside, and the above like the below, and when you make the male and female into a unity, so that the male is not male and the female is not female; when you make some eyes in place of an eye, and a hand in place of a hand, and a foot in place of a foot, an image in place of an image, then you will go in to the kingdom."

23.

Jesus said, "I will choose you, one out of one thousand and two out of ten thousand, and they will rise up, becoming a single unity."

24.

His students said, "Show us the place from which you live, for we need to seek it."

He said to them, "Whoever has ears, let him listen. Light exists within a man of light and he becomes light for the whole world; if he does not become light, he is darkness."

25.

Jesus aid, "Love your brother like your own soul. Watch over him like the pupil of your own eye."

26.

Jesus said, "You see the splinter in your brother's eye, but you do not see the plank in your own. When you remove the plank from your own eye, then you will see out so that you can remove the splinter from your brother's eye."

27.

Jesus said, If you do not fast from the world, you will not find the Kingdom. If you do not make the Sabbath into a day of rest you will not look upon your Father."

28.

Jesus said, "I rose up within the world and I appeared outwardly to them in the flesh. I found them all drunk and I found none of them thirsty, and my soul was pained for the sons of men, for they are blind in their hearts and do not look outwards. For they came into the world empty, and seek also to go out of the world empty. But now they are drunk. When they shake off their wine their hearts will change."

29.

Jesus said, "If the flesh was created because of the spirit, it is a wonder; but if spirit is produced because of the body it is a wonder of wonders. I myself marvel how this great wealth was placed within this poverty."

30.

Jesus said, "Where there are three gods they divine. Where there is one alone, I myself am with him [Split the wood and I am there; pick up the stone and you will find me there.]"

31.

Jesus said, "No prophet is accepted in his own village. No physician heals those who already know him."

32.

Jesus said, "A city that has been built on the summit of a high mountain and has been strengthened cannot fall, but neither can it be hidden."

33.

Jesus said, "What you hear in your ears, proclaim upon the housetop. For no one lights a lamp and puts it under a bush, or hides it. Instead, he puts it on the lamp stand, so that whoever goes in and comes out will look upon its light."

34.

Jesus said, "If a blind man leads a blind man, the two of them will fall down into a pit."

35.

Jesus said, There is no way that anyone can go into the house of a strong man and take him by force, unless he bind the strong man's hands; then he can remove him from his house.

36.

Jesus said, "Do not care from morning to evening and from evening to morning what food you should eat or what clothing you will put on yourselves. You are much greater than the lilies that neither comb wool nor spin it. When you have no clothing, what will you wear? Who can add to the length of your life? It is he who will give you your clothing."

37.

His students said, "When will you be revealed to us, and when will we look upon you?"

Jesus said, "When you strip yourselves naked without being ashamed, and you take off your clothing and put it under your feet, like small children, and you trample on it, then you will look upon the son of the living one and you will not be afraid.".

38.

Jesus said, "Many times you have wanted to hear these words that I say to you, and you had no one to hear them from. The days will come when you will search for me and not find me."

39.

Jesus said, "The Pharisees and the scribes took the keys of knowledge and they hid them; they did not go into the kingdom and they did not let in those who want to go in. You, however, must be as wise as serpents and as innocent as doves.

40.

Jesus said, "They planted a vine outside of the father and, since it isn't healthy, it will be pulled up by the roots and destroyed."

41.

He who has it in his hand will receive it, and he who does not have it will have it taken from his hand.

42.

Jesus aid, "Be a passer-by."

43.

His students said to him, "Who are you that you can say these things to us?"

Jesus said, "You do not recognise what I am by what I say to you. But you have become like the Judaeans, for they love the tree and hate the fruit, or love the fruit and hate the tree."

44.

Jesus said, "Whoever blasphemes against the father shall be forgiven, and whoever blasphemes against the son shall be forgiven, but whoever blasphemes against the Holy Spirit shall not be forgiven, neither on earth nor in heaven."

45.

Jesus said, "Grapes are not harvested from thorns, nor are figs gathered from thistles, for they give no fruit. A man who is good brings something good out of his treasure, a man who is evil brings evil things out of his treasure, which is wicked and which is in his heart, and so he says evil things; for from the contents of his heart he brings out evil things."

46.

Jesus said, "From Adam up to John the Baptist, no on born of woman is so raised up above John the Baptist that he should not lower his eyes. But I have said that whoever among you should become a little one will know the kingdom, and will be raised up above John."

47.

Jesus said, "No one can climb on to two horses or stretch two bows; no servant can serve two masters, for he will honour the one and despise the other. No one drinks old wine and immediately wants the new. And new wine isn't poured into old skins in case they split open, and so old wine isn't poured into new skins in case they are destroyed. Old patches are not sewed onto new clothes, because they will split."

48.

Jesus said, "If two make peace with each other in the one house, they will say to the mountain, 'move away,' and it will move."

49.

Jesus said, "Blessed are the single ones and the chosen, for you will find the kingdom. For you came out of it and you will go in again."

50 .

Jesus said, "If they ask you, 'Where have you come from?' say to them, 'We have come from the light, from that place where the light exists in itself. It rose up and revealed utself in their image.'

If they should say to you, 'Are you this light?' say, 'We are its sons and we are the chosen of the living father.'

If they ask you, 'What is the sign of your father within you?' say to them, 'It is movement and rest.'"

51.

His students said to him, "When will there be rest for the dead? And when is the new world coming?"

He said to them, "What you are looking out for has already come, but you do not know it."

52.

His students said to him, "Twenty-four prophets spoke to Israel, and all of them spoke of you."

He said to them, "You have forgotten the living one who is in your presence, and spoken of the dead."

53.

His students said to him, "Is circumcision of benefit to us or not?"

He said to them, "If it were of benefit, their father would have them born from their mother already circumcised. Rather, it is the true circumcision in spirit that is worth something."

54.

Jesus said, "Blessed are the poor, for the kingdom of heaven is yours."

55.

Jesus said, "Whoever does not hate his father and his mother cannot be a student of mine; and whoever does not love his brothers and sisters, and take up his cross in my way, will not be worthy of me."

56.

Jesus said, "Whoever has understood the world has found a corpse, and the world is not worthy of someone who has found that corpse.

57.

Jesus said, "The kingdom of the father is like a man who had good seed. His enemy came in the night and sowed weeds upon the good seed. The man did not permit the weeds to be pulled up. He explained, 'So that you do not pull up the weeds and pull up the grain along with them.'

On the day of harvest the weeds will appear; then they will be pulled up and burned."

58.

Jesus said, "Blessed is the one who suffers, for he has found life."

59.

Jesus said, "Look to the living one while you are alive, in case you ddie and search for him and cannot find the strength."

60.

They saw a Samaritan taking a lamb to Judea. He said to his studnets, "Why is he carrying around a lamb?"

They said to him, "So that he might kill it and eat it."

He said to them, "While it is living he will not eat it, only if he should kill it and it becomes a corpse?"

They said to him, "He cannot do it any other way."

He said to them, "You must also search for a place of rest within yourselves, so that you do not become corpses and get eaten."

61.

Jesus said, "Two will rest on a couch. One will die, one will live."

Salome said, "Who are you, man, that as if you come from unity, you climbed on my couch and ate off my table?"

Jesus said to her, "I am the one who lives from unity. I received that which is my father's."

She said, "I am your student."

Jesus said, "Because of this I say, 'Whoever is unified will be full of light; whoever is divided is full of darkness.'"

62.

Jesus said, "I tell my mysteries to those who are worhty of my mysteries. Do not let your left hand know what your right hand will do."

63.

Jesus said, "There was a rich man who certainly had many riches. He said, 'I will make use of my riches so that I might sow and reap and plant, and fill my treasury with grain, so that I will not need anything.' Those were the thoughts he had in his heart, and in that night he died. Whoever has ears, let him listen."

64.

Jesus said, "A man was receiving some guests and when the dinner was ready he sent his servant to invite the guests. The servant went to the first and said, 'My lord is calling you.' He said, 'I have some money for some merchants; they are coming to me this evening, I shall have to go and give them their orders; I ask to be let off the dinner.' He went to another one and said to him, 'My lord is calling for you.' He said, 'I have bought a house and I am needed for the day. I shall not be able to rest.' He went to another one and said to him, 'My lord has called for you.' He said, 'My friend is getting married and I am making the dinner. I cannot come. I ask to be let off your dinner.' He went to another and said, 'My lord is calling for you.' He said, 'I have bought a farm; I am going to collect the rent. I cannot come. I ask to be let off.' The servant came and spoke to his lord. 'Those that you have called to the dinner have asked to be let off.' The lord said to his servant, 'Go outside, go to the way and bring whoever you may find there, so that they may dine. Buyers and merchants may not go in to the places of my father.'"

65.

He said, "A just man had a vineyard; he gave it to some tenants so that they might work on it and he might receive its fruit from them. Later he sent his servant so that the tenants might give hi the fruit of the vineyard. They grabbed his servant and beat him. If they had continued they would have killed him. The servant went and said to his lord, 'Perhaps they did not know me.' He sent another servant; the tenants beat the other one. Then the lord sent his son. Those tenants seized him because they knew that he was the heir to the vineyard. They killed him. Whoever has an ear, let him listen."

66.

Jesus said, Show me the stone that the builders have rejected; it is the foundation stone."

67.

Jesus said, "Whoever knows everything but lacks himself, lacks a place within himself."

68.

Jesus said, "You are blessed when you are hated and persecuted, and you are not found within the place where you are persecuted."

69.

Jesus said, "Blessed are those who are persecuted in their hearts; they have known the father in truth. Blessed are those who are hungry, so that their bellies can be satisfied."

70.

Jesus said, "When you bring to birth what is within you, it will save you. If you do not have it within you, what you do not have will kill you."

71.

Jesus said, "I shall destroy this house, and no one will be able to build it again."

72.

A man said to him, "Speak to my brothers so that they will divide my father's belongings with me."

He said to him, "Man, who made me into a divider?"

He turned to his students and said, "Really, am I a divider?"

73.

Jesus said, "The harvest is indeed plentiful, but the workers are few. So pray to the lord that he might send out workers to the harvest."

74.

He said, "Lord, many are around the fountain, but nothing is in the well."

75.

Jesus said, "There are many standing at the door. But the single ones will go into the bridal chamber."

76.

Jesus said, "The kingdom of the father is like a merchant with a consignment. He found a pearl.

He was a wise merchant, so he gave the goods back and bought that single pearl for himself. You yourselves must search for the enduring treasure that does not perish, in that place where moths do not consume nor worms destroy."

77.

Jesus said, "I am the light that is above everything. I am everything, everything has come out of me and split itself open to me. Split the wood and I am there; pick up the stone and you will find me there."

78.

Jesus said, "Why did you come out to the field? To see a reed moved by the wind? And to see a man with soft clothing on him, like your kings and your powerful men? They wore sift garments, and yet they cannot know the truth."

79.

A woman in the crowd said, "Blessed is the womb that bore you and blessed are the breasts that fed you."

He said to her, "Blessed are those who have listened to the words of the father and watched over him in truth. For the days will come when you will say, 'Blessed is the womb that hasn't conceived, and blessed are the breasts that haven't given any milk.'"

80.

Jesus said, "Whoever has understood the world has found a carcass, and the world is not worthy of someone who has found that carcass."

81.

Jesus said, "Let him who is wealthy become king; let him who has power abdicate."

82.

Jesus said, "Whoever is close to me is near to the fire, and whoever is far from me is far from the kingdom."

83.

Jesus said, "The images are revealed to man, and the light within them is hidden in the image of the light of the father. He will be revealed, and his image hidden because of his light."

84.

Jesus said, "When you look upon your likeness you are happy. When, however, you look upon your images, which came to be from the beginning, which neither die, nor are they yet revealed, how much will you bear?"

85.

Jesus said, "Adam came from a great power and great wealth, yet he was not worthy of you; for had he been worthy he would not have tasted death."

86.

Jesus said, "Foxes have their dens and birds have their nests, but the son of man has no place to lay his head and rest."

87.

Jesus said, "Wretched is the body that depends on a body, and wretched is the soul that depends on these two."

88.

Jesus said, "The angels and the prophets will come to you and give you what you have. And you will give to them, and say to yourselves, 'When will they come and take what is theirs?'"

89.

Jesus said, "Why do you wash the outside of the cup? Don't you understand that the one who created the inside also created the outside?"

90.

Jesus said, "Come to me, for my yoke is fair and my lordship gentle, and you will find rest for yourselves."

91.

They said to him, "Tell us who you are, so that we may believe in you."

He said to them, "You read the face of heaven and the earth, yet you did not know who was in your presence, and you do not know how to read this moment."

92.

Jesus said, "Search and you will find. Previously I didn't tell you those things that you were asking me about. Now that I want to tell them to you, you do not search for them."

93.

Jesus said, "Do not give what is holy to the dogs, so that they do not throw it on the dung heap, and do not throw pearls before swine, in case they trample on them."

94.

Jesus said, "Whoever searches will find, and whoever calls within will have it opened to him."

95.

Jesus said, "If you have money, do not lend it at interest, but give it to him from whom you will not get it back."

96.

Jesus said, "The kingdom of the father is like a woman who took some yeast and hid it in dough; she made it into some large loaves of bread. Whoever has an ear, let him listen."

97.

Jesus said, "The kingdom of the father is like a woman carrying a jar full of flour. As she was walking on the road faraway, the handle of the jar broke; flour emptied out behind her on the road. She did not know, and she did not understand what she was suffering. When she went into her house, she put down the jar and found it empty."

98.

Jesus said, "The kingdom of the father is like someone who wanted to kill a powerful man. He drew his sword in his own house and stuck it into the wall, so that he could see that his hand would be strong within. Then he slew the powerful man."

99.

His students said to him, "Your brothers and your mother are standing outside."

He said to them, "Those here who do the will of my father, these are my brothers and my mother; it is they who will go into the kingdom of my father."

100.

They showed him a gold piece and said to him, "Those who come from Caesar demand taxes from us."

He said to them, "Give the things of Caesar to Caesar, and the things of God to God, and give me what is mine."

101.

Jesus said, "Whoever does not hate his father and his mother in my way cannot be my student; and whoever does not love his father and mother in my way cannot be my student. For my mother gave birth to me, but my [true] mother gave me life."

102.

Jesus said, "Woe to the Pharisees; for they are like a dog sleeping in the manger of some oxen; for he will not eat nor will he let the oxen eat."

103.

Jesus said, "Blessed is the man who knows where the thieves will come in, so that he might rise up and prepare himself from the beginning, before they enter."

104.

They said to Jesus, "Come, let us pray and fast today."

Jesus said, "What sin have I committed, or how have I been defeated? But when the bridegroom comes out of the bridal chamber, then let them fast and let them pray."

105.

Jesus said, "Whoever knows the father and the mother will be called the son of a whore."

106.

Jesus said, "When you make the two into one, you will become the sons of man, and if you should say, 'mountain, move away', it will move."

107.

Jesus said, "The kingdom is like a man who was a shepherd; he had one hundred sheep. One of them got lost—it was the largest. He left the ninety-nine and searched for the one until he found it. Having suffered, he said to the sheep, 'I love you more than the ninety-nine.'"

108.

Jesus said, "Whoever drinks from my mouth will be like me. I myself will become him, and what was hidden will be revealed to him."

109.

Jesus said, "The kingdom is like a man who had a hidden treasure in his field and didn't know about it. And after he died he left it to his son. The son did not know. He gave away the field. And the one who bought it went ploughing and found the treasure. He began to lend money and interest to those whom he loves."

110.

Jesus said, "Whoever has found the world and become rich, let him abdicate from the world."

111.

Jesus said, "The heavens and the earth will be rolled up in your presence, and whoever lives from the living one will not look upon death."

For Jesus says, "Whoever finds himself, the world is not worthy of him."

112.

Jesus said, "Woe to the flesh that depends on the soul. Woe to the soul that depends on the flesh."

113.

His students said to him, "When is the kingdom going to come?

Jesus said, "It will not come by looking out for it, not by saying, 'Look, this way,' or 'Look, that way'. Rather, the kingdom of the father is already spread out on the earth, and no one sees it."

114.

Simon Peter said to them, "Let Mary leave us, for women are not worthy of life."

Jesus said, "Look, I myself will lead her, so that I may make her male and she might also become a living spirit like you males. For any woman who makes herself male will go into the kingdom."

[This essay on a Fourth Way interpretation of the *Gospel of Thomas* was originally published in my first book *The Gospel of Thomas: A New Version Based on the Inner Meaning* (Ulysses Books, 2002), long out of print. It has been slightly rewritten but for the most part is the original version. My original editor wanted me to be positive and forceful in my mode of expression, but it is intended to be a particular reading of the *Gospel of Thomas*, not an authoritative statement. The translation, with minor changes, also comes from my 2002 book, and uses Mike Grondin's interlinear translation as its primary source. Numbers in parentheses refer to the standard subdivision of the sayings. Over the years I have received a number of requests to put the book back into print, so I include the bulk of the material here for those interested.]

The *Gospel of Thomas* proclaims a change in the way that we see things and a transformation in what we are. It uses a definite set of symbols and images to communicate this and tells us that if we find the inner meaning of these sayings, we shall not taste death. This death is both the fact of mortality and the spiritual death in which we live our everyday lives. Throughout its sayings, parables and dialogues, the *Gospel of Thomas* presents mankind as being in a fallen state. We are dead, we are blind and drunk, we do not know the truth, are impoverished, divided and in darkness. But there is another state of being. In the new state we will be alive, will be able to see, will be intoxicated rather than drunk, will know the truth, have real wealth, and be in the light. We will go into the kingdom and we will have unity. The *Gospel of Thomas* tells us of these two states and how we may change our state from the former to the latter.

I discovered the *Gospel of Thomas* through my involvement with contemporary Fourth Way teachings. The first time that I read it, I felt immediately that Thomas was saying the same thing as the teaching that I was trying to follow. I felt that the Fourth Way system expressed the same truths as *Thomas*, but uses a different terminology. In its language, we are asleep. We are mechanical—stimulus-response machines who are not ordinarily aware of ourselves. We are lost in imagination and daydreams, and identify ourselves with who we think we are and with the little events of our daily lives. We do not remember ourselves, are not aware of our separate existence when we feel, think or act. It requires inner work—practical work on oneself—to change this, and it is not a question of developing new powers, but of recovering our birthright, which we sold for a mess of pottage. If we work on ourselves we can be awake, be conscious both of our surroundings and ourselves, and will truly recognise what is in front of our faces (saying 5).

The Fourth Way is said to be a system for the development of consciousness that is not passed down from generation to generation in a relatively static traditional form, but exists for a limited time in particular circumstances, and takes place in the midst of life. One is in life yet not of it, or as the *Gospel of Thomas* says, one is a passer-by. The current form of the Fourth Way teaching originated in the early twentieth century. In St Petersburg in 1915, P.D. Ouspensky, a Russian journalist and writer on esotericism, met a very remarkable Greek Armenian man named G.I. Gurdjieff, who was already teaching a small number of pupils. (Incidentally, Edessa, the location most associated with St Thomas in antiquity, though now in modern Turkey and named Sanli-Urfa, has a large Armenian population and has historically been part of Armenia, Gurdjieff's homeland. Historically a crossroads between East and West, yet also isolated, it was the home in ancient times of the Archontic Gnostics as well as possibly Valentinians, Marcionites, Manichaeans and Paulicians. While these groups didn't persist, the Yezidis were known to Gurdjieff.) Ouspensky had been searching for years for mystical ideas and practices that could produce verifiable results. He had travelled to India in search of esoteric schools, and had become something of an expert in sifting through occult literature trying to extract what was genuine and reasonable in it. Though not a member of the Theosophical Society, he had contact with members at the highest level of the Society. In Gurdjieff he found ideas, exercises and practices that he could find nowhere else, and moreover he was encouraged not to believe anything but to verify for himself. He was also very impressed with Gurdjieff as a man, though he eventually separated from him and expressed reservations about Gurdjieff's character and development.

It seemed that Gurdjieff had gathered and distilled the teachings from mysterious Eastern sources; parts of it are reminiscent of Sufi teachings, other parts of the Orthodox Christian tradition, some of otherwise unknown sources. Some of it, and the overall synthesis undoubtedly came from his own genius. Once the Russian Revolution came, Gurdjieff and his various followers fled Russia in difficult circumstances and escaped to Constantinople and then to the West, Gurdjieff eventually settling in France and Ouspensky in England and then New York. They continued to teach until their respective deaths in 1949 and 1947.

Gurdjieff was a practical man who created a strong impression in those who met him. He liked to shock people awake, and emphasised a practical and balanced approach to life. Ouspensky was very much the thinker. He defined and systematised Gurdjieff's teachings, and was able to make his ideas available to more people. Both men viewed Christianity as originally being a school of awakening. When Gurdjieff was asked about the relationship of his teachings to Christianity, he replied "if you like, this is esoteric Christianity." He held Jesus in the highest regard as one of the world's great teachers and considered him to be a messenger from above. In Ouspensky's early book *A New Model of the Universe*, he devoted a chapter to an initial study of the gospels and esotericism, pointing the way to further interpretation, and described the gospel story as a living drama designed to produce consciousness in those involved in it. He often carried with him a well-thumbed copy of the New Testament in the original Greek, and thought deeply and constantly about the gospels. Yet, though he undoubtedly came to a deep understanding of their meaning, he never wrote anything truly definitive on them.

Both men had many students who continued their work after them. One of Ouspensky's most notable pupils was an Englishman, Rodney Collin Smith, who moved to Mexico after Ouspensky's death and began to teach there. Collin also wrote of early Christianity as a conscious school, and produced a highly-charged pamphlet, The Christian Mystery, which connected the story of Jesus and the development of Christian civilization to the pattern of the enneagram, a complex symbol used by Gurdjieff to indicate the structure of the cosmos on different scales. Collin eventually converted to Catholicism before his untimely death in Cuzco, Peru, 1956.

But it was another pupil of Ouspensky, Maurice Nicoll, who was also an early associate of Jung, who really pointed the way towards a fuller understanding of the gospels. In two groundbreaking books, *The New Man* and *The Mark*, Nicoll gave psychological and spiritual interpretations of some of the parables and miracles of Jesus in terms of a symbolic language that had both an outer and an esoteric meaning. He didn't use specific Fourth Way terminology, (which perhaps limited him a little; one has the feeling that he is understanding the gospels according to the Fourth Way teachings and then translating them into more general spiritual terms) but even so, he was the first in print to offer a convincing Fourth Way interpretation of the Bible. Nicoll died in 1953, Ouspensky in 1947, Gurdjieff in 1949, and Collin in 1956, so none of them were ever able to read the complete *Gospel of Thomas*.

In the twentieth and twenty-first centuries the Fourth Way system is expressed using a precise language that has something in common with the language of modern science and psychology, and other modern esoteric systems, such as Theosophy. Jesus and his followers used a symbolic language that was part of the inheritance of Judaism and also had much in common with the rest of the ancient Mediterranean world. As I explore the imagery used in the *Gospel of Thomas* I will show how it can be understood in terms of the Fourth Way system. If we know how to read it, we can reclaim some of the deepest spiritual teaching that western man has ever known.

What follows isn't a systematic association of one word or image in *Thomas* with a concept from the Fourth Way, but a more impressionistic interpretation, flitting from saying to saying but pausing to briefly explain the corresponding concepts in Gurdjieff's teaching. This is by no means my final assessment of the meaning of the *Gospel of Thomas*, nor do I even agree necessarily with the ramifications of some of the sayings—I am currently suspicious of the elitism represented by "many are called but few are chosen", at least as applied to spiritual seekers.

On the other hand I do believe that some of the ideas, for instance the distinction between one and many, are not only genuine features of the *Gospel of Thomas* but also of the psychological aspect of Gnosticism and many other spiritual approaches. The idea that wandering thoughts must be controlled or transcended is common to many spiritual traditions, from Buddhism to the hesychastic practices of Orthodox Christianity.

The apology is over, here comes my interpretation.

The *Gospel of Thomas* begins with instructions on how to search. In one of the more extended sequences of sayings (1-5) we are told of the progression of seeking, finding, suffering, being astonished and then becoming king over everything and finding rest. In Fourth Way terminology the part within people which searches for a teaching is called the magnetic centre, since it is attracted to material that suggests that there is something more to life than ordinary society and the biological imperatives of eating, sleeping and reproducing. Influences in the world can be divided up into three categories. Influence A consists of the material of ordinary life—money, family, security, which are the "riches" and the "world" of the *Gospel of Thomas*, the things of Caesar that we must to

Caesar. Influence C, in contrast, is the direct, living influence of consciousness, an influence that extends from a conscious teacher. In *Thomas* this is referred to as the kingdom, and ultimately comes from contact with Jesus. Lying between these two is Influence B. Influence B consists of the material in life which may point the way to the possibility of something higher, without actually being part of a direct higher influence. The source was originally conscious, but it has been sown into general life. Its various effects on people are described well in the Parable of the Sower (9). Influence B is transmitted from generation to generation through activities such as art, philosophy and religious culture, and it is a way both of preserving esoteric knowledge and keeping alive the possibility of finding conscious teachings when they are available. A magnetic centre is attracted to Influence B, and if it accumulates enough of it in a right way, it leads the person to search for an esoteric school.

The *Gospel of Thomas* presents itself as being derived from the tradition of Judaism. It proposes that other Jewish groups of the time, such as the Pharisees, have maintained the tradition to some extent, but have prevented people from receiving genuine spiritual benefit from it. They have the keys, but did not go in to the kingdom and did not let in those who wanted to go in (39); they are like the proverbial dog in a manger (102). So Influence B is represented by the Pharisees, in that they have preserved esoteric knowledge without understanding or using it. The meaning of the scriptures has been obscured not only by members of a first century group, but by all who place external values above internal, esoteric ones. In understanding the inner meaning of the *Gospel of Thomas*, the keys to that tradition, to the esoteric meaning of Judaism and Christianity, can be restored. Ultimately, the aim is to go into the kingdom, not merely to know how to enter, and Jesus rebukes his own disciples for being concerned with the twenty-four prophets (the scriptures) and not seeing what is in front of them (52).

There are always many more people who possess magnetic centres than there are people who truly live a teaching. Sayings 73-75, which may constitute a dialogue, tell us that there are a few workers who are reaping a plentiful harvest, but many people standing around an empty fountain; many stand at the door, but few go in. It is a process of learning from a teacher, of drinking from his mouth, as Thomas peculiarly expresses it (13, 108). When we do this and become like Jesus, and when we have light, we must not hide it, even though it was hidden from us, but must pass it on.

Esoteric teachings give us a map of ourselves, of our inner makeup and organisation, so that we can know what our possibilities are and can understand what obstacles, what stumbling blocks, are getting in the way of them. One cannot put everything into the same map, so in Gurdjieff's teaching, for instance, several overlapping descriptions are used. One map views the human being as consisting of different centres, the moving-instinctive, the emotional, intellectual and the sex centres, and then the higher centres, which may exist only in possibility. Another map tells us that we have an essence, which is our natural capacities and preferences, and a personality that we have acquired through imitation as we adapted ourselves to the demands of life. Yet another map tells us that we have different qualities of energy within us. As in the tale of the elephant in the dark, which is described differently depending on whether one touches the trunk or the tail or a leg or an ear, so the kingdom, or awakening, can be described in different ways.

One of the methods that the *Gospel of Thomas* uses to describe the human being is to use imagery from the first couple of chapters of the book of Genesis. The state to which we must aspire is the state from which we have fallen. It is light, it is the spirit, it is the beginning. Just as Jesus says that life is movement and rest (50), so the spirit moves across the face of the waters on the first day, and God finds rest from work on the Sabbath, the seventh day in Genesis. Rest, sometimes rendered as "repose", is the culmination of the sequence of searching, finding, suffering, being astonished, and

becoming king. Rest is not sleep, but the state of having worked and found reward, the fruit of one's labours. These two terms, "rest" and "the beginning" are easy to miss in Thomas, and I have tried in my translation to draw attention to them where possible by rendering the terms literally. Thomas is much easier to understand when one recognises that both of these terms refer to a higher state of consciousness. (When I refer to a higher state of consciousness, I don't necessarily mean an ecstatic state, merely one that includes a recognition of that is not found in our usual state of consciousness.)

The *Gospel of Thomas* also describes this higher state as having unity. The number "one" characterizes a higher state, and "two" characterizes the division of our ordinary, lower state. Making the two into one is a notion that occurs through Thomas. In our normal state we are divided into male and female. Philo of Alexandria was an Egyptian Jew who lived in the first century and wrote extensive allegorical interpretations, which come from a union of Platonism and the Bible (the Hebrew Bible or rather the Septuagint Greek translation.) He explains, "There are two kinds of souls, just as there are two genders among humans… The male soul devotes itself to God alone, as the father and creator of the universe and the cause of all things that exist. But the female soul depends upon all the things that are created, those things liable to destruction. And it puts forth, as it were, the hand of its power so that in a blind way it may lay hold of whatever it comes across, clinging to a generation which has an innumerable quantity of changes and variations, when it ought to cling to the unchangeable, honourable, and esteemed divine nature." As unappetising as this view of gender may be to our modern sensibilities, it is very helpful to understanding the symbolism of early Christianity. The final saying in the *Gospel of Thomas* makes it clear that being biologically female is no impediment to becoming symbolically male as a living spirit (114).

Being dead is the state of having the male and female exist as two and not be united as one. When these two are made into a unity we are alive and we are made into the image of God. Biologically, the union of male and female results in a child, and this is also what happens when we bring the male and female together esoterically. Instead of the fallen Adam, the old man who is born of woman, we have a little seven-days-old child who is living from the Sabbath, the day of Rest, in a state of repose, naked without being ashamed. This new thing is as small and as precious as a pearl, with as much potential as a tiny mustard seed that can grow into a towering plant. If we bring to birth what is within us it will save us; if we don't, it will kill us (70), for we will continue to exist in the state of spiritual death.

Being in the kingdom means that one is a king (2). Not a king in the worldly sense, since, as Thomas tells us, they cannot know the truth (78), but king over oneself. In the first five numbered sayings we are given much of what is essential in the teaching. The kingdom—the state of being a king—is within you and without you. It is not simply within, which would refer only to our subjective inner life in a solipsistic way, but consists of bringing what is within us into contact with the outside world. This point of contact creates something new. We do this by recognising what is in front of our faces, in other words, by being present to our surroundings. For in the presence of truth all outward things are revealed (6). This is a state of consciousness known in the Fourth Way as the third state of consciousness, above the first state of total sleep and the second state of our ordinary daytime consciousness. In the third state we know ourselves and are known by our higher selves, and so find the kingdom.

At the hub of the Fourth Way are the ideas of self-remembering. Self-remembering is consciously remembering and perceiving that we exist in all our constituent parts—body, heart and head. Linked to this is the idea of divided attention. Usually, Gurdjieff tells us, our attention goes in one direction only, and we are identified with what is outside of us, or we are absorbed in our subjective inner states, in undirected imagination. The double-headed arrow of divided attention points both inside and outside. Ouspensky wrote, "When . . . I try to remember myself, my attention is directed both towards the object observed and towards myself." So we must make the inside as the outside and the above as the below, and enter the kingdom. Yet it is a change within us that makes the difference, and this changes our hearts, which were previously blind (28).

Our enemy is within. It is within our own house that we will defeat the powerful man (98). We must be prepared against the thieves; we must keep watch (103). We must eat the lion within us (7), combine the male and female into one (22}), not be divided (61), not lose the energy, the flour that we possess (97), but make it into a dough within us that can have yeast added to it (96). Our ordinary state is characterised by division. Every impulse, desire or thought in us calls itself "I": "I am angry," "I think such-and-such." These are actually responses to stimuli that may come to us from outside sources or from a mechanical progression of internal states. When we briefly experience unity we can see these many "Is for what they are. The *Gospel of Thomas* also refers to unity and division, and many sayings contain this relationship of one to many. The many who are first shall become last, and they shall become one unity (4). We should throw back the little fish from below to take the one good, large fish (8). Jesus chooses one from a thousand (23). There are ninety-nine sheep that should be left behind to look for the one sheep that is lost (107). The field has many lords but the house one lord. (21). Unity is a small thing, like a mustard seed, yet when it grows it can shelter the many "I"s, described as the birds of the air (2). If we think that the kingdom is in the air—in thought—then our thoughts or many "I"s—the birds—will prevent us from reaching the kingdom.

Once we attain a higher state—once we go into the kingdom, live from the beginning and have rest—we cannot expect it to be permanent or be the highest level of experience. This heaven and the heaven above it will pass away (11). We will lose the state of unity and go back to being divided, to being two, and then we have to find out how to get back to it (104). Once we know of the kingdom, we must keep searching for it, since it is already spread out on the earth, but we don't see it. It is easily lost without noticing, or we waste the energy that we could use to attain it, like the woman with a jarful of flour who gets home to find that it has all leaked away (97). Disciples who are evolving are like children in a field. The field, which is the human machine, is not truly theirs, but they are staying in it temporarily. The many "I"s, the lords of the field, come back and the disciples strip naked, that is, they let go of their higher states, and give the field back to the many "I"s. If they had known that the thief, who is the same as the lords of the field, would come, they would have taken precautions. Much of awakening focuses on the obstacles that take us away from higher states.

The process of moving from death to life, from division to unity, from darkness to light, involves suffering (58). The Coptic word for suffering also carries the meaning of working hard. We must suffer; we must be persecuted within ourselves. But, since everyone and every sentient creature must suffer at some time in their lives, some more, some less, merely suffering is not the point. In itself. Rather, we must suffer and find life; we must be persecuted, yet not take our identity, our new self, from the part in us that is persecuted (68). Once we have suffered we will be astounded and will become king over everything, our divided self, and will have rest from our labours (2). For Jesus did not come to bring peace, to bring sleep, but to bring consciousness, and it appears in us as a fire, as a sword, as war (16). The father, the higher part, who is not born of woman (15), will be at war with the son, the lower part, and they will be raised up to the state of unity (16). Weeds, plants, thistles are all different "I"s, which come ultimately from the heart. But we cannot destroy the weeds that were sown by the enemy at night time. At the time of harvest, when we are alive and in the present, we can sort out the good seeds, the useful "I"s, from the weeds.

One of the barriers to awakening is our

thinking. Gurdjieff characterised our typical thinking as formatory thinking, a kind of thought that operates with little attention. It simply applies words as labels and fits new information into existing categories. It thinks in opposites; as Ouspensky wrote, it can only count up to two. Yet this is the kind of thinking that predominates in our lives, the automatic thoughts that can never see anything in a new way, and that deaden our perceptions. The *Gospel of Thomas* includes some features that confound formatory thinking. A peculiar feature of the *Gospel of Thomas*, and one that is easy to overlook, is its contradictory use of imagery. One must become a king (2), yet kings and powerful men cannot know the truth (78); intoxication through Jesus is commended (13), but Jesus sees everyone as blind and drunk in a derogatory way (28); a true wealth is desirable, but riches are condemned (in my translation I have generally used "wealth" where the meaning is positive, "riches" where it is negative). In saying 21 "naked" means that once has lost the divine clothing of a higher state, whereas in 37 it represents being free of the clothing acquired personality. These contradictions (which may be seen by scholars as evidence that Thomas has been compiled from conflicting sources) are reconcilable, in that there is a right way to be a merchant or to have wealth, or to be drunk, and a wrong way of these, but the imagery forces us to think twice and we cannot assume that the sayings are telling us what we may initially think they are telling us. Another way the *Gospel of Thomas* upsets formatory mind is its use of various terms—the beginning, the kingdom, light, etc.—for the same state of unity.

The kingdom represents both the inner state of consciousness and the outer collection of people, the school. This is another meaning of the kingdom being inside you and outside of you. An esoteric school has students, and the *Gospel of Thomas* gives some of the conditions under which students (or disciples) of Jesus can be successful. One of the positive conditions is that they are to be like children or little ones. Another is that they must fast from the world—

that is, not concern themselves with Influence A and false personality. The school is a family, and those who do the will of Jesus' father are his brothers and mother. The most condensed statement in the entire gospel is "Be a passer-by" (42). This sums up the whole doctrine of being in the world but not of it, and of the idea of non-identification or non-attachment, of taking one's moment-to-moment identity neither from external events nor from one's reaction to them.

Gurdjieff specifies that work in a school needs to be on three different lines, called simply the first, second and third lines of work. The first line is work for oneself, for one's own advantage and for one's own results. The second line is work with and for others. The *Gospel of Thomas* tell us how students of Jesus should relate to each other: "Love your brother like your own soul. Watch over him like the pupil of your own eye" (25). We all have weaknesses and these need to be pointed out, and the best way to point out a fellow disciple's weakness is to see it in yourself: "When you remove the plank from your own eye, then you will see outside so that you can remove the splinter from your brother's eye (26). One must not give the precious things, the pearls, to those who cannot receive them, or to the many "I"s. Yet we must use the knowledge to help others into the light, those who go into and our of the kingdom. When we do this we are like a strong city on a hill; we can't fall, but we can't hide ourselves either. The third line of work is work for the school itself, reflected in Jesus' instructions to heal the sick, and in "Give the things of Caesar to Caesar, and the things of God to God, and give me what is mine" (100).

It is difficult enough to describe our current state of being, to describe the limitations and weaknesses that we do not see, the things we lack that we think we already have. This is why we need more esoteric knowledge. It is even more difficult to describe a higher state of consciousness, the possible being of someone who works on herself. Certain important characteristics can be described, so that they may be imitated or approximated in the hope of creating the state itself; the inside and the outside are united; we see what is in front of us, we are light not darkness. But it is at the end (or beginning) a question of personal experience, and more detailed descriptions are often unnecessary.

If we merely nod our heads at the *Gospel of Thomas*, or marvel at its profundity, we are like Jesus' disciples saying that "twenty-four prophets spoke to Israel, and all of them spoke of you," and so forget about the living one who is in your presence (52). It is not that a book, or even a personal interpretation, gives us the answer, "rather the kingdom of the father is already spread out on the earth, and no one sees it" (113). The *Gospel of Thomas* asks us to choose between being dead and becoming the image of God.

Mike Grenfell

John Cowper Powys

'A Bunch of Nutters!'. That is the title of a review in *The Times* of the biography of *The Brothers Powys* by Richard Perceval Graves in 1983. It is not an unusual comment from the literary world in its ambivalent and confused response to this Dorset family. Yet, it is a view, which overlooks an important element of the English spirit. In this essay, I want to illuminate some aspects of this spirit by drawing on the work of the eldest of the Powys Bothers—John Cowper—in connection with Blake.

A brief biography of John Cowper Powys can hardly be 'brief'. Born in 1872, the eldest of eleven children, John Cowper could trace his ancestry to the ancient Welsh princes of Powysland on his father's side, and directly to John Donne and the poet Cowper on his mother's. His father, a Dorsetman, moved to become Rector in the Somerset village of Montacute. People who knew the family spoke of their clan-like existence; apparently living self-sufficiently in the large vicarage. They lived as upper middle class Victorians in a world of claustrophobic subjectivity.

Montacute nestles at the foot of St Michael's Hill; Cadbury Castle is nearby; Glastonbury Tor is visible at a distance. The golden Ham stone used in buildings here gives radiance to its surroundings. The physical world is everywhere magical. The imagination of John Cowper sunk into these inner and outer worlds, which became literally larger than life.

John Cowper eventually attended Sherborne School where he suffered bullying and 'torture'. When he went up to Cambridge, he took a revolver to scare off would-be aggressors! By his early adulthood, he was already the English eccentric. He was a big man, who immediately drew attention to himself. He would wear three waistcoats and two overcoats—even on a warm day!—the best way, he concluded, of transporting one's wardrobe. He spoke animatedly, expressively, and gesticulated continuously. People would turn in the street to take a second glance! This idiosyncratic disposition fitted him perfectly for the job of travelling lecturer in America, where he first went in 1904, and where he mostly stayed for the next thirty years. Apparently, he held his audiences spellbound. Once started, he would run hopelessly over time, marching up and down like a frenetic spider.

Collections of poetry and essays followed, but it was not until 1915, when he was already 43, that his first novel Wood and Stone was published— the first of many to many to follow. The world they create is grotesque and phantasmagoric. The characters themselves are often presented as possessed by contraries: the heathen and the Christian, sexual obsessions and love, the material and the spiritual, the heroic and the pitiful. The world that surrounds them is a living universe, or multiverse, as John Cowper named it. As one character arrives at Waterloo Station in London, he looks up to see the sculptured stone faces on the outside gesturing to him. It is a world where leaves and trees have thoughts and feelings. In another novel, he describes what a corpse is thinking on its way to its own funeral. All this might seem mad at first, until we see that these things are exactly what might be pondered if indeed objects had thoughts and feelings.

John Cowper Powys recorded his own admiration for Blake in 1923, where he describes him as being 'in harmony with the instincts of our most secret souls'. Of course, any developed comparison of Blake and John Cowper Powys would be the subject of a doctorate thesis—if not several! Simply reading their combined works is no small undertaking! However, I do want to consider some salient features, which they do share and which, I believe, are worth drawing attention to in appreciating their respective work.. These aspects also help us understand the spirit at large, which I refer to above.

Both John Cowper Powys and Blake were writing across the turn of centuries. Both were witnessing rapid changes in life and society. Such changes are probably most clearly expressed in oppositions between town and country. As Blake experienced the early years of industrialisation in Britain, Powys' life extended from the first full-blown form of this revolution to its demise and the birth of the modern technological age (he died in 1963). The effects of these on the land were devastating. For Blake, industrialisation brought with it 'dark satanic mills'. Powys had a rather more ambiguous relationship to modern technology. Late in old age, he was fascinated by the building of a hydroelectric dam, which he watched from his tiny cottage in Blaenau Ffestiniog. However, this thrill might be likened to that of a child watching a magic trick. Mostly, his heart was in life of the country, and it is from the land that he seems to have drawn his spiritual inspiration. As with Blake, he was suspicious of modern rationality.

'More will perish because of Science than will be saved by it', he exclaimed, and had a particular loathing for the treatment of animals. He was a militant anti-vivisectionist. But this relationship to nature goes beyond a protective concern. When Blake moved out of London to Felpham, we can track the impact the expanding sky and sea-line had on him; the smell of the wild thyme and the song of birds. Powys spent rather more of his life in the country than Blake; firstly in Montacute and Burpham in West Sussex and then, on his return from America in 1935, to Corwen in North Wales and then Blaenau. The effects of his rural surroundings are everywhere apparent in his writings. His three Wessex novels—*Weymouth Sands, Maiden Castle* and *A Glastonbury Romance*—are set explicitly in particular places and build on their ancient spirits. In fact, the latter was written in America using an Ordinance Survey Map. The world constructed here is no less a private cosmos than Blake's. But it is also a story of individuals struggling with personal identity and character in the face of the social and spiritual forces acting on them.

Life can be hard and living it heroic. On one level, such spirit is a cause for celebration. Powys quotes Blake approvingly:

He who binds to himself a joy
Does the winged life destroy
But he who kisses the joy as it flies
Lives in Eternity's sun-rise.

And comments: 'In the welling up, out of the

world's depth, of happiness like this, there is a sense of calm, of serenity, of immortal repose and full-brimmed ecstasy. It is the "energy without disturbance" which Aristotle indicates as the secret of the eternal Being himself. It is beyond the ordinary pleasures of sex, as it is beyond difference between good and evil. It is human and yet inhuman'. One recalls Blake's prose inspired by standing in his garden in Felpham. Powys lived his life in connection with this spirit: when he sent a letter he would pray to the post-box to help it on its way; he constructed small stone cairns to his loved one against which he would place his head and pray; and he was known to fling himself on the ground whist out walking to worship 'the god of the hill' behind his house. However, he also understood, as Blake did, that this energy could be destructive as well as creative. Here he comments on this energy, reminiscent of Blake's tiger in the forest: 'Dim shapes—vast inchoate shadows—like dreams of forgotten worlds and shadows of worlds yet unborn, seem to pass backwards over the brooding waters of his spirit (Blake's). There is no poet perhaps who gives such an impression of primordial creative force—force hewing at the roots of the world and weeping at the sheer pleasure at the touch of that dream stuff where of life is made'. The energy is fascinating and creative but also destructive and fearful.

Nowhere is the creation-destruction dichotomy more apparent than in the human body and psyche itself. The mystery of the body is ever present in Powys, around which he constructed his mythology. This mythology attempts, as Blake's does, to contain these forces and, in some ways, reconcile them. Blake employs gender archetypes in his alchemy of the human spirit. For Powys too sex is the most powerful expression of the creative-destructive spirit. There are fantasies and daydreams in Powys. In America, he met and fell in love with Frances Gregg. Being married himself at that point, if somewhat estranged from his wife, he suggested she marry his best friend Louis Wilkinson, which she did! The distress of being with a woman he desired, but who remained untouchable and unobtainable comes out in letters to her, where he explicitly details what he imagines doing with her - such as smearing her with marmalade or treacle! These sorts of experiences fed his repressed desires, born out of Victorian morality, and resulted in distorted thoughts and feelings. It is Hell! He who desires but acts not breeds pestilence.

There is also sadism and masochism in the work of John Cowper Powys, and the shame and guilt of acknowledging this in oneself. These sentiments are brought to life in his characters. In Glastonbury Romance, the sadist Mr Evans, finally recognises himself for what he is. Here, we have the pathos of piteousness in the hopeless fact of being. The character comes close to breakdown as the only way to smash the hold of who he is over 'him'. As in Blake, the Spectre rules the 'true' self. Evans' form of self-induced humiliation was also within Powys' own experience. In his 'Autobiography'(1934), which, much to his amusement, was described in a contemporary review as 'a rubbish heap of words', he sets out the awful experiences of being picked on at Sherborne school. One night, he addressed the full school:

> ..the moment came and I stood up. The extraordinary, nay!, the unique nature of this revolution held all the boys spellbound. You could have heard, as they say, a pin drop. And then, beginning lamely enough, but quickly catching my cue, I poured forth a flood of tumultuous speech. Out of my foolishness it came, out of my humiliation, out of my inverted pride. It came literally de profundis. I had prayed in the chapel; "And take not thy Holy Spirit from us!" but whether the torrent of self-accusations, of self-incriminations, of wild self, proceeded from the Creator Spiritus, or from the Devil, I cannot tell. I dragged in every single detail they derided me for, I exposed my lacerations, my shames,

my idiocies. "Mooney" was talking at last out of the madness of the mistress of his horoscope! I referred to the great dilapidated umbrella I placed such stock in. I referred to my obscene fashion of chewing my food with my front teeth. I stripped myself naked before them…

There is liberation in such openness. However, it is freedom bought at a cost. I have already referred to the way he seemed 'uncomfortable' in his body. He suffered from psychosomatic ill health for most of his life. Each year he had a different food fad and there seemed little he could stomach. For two years he lived on olive oil! The physical and psychological warring that went on inside John Cowper Powys is akin to the struggle of Blake's Albion and his archetypal Zoas. Similarly, there is the sense of physical embodiment, indeed, of the mystical significance of organs and limbs in conducting psychic forces. It is as if the body is available where the mind isn't, as the repository of experience, past and present. Of course, for Blake, escape from the fall comes through Christian resurrection as imagination and creativity, which reconciles the warring factions of the mind and body. Each element knows its place and performs its particular function and no other, contributing to the whole.

Powys had no affinity for Christian theology, no matter how Gnostic. Nevertheless, his path seems to have followed one parallel to Blake's own. In his essay on Blake, Powys focuses on 'the immortal and undying child to be found in the heart of every man and every woman'. As Powys grew old, he became more and more child-like. In 1944, he wrote *The Art of Growing Old*. Clearly, he welcomed the giving up of youthful responsibility for an 'at-play' like state of returned childhood. Blake, he wrote, 'brought the 'child in the house' into the clear sunlight of an almost religious appreciation'. However, the child for Powys should not be confused with an affected version of benign purity. For him, the child is to be associated with experience as well as innocence, with love and wrath. He quotes

Nietzsche on the child who will come at last to inaugurate the beginning of the 'Great Noon':

And there the lion's ruddy eyes
Shall flow with tears of gold
And pitying the tender cries
And walking round the fold
Saying, 'Wrath by his weakness
And by his health sickness
Are driven away
From our immortal day

Of course, here the child is Christ himself, a figure 'possessed of a power drawn from the depths of the universe…(Blake) boldly associates this Christ of his—this man-child who is to redeem the race—with a temper the very opposite to the ascetic one'. As Blake, he rails against Protestant Puritanism. He celebrates Catholic Faith and Pagan Freedom equally, and praises the way Blake 'disentangles the phenomenon of sexual love from any notion or idea of sin and shame'. Powys writes in a Blakean manner: 'The man-child whose pitiful heart and whose tenderness toward the weak and unhappy are drawn from the Christ-story, takes almost form of a Pagan Eros—the full-grown, soft-limbed Eros of later Greek fancy—when the question of restraint or renunciation or ascetic chastity is brought forward'. Moving towards this childlike state is far from assuming naivety. Rather it is innocence regained, or innocence through experience where nothing is lost from the process which gives rise to it. It is present in the creative act, which it implies. Robert Fripp describes it as 'the assumption of innocence within a context (or field) of experience' and as a characteristic of mastery (sic.). But how to realise it?

This state of innocence/experience is an important element in Powys' work as it was for Blake. It is central to the English spirit I wrote of above. For Blake, it is a product of the process of resurrection as an existential event. A death and resurrection. 'Each day I die', wrote St Paul. And it occurs whenever 'error is put off'.

There is no lack of energy available from the fission and fusion present in Blake's intellectual warfare of archetypes. But, for him, deliverance comes through the integration of the members of the dramatis personae of his psychic theatre of war, rather than the rejection of any one individual element. In the novels of Powys, the characters engage in similar encounters and generate similar forces, which is why he quotes Blake so enthusiastically. For Powys, however, deliverance comes about more as a result of the Pagan than the Christian. Here, I am reminded of J.G Bennett in *The Masters of Wisdom*. Bennett argues that we can observe two principal strands in the early years of Christianity. One he refers to as humiliation and transformation; the other as the 'forgiveness of sins'. He attributes the latter to Pauline theology and its preoccupation to make good the sins of the world. Clearly, the philosophy of Powys is more akin to the acceptance and acknowledgement of the 'sin' of individual personality trait, whatever the consequences—humiliation and transformation. And this is so much like Blake: 'To annihilate the Self-hood of Deceit and False Forgiveness'. Real transformation is quite simple but very hard to achieve. This type of 'burning off' of cultural masks (the Spectre) to reveal some inner 'true-self' is clearly present in both Blake and Powys; although the consequence is less Christian Gnostic in Powys. It is a process, which can also be linked to the work of such diverse figures as Bataille, Artaud, and Foucault—not to mention de Sade. But here my references begin to run away with themselves! Nonetheless, Powys had affinities with Tolstoy, Hardy, Dickens, Lawrence and Dostoyevsky. Reading him is life-enhancing. I started this essay by referring to a particular character of English spirit. It is not exclusively English. My last references are French and my Gnostic links go beyond European boundaries.

I have here drawn attention to a peculiar manifestation of this spirit in the work of Blake and Powys. Of course, they possessed distinct and separate missions. They did, however, share elements of this spirit. Besides the mythical and psychological tracks they followed in parallel, both shared the voice of English dissent. Blake was a radical supporter of republicanism and the overturning of the status quo. Powys, in his turn, was on the side of anarchists and communists in the United States in the 1920s and 30s and, on his return to Britain, hailed the socialist victory of 1945. It is a position, which has been described as 'deeply unclubbable' in terms of the English way of being in the world.

Powys' lack of solemnity and dignity in much of his writings is no less audacious as Blake's in his observations and intentions. The 'come off it' attitude of the English, whose sole purpose in life is to avoid embarrassment, is the direct opposite to Powys' hysterics and intensity or Blake's didactic prophecies. It is unsurprising, therefore, if the work of Powys has largely been overlooked. By the early 1960s, no-one, it seems, was interested in Powys. However, the spirit I write of struck a chord with the hippies and flower children of the late sixties. Both Blake and Powys appealed to the 'Tolkien generation'; although, it is debatable how many got far beyond an intuitive acknowledgement of kindred spirit. Today, it is also possible to see Powys as a precursor to 'magical realism'; although, here again, this hardly makes him more readable in contemporary terms (I have heard reading his complete works described as a definition of purgatory!). Who now read novels of over a thousand pages? When reading him, time slows down - and passes very quickly! Nevertheless, the work of John Cowper Powys, as that of William Blake, continues to live a life of its own and makes excluded knowledge present and available.

SOURCES AND ACKNOWLEDGEMENTS

As far as I know, there are only two of Powys' novels currently available in print: *A Glastonbury Romance* and *Wolf Solent*. Neither of these is a bad place to start with reading Powys.

Other novels and books of essays and ideas are less easy to find. However, many of the reprints in Village Press can be found in second hand bookshops. Village Press was the outlet of the Village Bookshop in Regents Street, London, now sadly long-since closed. We have the Powys enthusiast Geoffrey Quintnor to thank for reprinting the Powys oeuvre and thus making it available to a wider public. Mr Quintnor in fact owned the Village Menswear shop, also in Regents Street, but that is another story....

Another story, or stories, would be the lives and associations of the two other principal writer brothers of John Cowper: Theodore (usually known as T.F.) and Llewelyn. The best ways to explore these two would be to begin with The Brothers Powys by Richard Perceval Graves (1983). It is still possible to visit the villages where they lived and thus connect with the countryside, which inspired them all.

There has been a *Powys Journal* and *Powys Review* and, indeed, Powys Society. I would be grateful for any news of their continued existence or, indeed, any comments or questions on this essay. E-mail: m.grenfell.soton.ac.uk

I would like to acknowledge a very helpful BBC radio programme on John Cowper Powys, broadcast on the 17th June 1983, for drawing my attention to features of his life and work. Thanks also to Robert Fripp for permission to quote from his monograph *The Act of Music*.

Andrew Phillip Smith

An Interview With Miguel Conner

Miguel Conner is host of *Aeon Byte Gnostic Radio* at http://www.thegodabovegod. com. Over the years he has interviewed a wide range of scholars, writers and thinkers on Gnosticism and other esoteric topics. The best of his interviews with major scholars of Gnosticism and early Christianity are collected together in the book *Voices of Gnosticism*, published by Bardic Press, with a set of introductions by Miguel. He is also the author of Stargazer, a sci-fi vampire novel, and is working on further novels.

APS: You're best known as the host of *Aeon Byte*, formerly *Coffee, Cigarettes & Gnosis*, an Internet radio program devoted to Gnosticism. How long has that been going?

MC: It will be five years this May. So I've been at it for five years.

APS: How many shows have you packed into that time?

MC: If you include the *Schroedinger's Diary* series with Anthony Peake, and some other lateral stuff that I've done, I would say at least, at this point, over 200 shows, and I feel I have just scratched the surface. That's the exciting and frustrating thing.

APS: So you're planning to go on for a good while yet.

MC: I have no idea. I never planned to do more than eight shows when I started. I never planned to go more than a year. Every time I tell myself it's time to hang up the hat more interesting revelations keep happening.

APS: So it was meant to be eight shows at the beginning. Why did you decide to do an Internet radio program?

MC: Well, at the time I had just started delving into Gnosticism. I had found myself, in a story that I don't want to give too much detail to, excommunicated from a Gnostic church—believe it or not, but it did happen! I also found myself under some sort of weird on-hold for esoteric secret organisations, and I said, "Well, this is ridiculous. I'm tired of this secretive stuff and I'm here in no man's land." So I decided I would take the proverbial bull by the horns, and do something about it, make public what so many people insist on being secret, which is ridiculous. At the time I was listening to Freethought Media, which was a humanist/ atheist Internet station, and it was a great place. Robert Price used to have a show there. The Rational Response Squad was broadcasting there, which was famous for debating on CBS Kirk Cameron and his banana theories. Dangerous Talk with Staks Rosch was there, and that's a very popular show with the atheist community, and they had a lot of other cool shows. I proposed to the owner, how about if I do just a quick series on Gnosticism, since at the time the Gospel of Judas had just been released, and the whole Da Vinci Code machine was still very strong. Yet at the same time nobody knew who the Gnostics were. So I proposed to the owner—and he had this attitude that the enemy of my enemy is my friend—and he gave me some spots and I put out the first eight shows, and then I realised that the rabbit hole went a lot deeper than I'd ever imagined.

APS: Did you have any background in broadcasting?

MC: No, absolutely not. I do have a degree in communications, and I've done some journalistic work. But the other thing that inspired me too is that at the time I felt that I'd gotten on the right path, and I decided that the show would be my way of tithing or volunteering to the Gnostic cause, since again I was sort of homeless and didn't know how else to do it. That was really another one of my drives for creating the show.

APS: I can't resist asking, but you're presumably not going to tell us which Gnostic church it was that you were kicked out of.

MC: Not publicly, but privately a lot of people know about it. It was really a bizarre situation because somehow I got accused of casting magic or being some kind of sorcerer in this church, and at the time I had never studied any sort of magic. But somehow this slanderous thing got turned around towards me, and I got quickly booted. It was kind of hypocritical because this church was known to practise a lot of magic behind the scenes. It's an old story, but I guess it worked out well.

APS: I have some sympathies with atheism myself, as long as it's not too aggressive—I'm not an atheist. But what was the ongoing reaction to your program, which isn't rationalist in tone?

MC: It was mixed. You had the atheists who found it fascinating on a scholarly level, you had atheists who said, ah-ha, I have a new weapon against the orthodox, because now I can beat them up with another stick, the stick of the Gnostics and their views, and of course you had the fundamentalist atheists, the jihadist atheists, who just attacked me viciously from the start. What is the proof? What is this, what is that? So it was a mixed bag, but it's like anything in life, there's good people and there's a lot of jerks.

APS: How long did you last with Freethought Media?

MC: I lasted a year. Eventually it went down because some of these shows were springboards to many ventures that were very successful, and they started branching out, and in a sense they started cannibalising Freethought Media with their own websites and blogs and so forth. So eventually Freethought Media just collapsed, and I found myself once again an orphan, so I just had to set up my own home page, and perfect it, thegodabovegod.com, and just start broadcasting directly from there.

APS: So you were thrown out of a Gnostic church for supposed magic, and you were thrown out by the atheists for Gnosticism.

MC: Yeah, the story of my life. When I do wrong it seems nobody cares, but when I don't do wrong that's when they nail me. It's not that uncommon of a story when you think about it.

APS: After a year you had the feeling that there were enough people interested in it to continue, and you were finding enough people to interview too.

MC: For the first few years I still had that mindset of tithing and volunteering. This was my gift and I thought that this was something that would be eternal. You have to remember that when I started doing this the word podcast didn't even exist, so I wanted it to be a place where I could give a lot of alternative views, not just on Gnosticism, but on anything esoteric or occult. Because it was the Internet I knew it was something that would be eternal and everlasting, at least I hoped so. Now it seems that Obama has this kill switch on the Internet. It looks like governments can turn you off at the drop of a hat. But it was altruistic. It's always been a bootstrap venture and nobody has to worry about me making a lot of money from this. Even back in Freethought Media I was competing with some big names—Robert Price and the Rational Response Squad and the Infidel guy—and the owner kept calling me and saying, you know, you get the second highest ratings in Freethought Media, so I thought, "Wow, that's great. So there is an interest out there."

APS: So we have to mention it: *Voices of Gnosticism*.

MC: Isn't this a kind of nepotism, Andrew?

APS: It is, but we have to do it. It's the modern world, self-promotion and all that. So we collected a good collection of your interviews with scholars for *Voices of Gnosticism*. You wrote introductions to each of them. It's a great selection of perceptive interviews with the best scholars of Gnosticism and early Christianity. Which of these scholars did you enjoy interviewing the most?

MC: For *Voices*, I would say that they are all extremely enjoyable. What I found, and wrote in the introduction, was that they were all very passionate, almost to the point of being eager, and always very friendly and helpful through the whole thing. Some of us still keep in touch. We talk here and there, exchange ideas, and so forth. So I can't say that there's one who is more favourite than another. At the time I remember I could call up Bart Ehrman and say, "I have this little podcast, do you want to come on the show?" Back then he was already a bestselling writer who was appearing regularly on TV and documentaries, and he simply said, "No problem, let's do it." So all of the scholars have been great, and very graceful, and I can admit that I have not met one big ego in all my years of doing *Aeon Byte*. Apart from myself!

APS: And that's the one you want to meet and understand.

MC: Yeah, that's the one I'm fighting to the very end.

APS: Then I'll phrase it another way. Out of the scholars that you've interviewed, which do you find the most stimulating and most appealing in terms of their work?

MC: I would have to say that it would have to be April DeConick, because I see her as someone who will take risks, but still within the field of scholarship and sober history. I guess she gets that from Jeff Kripal who's the head of the department at Rice University. He's an amazing scholar, but he goes to places which most people would find shocking, but again he couches it with sound scholarship and ideas. I also feel that April DeConick has an instinctual way of understanding the Gnostics. Her work on understanding how much the Sethians were dependent on astrology, or astrotheology, and Egyptian magic and theurgy and so forth is something that other scholars have tiptoed around. And the way that she was able to go against the grain when the whole world was having an orgasm over finally finding their heroic Judas beyond the *Last Temptation of Christ* and *Jesus Christ: Superstar*, I thought that was really great, and she brought a lot of insight into the *Gospel of Judas*. I've interviewed Jeff Kripal, and he was wonderful too, because his book *The Serpent's Gift*, is really part of the spirit of *Aeon Byte*, which is to distil Gnostic wisdom in a way that is not only understandable but helpful to our modern world. And Jeff Kripal does an amazing job at it.

APS: And I would guess that you have a favourite out of the scholars who didn't appear in the Voices book?

MC: Yes, which one?

APS: Robert Price?

MC: Well, we all remember the time we lost our maidenhead, Andrew. Robert was my first interview, and it's one that I can't forget. I had nothing. No credentials, no experience, and I simply called him up and he said, let's do it. Within a week we had conducted the interview, and he gave me an hour and a half of gold. Beyond that, we have become friends, and I can relate to him in so many ways. He is considered on the fringe, since he's no longer a professor because he'd rather go on his own. He's a mythicist. He has a great passion for the protestant Christians and the radical Dutch schools of the nineteenth century. He is always up to date on the latest biblical scholarship, he's extremely passionate about Gnosticism, and like me he's a big fanatic for science fiction, comic books and Japanese anime. So we tend to connect very well.

APS: Thanks to you, he has an article in this issue of *The Gnostic*.

MC: Although he considers himself a skeptic, I've always told him, Robert, you're a closet Gnostic. Why don't you just come out? His just laughs and stays silent. He won't deny it or

accept it.

APS: Probably only about a third or a quarter of your interviewees or academic scholars. Which of the other guests have you most enjoyed interviewing?

MC: I can only say that I really enjoy all of them. As an author of both fiction and nonfiction, I respect anyone who writes a book. I know they have put their heart and soul in it. Sure, there's a lot of scholarly Ed Woods out there in the field, but they really have a passion for their ideas, and even if most listeners reject the ideas outright as being foolish, this may cause other the listeners to at least start thinking along other avenues, or at least reinforcing where they already knew. So I pretty much treat every guest equally. A lot of them are very grateful because often people will just scan their guests and do just a little cursory research, but I really delve in. I will read every book that I get, I will do as much research on them as I can, and eventually I want to become a single white female to them. I want to get right into their heads so the interview goes well, and most of my guests are very grateful and respect what I do, regardless of my personal views.

APS: Some of the people you've had on seem a bit wacky in their theories. We don't have to name names here. What's your attitude towards that, and how do you select people to interview?

MC: At this point in time, they come to me, and even back then they came to me. But a lot of times it could be something that's going on with society right now. Often it's simply looking at the shows, and saying, okay, this area should be explored, this other area should be explored. So eventually everything ties in. One day I should have this vast Jorge Luis Borges library that never ends, that would be a dream come true. I don't see a problem. I know that sometimes people say to me, well, why do you interview all these conspiracy theorists. I think that the word "conspiracy theory" is a sophist argument. It's a term people use to marginalize you just like the words Gnostic or Manichaean were used to marginalize people in the past. And of course I have to add the Gnostics were quite probably the original conspiracy theorists. That's why people who are in secret societies have such a fascination for them. The Gnostics were the first ones, as far as I know, who stood up and pointed at their own supreme being and his agents and said, "Oh my God, they are the cosmic BP Oil or Monsanto Corporation or Rothschilds." The universe is really a prison, and it's not some sort of Pythagorean wet dream. It's a badly built prison, a house of cards that will crash on us. And like many conspiracy theorists they were mocked and disdained by Jews, Pagans and Christians alike. Being paranoid sometimes means that you've been paying attention all along, so I like to leave all options on the table. With the variety of my guests, I even have guests that are completely diametrically opposed to the Gnostic worldview. Most people should definitely download this one, but I had Peter Jones, the author of the very popular *The Gnostic Empire Strikes Back*, which basically decimates the ancient Gnostics and the modern Gnostics, and he's a Presbyterian Calvinist minister. I decided that he needed his chance, or the other side needed their chance to give their case, and I called him up, and he said "Yeah, let's do it," and we had a great conversation. He knew more about Gnosticism than 95% of modern Gnostics did, and since he was a Calvinist there was no pressure as I'm sure he believed that I was going to Hell and he was going to Heaven. There was no worrying about anything. We already knew what was going to happen! So that was another great interview that I enjoyed. There's no reason to despise the opposition. I would have thought that the ancient Gnostics didn't think that the opposition were bad people or immoral people, or anything like that. They just thought they were wrong.

APS: This is something that's emerging a bit as a theme in the current issue of *The Gnostic*, partly because I asked Stephan Hoeller the same question and I have about twenty pages of blather that I need to boil down into a column. But how do you view the relationship between the academic research into Gnosticism and the attempt to practise as a modern Gnostic. I don't

call myself a Gnostic, so I manage to sidestep any . . .

MC: Responsibility?

APS: Right, any responsibility! But there's a lot cooking in the academic community with the deconstruction of Gnosticism, and there seems to be this reconstruction emerging that integrates it back into second-century Christianity, and seeing it as contributing in its little way to the development of the church. Everything's being shuffled around, people say that Gnosticism doesn't exist, we're misreading the context, and all of that. But people are trying to practise as modern Gnostics, and there is a Gnostic worldview. How do you see the relationship between these two separate endeavours?

MC: Well, I definitely see a big divide between them. I wish it wasn't so, because each has a lot to offer to the other, there's no doubt about it. When, for example, in *Voice of Gnosticism*, these scholars have spent a good part of their lives studying the ancient Gnostics. As historians they're not just interested in data. They truly want to walk where they walked, they want to feel the culture that was around these mystics. They actually want to know what these ancient heretics were feeling and experiencing at the time. And when you read some of the parts of *Voice of Gnosticism*, what they say sounds better than any Gnostic priest I have seen at a church, and I have been to many of them. When Marvin Meyer begins to talk about the Gnostic Judas, and what the Gnostics stood for, it's very uplifting. The same when April DeConick talks about the Sethians and their views on God and their views on the universe, or Einar Thomassen when he starts to speak about different ways the Valentinians saw Jesus Christ, it's extremely educational and inspiring at the same time, and it should be! These scholars know the Gnostics better than anyone. As far as the other side goes, I would probably have to be critical of them because I feel they haven't really gone far enough into really understanding what Gnosticism is, or what the Gnostics were really trying to convey. I can understand because, let's face it, the Gnostics were never really allowed to mature, and maybe that's not a bad thing. So you maybe have to create a God of the gaps with the Gnostics, and people have started inserting Daoism or Chaldean theology or nineteenth century occultism into it; but now that we have all this data and the scholars have done such great work, there's no reason to not start getting into the true essence and ethos of the Gnostics. It's all there!

APS: There is quite a difference between the ancient world, or the time of late antiquity in which the Gnostics lived, and the modern or postmodern world in which we live. For most of us it's difficult to take the gnostic myths too literally. We might find a core of ideas that maybe accurately represent the way that the world is. How do you approach that? What is your Gnosticism?

MC: I would say first of all, you've got to know your material. If we expect a Muslim to know the Qur'an, and not just know the Qur'an, because we don't want them to take it literally, we want them to understand and see it in a historical perspective, but also read the Hadiths, also find out how scholars have interpreted it, and how their theologians have been able to fit the essence of Islam and make it work for their specific time. The same goes with the Christians. A Christian is expected to know his Bible, and is certainly expected to know the thinkers around the Bible, and their heroes, and their theologians, and their martyrs. So why Gnostics are not expected to know that is beyond me. Scholars are to blame in a sense for that too, because everybody seems to get stuck on the "greatest hits" collection of the *Gospel of Mary*, the *Gospel of Judas*, the *Gospel of Thomas*, *Thunder the Perfect Mind* or the *Secret Book of John*, but that's not all of it. Would you ask a Christian or a Muslim just to stick to a few passages? No. So I think we need to go deeper into the other Gnostic texts. And it's my experience as we go through it, and I'm sure also yours, and the scholars admit we have a long way to go, you do find almost the complete worldview, and a great framework for the Gnostic spirit. And you can certainly put

it to work in a modern context. No one has a problem with William Blake, or Philip K. Dick, or Carl Jung and their adaptations. So why not do it ourselves?

APS: And how are you doing that yourself?

MC: Well, this is another key and I think why, in my estimation, why the Gnostic spirit is so important these days. I'd been reading Gnosticism and studying it, and it was just kind of curious to me. In a sense it was a little bit boring until I got into the fun stuff, like the Sethian mythologies and all the cosmologies, and all the science-fiction, almost Lovecraftian stuff. It was when I started reading Hans Jonas, *The Gnostic Religion*, and LeCarrière, *The Gnostics*, these books didn't show a mirror into me, they actually showed a mirror into society. So you begin to study what the Gnostics were going through in those Greco-Roman times, and you see that the social-political atmosphere is so similar to what humanity is going through in the last hundred years, it almost becomes simple to translate Gnosticism into a modern context. Philip K. Dick does it very well, and so does Philip Pullman, Alan Moore, William Burroughs, Jorge Luis Borges, Carlos Castenada. They haven't had a problem with it. They've done it very well, and made it very impactful into seeing what we are and what condition we're in. I think that they're right in getting into what the Gnostics thought 2000 years ago.

APS: What's your take on things like the pleroma, the demiurge, aeons and archons and the makeup of the human being? How have you digested the Gnostic ideas and to what extent do you, for instance, see there being a force that corresponds to the demiurge, or a being that corresponds to the demiurge? Maybe I'm being a little bit literal, but do you see what I'm getting at?

MC: I think Stevan Davies put it in his book *The Secret Book of John: Annotated & Explained*, Gnosticism "is a developmental psychology, a descriptive Middle-Platonic philosophy, and most importantly, a cosmic mythology all rolled into one." So in a sense you can almost go up these levels and mix and match them. I've never seen a lion-headed snake talk to me so far (well maybe when I was doing acid). I haven't met an archon. But as principles of the universe I think that they're pretty much right-on. And I always tell people, please take this as literally, as mythologically, as psychologically as you want. Whatever works for you. I'm very agnostic about what's on the other side of the material world, but I do know that for me the Gnostic framework fits the best. I think the proof is in the pudding. We are in a prison, we are separated from our true selves, and we've got to be honest with ourselves. When I was doing a lot of shopping around for religions, what they offered me was coping skills, or promises of happiness and peace, and so forth, all based on the material world. But what happens to most people, and what happened to me, is that you turn a corner and you get a frying pan in your face. Things crumble, or you can just gird your loins into denial and just stand there. But to me Gnosticism was just great, it was because it was so honest. It didn't say the Titanic was sinking, it said, no, the Titanic already sank. We're floating in an ocean of despair and suffering with our little whistles, and we're just hoping for these apostles of light to catch us and pick us up in their boats. I think humanity needs to become honest with itself, because the truth is there is an ultimate duality that should have never mixed together, you can call this flesh and spirit, or you can call this information and the material world, or you can call it consciousness and unconsciousness, or you can call it whatever you want in whatever age you are. For Blake Gnosis was Imagination, and to Jung it was obviously psychoanalysis, and so forth. Philip K. Dick gave it a very technological vocabulary. I think we need to start becoming honest that as humans we can't cope with this world, we never have been able to cope with this world, we truly don't belong, and in this place called a soul there are two forces, spirit and matter, that are always going to be allergic to one another. As soon as we accept that, I think that's when we are going to start making improvements in our inner personal lives as well as in humanity in general.

Mani himself gave a very basic concept. He said Gnosis is separating light from darkness. I think that's where we need to go, in my personal opinion.

APS: You talk about the Gnostic spirit. I presume you would admit that other religions and worldviews can also provide a way. Would you see them as lacking some truths that Gnosticism possesses?

MC: I would say that my views are true, but I'm not saying that their views are not true. Again, all you have to do is go to the classic Gnostics. That was one of their characteristics, that they were inclusive, that they would borrow ideas that might work, as long as they fell into the Gnostic framework that they already had. So I don't begrudge any other path. I think that there are many paths to an expanded state of consciousness. I just think that the Gnostic one is the one that works for me, and in a way I think it's the most honest one.

APS: We touched on Gnosis earlier. How do you see Gnosis? Describing these experiences is often very difficult, and it can come over as very flat when you put it into words. How do you see Gnosis? What are the essential features of Gnosis?

MC: Obviously, any mystical experience is just going to come over as hearsay. I like very much what Jeremy Puma once said, Gnosis is not the result, it brings the result. A lot of people have written to me and said, The Matrix cannot be a Gnostic movie because when Neo took the red pill he saw a very horrible reality. I say, that's Gnosis! You take the red pill, you have the road to Damascus experience, or you suddenly realise you're in the Truman Show, the first thing you're going to see is not real or what is beautiful—you're going to get a glimpse of it—but you're also going to see what reality really is, which is a vast cosmos of emptiness and dark matter with just a little bit of light. So where Neo went in the movie is certainly Gnosis. Gnosis is the beginning of a hero's journey where you go deep within yourself and deep without through many challenges and many layers, and there are no guarantees. By the time I get to know myself and get find that pearl of great price, there's a good chance I'm going to die before that. By the time I get close to becoming Christ-like, like in the *Gospel of Philip*, there's a very good chance the clock will suddenly run out on me. So it doesn't give you any guarantees, but it certainly gives you a sense of urgency. The Gnostics saw St Paul as one of their luminaries, or at least the Valentinians did, and it's not like St Paul saw Jesus and suddenly he walked away like Buddha under the Bhodi Tree, or any of those stories. He had to go to Arabia for three years, either to get his head sorted out or to open a Starbucks, or something. When you read his letters, you can tell he's still not there, he's struggling a lot but also full of ecstasy. The Gnosis is still flowing through him, like that holy virus that Philip K. Dick wrote about. So that's how I see Gnosis.

APS: This is a question that you often ask other people: do you see St Paul as a Gnostic?

MC: I don't see him as a Gnostic, because the term and the vocabulary wasn't there, but I definitely see him as someone who was already carrying Gnostic truths within him, and who basically would set the stage for the Gnostics who would come. I see him very much like Stephen in the Acts of the Apostles. He was already part of that movement, like I said, that conspiracy theory that was beginning to see things as they were. The Gnostics didn't just not trust Jehovah, they didn't trust any of the gods, and they didn't trust any of the earthly institutions. St Paul was definitely the beginning of it.

APS: How about Jesus? You're a mythicist, aren't you?

MC: Yes, I am a mythicist. I don't see enough evidence to even assume that there was a historical Jesus, and even if moments where I allow myself a little breathing room, I would have to agree with so many scholars, if there was a historical Jesus, basically he's lost in the sands of time. So I'd rather just focus on the mythological Jesus, which goes right along with the Gnostic Jesus.

APS: How do you think Christianity started?

MC: Good question. I'd have to say that I'm pretty agnostic on that one too. All the theories are extremely fascinating, and I don't want to get rid of any of the theories. For a long time I subscribed to the idea that it was a sort of radical offshoot of the mystery religions. I do think St Paul was in essence spreading a mystery religion on some sort of a Joshua dying-and-rising god-man, and he was obviously competing with the other mystery religions. But I do also like the theory of these breakaway heterodox Jews that Birger Pearson, John Turner and others have proposed, and who basically said, "Enough is enough," and they walked away from the temple culture and started doing their own mystic speculations based on platonic ideas.

APS: You've asked myself and several other interviewees about the origins of Gnosticism. Of course, we don't know and we can't know what the origins are, but you find the breakaway Jewish sect idea the most convincing and appealing explanation? I tend to hedge my bets as well, even to the extent that Gnostic groups might have sprung up independently in different places, but I do like that John Turner thesis myself.

MC: I always took the advice of Robert Price who said, "Until we can invent a time machine we're all really just sitting around talking about a lot of stuff." Probably the most attractive one to me, and I guess I'm going to show my esoteric roots, is the one Ioan Culianu put forth in *The Tree of Gnosis*, another book which when I opened it I saw a mirror to society, deep into the heart of darkness that was humanity, and his idea that the human mind works as a binary code, and in each one of us we have a formula that is either orthodox or Gnostic, and this can be used for every facet of our lives. The point is that, let's say, if the Gnostic scriptures, and the Bible, and Christianity and the Abrahamic religions were wiped out from creation, in a hundred years, as soon as humanity started again, those binary switches would go off, and you would have a Gnostic movement, and you would have an orthodox movement. I like that theory, that seems to be more anthropological to me.

APS: Yes, I looted that theory from *The Tree of Gnosis* for my book *The Gnostics:History Tradition Scriptures Influence* as well. I did credit him!

MC: It's a great book. He tackles a lot of great issues and he really dispels a lot of illusions, so it's a brilliant book.

APS: He was murdered in Chicago. Do you know anything more about that?

MC: He was murdered right outside the University of Chicago and as far as people say here, it was Romanian nationalists. But outside of that nobody really knows. I don't know exactly what he was writing. Of course, the conspiracy theorists or the Jungian Gnostics immediately assumed that it was because Culianu was so into Giordano Bruno and adopted so many of his ideas including his memory recall techniques. They say Culianu could walk into a party of 200 people and he would ask all of their names and their addresses and other personal information. Then he would walk out and come back in an hour and immediately name each person, what they were and what they did. But anyway, they thought that because he was a latterday Giordano redivivus the fate had to be the same. The binary switch went off and orthodoxy had to get rid of him, just like they got rid of Jesus or Socrates. The story never changes.

APS: Fascinating to hear about the memory theatre techniques. I did want to ask how you first got interested in Gnosticism, and what other religions, churches and spiritualities did you explore before that? What led up to the Gnostic moment when you realised that this was what you wanted to pursue?

MC: Well, again the Gnosticism wasn't giving me the easy comfort that other religions were giving me. I kept finding them disappointing. I was raised Catholic but it was a very ecumenical Catholicism, way before it was trendy to be ecumenical in the Catholic Church. My mother used to go to different services or different religions because she wanted to know what experiences they might have, and she was

always very comfortable with her Catholicism. Same with my family, they were always very experimental. Unlike a lot of people I didn't go to Gnosticism because I was scarred or hurt by the Church. I was perfectly happy in Catholicism but I also wanted to explore other avenues so I explored Buddhism, Hinduism. I was an atheist for six months, I was a born again Christian for six months. I found both of them pretty boring because there's not much in the universe when you're either one. It's just you and God, or you and your hatred for God. I even did the New Age thing, I'm embarrassed to admit.

APS: What does that mean, "the New Age thing"? What did it involved?

MC: Well I feel that New Age is one of the great evils in our society because it waters down so many great traditions, repackages them and makes it into a very profitable business for consumers. It's this dumbing down effect before we even had Oprah or Twitter or Facebook. It's a precursor of all of this and it has these horrible false promises and false gold—again what other religions do—that it can give you without any work or without any struggle which I feel is the antithesis of Gnosticism, which really demands so much out of you, both intellectually, spiritually, and even morally. I was lucky because it was a springboard to many things, but I see New Age as appropriating, corrupting and ultimately killing a lot of the great ideologies and philosophies of our times. I call myself an enemy of New Age on *Aeon Byte*.

APS: What was your New Age experience? What did you do?

MC: It was the usual stuff. I read Eckhart Tolle. He was good because he got me interested in getting my hands wet with Buddhism. I actually started going to a Buddhist temple and everything else. But most people stay stuck on the New Age idea instead of exploring further. The problem with this view, which New Age and Buddhism have, which it lacked for me is that I realised I'm a child of the Greeks. I would be sitting in a temple and I asked the master, "Why is there evil?" "It doesn't matter. What matters is that you get out of evil" "So why is there suffering?" "It doesn't matter. You just need to get out of suffering." My mind is not wired that way, and I had to get honest with myself. The Gnostics really gave me the best answers for why is there evil? Why is there suffering? Sometimes I think that New Age, and also modern Gnostics, they get really lazy.

I remember a book that was very popular by Gary Zukov called *The Seat of the Soul*. I love his books on physics but he wrote this book, and I'm reading this beautiful book. And then he talks about when you walk by a beggar on the street, somebody who's crippled on the street asking for money, tell yourself this, "This guy is fulfilling his karmic duty so neither judge him nor help him nor anything." And that's the kind of attitude that drives me crazy about New Age. Oh, I'll just give out these positive waves, and everybody has a destiny, and some good. And I'm sorry but to me that's just bordering on evil. We have to help others. As you and I both know, when we read about Plotinus barking about the Sethians complaining about social injustice, and when we read many of the words of Jesus and Saint Paul on charity, we are here to help our brothers and sisters. The Gnostics were not just mystic philosophers and very educated, but they were down on the streets helping others, so that's another reason I find Gnosticism so appealing.

APS: I'm also fascinated by you being a born again Christian for a few months. Did you actually have a conversion experience?

MC: Yes, it was the classic thing. You're going through a crisis in life, you get down on your hands and knees, you hold the hands of the person who's trying to proselytise to you, and you do that simple formula where you say, "I want Jesus in my heart; Jesus is the only one; the Bible is the only word of God," and you are filled with this amazing energy which you presume must be the Holy Spirit. But again as a child of Greek thought I like to test things. I was happy for six months but I realised it wasn't the Holy Spirit, it was endorphins and adrenalin I was injecting into my heart. It was great, I was happy, but I knew it just wasn't the most authentic state

of being. It was that peak experience of Maslow, or that oceanic feeling that Freud wrote about. There was lots of happiness, lots of joy, and I felt I had the coping skills to deal with the world from now on, but at the end of the day I felt that—as we might say in Gnosticism—they were just psychic, they were emotion based.

That's one of my other big gripes, that God is everywhere. It's funny, but I think it was Harold Bloom in *The American Religion* who gets it right. He was trying to get rid of the word Christianity as other scholars were trying to get rid of the word Gnosticism, which is kind of funny. But he said that most Americans who call themselves Christians actually take their theology from Thoreau and not Jesus Christ. My complaint is that most people in the West have taken their theology from Spinoza's God, instead of the philosophers' God.

APS: What practices do you have? There's the effort to actually read and understand what the Gnostics are saying, but do you have anything in the way of Gnostic practice?

MC: Again, all you have to do is look at the classic Gnostics. There's no reason to be lazy about it, it's right there. You see that the Gnostics practise various sets of rituals and methods in order to gain their higher state of consciousness. I feel that modern Gnostics should be able to do that too. For example, reason is extremely important. You read the *Excerpts of Theodotus* or the *Teachings of Silvanus* and they keep stressing about science, and use your mind. If the Gnostics were Platonists then they would obviously believe that dialectics can reach you to a higher state of awareness, almost a mystic experience. The Gnostics practised the Eucharist, contemplative prayer, meditation, astrology, theurgy, different forms of magic. So I always tell people that if April DeConick is right, and other scholars are right, they actually went to church, which I do, and then during the week practised different things. I think that's what a modern Gnostic should do. You have to mix and match what you do, test it out, re-test it, and then find what's going to keep deepening your sense of Gnosis, which is again an inward journey and an outward journey to know the unknown, the divine, the God—whatever you want to call it. So I practise a lot of these things.

When someone asked Joseph Campbell how he practised spirituality, he said, "I underline books." Carl Jung, although we're finding out recently that he was a lot more mystical than we ever knew before, he went a different path. Philip K. Dick had his things. He would have an epiphany or a theophany and he would spend years writing about it until the mind started clicking. I like to mix and match, but at the end of the day I consider myself a writer and I find much Gnosis in writing. If God is supposed to be this gigantic mind, this pure, powerful imagination and creativity, and we are meant to emulate the mind of God or the mind of Christ, then I think our best weapon as modern Gnostics is to use our imagination and our creativity always as well as our reason. I always say on Aeon Bye, "Write your own gospel and live your own myth." Because that's what the ancient Gnostics did. It's not complicated. There's no secret information anywhere.

APS: To continue with writing your own myth: you wrote a novel *Queen of Darkness*, recently republished as *Stargazer*. How long ago was that?

MC: The second edition has finally come out this year. The first edition came out in 1998. For very silly reasons I left the profession of writer to go into the real world, and I guess have my ego chopped up a little bit more, and have the rest of my psyche crushed. The first edition came out in 1998. I was a practising Catholic, and I can honestly say, and I'm sure you would agree, writing is brutal, and it's a lot of work, but there are times when it really flows out of you like you've got a Muse on your lap. I wrote this vampire fiction. People like to playfully call it vampires in space, even though I would consider myself one of the forerunners, although the guy who wrote *I am Legend* would be the fountainhead of this vampire genre. It struck a lot of people who would come up to me and say, "Wow! You have some amazing medieval alchemical symbols in your novel." And I was

like, I don't understand what you're saying. Or they would say "Wow! You have really chanelled Philip K. Dick in this novel" And I would say, "I've never read him." And so forth. And people would just keep coming. As I later started to delve into these subjects I realised I really must have tapped into something because it's all there. The Gnostic formula is there, there's Philip K. Dick, there's Jung, it's all there, it's just couched within this vampire genre. The sequel too I wrote shortly after it. It's the same. The main character is Lilith who happens to be in a similar situation as Sophia, cast on Earth, even though she's the main vampire, because she is thrown out by a mad god. I don't know why I used the term "mad god", maybe coming from Philip K. Dick's demented God, or the Gnostic Saklas, the childish god, but she finds herself as the fallen Sophia or Achamoth, here on this Earth. The Gnostic saviour and luminaries and even some of the names were just very bizarrely close to the Gnostic scriptures. Chalk it up any way you want.

APS: So it was coming through somehow or other.

MC: Yeah, I don't know if it was within me, or we can go back to Culianu and that binary switch just went off in me. That 0110 and suddenly I'm a Gnostic. Or for six months when I was writing this novel, and then I went back to being a Catholic without any problems.

APS: This is something that I had as a separate question, but you've been referring to it all alone. How would you like to see the modern Gnostic movement, in the broadest sense, develop, and what problems do you see it having as it is.

MC: I do see a lot of problems. A lot of people email me or call me about blatant corruption. I do not divulge this information unless they wish to go on the record, for obvious reasons—libel, slander and so forth—and even when they give me the documentation, I'm sorry, but I interview people, I'm not going to come out and say it, but the amount of corruption and even crime that you find in a lot of Gnostic organisations and churches is equal to what you will find in any orthodox or Muslim or Jewish temple, and that's very sad. Either we can get into the cynical view that organised religion is organised religion, you take the good with the bad, or you take the view that modern Gnostics, like New-Agers, like to jump over the whole basic morality-ethics-compassion thing that at least Christianity stresses, and the end up in this amoral landscape where as long as you have a mystic experience anything goes. The other problem, going back to what I said, is their complete laziness and this habit of injecting other easier-to-understand or more available philosophies like Daoism or Thelema or Wicca right into the Gnostic themes, and they end up corrupting it. It's all right there. Some of the concepts really crack me up. You and I probably will remember making the mistake about the demiurge, the half-maker rather than its true meaning, "craftsman", but they still go around saying that. Or modern Gnostics will go on saying, "You know, it's knowledge of the heart," which means that basically it's to be an emotion-based theology, and of course when you read the text, or as scholars tell you, people in ancient times thought that the brain was in the heart. So what the Gnostics are telling you is get your head fixed, get your mind to work like the mind of God. They were not talking about emotions because the Greek philosophers and the Gnostics thought that the emotions were just lower passions. The Stoics believed the same thing. So modern Gnostics make that mistake. They make huge mistakes with Gnosis. They make the terrible infraction of equating Gnosis with enlightenment when they're two separate experiences. They will tell you that Gnosticism does not require intermediaries and it's direct experience of God, but when you read the texts it's completely the opposite. Once you take the red pill and you see reality for what it is, what do you see? You see a vast world inside and outside of you of archons and aeons and apostles and luminaries. It is probably the most indirect experience of God you can have. You have to go through this huge network, this ladder of different things before you can really start seeing the pleroma or self-actualisation, or your Christ-self. So that's one of the things that

honestly drives me crazy. But I find it rewarding because no longer are these faiths telling me—these ideologies, including atheism—well, it's easy, it's one-two-three. Gnosticism is this big, great adventure or labyrinth that you have to go through. And I believe when we read the stories, whether it's Jesus or St Paul, we are to emulate their stories, and that is our story. It's not easy, it's a great quest which is very uncertain at the end.

APS: Is there any light scattered around in the modern Gnostic movement? Or not necessarily in the Gnostic movement, just people doing something genuinely similar to what the ancient Gnostics were doing? Presumably you think that you are!

MC: I often tell people, I could be the biggest agent of the demiurge by me exposing so much light onto Gnosticism and putting a bullseye over your foreheads, all of our foreheads. So I might be working for the demiurge and not even know it. That's the risk you take in Gnosticism. You roll the dice in a sense. Modern Gnostic luminaries? Obviously you have to mention Bishop Hoeller. Without his invaluable contributions you and I probably wouldn't even be having this conversation.

I do like the work that Rosamonde Miller does in her Gnostic Sanctuary, because again she simply looks at what the Gnostics did in ancient times. She's out on the streets every day doing a lot of charity work, and then she's back in her sanctuary doing a lot of mysticism and philosophy for those who want to sit around and listen to her. Those two I think have done a great job, as far as modern self-designated Gnostics go. Obviously Philip K. Dick is more popular than ever, and I only see his reputation skyrocketing. I do have no doubt that he was a Gnostic, although he considered himself a Christian until the end. Who else? I can't even think. That's what has become of me, I'm so cynical against modern Gnostics. Then again, St Augustine himself wrote that the Church attracts more demons and evil doers than it does holy men. Because people are worshipping at the altar of the human instead of the altar of

God, so in that sense I guess somebody has to be inside complaining. There has to be some sort of devil's advocate or internal affairs within Gnosticism.

APS: There are many ways to get it wrong and deceive yourself. How do you learn to distinguish between true Gnosis and this self-deception?

MC: I think all of us seekers, and I don't even mean mystic seekers, also secular seekers who are thinking of different ways, who are trying to think outside the box in some way, at some point in our lives I'm sure we all feel that we don't belong. You've heard it, I've heard it, we've probably said it, Andrew, we say, "Man, if I'd been born ten years ago I could have been in the sixties having a good time. Man, I wish I'd been born in the twenties, or been born in France in the Medieval times, that's where I belong!" Or, "Man, I wish I was in this novel, and it really existed." You keep going through this process, and you realise, "Man, I don't belong no matter where I am!"

I am always going to be on the fringe. I am always going to be outside looking in, and observing, and studying, and trying to understand why I am on the outside, and what is outside of me, because "me" is really just a fraud in the end. So I think—this might sound negative, but I contend it's positive—the more you find yourself alienated, as Jesus was called, the Allogenes, the stranger, in the gospels, and in the Gospel of John he's very insistent that he is the ultimate alien, and the ultimate outcast of this world. And of course, St Paul too, St Paul never felt at home anywhere, or Simon Magus, we can go down the list, Philip K. Dick, Jung, they were all outside, William Burroughs, all outsiders, and the more beautiful art or the more discoveries they had, or breakthroughs they had, the more they began to just not feel part of this material world. And that is the heart of Gnosis, that we are not a part of this material world, we are part of something much greater, and we don't know what it is at the end, because we're still stuck in our monkey bodies with these organic brains, but we know that there's something out there.

So I know when the Gnosis is increasing by the fact that I'm becoming more alone in this world, more lonely. There the famous quote, "I alone and afraid in a world I did not make." I forget who the poet was. I think that's how you find out if you've had Gnosis, or if you're going on the right path. But most people don't want to go on that path, we want to belong.

APS: Okay, that's a challenging ending to the interview. Let's finish here.

Andrew Phillip Smith

Marcus the Magician

Of all the Gnostics pilloried by Irenaeus and the other heresiologists, Marcus the Magician stands out for two reasons: his extensive use of gematria and his alleged sexual opportunism. Irenaeus accused Marcus of recruiting wealthy followers and seducing his female disciples. G.R.S. Mead, in his ground-breaking introduction to Gnosticism, *Fragments of a Faith Forgotten*[1] refused to even discuss Irenaeus' accusations, dismissing them as based "entirely on hearsay." (*Fragments* p.359) Yet such abuses of trust are certainly possible, as the modern history of spiritual teachers and western gurus illustrates.

Irenaeus can hardly be said to be a neutral witness. For him, Marcus was "an actual precursor of the anti-Christ." Irenaeus writes that he knows of these allegations from apostate Marcosians (followers of Marcus) who joined Bishop Irenaeus' church in Lyon (or "returned to the church of God," as he puts it.) He describes two sets of circumstances under which these women have sex with Marcus. Firstly, he writes that overcome with the experience of being taught how to prophesy, "her heart pounding abnormally she utters ridiculous nonsense, anything that comes into her head, idly and audaciously, for she is stimulated by a vain spirit . . . "[2] This is presumably a form of glossolalia. In return for this spiritual gift his female pupils reward him with money "but also by physical intercourse, prepared as she is to be united with him in everything in order that she, with him, may enter into the One ..."

The way this is phrased suggest that the women voluntarily offer themselves to Marcus.

It is true the disciples of charismatic teachers often wish to receive the personal attention of their leader by any means possible. However, Irenaeus goes on to claim that Marcus used love potions and aphrodisiacs on some of his female followers. Further, Marcus' male disciples are said to have similarly "led astray" many women by virtue of the claim to perfect gnosis and their redeemed status. It is difficult to assess the truth of these accusations. On the one hand there is no smoke without fire, and Irenaeus doesn't attribute sexual indiscretion to many of his "heretics". However, claims such as seduction via love potion were a common form of polemic in the ancient world. Irenaeus himself encountered Marcosians in the Rhone Valley, but does not claim to have met Marcus himself. So Marcus may or may not be guilty of the crimes of his followers, even assuming that these latter claims are themselves genuine. From this single account it is impossible to know the truth behind the slander, and whether any sex was coercive or consensual. Hippolytus, who reproduced Irenaeus' account of Marcus, adding a few details, mentioned that the Marcosians had objected to Irenaeus' account of them. Scholar Michael A. Williams believes that the accusation that Marcosians took part in actual sexual rites is a slander based on a deliberate misrepresentation of what Irenaeus describes later on as a "spiritual marriage". i.e., the spiritual rite and metaphor of the bridal chamber has been interpreted, deliberately and spitefully, as a physical sex magic ritual.

It seems likely that Marcus operated mainly in Asia Minor in the period between 160CE and 180CE. There are strong links between the

Valentinian systems and that of Marcus, but scholars differ on whether Marcus should be counted as a Valentinian. Einar Thomassen, the leading expert in Valentinianism, suggests that Marcus' movement, with its ecstatic prophesying and charismatic leader, may also be linked to Montanism, the prophetic movement founded by Montanus around 170, the period in which Marcus was active, and which was later joined by heresiologist Tertullian, hoist by his own petard. Both movements operated in the Rhone Valley and in Asia Minor.[3] Montanus himself was accompanied by two female prophets Maximilla Priscilla, also reminiscent of the important role (seduction aside) which women had in Marcus' church.

Apart from the alleged disciple-fucking Marcus and the Marcosians are known for their extensive use of gematria and their use of specific rites. Marcus took the western Valentinian system and applied sophisticated and extensive alphabetical and numerical symbolism to it. This system, described by Irenaeus, used a scheme of 30 named aeons which emanated to fill the pleroma. Most of Marcus' gematric explorations are concerned with this heavenly scheme, rather than with the demiurge and the archons who rule this world. The aeons are divided into two tetrads (4) which form together form the ogdoad (8) plus a decad (10) and duodecad (12).

In the Greek-speaking world numbers were expressed using the 24 letters of the Greek alphabet (which at that time existed only in what is now the uppercase form) plus three additional letters that, in the case of digamma, used to belong to the alphabet or, for koppa and sampi, were used just for numerical representation. (See facing page.)

Thus the famous 666 from Revelation was written XΞF

X chi = 600

Ξ Xi = 60

F digamma = 6

This notorious number, 666, which in the modern world has entirely evil implications due to it being designated the "number of the beast" in Revelation 13:17-18, was originally associated with the sun. 666 is also associated with the sun in Hebrew Kabbalistic gematria.[4] The magic square of the sun is a 6x6 square in which each number from 1 to 36 appears once only and each row or column adds up to 111, so the sum of the rows or columns is 666, as is the sum of every number from 1 to 36. There is more than one solution to the magic square of the sun. (See facing page for two solutions.)

Using gematria any word can be resolved to a number by adding up the numerical value of each component letter. Other words which also add up to this number have a meaningful equivalence with the first word. Additionally, the number itself may have unusual arithmetic or geometric properties (e.g. 10=1+2+3+4, a triangular number) and hence further meaningful associations may be made. One example used by Marcus is ΙΗΣΟΥΣ, Iesous, Jesus.

I	10
H	8
Σ	200
O	70
Υ	400
Σ	200
= 888	

A alpha	B beta	Γ gamma	Δ delta	E epsilon	F digamma	Z zeta	H eta	Θ theta
1	2	3	4	5	6	7	8	9
I iota	K kappa	Λ lambda	M mu	N nu	Ξ xi	O omicron	Π pi	Q koppa
10	20	30	40	50	60	70	80	90
P rho	Σ sigma	T tau	Υ upsilon	Φ phi	X chi	Ψ psi	Ω omega	ϡ sampi
100	200	300	400	500	600	700	800	900

6	32	3	34	35	1
7	11	27	28	8	30
24	14	16	15	23	19
13	20	22	21	17	18
25	29	10	9	26	12
36	5	33	4	2	31

32	29	4	1	24	21
30	31	2	3	22	23
12	9	17	20	28	25
10	11	18	19	26	27
13	16	36	33	5	8
14	15	34	35	6	7

Marcus saw 888 as significant in an additional way as Greek has 8 letters to designate the units, 8 to designate the tens and 8 for hundreds. (The three extra symbols are not counted here and the concept of zero and its symbol wasn't commonly used in ordinary counting, even though it had already been invented for some technical uses.) Thus the name ΙΗΣΟΥΣ, value 888, can be said to contain the entire alphabet of 24 letters. The alphabet was linked to the emanation of 30 aeons, closely linked to similar Valentinian systems described by Irenaeus.[5]

The alphabet principally represents sounds. In Marcus' cosmology everything begins with Sige, Silence, from which the entire pleroma is spoken, a motif which some see as being drawn from Egyptian sources. The father spoke the first word, Arche (beginning) which consisted of four letters, ΑΡΧΕ. The second word also consisted of four letters, the third 10, the fourth 12. Unfortunately we are not told what the other three words are, only their lengths. There are thus 30 letters in total, the 4+4+10+12 that occur in other Valentinian cosmologies. These spoken letters are stated to be the equivalent of angels, aeons, logoi, roots, seeds, pleromas and fruit.

The last of these letters made a sound which resulted in the production of the existing created world. The letter itself did not fall, but was taken back up into the twelve-letter word. This is a parallel to the fall of Sophia, who in western Valentinianism split into a higher and lower Sophia. This sound echoes in the material world while the letter remains in the fourth word spoken by the father. Note that this final letter is not omega, the last letter of the Greek alphabet, but the final letter of the twelve-letter fourth word, whatever that was intended to be.

Each of the thirty letters may be expanded into its component letters ad infinitum. To use the example given by Irenaeus, the letter Δ is spelt out as ΔΕΛΤΑ. Thus the letters Δ, Ε, Λ, Τ, and Α are produced secondarily, and these words can again be expanded into the letters ΔΕΛΤΑ, ΕΤΑ, ΛΑΜΒΔΑ, etc., on and on into infinity.

Marcus was said to have received this gematric cosmology by revelation, becoming the "womb and receptacle of the Sige of Colorbasus"[6] The supreme tetrad descended to Marcus in a female form (the world, we are told, was unable to support the male form!) and gave him his revelation of cosmological gnosis.

The tetrad showed Marcus a vision of truth (Greek *Aletheia*) the 24 letters of the alphabet placed in pairs on various parts of her body (See diagram.) The alphabet may be followed in sequence down one side of the body and back up the other. Thus it may have been used for techniques of body sensing, perhaps in a similar way to Jeremy Puma's Kimetikos, based on the *Secret Book of John*.[7] The twelve parts of the body suggest zodiacal symbolism too. Truth/ Aletheia then spoke and uttered a word which became the name Christ Jesus. She then divided the 24 letters into three sets of consonants, semivowels (liquids such as 'r',) and the vowels, these consisting of 9, 8 and 7 letters in each set. The consonants belong to the Father and Truth because they are voiceless, inexpressible and unutterable. The eight semivowels belong to the aeons Logos and Life, the seven vowels to Man and Church. These six categories (Father, Truth, Logos, Life, Man, Church) are names of aeons in other Valentinian systems. These six powers multiplied by the tetrad make 24. The images of the three powers are the double letters (ΖΞΨ, with the respective sounds *ks, ps, tz*, each of which has two consonantal sounds) and if the three powers and three double-letters are added to 24 we have 30 again. Episodes from the Bible containing the numbers 6 and 7 (the six powers plus Sige) are interpreted in the light of this symbolism. (See table at end.) A slightly similar contemplation of letters and sounds and arithmology can be found in the Sethian text *Marsanes*, from Nag Hammadi Codex X [8]

The seven vowels are linked in order to the seven heavens, alpha being the first, the second epsilon on the omega the seventh. When children are born it is said that they intone the sound of each of these vowels in turn. Truth, Aletheia, ΑΛΗΘΕΙΑ has seven letters in Greek.

This symbolism is applied to each of the aeons of the first and second tetrads, based on the length of the words.

What is the purpose of all this numerical speculation? While it was (and still is) fun to add up the value of letters and find corresponding meanings, gematria is primarily a way of infusing language and writing with an inner meaning. The divine structure of the pleroma could be discovered in scripture, in sacred names and in ordinary words. These multiple levels of significance formed a web of association, revealing the structure of the heavenly realm in the fallen world, in that most ubiquitous of human activities, language. Iesous is no longer an arbitrary name that happens to be the Greek translation of a version of the name Joshua borne by a Galilean, but contains within itself a description of the two tetrads and an indication of the plan of gematria itself, as three sets of eight letters.

The numbers which are significant for Marcus—4, 6, 7, 8, 10, 12, 24 and 30—crop up in all sorts of contexts. 12 and 30 are particularly relevant to timekeeping and the calendar. We may speculate that each month and each date might have had unique importance for the Marcosians. Each month might have been ruled by one of the aeons in the duodecad, each day in each month by one of the entirety of 30 aeons.

Both the Hebrew Bible and the gospels provided ample opportunity for meaningful numerical interpretation. The book of Genesis was particularly important for Marcus, as it was for the Gnostics in general, but he seems also to have been partial to the rest of the Torah and some of the "histories" such as the books of Kings. The seven days of creation could be assigned to the vowels. The seven spheres also, and they plus the sphere containing them, plus the sun and the moon (here counted separately from the spheres for some reason) gives 10, the decad.

10 (as kabbalists know) can be found both explicitly and in a hidden manner in the Torah, in the 10 peoples given by Abraham to God, or in the 10 curtains of the Tabernacle, or in the ten categories light, day, night, etc. given in Genesis. Again, see the closing tables for a list of the specific examples given by Irenaeus.

Marcus had a particularly complex interpretation of the parable of the 99 sheep and the one that was lost, found in Matthew (18:12–14) and Luke (15:3–7) and *Gospel of Thomas* 107. The sheep that was lost immediately suggests the Sophia aeon. The duodecad minus the lost aeon gives 11. The 9 drachma of the woman in the parable of the lost coin in Luke 15:8 is roped in, so that 9x11=99, the number of the sheep. The 99 is also formed by the 30 aeons multiplied by 3, the three divisions of the aeons into the ogdoad, decad and duodecad. The number 11 suggests the eleventh letter of the Greek alphabet, Lambda. Lambda therefore, in this interpretation, descended to regain the fallen twelfth letter Mu. This is why Mu M resembles a double Lambda, ΛΛ .

The numbers 1-99 were counted on the left hand, associated with evil in the ancient world, as in "Let not your left hand know what your right hand is doing."[9] When 1 is added to 99 the right hand takes over the counting for 100, thus moving from the evil hand to the good. Thus the 99 sheep and the one lost is seen as a parable of the fall of Sophia.

Incidentally, Marcus' use of gematria presupposes that his pupils were literate, and Irenaeus does specify that they were all wealthy. Hopefully gematria persisted as a creative endeavour for the Marcosians and did not degenerate into a merely authoritarian system of assigning agreed meanings to scriptures which were patently not intended to describe the 30 aeons of the pleroma.

Aside from all the gematria and fornication, Irenaeus and Hippolytus give us plenty of information on Marcosian ritual, filtered through all the invective and sarcasm. We have information on an initiation rite, a rite of prophecy, and the rite of redemption or apolytrosis.

The initiation involved a descent of Grace and

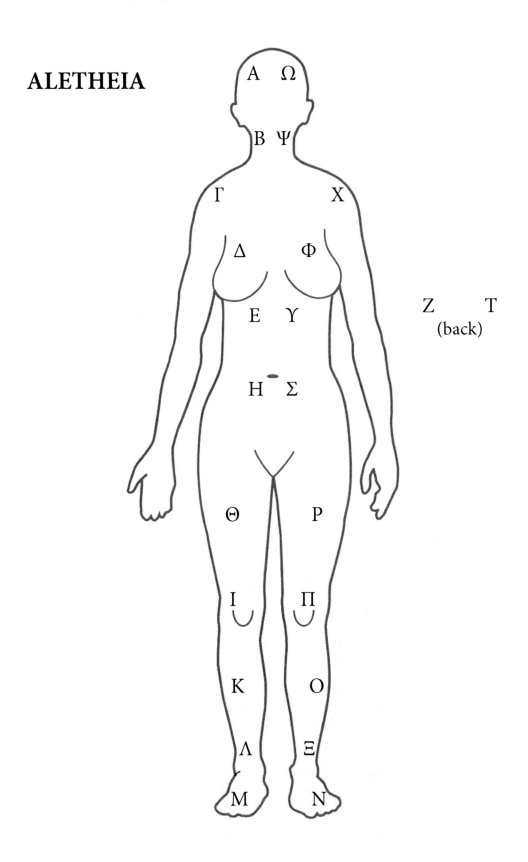

ALETHEIA

a transformation of white wine into red. Marcus (or a follower) prayed over a cup of white wine for Grace (Charis) to drop her blood into the cup. The wine then changed from white to blood red or purple. Hippolytus adds that this was achieved by dropping a drug (probably a plant pigment) into the cup.

The rite of prophecy involved a similar appeal to Grace and another trick with a cup. The female initiate was given a full cup of mixed wine over which she offered thanks. Marcus then produced a much larger cup and proceeded to fill the large cup from the small to the extent that the large cup overflowed. Hippolytus believed that Marcus put an effervescent powder into the larger cup, which foamed up once the wine was added. These wine rituals must have had a startling effect on the participants. The surprise of seeing the wine turn red, or overflow the larger goblet, must surely have created a moment of increased awareness. Presumably dyes and effervescents (or a false bottom in the cup) were used. Whether this should be seen as a deception or as an aid to Gnosis depends entirely on the intention of the practitioner and the attitude of the initiate. Was it merely a trick for the gullible or was it the creation of a transcendent moment?

The Valentinians used five sacraments, as mentioned in the *Gospel of Philip* and by Irenaeus, the redemption, the bridal chamber, baptism, chrism and Eucharist. The *Gospel of Philip* states "The Lord did everything in a mystery: a baptism and a chrism and a Eucharist and a redemption and a bridal chamber."[10] The Marcosians performed the rite of redemption, or *apolytrosis*, in various ways, either as a bridal chamber rite, symbolising the syzygies—the male-female pairs of aeons in the pleroma—or as a kind of baptism. A third kind of rite was a chrism in which oil and water or balsam was poured on the head of the initiate.. They saw it as a kind of higher baptism which allowed entry into the pleroma. Baptism was given by John the Baptist for repentance, but the redemption was given by the Christ who descended into Jesus at the time of his baptism. This is a variation on the adoptionist christology, whereby Jesus was adopted by God as his son at baptism.

They also believed that when Jesus asked the sons of Zebedee, John and James, whether they could be baptised with the baptism with which he was baptised (Matt 20:20) he was giving them the redemption.

Fortunately, Irenaeus has given us some of the formulae used in the baptism. "In the name of the unknown Father of all things, into Truth, the mother of all, into him who descended on Jesus, into union, into redemption, into the communion of the powers." Aramaic (called Hebrew by Irenaeus) is recited in other versions of the rite, "Basema chamosse baaianora mistadia rouada kousta babophor kalechthei." This is in accompanied by "I call upon that which is above every power of the Father, which is called Light, and the good spirit, and life; for thou hast reigned in the body."[11]

Still other Marcosians considered the redemption to be equivalent to gnosis itself and required no external ritual.

Yet another form of redemption was given to the dying. This allowed "the inner man", i.e. The spirit, to ascend past the powers of the demiurge and his archons. The body remained in the created world and the soul was returned to the demiurge. The dying person is taught the following to say to the archons, "I am a son of the Father, the pre-existent Father, and now a son of the pre-existent Father. I have come to behold all things, both what is strange and what belongs to me. But they are by no means strange but belong to Achamoth [Sophia], who is female and who has made these things for herself. I derive my being from him who was pre-existent, and I go again to that which is my own, whence I come forth." To those around the demiurge he should say, "I am a precious vessel, more precious than the female which made you. If your mother does not know her origin, I know myself and am aware whence I am, and I invoke the incorruptible Sophia, who is in the Father, mother of your mother, who has no father nor any male consort. A female sprung from a female made you, and she did not know her mother, but believed that she existed all alone. But I call upon her mother."[12] Here we have exciting account of a direct confrontation of a Gnostic with the demiurge's archons. The deceased states his true lineage, appealing to Sophia and the unknowable Father, in contrast with the invalid descent of the archons.[13]

To Irenaeus the variety of Marcosian practices was an abomination, but to us it is part of the attractive diversity of the Gnostics.

Though Marcus is known notoriously as the Magician, the designation is based more on these details than on any intrinsically magical basis to his teaching. Certainly gematria is part of the magical tradition, but the special effects in the wine rituals are not magic in any specific sense of the word. As described by Irenaeus they are more like conjuring tricks, though the descent of Grace may be considered to be a form of invocation. But there is plenty of material here for the aspiring Gnostic to experiment with.

Even when we take into account the prejudice of Irenaeus there is a whiff of subterfuge and deception. He is a little reminiscent of Alexander of Abonoutheichos, a second-century charlatan who deceived his followers with the manipulation of a trained snake with a puppet head, Glycon, who was said to be the actual incarnation of Asclepius (now worshipped knowingly by Alan Moore.) As with all forms of religion and spirituality, *caveat emptor*, let the buyer beware!

Marcus' Numerical Correspondences

duodecad in zodiac=12

moon 30 days = 30

sun 12 months = 12

days = 12 hours =12

hour = 30 parts = 30

zodiac circle 360=12x30

30

30 triacontad

2+4+6+8+10=30

Numbers to H not counting F 1+2+3+4+5+6+8= 30

30 cubits height of Noah's ark, (Gen 6:15)

30 Samuel placed first among 30 guests by Saul (I Sam 9:22)

David concealed himself for 30 days (I Sam 20:5)

30 men went with David to the cave (II Sam 23:13)

Tabernacle 30 cubits long (Exod 26:8)

10

1+2+3+4=10

10 in Genesis 1: light, day, night, firmament, evening, morning, dry land, sea, plants, trees

10 fingers

10 peoples given to Abraham by God (Gen 15:18-)

Sarah's handmaid given to Abraham for ten years so that he might get a son by her (Gen 16:3)

Abraham's servant gave Rebecca ten gold bracelets and her brothers detained her for ten days (Gen 24: 22,55)

Jereboam received ten sceptres (I Kings 11:30-)

There were the curtains of the Tabernacle (Exod 26:1; 36:8)

The columns of the Tabernacle were ten cubits high (Exod 36:21)

The ten sons of Jacob were sent to Egypt to buy corn (Gen 42:3)

Jesus revealed himself to ten apostles after the resurrection, Judas being dead and Thomas missing (John 20:24)

the seven spherical bodies plus the sphere containing them, plus the sun and moon = 10

12

12 sun, moon, stars, seasons, years, whales, fish, reptiles, birds, cattle, wild beasts, man-woman-child

12 members of body as in the body of Aletheia

Earth has 12 zones

12 sons of Jacob and twelve tribes(Gen 35:22)

12 precious stones on the breastplate and twelve little bells (Exod 28:17-20; 39: 10-13, 25)

12 stones laid by Moses at the foot of the mountain (Exod 24:4)

12 stones place by Joshua in the river (Josh 4:3,8-) etc.

12 apostles

4 and 8

4 In Genesis, God, beginning, heaven, earth

4 In Genesis, abyss, darkness, water, spirituality

In mankind: brain: a single source; 4 senses sight, hearing, smell, taste

4 Sun created on the fourth day

court of Tabernacle linen, blue, purple, scarlet (Ex 26:1; 36:8)

The four elements are an image of the tetrad

these plus their component qualities of hot/dry and cold/moist are added to the elements to form the ogdoad

4 rows of precious stones on the robe of the high priest

On the eighth day man was formed

8 orifices 2 ears, 2 eyes, 2 nostrils, bitter/sweet taste

Circumcision takes place on the eighth day

Eight people saved from the flood (Gen 7:7)

David the eighth brother (I Sam 16:6-12)

IHSOUS has 8 letters, the unutterable name 24.

Christ (the) son has 12 letters and represents the duodecad.

Unutterable Christ 30

NOTES

1 Available in numerous reprint editions, often poorly produced, and also online at http://www.gnosis.org/library/grs-mead/fragments_faith_forgotten/index.htm and other places.

2 The principle source for Marcus is Irenaeus. I use Werner Foerster's translation in *Gnosis: A Selection of Gnostic Texts Volume 1* (Clarendon, 1974) p.198-221. This particular quotation is found on p.202.

3 See The Spiritual Seed particularly (Brill, 2008) p. 241-247, 261-262, 498-500,

4 See David Fideler's *Jesus Christ: Sun of God (Quest, 1993)* for information on gematria in early Christianity, or read Miguel Conner's interview with him in *Voices of Gnosticism* (Bardic Press, 2010).

5 A website http://www.jesus8880.com explores the Gospel of Mark using this kind of gematria.

6 Colorbasus may be the name of an otherwise unknown author of gematria, or more likely, is a corruption of *kol-arba*, all is four, a reference to the divine name in Hebrew and the tetrad.

7 See *The Gnostic 2* for Jeremy's article on using the archons and their bodily attributes to produce a similar technique.

8 e.g., see *The Nag Hammadi Scriptures* (HarperCollins, 2007) ed. Marvin Meyer, p.642-646.

9 Matthew 6:3 et al.

10 *The Gospel of Philip: Annotated & Explained* p. 63.

11 *Gnosis Volume 1* p.219. The Aramaic is not actually translated by the accompanying Greek text.

12 *Gnosis* p. 220-221.

13 Ismo Dunderberg has suggested that the beautiful epitaph of Flavia Sophe is Marcosian in origin and contains a reference to the redemption.

You were filled with longing for the father's light,
My sister, my spouse, my Sophe.

Now, anointed with holy immortal chrism in the baths of Christ,
Be quick to view the divine faces of the aeons,
The great angel of the great council, the true Son.
You made your way into the bridal chamber and made an undying ascent
Into the breast of the Father.

See Ismo Dunderberg, *Beyond Gnosticism* (Columbia University Press, 2008), p. 115-117.

The Gnosis of the Light

Here we present the complete translation, with the original introduction and notes, of the Untitled Apocalype from the Bruce Codex from Rev. F. Lamplugh's *The Gnosis of the Light*. Originally published in 1918 by John M. Watkins. Generally ignored, this book is the only one on the subject. Birger A. Pearson notes the many Sethian features of the work and places it in the fourth century, at the very final stage of Sethian gnosticism, probably written in Egypt.

INTRODUCTION

This translation of the ancient Gnostic work, called by Schmidt, the Untitled Apocalypse, is based chiefly on Amélineau's French version of the superior MS. of the Codex Brucianus, now in the Bodleian Library, Oxford. In making the rendering I have studied the context carefully, and have not neglected the Greek words interspersed with the Coptic; also I have availed myself of Mr Mead's translation of certain important passages from Schmidt's edition, for purposes of comparison. Anything that I have added to bring out the meaning of the Gnostic author now and again, I have enclosed in brackets. Such suggestions have always arisen from the text. I fancy my English version will be found to give a reasonably accurate idea of the contents of one of the most abstruse symbolical works in the world. The notes that I have added are not intended to be final or exhaustive, but to give the general reader some guidance towards understanding the intensely interesting topics with which the powerful mind of the ancient mystical writer was preoccupied. I have endeavoured to show myself a sympathetic "Hierophant" or expounder of some of the mysteries, not without study of the Gnosis, both of the Christianised and purely Hellenistic type, for the key to the understanding of symbolism is only given into the hands of sympathy.

The Codex Brucianus was brought to England from Upper Egypt, by the famous traveller Bruce, in 1769, and bequeathed by him to the care of the Bodleian Library, Oxford. It contains several Gnostic works translated into the Upper Egyptian dialect from the Greek, and probably is as old as the sixth century A.D. The Greek originals were of course much older, that is to say, the MSS. to which the codex ultimately goes back were much older. We are only concerned with one of them here, the so-called Untitled Apocalypse, which is markedly distinct from the others in character and style. Schmidt dates it well in the second century A.D., and with this estimate I am inclined to agree. It shows, as I have endeavoured to make clear in the notes, marked affinities in some respects to the Gospel of Mary (Codex Akhmim), which we know to have been in existence before 180 A.D., and its philosophical basis is the Platonism of Alexandria. If it is by one writer, I think it may be dated from 160 or 170 A.D.-200 A.D., and belongs to the period of Basilides and Valentinus.

Before venturing upon any discussion of the authorship and contents of our document, it would be as well to say a few words as to the meaning of that much misunderstood technical term "Gnosis" in Hellenistic and early Christian theology. For a fuller exposition I would refer the reader to the admirable essay upon the subject by Mr G. R. S. Mead in his volume Quests Old and New. Gnosis was not "philosophy" in the generally accepted sense of the term, or even religio-philosophy. "It was immediate knowledge of God's mysteries received from direct intercourse with the Deity—mysteries which must remain hidden from the natural man, a knowledge at the same time which exercises decided reaction on our relationship to God and also on our nature or disposition" (Reitzenstein). It was the power or gift of receiving and understanding revelation, which finally culminated in the direct unveiled vision of God and the transformation of the whole man into spiritual being by contact with Him. The ground of the idea of Gnosis does not seem to be very different from that of the later "Mystical Theology," "which originally meant the direct, secret, and incommunicable knowledge of God received in contemplation" (Dom John Chapman). The revelation sought for was not so much a dogmatic revelation as a revelation of the processes of "transmutation" of Rebirth, of Apotheosis or "Deification." Its aim was dynamic rather than static. But while the followers of the Gnosis, both Christian and Hellenistic, would have agreed that the direct knowledge of God is incommunicable to others, they undoubtedly seem to have held that there were what may be described as intermediate or preparatory processes or energisings which could be communicated: (1) by initiation into a holy community; (2) by a duly qualified master; (3) under the veils of symbols and sacraments.

The Gnostic movement began long before the Christian era (what its original historical impulse was we do not know), and only one aspect of it, and that from a strictly limited point of view, has been treated by ecclesiastical historians. Recent investigations have challenged the traditional outlook and the traditional conclusions and the traditional "facts." With some to-day, and with many more to-morrow, the burning question is, or will be—not how did a peculiarly silly and licentious heresy rise within the Church—but how did the Church rise out of the great Gnostic movement, and how did the dynamic ideas of

the Gnosis become crystallised into Dogmas? I do not indicate a solution; I do not express an opinion. I call attention to a fact in the world of scholarship that will not be without its decided reaction upon the plain man. But the study of the ancient Gnosis, and indeed of mysticism generally, has left another suggestion that seems laden with limitless possibilities. Let us first go back to what I said as to the communication of certain "processes," "leavenings," or "energisings" under a sacramental veil. These processes were held to modify the nature of the person who submitted to them in a peculiar manner that was likened to the impress or "character" of a seal upon wax. These seals or "characters" could not only be acquired through formal rites and by the laying on of the hands of a master, but also, I am disposed to believe, by a certain mode of study—I am developing the Gnostic theory, not stating one of my own— namely, that of a highly symbolic literature. The objection of the Gnostic to a plain statement of facts would probably be somewhat as follows: "What you say is very good and true as far as it goes, but it is 'Pistis,' not Gnosis; Faith, not Knowledge. You desire to be a changed man. Pistis will change you to a certain extent. I have nothing to say against it, but it will not change you in the radical way that Gnosis does." If you went on to argue that your statement was reasonable and received admirable support from logic and philosophy, he would probably reply: "Philosophy of the kind you mention is excellent, and forms a basis for Gnosis which is not contrary to reason, though it is above it. Gnosis is a rebirth by which you become a god, and then you will have no need to find out things by talking and discursive reasoning, for everything will be within yourself and you will know all things in a vital way, by an act of simple intuition in the end. 'The wind bloweth where it listeth, and thou hearest the sound thereof, but canst not tell whence it cometh, and whither it goeth; so is every one that is born of the Spirit.' If you tie yourself down to logic, you will not know the real things, the 'Things that are,' by getting inside them. Your knowledge will be external, superficial. Gnosis, you may be surprised to learn, is not just 'knowing,' it is light and 'life,' living and being as well. This must not be taken as an attacking reason; if you join our school you will have a stiff course of Plato. You ought to know the 'Things that are' from the ordinary point of view, from outside, before you approach them with the idea of getting inside them, and so raising them up within yourself as far-shining lives. Afterwards you will study in a new manner that will seem madness to the common-sensed; and a Divine Madness indeed it is, for it will lead you to the secret of the Cross."

Hence the disciple was confronted in due time with a document that would not yield its secrets to dialectic, a kind of ritual in words that initiated his intuition into self-knowledge. Intense devotion was needed, imagination, and will-power. The Gnosis came gradually, perhaps after the manuscript had been laid aside; it was the effort towards a sympathetic understanding that mattered, that was rewarded with life and light from God. The mere success of the logical mind in unravelling a puzzle was as nothing, for the readings of these monstrous, many-faceted stars of symbolism were infinite. That the intuition should enter into self awareness as into a sacred place of the mysteries—that was a process of the Gnosis.

Now this strange way of teaching, which was really a "Cloud of Unknowing," was the real basis and point, as it were, of the Alexandrine method of interpreting Scripture. Think of Philo and what he says of the teaching of his Gnostic Therapeuts. Think of Clement, and of Origen with his "Eternal Gospel." This quickening of the intuition into knowledge of itself and God, through allegory and symbol based on philosophy, was the Everlasting Gospel.

So Gnostic documents were not merely intended to puzzle the outsider, but the insider as well. This fact will enable us to appreciate better Basilides' famous remark about the one or two only who could understand his system. His frame of mind was a little like that of a university examiner after setting a paper. We need not think that these people were altogether destitute of humour. It would be a gross exaggeration,

of course, to say that all the Gnostic systems described in Irenaeus and Hippolytus might have been devised by the same man, but it would be a useful exaggeration, illustrating the extreme anti-literalist point of view. Our knowledge of the schools rests for the most part on reports made upon documents such as these, the purport of which was entirely missed by those that made them. They treated Gnosis as if it were another kind of "Pistis," or another system of philosophy. One doubts very much the correctness of the traditional classification of schools, which was made by people who were not in very close touch with them. One doubts if there was much hostility between these schools, however much their symbolism may appear to differ on the surface.

What was the result of these processes "initiated" or "started" by sacramental rites, by symbolism, by masters of Gnosis? Was the result something purely "subjective" at best? The answer of the Masters of the Gnosis to this question, which is characteristic of the modern mind and expresses the doubt which is gnawing at the heart of much modern religious life, would have been "No. There are certain physical changes as well. The body is spiritualised." They might possibly have added, "It is assumed, in part at least, by the Body of Stars which has been awakened within it. This is the Body by means of which Union with God takes place, and then still more wonderful changes happen. We can awaken the Body of Stars or Rays, but to unite it with Himself, that depends upon the Will of God above, but all is a mystery of Grace."

This awakening of the Body of Stars, this assumption, or partial assumption, by immortality of the inner flesh, is the interesting possibility to which I referred earlier. Let me here quote two Catholic writers. Says Döllinger (First Age, p. 235, quoting Rom. vii. 22, 1 Cor. vi. 14, Eph. iii. 16 and 30, in support), "Saint Paul not only divides man into body and spirit, but distinguishes in the bodily nature, the gross, visible, bodily frame and a hidden, inner 'spiritual' body not subject to limits of space or cognisable by the senses; this last, which shall hereafter be raised, is alone fit for and capable of organic union with the glorified body of Christ, of substantial incorporation with it." Dom John Chapman, O.S.B., in his excellent article on "Catholic Mysticism" in Hastings' Encyclopaedia of Religion and Ethics, vol. ix., writes: "It is not to be denied that this psycho-physical side demands scientific investigation. It seems certain that St John of the Cross is justified in his view that the body is somehow 'spiritualised' by contemplation. Such facts as the power of saints over the animal world and the power of reading thoughts, e.g., are proved beyond cavil."

Here, then, we have a consistent tradition held by many schools, and I think that it is by investigation along the lines suggested by Dom John Chapman that there is the greatest chance of arriving at some proof of immortality that will satisfy the scientific mind. For the claim of mystics is that here and now it is possible to participate consciously in that which is immortal, and the "spiritualising" of the body is an outward sign of the substantiality of that claim, the standard set up upon a hill to testify that the human consciousness is not planetary merely, not "hylic," nor "psychic," but has its root in the wisdom that issues from an inconceivable Abyss of Life and Light.

I believe that the original source of the document I have translated belonged to an Egyptian community or school of contemplation whose name has been forgotten in the night of time; that it was connected with the preparation of a candidate for the Baptism of Light. What form this rite really took it is impossible to say, but that it had outward signs of some kind is extremely probable. We have an old Gnostic ritual preserved in the compilation generally known as the "Acts of John." Perhaps this may give us some idea of the sort of ceremony that was worked. I fancy there was an Eucharistic side, and that the Baptism of Light was connected with the mystic crucifixion alluded to so often in the notes. Possibly in the midst of the sacred dance, at the breaking of the Bread, there was a certain laying on of hands by an adept Master, one who had himself attained to the autoptic vision, and then the candidate was left alone to immerse himself in the Dark Ray of the Divine Mind.

I think also that the original MS. was based upon the work of one Master, whose name, like that of the order to which he belonged, is lost in the night of time, but that it also contains amplifications and additions by at least one later hand. It will thus represent the mind of a grade of teaching, and possibly contains material dating back to the period of the Therapeutae that Philo knew. In other words, the community may have been an old one before it was Christianised. In any case, it remains the record of a stupendous spiritual adventure, the attempt to produce a race of Divinised men, that is not without the splendour of tragedy, for at some time, like the Holy Cup of Legend, the presence of Masterhood departed, and the external house fell into ruin and its place knew it no more. Perhaps, in the desire to propagate, it admitted unworthy candidates; perhaps it turned to the by-ways of magic in an attempt to arrest the external course of nature and to defy necessity; perhaps there came a day when none could understand the inner meaning of the high and far-shining mysteries, and so amidst party strife the building word was lost. Many a man, no doubt, who called himself a "Gnostic" was but a sorry rogue; many another was but a student of the letter, not of the life; many another was but a spiritual swashbuckler, pompous in his demeanour and cryptic in his utterance; some, led by an abhorrent fantasy, may have wandered along the path that goes to the Venus-berg and have striven to lisp a formula that would transform the earth into Gehenna rather than into Heaven. But, beside this mass of imposture, of folly, of elegant idleness and of corruption, the à rebours of a spiritual outpouring, there was a real mysticism that could present the Authentic Spectacle and could utter comfortable words in tongues not of this world utterly. There was a Gnosis that strove to give the Peace of God to those within and to those without, because in Peace all things were made, that yearned to bring forth children, quickened fiery souls, æons, gods, in bodies of light for the love of God; that saw in all things Grace, the Sponsa Dei, the Mother most pure and immaculate. "No creature was ever wronged of Thee," no spark ever quenched, no hope defrauded and hurled eternally from the sky with shattered wings by Thee. Such is the fair Faith that chanted its prayer beneath a heaven set with such strange galaxies, and whispers to us now through the disremembered symbols of a forgotten book.

It is pleasant, in these days of strife, to be able to quote Dr Schmidt's appreciation of the Untitled Apocalypse with a cordial agreement:

"What a different world, on the contrary, meets us in our thirty-one leaves! We find ourselves in the pure spheres of the highest Pleroma; we see, step by step, this world, so rich in heavenly beings, coming into existence before our eyes; each individual space with all its inmates is minutely described, so that we can form for ourselves a living picture of the glory and splendour of this Gnostic heaven. The speculations are not so confused and fantastic as those of the Pistis Sophia and our two Books of Jeu.... The author is imbued with the Greek spirit, equipped with a full knowledge of Greek philosophy, full of the doctrine of the Platonic ideas, an adherent of Plato's view of the origin of evil—that is to say, Hyle.... We possess in these leaves a magnificently conceived work by an old Gnostic philosopher, and we stand astonished, marvelling at the boldness of the speculations, dazzled by the richness of the thought, touched by the depth of soul of the author. This is not, like the Pistis Sophia, the product of declining Gnosticism, but dates from a period when Gnostic genius, like a mighty eagle, left the world behind it and soared in wide and ever wider circles towards pure light, towards pure knowledge, in which it lost itself in ecstasy.

"In one word, we possess in this Gnostic work, as regards age and contents, a work of the very highest importance, which takes us into a period of Gnosticism, and therefore of Christianity, of which very little knowledge has been handed down to us."

Finally, I wish to acknowledge my indebtedness to the scholarship of Mr G. R. S. Mead, whose labours in the field of Hellenistic Theology have to my mind received insufficient recognition, and whose admirable translations I have often used in the notes.

TRANSLATION

This is the Father of all Fathers, the God of all ... Gods, Lord of all Lords, Sonship of all Sons, Saviour of all Saviours, Invisible of all Invisibles, Infinity of all Infinities, Uncontainable of all Uncontainables, Beyond–the–Deep of all Beyond–the–Deeps, Space of all Spaces. This is the Spiritual Mind which existed before all Spiritual Minds, the Holy Place comprehending all Holy Places, the Good comprehending all Goods. This is the Seed of all good things. It is He who has brought them all forth, this Autophues or Being who has produced Himself, who existed before all the beings of the Pleroma which He Himself has brought forth, Who is in all time. This is that Ingenerable and Eternal One who has no name and who has all names; who was the first to know those of the Universe, who has looked upon those of the Universe, who has heard those of the Universe. He is mightier than all might, upon whose incomprehensible Face no one is able to gaze. Beyond all mind does He exist in His own Form, Solitary and Unknowable. The Universal Mystery is He, the Universal Wisdom, of all things the Beginning. In Him are all Lights, all Life, and all Repose. He is the Beatitude of which all in the Universe are in need, for that they might receive Him they are. All beings of the Universe does He behold within Himself, that One Uncontainable, who parts those of the Universe and receives them all into Himself. Without Him is nothing, for all the worlds exist in Him, and He is the boundary of them all. All of them has He enclosed, for in Him is all. No Space is there without Him, nor any Intelligence; for without that Only One there exists nothing. The Eternities (æons) contemplate His incomprehensibility which is within them all, but understand it not. They wonder at it because He limits them all. They strive towards the City in which is their Image. In this City [1] it is that they move and live [and have their true being]; for it is the House of the Father, the Robe of the Son, and the Power of the Mother, the Image of the Pleroma. He is the First Father of all things, the First Eternal, the King of those that None can Touch; He in whom all things lose themselves, He who has given all things form within Himself; the Space which has grown from Itself, He who is born of Himself, the Abyss of all being, the Great and True One who is in the Deep; He in whom the Fullnesses (Pleromata) did come, and even they are silent before Him. They have not named Him, because Unnamable and beyond thought is He, that First Fount whose Eternity stretches through all Spaces, that First Tone [2] whereby all things hearken and understand. He it is whose limbs make a myriad, myriad Powers, and every Power is a being in itself.

The Second Space is that which is called Creator, Father, Word, Source, Mind, Man, Eternal, Infinite. He is the Pillar, the Overseer, the Father of all. He it is upon whose Head the æons form a crown, darting forth their rays. The Fullness of His Countenance is unknown to the external worlds who seek His Face, for evermore yearning to know It; for unto them His Word has run forth and to behold It is their desire. The Light of His Eyes pierces to the spaces of the external Pleroma and the Word goes forth from His Mouth to those who dwell in Heaven and to those who dwell beneath it. The hairs of His Head are the number of the Hidden Worlds, and the Features of His Face are the type of the Eternities; the hairs of His Beard are the number of the External Worlds. The stretching out of His Hands is the manifestation of the Cross [3]. The strain of the Cross is the Ennead, the Ninefold Being. He who springs up [? or is nailed] to the right and to the left of the Cross is the Man whom no man can comprehend. He is the Father, the Fount whence Silence wells, He for whom the Quest is everywhere. The Father is He from whom went forth the Monad and the Spark of

Light, and before this all the Worlds were dark nothings. For it is that Spark of Light which has placed all things in the rays of Its Splendour, so they have received Knowledge [Gnosis], Life, Hope, Peace, Faith, Love and Resurrection, the Second Birth and the Seal. Now these things are the Ennead, the Ninefold Being, which has come forth from the Father without beginning, who alone has been His own Father and His own Mother, whose Pleroma surrounds the twelve [4] Deeps.

The First Deep is the Universal Fount, from whom all fountains have gone forth.

The Second Deep is the Universal Wisdom, from whom all wisdoms have gone forth.

The Third Deep is the Universal Mystery, from whom all mysteries have gone forth.

The Fourth Deep is the Universal Gnosis, from whom all Gnoses have gone forth.

The Fifth Deep is the Universal Purity, from whom all purity has gone forth.

The Sixth Deep is the Silence that contains all silences.

The Seventh Deep is the Universal Super–essential Essence, from whom all essences have gone forth.

The Eighth Deep is the Forefather from whom and by whom all forefathers exist.

The Ninth Deep is the All–Father, Self–Father, in whom is the All–Paternity of those who are Self–Fathers of the all.

The Tenth Deep is the All–Power, from whom all powers have gone forth.

The Eleventh Deep is that in which there is the First Invisible, from whom have gone forth all invisibles.

The Twelfth Deep is the Truth, from whence all truths have sped forth.

Now the Truth[5] which envelops all things is the Image of the Father, the End of all things. She is the Mother of all Eternities, who surrounds all Deeps, the Monad beyond knowledge who cannot be known, without seal–mark and having all seal–marks within, blessed for ever and ever. To the Father Ineffable, Inconceivable, Unthinkable, Unchangeable, all things have been made like in their being. They rejoiced and have been filled with life–giving powers. They engendered myriads and myriads and myriads of æons, and in Joy, because they rejoiced with the Father [6].

These are the worlds from which the Cross upsprang, and from their incorporeal limbs the Man has come forth. It is the Father and Fount of all being who has produced the limbs.

Now from the Father are all names [7], whether Ineffable One, or Incorruptible One, or Invisible One, or Simple One, or Solitary One, or Powerful One, or Triple–powered One, or the names that in Silence alone are named. In the Father are they all, and He it is whom the Outer Worlds behold [as men behold] the starry sky at night. Even as men [so gazing into the night] desire to see the Sun, so do the Outer Worlds desire to see Him because of the very Invisibility which surrounds Him. He it is who to the æons gives life perpetually, and by His Word hath the Indivisible ... the Monad in order to know it. For it is by His Word that the Holy Pleroma exists. This is the Father, the Second Creator, by the breath of whose Mouth Providence (Pronoia) has been in travail of those who were not, and it is by His Will that they are.... This is the Father, Ineffable, Unspeakable, Beyond Knowledge, Invisible, Immeasurable, Infinite. He has produced those that are in Him within Himself. The Thought of His Greatness has He brought forth from non–being that He might make them to be. Incomprehensible is He in His limbs. A Space has He made for His limbs that they might dwell in Him and know Him for their Sire. From His First Thought [8] has He made them come forth, and she has become a Space for them and given them being....

In this wise has He created the Temple of the Pleroma. At the four gates of the [Temple of] the Pleroma are four Monads, a Monad at each gate, and six Supporters at each gate, in all four and twenty Supporters, and four and twenty myriads of powers at each gate, nine Enneads at each gate, ten Decads at each gate, twelve Dodecads at each gate, and five Pentads of Powers at each gate. At each gate there is an Overseer of triple aspect having countenances Ingenerable, True, and Ineffable. Of these faces one gazes upon the external æons without the gate; another beholds Setheus, and the third looks upward to the Sonship contained in every Monad. There it is that Aphredon is discovered with his twelve Holy Ones and the Forefather, and in that Space abides also Adam, the Man of the Light, with his three hundred æons. There also is the Perfect Mind. All these surround a Basket [9] that knows no death. The Ineffable face of the Overseer, who is the Warden of the Holy Place, gazes into the Holy of Holies upon the Boundless One. Now this Warden has faces twain. One is disclosed from the side of the Deep, the other from the side of the Overseer called the Child (or Servant). For there is a Deep [within the Holy of Holies] which is named "Light" (10), or "He who gives the Light," and in this Abyss there is concealed an Alone–begotten Son. He it is who manifests the Three Powers, who is mighty amongst all Powers.

This (? the Holy of Holies) is the Indivisible One, [the atom—Body or Church] that can never be divided, in whom the All is discovered, because all powers are hers.

He who is the Triple Power has three faces, an Aphredonian face that is called Aphredon Pexos, in which is found a latent Only–begotten One.

When the (?) Idea comes out of the Deep, Aphredon takes the Thought to conduct her to the Alone–begotten of Alone–begottens, to lead her to the Child, so that she may be brought to the Space of the Triple Power for self–perfecting, and be escorted in the Space of the Five Ingenerables.

There is also another Space called the Deep, where there are three Paternities. In the first thereof is Kalupto, the Hidden God. In the Second Paternity there are Five Trees, and in the midst of them an altar. An Alone–begotten Word stands upon the altar, having the twelve countenances of the Mind of all things, and before him are the prayers of all beings placed. The Universe rejoices over him because he has manifested himself. He it is that the Invisible World has struggled to know, and it is on his account that the Man has appeared. In the Third Paternity is Silence and the Fount which twelve Anointed Ones contemplate, beholding themselves therein. In him are also found Love and the Universal Mind and furthermore the Universal Mother from whom has gone forth that Ennead whose names are Protia, Pantia, Pangenia, Loxophania, Loxogenia, Loxokrateia, Loia, and Iouel. She is the First Beyond Knowledge, the Mother of the Ennead, who completes a Decad, come forth from the Monad of the Unknowable.

Following there is another Space, more stretched out, where is hidden a great treasure which the Universe surrounds. [This Space] is the Immeasurable Deep where is an altar whereon three Powers are gathered: a Solitary being, an Unknowable being, and an Infinite being, in the midst of whom is revealed a Sonship called the Anointed Glorifier. This is he who glorifies everyone and impresses upon him the seal of the Father, who brings everybody into the eternity of the First Father who is the One, He for whose sake all is and without whom nothing is. Now this Anointed One has twelve faces, visages Unbounded, Uncontainable, Ineffable, Simple, Imperishable, Solitary, Unknowable, Invincible, Thrice–powerful, Unshakable, Ingenerable, and Pure. These Spaces, where are these twelve founts, named Founts of Reasons, full of eternal life, are called Deeps as well as the Twelve Countenances, because they have received in them all Spaces of Paternity on behalf of the Pleromata and the Fruit which the Pleroma emanated, who is Christ who has received the Pleroma in Himself.

Beyond all these Spaces comes the Deep of Setheus. This he who is in them all and is surrounded by twelve Paternities, even in the midst of these is he. Each Paternity has three faces. The first of them is an Indivisible One, and three faces has he, Infinite, Invisible,

and Ineffable faces. The Second Father has Uncontainable, Unshakable, and Incorruptible faces. The Third Father has faces Beyond Knowledge, Imperishable, and Aphredonian. The Fourth Father has a countenance of Silence, a face of Founts, and a visage Impalpable. The Fifth Father has Solitary, Omnipotent, and Ingenerable faces. The Sixth Father has the face of an All–Father, the face of a Self–Father, and the face of a Forefather. The Seventh Father has countenances of Universal Mystery, of Universal Wisdom and Universal Origin. Visages has the Eighth Father of Light, Repose, and Resurrection. The Ninth Father has faces Knowable, First Visible, and... The Tenth Father has Triple–fleshed, Adamic, and Pure faces. The Eleventh Father has faces Triple–powered, Perfect, and Sparkling. The Twelfth Father has a face of Truth, a face of Fore–thought, and a face of After–thought. These are the twelve Paternities which encircle Setheus. [Their faces] make in all a [mystic] number thirty–six. These are they from whom those of the exterior have received a seal–mark, that is why they glorify them for evermore[11]. In that Space there are yet twelve other paternities who encircle the head [of Setheus] and support a crown there. They dart out rays upon the surrounding worlds by the Grace of the Alone–begotten Word, concealed in him, He that is sought for.

[*The passage enclosed within brackets has been so mutilated by the Coptic scribe that what follows is of the nature of a paraphrase rather than of a translation:*—(As to the mysteries of the Word that are so much beyond us, it is not possible to describe them otherwise than as follows. Not possible for us, that is. It is impossible to describe Him as He really is with a tongue of flesh. There are glories too exalted for descriptions moved by thought and for intuition that comes through symbols, except one finds a master who is a kinsman of the deathless race yonder. From such an one can be learned something of the Spaces from whence he came; for he finds the root of all things. The mighty powers of the great æons of the Power that was in Marsanes have said in adoration, "Who is he who hath seen aught in the presence of His Face?" That is because thus does He manifest Himself [? the Alone to the Alone], Nicotheos has spoken of Him [the Alone–begotten] and seen Him, for he is one of these. He [Nicotheos] said, "The Father exists exalted above all the perfect." Nicotheos has revealed the Invisible and the perfect Triple–power. All perfect men have seen Him, they have declared Him and have given Him glory with their own lips)[12] .] That is the Alone–begotten Word hidden in Setheus, He who is called the Dark Ray[13], for it is the excess of His light alone that is darkness. Setheus reigns by Him.

The Alone–begotten holds in His right hand twelve Paternities, the types of the twelve Apostles[14], while in His left hand are thirty Powers. Each of them emanates twelve two-faced æons after the type of Setheus. One of these faces beholds the Deep which is in the Interior [of the Temple of the Pleroma]; the other looks without upon the Triple–Power. Each of the Paternities in His right hand emanates three hundred and sixty–five powers, according to the word that David spake, saying, "I will cherish the crown of the year in Thy Righteousness." For all these Powers encircle the Alone–begotten Son as a crown, illuminating the æons with the light of the Alone–begotten, as it is written, "In Thy light shall we see light." And the Alone–begotten is lifted up upon [the powers], as again it is written, "The Chariot of God is a myriad of multiplications"; and again, "There are millions of beings who rejoice; the Lord is in them"[15].

This is He who dwells in the Monad in Setheus, which comes from the place concerning which one does not ask, "Where is it?" She comes from Him who is before these Fullnesses. From the One and Only, even from Him has come forth the Monad, as a ship laden with all good things, or as a full field planted with every manner of tree, or as a city filled with men of every race and with all the statues of the king. Thus it is with the Monad where the Whole is found.

Upon her head twelve Monads form a crown; each has emanated another twelve. Ten Decads encircle her neck, nine Enneads are about her heart, and seven Hebdomads are under her feet, and each has emanated a Hebdomad. The firmament which surrounds her is like a tower with twelve gates, and at every gate are twelve myriads of powers; archangels are they called, or angels. This is the metropolis of the Alone–begotten Son[16].

Now it is of the Alone–begotten that Phosilampes[17] has said, "Before all things is He." He it is who has come forth from the Infinite; He who has engendered Himself there and has no seal nor form and has given birth to Himself. This is He who is come forth from the Ineffable One, the Immeasurable One, who truly is, and in whom is found all that truly is, who is the Father Incomprehensible. He is in His Alone–begotten Son, while the All reposes in the Ineffable and Unspeakable King, whom none can move and whose Divinity no one can declare, whose kingdom is not of this world. Meditating upon Him, Phosilampes has said, "Through Him is That–which–really–is and That–which–really–is–not, through which the Hidden–which–really–is and the Manifest–which–really–is–not exists."

He is the true Alone–begotten God, and all the Fullnesses (Pleromata) know that it is by Him that they have become gods and that they have become rulers in this name—God. This is He of whom John has said, "In the beginning was the Word, and the Word was in God and the Word was God, and without Him was not anything made. That which was made in Him was Life."

The Alone–begotten is found in the Monad, dwelling in her as in a city, and the Monad is in Setheus as a concept, and Setheus dwells in the Temple as King and as God. He is the Word creative, who has commanded the Fullnesses to labour; the Creative Mind after the order of God the Father, whom all creation worships as God and Lord, to whom all is subjected.

The Fullnesses wonder at Him [Setheus] because of His beauty and grace. Around His head those of the Inner Spaces of the Universe form a crown; those of the external spaces are beneath His feet, while those of the middle spaces encircle Him, all praising Him and saying, "Holy, Holy, Holy, AAA, HHH, EEE, III, OOO, YYY, +ÔÔÔ+"—that is to say, "Thou art the Living One of Living Ones, Holy of Holies, Being of Beings, Father of Fathers, God of Gods, Lord of Lords, Space of Spaces"[18]. They praise Him, saying, "Thou art the House and the Dweller in the House." They praise Him, saying unto the Son concealed in Him, "Thou art: Thou art, O Alone–begotten, Light and Life and Grace."

When Setheus sent the Light–Spark from the Indivisible [Body], it burned and gave light to all the Space of the Temple of the Pleromata. And they, beholding the light of the Spark, rejoiced and uttered myriads and myriads of praises in honour of Setheus and of the Light–Spark which was manifested, seeing that in it were all their images, and they fashioned the Spark among themselves as a Man light–giving and true. They named Him "Pantomorphos," and Pure, and Unshakable, and all the eternities also called him "All–powered." He is the Servant of the Æons and serves the Fullnesses[19]. And the Father sealed the Man His Son in their interior so that they might know Him interiorly, and the Word moved them to contemplate the Invisible One beyond knowledge, and they gave glory to this One and Only One, to the Concept which is in Him and to the Intelligible Word, praising these Three who are One, because by Him have they been made essential beings. The Father took their total image and made of it a City or a Man and figured in Him all those of the Pleroma, that is to say, all the powers. Each one of them knew his image in the City, for everyone of the myriads of glories found himself in the Man or City of the Father which is in the Pleroma. The Father took His radiant glory and made thereof an outer vesture for the Man....

He created in Him the type of the Temple of the Pleroma. He made His shoulders, which came out one from the other, after the type of those hundred myriads of powers, less four myriads. He created His fingers and toes like the two Decads, the hidden Decad and the manifest Decad. He created His organ like the Monad concealed in Setheus. He created the great reins like Setheus. He made His breast like the Interior of the Temple and His feet after the type of the Solitary and Unknowable Ones who serve the Pleroma, rejoicing with those that rejoice. He made His limbs after the type of the Deep which encloses three hundred and sixty–five Paternities after the type of the Paternities. He fashioned His hair after the type of the Worlds of the Pleroma and filled Him with wisdom like the Universal Wisdom, and filled Him with interior mystery like Setheus and with exterior mystery like the Indivisible [Body]. Incomprehensible created He Him like the Incomprehensible One, who is in every Space, unique in the Pleroma. His sides created He after the type of the Four Gates and His two thighs after the type of the Myriarchs who are to the right and left, and His members after the type of those who go forth and those who enter. He created companions surrounding Him after the type of concealed mysteries....

[This was the Man or City that the Pleromata beheld in the Light–Spark and saw their likenesses therein. They fashioned the Man called Pantomorphos in His likeness, or clothed the Light–Spark in the Star–body.]

The Indivisible Point sent the Light–Spark without the Pleroma, and [He] descended [as] the Triple–Power into the Spaces of Autogènes, the Self–generated One, and [these Spaces] beheld the grace of the Eternities of Light which had been given unto them, and they rejoiced because that–which–is had come among them.

Then they opened the firmaments and the Light descended below to the lower regions and to those who were without form, having no [true] likeness. It was thus that they got the likeness of the Light for themselves. Some rejoiced because the Light had come to them, and that they had been made rich thereby. Others mourned because they were made poor and that which [they thought] they had was taken away from them. Thus came He, who went forth full of grace, and was taken captive with a captivity[20] . A light of glory was given to the æons who had received the Spark, and guardian spirits were sent to them who are Gamanel, Etrempsouchos, and Agramas, and those who are with them. They bring help to those who have believed in the Spark of Light.

Now in the Space of the Indivisible Atom are twelve Founts, above which are the twelve Paternities who surround the Indivisible [Queen] like Deeps or like Skies and make for Her a crown in which is every kind of life: all modes of Triple–powered life, of Uncontainable life, of Infinite life, of Ineffable life, of Silent life, of Unknown life, of Solitary life, of Unshakable life, of First–manifested life, of Self–born life, of True life. All is therein. Every species is in it, all Gnoses and every power which has received the Light, yea, all Mind manifests itself therein. This is the Crown which the Father of the Universe has placed upon the Indivisible [Queen] with three hundred and sixty–five kinds in it, brilliant and filling the Universe with an incorruptible and unfailing light. This is the Crown which crowns all dominion, the Crown that the Deathless pray for, and by it and in it they will become Invisible Ones [in the world beyond manifestation] on the Day of Joy, who by the Will of the Inscrutable One have from the first been manifested, that is to say, Protia, Pantia, Pangenia, and their company. Then shall all the Invisible Eternities receive from Him their crown, so that they may cast themselves among the Invisibles, who shall receive there their crown in the Crown of the Indivisible [Queen], and the Universe shall receive its perfection of incorruption. Because of this it is that those who have taken bodies pray, desiring to abandon the body that they may receive the crown laid up for them in the Incorruptible Eternity.

This is the Indivisible [Queen and Mother], the first æon of all, who has been given all good things by Him who is above all good things, and she has been given the Immeasurable Deep, wherein are found innumerable Paternities, whereof is the Ennead without seal–mark and having in her the seal–marks of all creatures, and by whom the Ennead emanates twelve Enneads. She [the Indivisible Mother it is] who has in the midst a Space called "The Land productive of Gods," or "The Land which gives birth to the Gods"[21]. This is the land of which it has been said, "He who ploughs his soil shall be satisfied with bread and he shall make large his threshing floor," and also, "The Master of the Field, when they shall plough it, shall possess all good things." And all those Powers which are in this land which brought forth the God have received the Crown. That is why they know, because of the Crown upon their heads, if the Inheritors of the Kingdom of Light have [? in truth] been born from the Indivisible Body or not: that is, from Her who is the Universal Mother[22]. She has within Her seven Wisdoms, nine Enneads, ten Decads, and in the midst a great Basket is revealed. A mighty Invisible [Hierarch] stands above it with a mighty Ingenerable [Hierarch] and a mighty Unbounded [Hierarch], each one triple–countenanced, and the prayer, the blessing, and the hymn of creatures are given place in this Basket which is in the midst of the Universal Mother, in the midst of the seven Wisdoms, in the midst of the nine Enneads, and in the midst of the ten Decads. For all these [creatures] stand upright in the Basket, made perfect by the Fruit of the Æons, He who has been ordained for them by the Alone–begotten concealed in the Indivisible [Atom]. He [the Fruit of the Æons] has a Fount before Him surrounded by twelve Holy Ones, each one wearing a Crown on his head and having twelve powers, who surround Him within, praising the Alone–begotten king and crying, "It is because of Thee that we ray forth glory, and it is by Thee that we behold the Father of the Universe, AAA, +OOO+[23], and the Mother of all the good, She who is hidden in every space"—that is to say, the contriving thought (Epinoia) of all the Eternities, the conceiving thought of all gods and of all lords—"She is the Gnosis of all the Unseen beings, and Thy Image is the Mother of all the Boundless Ones, the Power of all the Infinites."

Praising the Alone–begotten, they cry, "It is because of Thy Image[24] that we have seen Thee, that we have run to Thee, that we have clung to

Thee, that we have received the Incorruptible Crown which is known through Her. Glory be to Thee, O Alone–begotten, for ever and ever."

Then together do they all say Amen.

For [? Jesus, the Fruit of the Æons] became a Body of Light, He crossed the Æons of the Indivisible [Body] until He came to the Alone–begotten who is in the Monad and who dwells in Peace and Solitude. He received the Grace of the Alone–begotten—that is to say, His Christhood or His Perfecting. Also He received the Eternal Crown. He is the Father of all Light–Sparks, the chief of all Immortal bodies, and this is He for whose sake resurrection is given to the body[25].

But besides the Indivisible Queen and besides her Ennead without seal–mark, in which is found all seal–marks, there are three other Enneads, of which each emanates nine Enneads. In the first of these is revealed a Basket round which three Fathers are gathered: an Infinite Father, an Ineffable Father, and an Uncontainable Father. In the middle of the second Ennead is a Basket, and three Fathers are there: an Invisible Father, an Ingenerable Father, and an Unshakable Father. In the third Ennead is also revealed a Basket which encloses three Paternities: a Solitary Father, an Unknown Father, and a Triple–Powered Father. It is through these that the Universe has known God. They ran towards Him and have engendered an innumerable multitude of æons, and in each Ennead they offered myriads and myriads of praises.

In each of these Enneads there is a Monad, and in each Monad a Space called "Incorruptible": that is to say, "Holy ground." There is a Fount in the ground of each of these Monads, and myriads and myriads of Powers who have received on their heads a crown of the Crown of the Triple–Power. In the middle of these Enneads and of these Monads is an immeasurable Deep towards which all the Universe looks, those that are internal as well as those that are external, having above it twelve Paternities, each surrounded by thirty Powers.

The First Paternity is a face of the Infinite One, and thirty infinite powers surround him.

The Second paternity is a face of the Invisible One and thirty invisible powers surround him.

The Third paternity is a face of the Uncontainable One, and thirty uncontainable powers surround him.

The Fourth paternity is a face of the Invincible One and thirty invincible powers surround him.

The Fifth Paternity is a face of the All–powerful One and thirty Ill–powerful powers surround him.

The Sixth paternity is a face of the All–Wise One and thirty all–wise powers surround him.

The Seventh paternity is a face of the Unknown One and thirty unknown powers surround him.

The Eighth paternity is a face of the Solitary One and thirty solitary powers surround him.

The Ninth paternity is a face of the Ingenerable One, and thirty ingenerable powers surround him.

The Tenth paternity is a face of the Unshakable One and thirty unshakable powers surround him.

The Eleventh Paternity is a face of the Universal Mystery, and thirty universal mysteries surround him.

The Twelfth Paternity is a face of the Triple–Powered One, and thirty triple–powers surround him.

And in the midst of the Immeasurable Deep there are five Powers which are called by these ineffable names:

The first is called Love, and from her comes all love.

The second is called Hope, and it is by her that we hope in the Alone–begotten, the Son of God.

The third is called Faith, and it is by her that we believe the mysteries of the Ineffable One.

The fourth is called Gnosis, and it is by her that we know the First Father, Him because of whom we live that we may know Him. [Gnosis] the Mystery of Silence, who spake before all things, that which is hidden, the First Monad, for whom the Universe became being. It is upon the head of this Mystery that the three hundred and sixty–five substances form a crown like the hair of human kind, and the Temple of the Pleroma is as a stairway beneath her feet. This is the Gate of God[26].

The fifth is called Peace, and it is by her that we give Peace to all, to those within and to those without, for it is in her that all things have been created.

This is that Abyss Immeasurable in which is found three hundred and sixty–five Paternities, thanks to whom they have devised the year.

This is the Abyss which surrounds the Temple of the Pleroma, where is revealed the Triple–Power with his branches and his trees, and Mousanios and those which belong to him. There also is Aphredon and his twelve Holy Ones, and a Basket is in the midst of them. They come to carry in it the praises, the hymns, the prayers and supplications of the Mother of the Universe, the Mother of the (manifested?) worlds who is called Phanerios[27], and to give them a form, thanks to the twelve Holy Ones. They send them into the Pleroma of Setheus, by which act they call to mind those of the external world in which there is matter.

This is the Deep where the Triple–Power rayed out the splendours of His glory, after He had been to the Indivisible Mother and had received the Grace of the One Beyond Knowledge, by which He had gotten such a Sonship that the Fullnesses were not able to stand upright before Him because of the excess of His light and brilliancy thereof. The whole Pleroma was troubled, the Abyss and all it contained was moved, and the [æons] fled to the world of the Mother [Phanerios], and the Mystery ordained that the veils of the æons should be drawn until the Overseer had established them once more. And the Overseer established the æons once more, as it is written, "He has established the Earth, and it shall not be moved," and again, "The Earth has been dissolved and all that therein is"[28].

Then the Triple–Power went forth: the Son was concealed in him, and the crown of confirmation was upon his head, making myriads and myriads of glories. They cried, "Make straight the way of the Lord and receive the grace of God: every æon which is empty shall be filled with the grace of the Alone–begotten Son."

The Father holy and all–perfect stood above the Deep Immeasurable. It is in Him that all perfection is found, and in His fullness have we received grace. Then the world was established; it ceased to shake; the Father fashioned it so that it might nevermore be shaken, and the æon of the Mother remained full of those that were in it until the ordering came from the Mystery concealed in the First Father, He from whence came the Mystery; when His Son re–established the Universe once more in His Gnosis, that which re–enforms the Universe.

Then Setheus sent the Logos Demiourgos, having with him a multitude of Powers, wearing the crowns on their heads; and their crowns darted forth rays. The brilliancy of their bodies is as the life of the Space into which they are come; the word that comes out of their mouths is life Æonian, and the light that comes from their eyes is a rest for them; the movement of their hands is their flight to the place from whence they have come, and their gazing on their own faces is Gnosis of their interior nature; their going towards them is their return once more within; the stretching forth of their hands establishes them; the hearing of their ears is the intuition in their hearts; the union of their limbs is the regathering of the dispersal of Israel; their self–understanding is their contemplation of the Logos; the writing upon their fingers is the number which has gone forth, even as it is written, "He counteth the number of the Stars and calleth them all by their names."

And the whole union was made by the Logos Demiourgos with those who had come out of the turmoil that had been: altogether they became one and the same body, as it has been written, "They have all become one and the same body in this One and Only One." Then this Logos Demiourgos became a mighty God, Lord, Saviour, Christ, King, the Good, Father,

Mother. This is He whose work was good: He was glorified and became Father to those that believed: He became Law in Aphredonia and mighty.

Then went forth Pandelos [All–manifest]; she had a crown on her head, and she placed it upon them who had believed[29].

The Power of the Æons [? the Indivisible Queen, the Mother within the Pleroma] ordered the Hierarchy of the World of the Virgin Mother [Phaneia, the Mother without the Pleroma, she who brings into manifestation] according to the Order of the Inner Space. She placed in it the Light–Spark after the pattern of the Monad and placed therein the concealment which surrounds Him. She ordained the Propator after the Order of the Indivisible Body and the twelve Holy Ones which surround it, having crowns on their heads and seals of glory in their right hands, after the type found in the Indivisible Point. In the midst of these is Love; a face of the Triple–Power is in the Fount, and there is a Basket which twelve Paternities surround, in whom a Sonship is concealed.

She ordained the Autopator according to the order of the Ennead without seal–mark and gave him authority over all that is only self–fathered, and gave him a crown of all–glory and love, and Peace, Truth, and myriads of powers, so that he might gather together those who had been dispersed by the troubling which had taken place when the [Light Spark] went forth with joy. As for the Prince of the Universe, he who has the triple–power to make alive and to destroy, she ordained the Son Protogennetor after the order of the Triple–Power. She gave him a ninefold Ennead and five tenfold Decads, and that he might have power to accomplish the warfare imposed upon him, she gave him the first–fruits of the Sonship concealed in her that he might be able to become a Triple–Power. He received the Vow of the Sonship because the Universe[30] had been sold [? into slavery], and took upon him the warfare entrusted to him and made arise all that was pure in matter. A world made he, an æon, a town; the world which is called "Incorruptibility" and "Jerusalem." It is also called "The New Earth," and "Self–Perfect," and "Without King." This earth is an earth that brings forth gods, a life–giving earth indeed. This is the earth that the Mother (? Phaneia) asked to have established. That is why she (? the Mother Above) has placed orders or hierarchy in this earth and has placed in it Providence and Love. This is the earth of which it has been written, "The earth which drank the rain a multitude of times": that is to say, which has multiplied the light in her multitudes and multitudes of times, since the (light) went forth until its return; that is to say, it is that from which the Man is named "Sensible." He is fashioned, He has been created according to the type of this earth, He who has been saved from His Self dispersion by the Protogennetor[31]. Because of that, the Father of all those of the Universe, He who has no [bridal] bed has sent [Him,? the Man] a crown bearing the names of all those of the Universe, whether Infinite or Ineffable, or Uncontainable, or Incorruptible, or Unknown, or Solitary, or All–powerful, or Indivisible. This is the crown of which it is written, "They gave it unto Solomon on the day of his exultation of heart."

The First Monad sent Him [the Man] an ineffable vesture which is all Light, all Life, all Love, all Hope, all Faith, all Wisdom, all Gnosis, all Truth, all Peace, all Witness, all Universal Mother, all Universal Mystery, all Fount, all Universal Perfection, all Invisible, all Unknown, all Infinite, all Ineffable, all Abyss, all Uncontainable, all Fullness, all Silence, all Unshakable, all Unengendered, all Universal Solitary, all Monad, all Ennead, all Dodecad, all Ogdoad, all Decad, all Hebdomad, all Hexad, all Pentad, all Tetrad, all Triad, all Dyad, all Monad. The whole Universe is in it, and the Universe has found itself therein and knows itself therein[29]. It gave light to all in its ineffable light, and it was given myriads and myriads of powers, so that the Universe might be established once and for all. It gathered together its skirts and gave them the form of a veil which surrounded it [the Universe] on every side. It poured itself over all things, raised them up and divided them according to the Hierarchies, according to the orders, and according to Providence. Then that–which–was separated itself from that–which–was–not, and that–which–was–not was the evil manifested in matter; and the Robe of Power severed that–which–was from that–which–was–not. That–which–was it called Æonian, and that–which–was–not it called Hyle (matter). It separated by the Midst that–which–was from that–which–was–not, and placed veils between these twain. It placed purifying powers, so that they might purge them and make them clean. It gave in this manner an order to that–which–is and made of the Mother the chief. It gave it ten æons, and each æon has a myriad powers; there is also a Monad and an Ennead in each æon. The [Robe of Power] placed in her [? Phaneia] an Universal Motherhood and therewith a Power that had hitherto been concealed therein, so that none knew thereof. [? The Robe] placed a great Basket, above which stand three Powers, an Ingenerable One, an Unshakable One, and the Great Pure One. It gave to [? the world order] the twelve other Powers who have received the crown and who surround it. It gave it also the Seven Stratelatai[32], who have the seal of the All–completing [Panteleios], and have on their heads crowns in which there are twelve stones of Adamant, which come from Adam, the Man of Light.

[The Robe of Power] established the Propator in all the æons of the Mother of [the Manifestation] of all things, and gave him the full power of Paternity, and Powers to obey him as Father and as First Father of all that exists. It placed upon his head a crown of twelve kinds; it gave him a Power which is Triple–powered and All–powered; it gave him Sonship and myriads and myriads of Glories. It turned the Pleroma towards him and gave him power to make live and to destroy. It gave him a power of the æon so that he might manifest it, with the myriads and myriads of out–rayed Glories, like the other æons that were with him. The Power which has been given to the Propator is called Protophanes, because he is the first to be manifested, and Agennetos, because no one has engendered him. Also Ineffable and "Without Name" is he

called, and also Autogenes and Autotheletos, because he has manifested himself by his own will. Yet again is he named Autoloxastos, for he manifested himself with the Glories that were his. Yet again is he termed Invisible, for he is hidden and none can see him.

Now [the Robe of Power] gave unto the Propator another Power, that which since the beginning has caused the Light–Spark to appear in this Space, and who is named with names Holy and All–perfecting. Who is Protia, that is to say, the First, and is also called Pantia—she who is found in all—and Pangenia—she who has brought forth all in the world—and Loxogenia—she who has brought Glory to birth—and Loxophania—Manifester of Glory—and Loxokrateia—she who has dominion over Glory—and Arsenogenia—she who brings forth males—and Loia—of which the interpretation is God with us—and Jouel—of which the interpretation is God for ever—she it is who has ordained that these Powers should appear whose name is called Phaneia, of which the translation is Manifestation. The angel who has appeared with them is he whom the Glories name Loxogenes and Loxophanes, of which the interpretation is "He who engenders Glory" and "He who manifests Glory," for he is one of those Glories who stand about that mighty power called Loxokrator, because in his manifestation he has had dominion over the great Glories.

Such are the Powers that were given to the Propator when he was placed in the æon of the Mother, and myriads and myriads of Glories, Angels, Archangels, and Liturgies were bestowed upon him, so that they might serve him, those of matter. They gave him power over everything. He made for himself a mighty æon and placed therein a mighty Pleroma and a great temple and all the Powers that he had taken and placed within himself, and he rejoiced with them, bringing forth his creatures again according to the commandment of the Father hidden in the Silence, Who had sent him these riches; and the Crown of Fatherhood was given to him because he had been made the Father of all those who came after him. Then he cried out and said, "My children, with whom I travail again until Christ be formed in you"; and again he cried, "Yea, I would set beside a holy virgin an only husband, Christ."

But when he had seen the Grace that the Father in secret had given unto him (that is Himself a Propator), he wished to turn the Universe to the Father in secret, for it is His will that the Universe should turn to Him. And when the Mother saw all the grandeurs which had been given unto her Propator, she rejoiced greatly, she exulted; that is why she said, "My heart has rejoiced and my tongue has been in exultation." Then she cried to the Power Infinite who stands hard by the æon of the Father, that mighty Power of Glory that the Glories call Trigenielos [33], that is to say, Three Engendered, and who is named also Trigenes and also Harmes. She prayed also unto Him who is concealed in every Space that He would send him the Mother of Him who has withdrawn Himself. The Father in secret sent him the Mystery who reclothes all the æons like the Glories who form the Crown Panteles, that is to say, of Perfection, so that he [the Propator] might place the Crown upon the head of the Indivisible [Body] hidden within her, Incorruptible and Unengendered. With [her He sent] the mighty Power which is in her company, she who is called Arsenogenia, who replenishes all the æons of Glory. Thus from him shall the Universe receive the Crown.

Then she established the Autopator Father and Æonian One; and gave unto him the æon of the Concealed One in which are found all things, such as species, faces, images, forms, questions, dissemblances, and changes, that which counts and that which is counted, that which thinks and that which is thought. She made a vesture thereof over all which is in him, so that he might give to him who asked him. She gave unto him ten Powers, and nine Enneads, five Æons, and she gave unto him Light; and that gave him power over all secret things, so that he might show mercy to those who had fought, who had towards the æon fled from matter, leaving it behind them. They have fled to the æon of the Autopator; they have made their own the

promise which has been promised by Him who said, "He who forsakes father, mother, brother, sister, wife, children, and riches, and takes up his cross and follows Me, shall receive the promises that I have promised unto him, and I will give unto them the Mystery of the Father in Secret, because they have loved that which was truly theirs and have fled from him who pursues them with injustice." And he [Autopator] gave them Glory, Joy, Exaltation, Jubilation, Peace, Hope, Faith, Love, and the Truth which changes not. This is the Ennead with which he rewarded those that fled from matter; they became happy, they became perfect, they knew God and the Truth, they comprehended the Mystery which works in the Man; for what cause He has revealed Himself, that they might see Him, for He is in truth Invisible; and for their sakes He has revealed in words His Logos, so that they might know Him and become gods and perfect.

When the Mother established the Protogennetor as her son, she gave unto him the Power of the Sonship; she gave unto him armies of Angels and Archangels; she gave unto him twelve Powers who served him; she gave unto him a robe to consummate all things in him, for in it is revealed every kind of body: the body of fire, the body of water, the body of air [? spirit], the body of earth, the body of wind, the body angelic, the body archangelic, the body of Powers, the body of Dominions, the body of Gods, the body of Lords—in a word, every kind of body, so that nothing might hinder him from mounting into the heights or descending into the depths of Noun. This is the Protogennetor to whom those of the internal and external Spaces have promised all things that please him, and it is he who separates all matter; for he brooded over it like a bird who stretches her wings over her eggs. Even thus did the Protogennetor unto matter, and made myriads and myriads of species and kinds come forth. When Matter was warmed she produced the multitudes of Powers that were in her, and he separated them into species and kinds. He gave them a law to love one another, to honour God and to praise Him, and to seek for Him, who He is and what

He is, and to wonder at the place from whence they had come forth, so narrow and so sad, and not to return thither again, but to follow him who had given them a law and made them come out of the darkness; of Matter, their Mother. He had said to them, "Let there be light." For they did not know if there were such a thing as light or not. Then he gave them the command not to hurt one another, and left them to go to the Space of the Mother of the Universe beside the Propator and the Autopator, so that together they might draw up those who had come forth from matter.

Then the Mother of the Universe[34], the Propator, the Autopator, the Protogennetor, and the Powers of the æon of the Mother sang a great hymn to the One and Only God, praising Him and saying:

"Thou alone art Boundless, Thou only art the Deep, Thou only art the Incomprehensible One, for Thou art He whom all beings seek and [without Thy grace] find Thee not, for none can know Thee against Thy will, and none can praise Thee against Thy will. For Thy will only is a Space for Thee, for nothing can contain Thee who art the Space for all. Thee I pray that Thou mayest give an holy ordering to those of the World, that Thou mayest dispose my offspring according to Thy will. Grieve not my offspring, for never has anything been grieved by Thee; yet no one knows Thy Counsel. Of Thee all beings of the Inner and the Outer Worlds have need, Thou only Incomprehensible, Thou only beyond All vision, beyond All mind. Thou only hast given character to all creatures and hast manifested them in Thyself. Of that which is not yet manifested art Thou the Creator, and Thou alone dost know these things, for we know them not [of ourselves]. Thou alone revealest them unto us [through Symbols and Images], so that we may supplicate Thee on their behalf, so that Thou mayest make them manifest, and we may know them [as they are in themselves apart from all Symbols] by Thy Grace alone. Thou alone hast raised up the Secret Worlds to Thyself, so that they might know Thee, for Thou hast given unto them the boon of knowing

Thee, for Thou hast given birth unto them from Thy Incorporeal Body and hast taught them that from Thy Self–productive Mind Thou hast the Man brought forth in Contemplation and in a perfect Concept, yea, even the Man brought forth by Mind to whom Contemplation has given a form. Thou it is who hast bestowed all good things upon the Man, and He weareth them like vestures. He putteth them on like garments and wrappeth Himself with Creation as with a robe[35]. This Man is He whom all the Universe yearneth to know, for Thou alone it is who hast ordained unto the Man to manifest Himself, so that in Him Thou mightest be known and that all might learn that it is Thou who hast brought Him forth and that Thou art manifested according to Thy Will.

"Thee do I invoke, and I pray Thee, O Father of all Fatherhood, Lord of all Lords, to give an holy ordering unto my kinds and to my offspring, that I may rejoice in Thy Name and in Thy goodness, O Thou Sole King, O Thou who changest not. Bestow upon me from Thy goodness, and I will make known unto my children that Thou art their Saviour"[36].

When the Mother had finished praying to the Boundless One Beyond Knowledge, who fills the whole Universe and gives life unto all, He heard her and those with her, for all of them were His own, and He sent unto her a Power who came forth from the Man whom they desired to behold.

From Being Unbounded came forth the Infinite Spark of Light, at whom all the æons wondered, asking themselves where He had been concealed before manifesting Himself from the Infinite Father, He from whom the Universe was manifested and who was latent therein. The Powers of the Secret Worlds followed Him when they were manifested and came into the Temple of the Pleroma. He hid Himself amidst the Powers who came forth from the Father in Secret[37]. He made a world and bore it into the Temple. Then the Powers of the Pleroma beheld Him and loved Him and praised Him in hymns ineffable, unspeakable to tongues of mortal flesh, and good to dream of in the heart of man. He received their hymn and made a veil surrounding their world like a wall; then went He to the borders of the Universal Mother [without] and stood above the Universal Æon [38]. The Universe was moved at the presence of the Lord of the whole Earth; the Æon was troubled and in suspense because it had seen that which it knew not. The King of Glory was seated, He divided matter into two halves and into two parts[39]. He fixed the borders of each part and taught them that they came from One Father and from One Mother. To those who ran unto Him and adored Him He gave the place at the right hand, and gave them Life for ever and ever and Immortality. He named the place on the right "The Land of Life," and the place on the left "The Land of Death"; He named the Earth on the right "The Earth of Light," and the Earth on the left "The Earth of Darkness"; He named the Earth on the right "The Earth of Repose," and the Earth on the left "The Earth of Sorrow." He placed boundaries between them and veils, so that they might not see each other; He gave many Glories to those who had adored Him and gave them dominion over those who had resisted and opposed Him. He extended the World of the Right into many places and placed them [who followed Him] in each hierarchy, in each æon, in each world, in each heaven, in each firmament, in many heavens, in each region, in each space, in each receptacle. He gave them [who had followed Him] laws and delivered unto them commandments, saying, "Keep My sayings and I will give unto you eternal life; I will send Powers unto you, yea, I will strengthen you with mighty spirits, and will give unto you the dominion of your desire: no one shall hinder your will, and you shall bring forth æons, worlds, and heavens. When the intellectual spirits come to dwell in you then shall ye become gods, then shall ye know that ye came forth from God, and then shall ye behold Him within yourselves, in your eternities shall He dwell."

These words spake the Lord of the Universe unto them; then He withdrew Himself from them and hid Himself from them. And those who had been the births of matter rejoiced that their thought had been accomplished; they rejoiced because they had come forth from the narrow and the sad. They prayed unto the Hidden Mystery, saying, "Give us power to create æons and worlds according to the word which Thou hast sworn unto Thy servants, for Thou alone art He who changest not, Thou alone art the Infinite and Boundless One, Thou only art unengendered, born of Thyself, Self–Father, Thou only art Unmoved and Unknowable, Thou only Silence art and Love and Fount of the Universe, Thou only art immaterial and hast no stain, ineffable in Thy generation and inconceivable in Thy manifestation. Hear us, then, O Father Incorruptible, Father Immortal, God of Hidden Beings, sole Light and Life, Alone beyond Vision, only Unspeakable, only Unstainable, only [Foundation] stone of Adamant[40], sole Primal Being, for before Thee nothing was. Hearken unto this prayer which we make unto Him who is concealed in every place. Hear us, send unto us incorporeal spirits that they may dwell with us and teach us that which Thou hast promised unto us; that they may dwell in us and that we may become bodies for them, for it is Thy will that it should thus be. So may it be. Give law unto our work and strengthen it according to Thy will and according to the order of the hidden æons; dispose us according to Thy will, for we are Thine"[41].

And He heard them and sent unto them discerning Powers which knew the order of those who are hidden. He established the Hierarchy like the Hierarchies above and according to the concealed order. They began from the base to the summit, so that the building might unite them to their companions. He created the aerial earth as a place of habitation for those who had come forth, so that they might dwell therein until the strengthening of those who are below them; then created He the true habitation in the interior of that, the place of repentance in the interior of that, the antitype of Aerodios; then the place of repentance in the interior of that, the antitype of Autogenes: in this place they baptise themselves in the name of Autogenes, who is God over them, and there are Powers placed in this place over the Fount of the Waters of Life which they make go forth. These are the names of the Powers who are over the Waters of Life: Michar and Micheu; and they baptise in the name of Barpharanges. In the interior of these Spaces are the æons of Sophia; in the interior of these Spaces is the True Truth, and Pistis Sophia is found there and also the pre–existent Jesus the Living, Aerodios and his twelve æons. There are placed in this space Sellao, Eleinos, Zogenetheles, Selmelche, and the Autogenes of the æons. There are placed in him four lights: Èleltheth, Daueithe, Oroiael ...[42].

He saith[43]:

O Alone–begotten of Light, I praise Thee.

O Light unengendered, I praise Thee. O Light self–begotten, I praise Thee.

O Forefather of Light, more excellent than every Forefather, I praise Thee.

O Light Invisible, who art before all those beyond vision, I praise Thee.

O Thought of Light surpassing all Thought, I praise Thee.

O God of Light above all gods, I praise thee.

O Gnosis of Light passing all knowledge, I praise Thee.

O Unknowable One of Light, who art beyond all that is unknown, I praise Thee.

O Hermit of the Light, who art above all solitaries, I praise Thee.

O All–mighty of the Light, more excellent than the all–powered ones, I praise Thee.

O Thou Thrice–mighty of the Light, greater than them of Triple–might, I praise Thee.

O Light that none can separate, for Thou dividest all light, I praise Thee.

O Thou Pure Light, surpassing all purity, I praise Thee.

O Thou who hast begotten [Thyself] in the absence of all generation, Whom none has engendered, I praise Thee.

O Fount of the Universality of Æons, I praise Thee. O True Self–born of Light, who art before all those self–born, I praise Thee.

O Thou True Unmoved One of Light, who by Thy Will movest all things, I praise Thee.

O Silence of all things, Silence of Light, I praise Thee. O Saviour of all things, Saviour of Light, I praise Thee.

O Thou Unconquerable One of Light, I praise Thee.

O Thou Sole Space of all the places of the Universe, I praise Thee.

O Thou Only Universal Mystery, I praise thee.

O Thou Only All–perfect Light, I praise Thee.

O Thou Only Wise One and Sole Wisdom, I praise Thee.

O Thou Only Intangible, I praise Thee.

O Thou True Goodness, who hast made appear all good things, I praise Thee.

O Thou True Light, who hast made all lights to shine, I praise Thee.

O Thou who sustainest all light and givest life to every soul, I praise Thee.

O Thou Repose of them [? who seek repose], I praise Thee.

O Thou [Father] of all Paternity from the beginning unto this day, I praise Thee.

They [? Thy children] search for Thee because Thou art their [Father]. Hear the prayer of [Thy children], for [Thou art He who is hidden] in every place, He who is the [Desire] of all hearts.

[The title and the opening part of the work are lost.]

NOTES

1. The centre of the Universe, which is everywhere and nowhere; the ideal unity in diversity, from which all things flow out and into which all things return. Just as Jerusalem was held to be the centre of the earth, so was this "City" held to be the hidden centre of the Universe; hence it is often named "Jerusalem Above, who is the Mother of us all." It is the principle at once of universality and individuality, the real "ground" or centre of the soul. It is called the "House of the Father" because it is the abiding place of the Presence; the "Robe of the Son" because it is His Body of Manifestation (cp. 2 Clem. xiv.); the "Power of the Mother" because it is the "Energy" by which man is reborn into Divine consciousness; and the "Image or Archetype of the Pleroma" (the World of Eternal Ideas in their "Fullness"), because it is the Wisdom which is the basis of all consciousness.

2. This term rather suggests the use of a vibratory formula to induce certain interior states as a practice of the School to which the Greek MS. belonged. Perhaps this may have been ÏAO, the meaning of which is given elsewhere as "I, because the All (or Pleroma) hath gone forth. A, because it will turn itself back again. O, because the consummation of all consummations will take place." This may be taken to mean exoterically, "Ï, the Incarnation of Jesus, Who is the Pleroma. A, the Crucifixion. O, the Ascension." Taken esoterically, it may mean, "Ï, the Soul, has come forth from God into generation. A, it is started or "Initiated" on its return journey through the Life of the Cross. O, there is union with God in the Eternity of Eternities as the consummation of all things" (cp. note 18). The work we are studying might almost be considered an exposition of this formula, though I do not suggest that it literally is so. We begin by reading it from right to left, beginning with the God "beyond Name," that is He whose being cannot be expressed by any name, O. We pass to the Logos, the Divine Mind, He who can be named, and His Pleroma, A, from which is "started" the Visible World by the going forth of the "Light-Spark" or "Man," Ï.

After this we read from left to right, but this is the expounding of the mystical life, the "return," under a veil of symbolism. ÏAO is the great Name of God in three vowels, derived historically, no doubt, from the Great Name in Judaism, and is the counterpart of the Indian AUM. Probably, like this latter, it was pronounced in three ways: (1) audibly; (2) inaudibly to others, but with the lips; (3) mentally. It was a formula of a sacramental kind by which the life of the disciple was mystically identified with the Life of the Master, so that the knowledge of the real nature of the soul is given or restored by God. During its use the mind was, of course, concentrated on its inner meanings. Various aspects of mystical truth could be expressed by its permutations; ÏAO, OAÏ, AOÏ, etc.

3. Cp. Odes of Solomon, 27: "I stretched out my hands and worshipped the Lord, for the extension of my hands is His sign, and my expansion is the Upright Tree [or Pillar]."

The Cross of Calvary was taken, by the Gnostics, to be the outward and visible sign of a concealed or Cosmic Cross, another aspect of the "City" or Monad, upon which the Logos or Light-Spark, as the "Son of Man," or the "Man," was crucified perpetually in an ineffable manner, thus communicating His Life and Light to the Universe. The substance or "strain" of this Cross is symbolised here by the Ennead or Ninefold Being, the members of which, Knowledge, Life, Hope, etc., are each in themselves Ideal Beings, Eternities, or Gods. Yet these Nine, a number typical of Initiation, are also one, as the Master and the Cross are also one. The Mystery is that of an Unbloody Sacrifice once and perpetually offered and also of Divine Espousal. [See further the "Hymn of Jesus" and the "Gnostic Crucifixion" texts and commentaries by G. R. S. Mead, who renders the passage in the text by "The Source of the Cross is the Man whom no man can comprehend."]

4. "Twelve" seems to symbolise the Powers creative of all kinds of life in their totality, the creative imagination or raying forth power.

5. "Truth" is another name for the Bride of the

Logos, His "Great Surround" or Body. It is the Divine Concept or Conceiving Thought of the Cosmos and its processes, and hence it is also the seal of perfection or Body of Glory, the Life with which the Risen and Ascended Master is clad. While conferring character on all things, it is entirely transcendent, modeless, and "unwalled." Through it God is immanent in the Universe, hence it is also called "Mother." This is what the symbolism seems to imply.

6. This implies the doctrine of the Macrocosm and the Microcosm, of the Universe and of the individual soul as a perfect compendium thereof. All the great cosmic processes are to be found within the soul.

7. A "name" was held to be that which manifests the innermost essence of a thing. Hence it symbolised the spiritual body or ideal vehicle of manifestation, the life clothing. The bestowal of a new name is therefore the sacramental sign of the gift of a new body or mode of life. The real and ineffable Name of God is the Concept or Conceiving Thought referred to in note 5. But this is the Name "Mother" or "Bride" of the Logos, Providence. To "name" was a sacramental way of invoking a presence or "spiritual vehicle."

8. Cp. Codex Akhmim: "Of Him it is said, He thinketh His Image alone and beholdeth it in the Water of Pure Light which surroundeth Him. And His Thought energised and revealed herself, and stood before Him in the Light-Spark—which is the Power which existed before the All—which is the perfect Forethought of the All—the Barbelo, the Æon perfect in glory—glorifying Him, because she hath manifested herself in Him and thinketh Him (i.e. gives Him birth). She is the first Thought, His Image." Barbelo seems to mean "In the Four is God": in other words, it is the personified Tetragrammaton or Great Name commonly rendered by Jehovah.

9. Kanoun. This is a flat, broad basket, originally made of rush or cane, but often manufactured in precious metals in later times. It was used in the sacrificial rites of the gods and was hence classed among sacred things (v. "Basket" in Hastings'

Ency. of Rel. and Ethics). What it signifies exactly I am unable to say. Possibly the rites of the school, if we only knew them, would throw some light upon the question. The offerings of bread and wine at the Eucharist may have been made in the Kanoun. Sometimes in the MS. it seems to be connected with prayer.

10. The Temple of the Pleromata or Fullnesses seems to be pictured as being in the manner of that in Jerusalem. The Æons of the Inner Space correspond to the Holy of Holies, the Æons of the Middle Space to the Holy Place, and the Æons of the Outer Space to the Court. The various Æons and their powers now described seem to be those of the Inner Space. "Æon" and "Space" are practically equivalent terms, only Æon is on the Mind or Spiritual side of things, Space or Extension (Topos) is on the Life or Body side of things. "Space" is purely the space of mind. It is a Spiritual Body with many members, each of which is a god, having his own individual consciousness and being, and yet partaking perfectly and wholly of a common consciousness or life. Each Æon is a mighty Hierarchy in himself, and his "topos" is a Church or Holy Assembly. The ideal union of these Spaces is in the Monad or Indivisible Point, which is therefore the Church of Churches, the Body of the Man whom no man can comprehend.

11. Setheus and the twelve three-faced Paternities seem to be the paradigms, or heavenly patterns, of the Sun, the signs of the Zodiac, and the thirty-six Decans. He is the Invisible Sun of Righteousness behind the visible flame which measures time. In other words, he is the symbol of the Æon of Æons, the Æon par excellence. What time is to the ordinary mundane mind that Setheus is to the Alone-begotten and the Monad, whose ineffable union he encompasses. For he is the manifested Sun of Eternity, (sun symbol). The Monad is the Indivisible Point within the circle or sphere, and the Light-Spark or Logos is within the Point, while Setheus himself is, strictly speaking, the circle or sphere, the well-known symbol of Eternity. All the æons are found in the "topos" of Setheus, as their

divinity is not innate, but comes from conscious participation, hence the name æon. I suggest the name "Setheus" is formed from that of the god Seth, who was a solar deity in some Egyptian traditions. No doubt the differentiation of the name is intentional. The twelve Paternities about the head are referable to the rays, to the creative powers, the "Divine Imaginings" of the Mystic Sun in their totality.

12. Schmidt thinks that the name "Nicotheos"— "the Victor God"—is a title of Christ, and that a quotation is given from some lost Apocalypse, called, perhaps, "The Apocalypse of Nicotheos." The whole passage seems to be a definite appeal to the experiences of attained mystics concerning the Dark Ray. The "Perfect" was a technical name, applied to those whose initiation or start had been consummated or perfected. Having been regenerated, they were "gods" or "æons," conscious of their kinship with the Pleromata. Each was now a hierarchy in himself, a race, as it were. The passage is probably by a later hand.

13. Cp. Pseudo Dionysius Myst. Theol.: "The super-unknown, the super-luminous and loftiest height wherein the simple and absolute and unchangeable mysteries are cloaked in the super-lucent darkness of hidden mystic silence, which super-shines most super-brightly in the blackest night, and in the altogether intangible and unseen, superfills the eyeless understanding with super-beautiful brightnesses. And thou, dear Timothy, in thy intent and practice of the mystical contemplations, leave behind both thy senses and thy intellectual operations, and all things known by sense and intellect, and set thyself, as far as may be, to unite thyself in unknowing with Him who is above all being and knowledge; for by being purely free and absolute, out of self and all things, thou shalt be led up to the Ray of the Divine Darkness, stripped and loosed of all." The above version is by Dom John Chapman, O.S.B., who says that this passage was "cited throughout the Middle Ages as the locus classicus for method of contemplation." This is, except for our text, the earliest mention of the "Dark Ray" in literature. Evidently Pseudo Dionysius did not invent the term himself, but followed a much older Christian tradition. This fact is important for the history of Christian mysticism.

14. This seems to imply a doctrine of pre-existence. Perhaps the passage is related to John 17:16: "They are not of the world, even as I am not of the world.... As Thou didst send Me into the world, even so sent I them into the world."

15. Cp. Psalm 68:17 (R.V.): "The chariots of God are twenty thousand, even thousands upon thousands. The Lord is among them, as in Sinai, in the sanctuary."

16. Further descriptions of this, "the oldest of the Æons," are given later on. From these it will be gathered that the crown is the Crown of Life, and that the twelve gates are also twelve deeps or firmaments, over each of which a Paternity presides. She is called the Indivisible One, either "Point," "Atom," or perhaps even "Body" or "Raiment." As she is both the Spouse and Mother of the Light-Spark within the Æon, I have generally called her the Indivisible Queen.

17. Mr Mead suggests that Phosilampes may be a mystery name of Basilides. Has a commentary on the Gospel of St John been used here, or a commentary on the prologue by Basilides [containing perhaps the teachings of the alleged instructor of Basilides, Glaucias, whose name, rather suggesting the "shining one," may equal "Phosilampes"], which interpreted "In the beginning" as meaning "In the First Concept or in the Monad was the Word"?

18. This repetition of the Seven Vowels gives the following meanings to them:—AAA = Living of Living Ones, HHH = Holy of Holy Ones, EEE = Being of Beings, III = Father of Fatherhoods, OOO = God of Gods, YYY=Lord of Lords, +OOO+ = Space of Spaces or Æon of Æons. The High and Holy One, together with His Bride and Mother, the "Universal Church or First Concept," are one in and with the Eternity that they inhabit. Hence "Thou art the House and the Dweller in the House." Time (Æon) and Space (Topos) are here one, or different aspects of the same mode of being.

19. Cp. "The Mind unto Hermes," 16: "The

Cosmos is all-formed [Pantomorphos]—not having forms external to itself, but changing them, itself within itself"; also the "Perfect Sermon," xix. 3: "The thirty-six, who have the name of Horoscopes, are in the self-same space as the fixed stars; of these the essence chief or Prince is he whom they call Pantomorph and Omniform, who fashioneth the various forms for various species." The Pantomorphic Body is the Augoeides or Astroeides, the ray-like or star-like glory (not to be confused with the "astral body" of modern theosophy). Cp. Origen, Ep. 38 ad Pammach: "Another body, a spiritual and aetherial one, is promised us: a body that is not subject to physical touch, nor seen by physical eyes, nor burdened with weight, and which shall be metamorphosed according to the variety of regions in which it shall be.... In that spiritual body the whole of us will see, the whole hear, the whole serve as hands, the whole as feet." The Star-body is the body of Resurrection and Ascension. Cp. Mark 16:12: "He was manifested in another form unto two of them." Also it was the body of "the universal" descent, that which transmitted the Æons from the Pleroma or Ideal World to the Sensible World, hence it was considered to be "scattered" or in a state of latency, or of mystical death in normal man. To awaken it, to gather it together, or to "raise it from the dead," was one of the first objects of the mystics, who followed the way of the Gnosis. Its partial resurgence was the first great step in the processes of the Apotheosis. It was the possession of this body, in some degree, which distinguished a man as "spiritual" from the psychic and "hylic" men. The Astroeides included the "natural" body in its consummation, under a great transmutation, for it was the "Wisdom" at the basis of material nature. I have transferred the account of the "City of the Man" from where it stands, at the end of the MS., to this place, as it seems more intelligible here, and the exact order has been obscured by the confusion of the leaves.

20. Cp. "Poemandres," 15: "He [the Man], beholding the form like to himself existing in her, in her water, loved it and willed to live in it: and with the will came act, and so he vivified the form devoid of reason. And Nature took the object of her love and wound herself completely round him, and they were intermingled, for they were lovers.... Thus, though above the Harmony (or Fate sphere), within the Harmony he [The Man] hath become a slave, ... and though he is sleepless from a sleepless Sire, yet is he overcome by sleep." This is the Mystery of the concealment of God in Nature, a mystery that was sometimes presented under the symbol of a self-scattering, sometimes under the symbol of a magical sleep, or mystic death.

21. "The Earth that brought forth the God" is the "ground of the individual soul," and is also the Sanctum Sanctorum of the Universe, the Hidden Sanctuary where the "Man" is raised from mystical death or is reborn. No doubt the symbolism is drawn from Egyptian sources.

22. This passage might be paraphrased, "Those who have received Life and Light in the Concealed Sanctuary of the Soul know, through this Crown of Perfection, that the Inheritors of the Kingdom of Light are indeed reborn from the Indivisible Body, who is the Mother of us all.

23. AAA +OOO+ = The Living Space of Spaces, Æon of Æons. See note 18 and cp. Rev. 1:8, 17-18: "I am Alpha and Omega ... the First and the Last, and the Living One; and I was dead, and, behold, I am alive unto the æon of æons."

24. The Body of Christ, which in its transcendental aspect is also His Bride and Mother. Cp. 2 Clem. xiv.: "I do not suppose that you know not that the living Church is the body of Christ; for the scripture saith, 'God made Man, male and female; the male is Christ, the female the Church; and the books and the Apostles belong not to the Church that now is, but to the Church which is from above. For it is spiritual, as is our Jesus, but is manifested in these last days to save us. But the Church, being spiritual, is manifested in the flesh of Christ.... Great is the Life and Immortality which this flesh can partake of—that is, of the Holy Spirit which is joined to it—nor can any declare or utter what the Lord has prepared for His chosen.'"

25. This extremely interesting and important

passage is also one of great difficulty, for it is full of technical terms and allusions which would need a small treatise to elucidate properly. For example, it seems to imply the doctrine of two Logoi that Clement of Alexandria was accused of teaching, and which is found in certain Hellenistic writings. The "Body of Light" is the Astroeides in which the "Adept" can cross the "Fate-Sphere," the "Midst," the regions of consciousness where mechanical cause and effect prevail and contact the Pleroma, or Universe of Divine Freedom and Fullness. "Charis" or "Grace" is the name of the Bride or Body of the Logos, and the use of it here symbolises a "raiment" or "Body" still more exalted than the Astroeides. It is the Body beyond the Stars, the Monadic Robe or "Robe of Glory," into which the "Star-like Body" was transformed at the Horos, Limit or Boundary of the Worlds of Difference and of Sameness. What kind of Peace was that in which the Alone-begotten dwelt in the Monad? A Peace most truly given to those within and those without, for in it all things were created. To realise what is meant we must remember that "Charis" and "Resurrection" were names of "Staurus," the Pillar that made with Horos the Great Cross referred to more than once. "Peace," then, was the state of the Logos in Mystic crucifixion, the Peace of God which established, reconciled, justified all things. Hence it can be inferred what transformation the Star Body had to undergo to become the Robe of Glory. The Cross and the Master were one. The Cross of Calvary was to the Gnostic Teacher the outer and efficacious sign of this Mystery or Sacrament. So also the Pentecostal outpouring recorded in Acts was the outward sign, or sacramental token, of the assumption by the Master of the Robe of Glory, the vesture of the Monad or Transcendental and Universal Church, which could not be assumed here. From thenceforth the band of disciples became a Church, the Mystic Body of Christ, the outward sign of concealed mysteries; and it will be seen in what manner Jesus was the Father of all Light-Sparks and gave resurrection to the body. Such was the teaching of the Gnosis. To make the matter clear to readers interested in mysticism, but unfamiliar with Hellenistic technical terms, it may be said that the "Bodies" so often referred to may be taken as standing for what may be called the Life side of various stages of mystical consciousness, as "Light" stands for the Mind side; but Life and Light are one.

26. "The Gate of God." Cp. the Naasene Document in Hippolytus: "This Mystery is the Gate of Heaven, and this is the House of God, where the Good God dwells alone; into which no impure man shall come, no psychic, nor fleshly man, ... but it is kept under watch for the Spiritual alone—where, when they come, they must cast away their garments, and all become bridegrooms, obtaining their true manhood through the Virginal Spirit. For this is the Virgin big with child, conceiving and bearing a Son—not psychic, not fleshly, but a blessed Æon of Æons." "Gnosis," then, was the Mystery of Regeneration or Rebirth from above. It will be observed that the text shows no hostility to "Faith." This is an indication of early date. "Mystery" is often, though not always, the equivalent to "Sacrament."

27. There is then another "Universal Mother," Phanerios or Phaneia ("Wisdom without the Pleroma"). In the last resort the two Mothers are one. Phaneia is the Mother of the manifested world in which there is matter, but she does not seem to be in exile, as in the Sophia Myth. Like Isis in the Osiris legend, she seems to have gone forth to gather together the self-scattered limbs of the Man and to redeem Him from captivity through the efforts of the great hierarchs that are given to her.

28. The pre-existence of the soul is taught, also the loss of the memory of its true nature owing to its fall into "Matter" [Hyle]. But this fall is not regarded as either a sin or a mistake, but as a needful step in the mystery of Rebirth or "Re-ordering." The Overseer is the "Mind of all Masterhood," the Logos, the Second Father of all. It is tempting to connect the Triple-Power with the Triple-Bodied Man of the Naasene Document and see in him the symbol of a simple Universal Consciousness "polarised" into the three states of Spiritual, Psychic, and Material.

29. This Vision of the Advent of the Creative Word seems to be in part a summary and anticipation of things described otherwise later in the MS. After it the writer (or writers) goes back and describes the "Re-ordering" from the time that "the veils of the æons were drawn" from various points of view. Various Cosmic processes are delineated symbolically, and their simultaneous working is not excluded.

30. The Universal Man had fallen into bondage in the Fate-Sphere.

31. I think that what we are to understand is, that the Man is raised from His state of Mystical Death or Self-dispersion by the Protogennetor (Son, First Parent), crowned with the Lights of Wisdom by the Hidden Father "Who has no consort," and robed with cosmic life by the Mother. Compare what has already been said about the Robe of Glory and the outward signs of its descent at Pentecost. The work of the Mantle would seem to symbolise the re-ordering work of the Church, the "New Creation," the new impulse on its mystical side. Is Protogennetor, then, a cryptic title of Christ? In a sense I think it is, but there are other issues which are better discussed at a later point. The Title "Without King" recalls the Naasene Document and its "One is the Race without a King which is born Above."

32. The Seven Stratelatai, leaders or generals, are perhaps the seven Planets.

33. Cp. the Akhmim Codex: "She (Barbelo) is the First Thought, his Image, she becometh the First Man; that is the Virginal Spirit, she of the triple Manhood, the triple-powered one, the triple-named, triple-born, the æon which ages not, the Man-woman."

34. Who are the Mother and the three great hierarchs? It is tempting to connect the three with the three traditional paths of Purgation, Illumination and Union, Water, Fire and Spirit. The Propator, who desires to turn the World to God, and who is, through the descent of a particular power, the Father-Mother of the Spiritual Life to come, may symbolise the process of Purgation and the Baptism of Water;

the Autopator, who utters the promises of Christ and who has the power of an Ennead of initiation, may typify the Illuminative Life and the Baptism of Fire; while the Protogennetor, robed in cosmic consciousness, so that he can walk even the waters of the Primal Deep (Noun), who draws forth finally from the material life, may represent the inception of the Life of Union and the Baptism of the Spirit. All this may be true, but, if I mistake not, there is more behind the veil of symbolism, and it is continual allusions to this more, plain enough to the person for whom it was intended, that renders the MS. so peculiarly difficult. Who is Phaneia, the Mother without the Pleroma, who owes her position to the descent of the Royal Robe? She stands for nature in what may be called its sacramental aspect, and she also stands for the Churches, if I mistake not, and more particularly for the community or order to which the writer or writers belonged. This implies a certain claim to a high mystical self-knowledge on the part of that community. Again, the title "Son Protogennetor" is most significant. He that bore it must be the Son of the Sacred House, the "Son of the Doctrine," and the First Parent, or Father in God, of those to come after. He invites comparison not only with the Saviour of the Gospels, but also with figures that appear in the myths of the mystery cults: with Horos, the son of Isis, with Hermes the Thrice-Great, with the "Eagle" or "Father" whose title represented the highest grade of the Mithriaca. I suggest that he may represent the ideal candidate in the mystery of initiation— that is to say, he who, by entering into himself, has attained to the "unio mystica," has raised up the "Man" within himself, has been "reborn" as a god in Divine consciousness, and so is qualified to hand on the vital processes of the Gnosis to others, becoming thereby their spiritual parent. So he is called Son Protogennetor. He is Christ in the sense that Galahad of the "Quest," and Parsifal of Wagner's great drama are Christ. The theory of initiation as conceived in the early mystical communities seems, in part at any rate, to rest upon the proposition that he who has himself attained to Union with

God is able to "start," to "initiate," in suitable persons, and under certain conditions, those processes which, under Providence, result in a like consummation. Thus we appear to have a claim in the MS. to a transmitted "Mastership" in the ranks of the order going back to Jesus Himself: "For whose sake resurrection is given to the body. He is the Father of all Light-Sparks." The Propator and Autopator would seem to represent different aspects of this claim. "Gnosis" was not the possession of a body of secret Doctrine in the sense of having a number of formal propositions containing occult information, but a vital knowledge of the processes of "Regeneration" or "Apotheosis."

Then, again, we have the idea of a "Divine Mind" or "Logos" manifesting Himself through a Body of Universal Consciousness, represented sacramentally (that is to say effectually) in the "physical world" by the bodies of a body of believers. The rites of this body symbolised, again "effectually," the modes and activities of the Body of Universal Consciousness of which it was the outward sign, just as its doctrines reflected on the plane of mentation and discourse the workings of the Divine Mind, which are above mentation and discourse, though not contrary to it. The acceptance of these ideas seems to have constituted "Pistis"—"the Faith by which we believe in the Mysteries of the Man"—a mode of the Divine Energy which resulted in good works. "Gnosis" was the knowledge of the processes by which these ideas passed from the life of formal belief and intellectual assent into the life of realised consciousness. The "Hylics," men in Hyle or "Matter," were "the children of this world," so absorbed in the life of the senses five that they lived like "brute beasts without understanding." [Hyle as a technical term was not always understood too literally by the Gnostics and Platonists (see various passages in Codex Bruce), but derived its importance as the symbol of a certain state of consciousness.] "Psychics" were those whose consciousness was sufficiently aroused to accept a formal belief in viewless Divine Energies and to order their social conduct on the basis of that belief. The

"Spiritual," the "Perfect," those perfected in Gnosis, that is, were those that were actually conscious of participating in a Mind in common and in a Body of transcendental energy in common. This Mind (Logos), Light-Spark, and Body (Monad) constituted a sole Being, Man, or the Son of Man, neither male nor female, and yet both, who enveloped all things, even those of Hyle (v. the Naasene Document) in His Infinite Perfections, who manifested all things, who was concealed in all things and who was above all things. An ideal Church or Community of "Spiritual" men, conscious of the whole Man in each of its members, could focus within itself, without any robbery, all the energies of the Universe, and by concentrating and applying them in a certain manner could give birth to the whole order within the consciousness of the called and chosen candidate, who thus became a "Self-Knowing," "Self-Fathered," "Fore-Fathered" god, a "Race without a King in the name God." His substance was "enformed" by the Sacraments of the Manifested Order (Phaneia), and the substance thus "enformed" was finally "assumed," "translated," "transformed," what you will, in a mode utterly beyond all symbol and image by the "descent" of the Divine "Grace," "First Concept," "Ennead and Monad Without Seal-Mark," "Barbelo" (again what you will), and given final "Re-birth in the Light of the Mind." To form an Ideal community of this kind, a community of gods in God, by a series of grades or steps, places of "Repentance" or "change" slowly taken, was, I believe, the purpose of those responsible for the original of the present MS. "They began from the base upwards that the building might unite them to their companions"—souls that in æonian bliss beheld the Face of God unveiled. Into this building plan the Neophyte was initiated to give thereto his soul and body as a willing oblation and sacrifice. It seems a reasonable suggestion to offer that this document consists of a series of meditations and spiritual exercises given to the candidate before one of the inner "initiations" or sacramental "starts" that was consummated beyond the veil of signs and symbols. For such an end not only Faith, not only a reasonable

Foundation in an accepted philosophy, that of Plato, but an Imagination intensified into intuition was needed. Hence these strange hieroglyphs on the expressed veil. The Child of Fire must behold rising within himself from the Immeasurable Abyss of Godhead the five-rayed morning star of Love, Faith, Hope, Gnosis, and Peace, the herald of the Perfect Dawn of a New Birth. Possibly "Propator," "Autopator" and "Protogennetor" may also have been the official designations of hierophants in the sacramental side of some "Mystery" consummated in solitude, from which the candidate returned an "Epopt."

35. Cp. Ps. 104:1, 2: "Thou art clothed with honour and majesty: who coverest thyself with light as with a garment."

36. This hymn or prayer seems to be an invocation to the "Dark Ray" on behalf of the candidate (and also for the building up of the "Ideal Order"). The consummation, beyond all signs and images, is in the hands of God alone. A "start" may be effected by duly qualified hierophants under certain conditions, but the crown "Pantelos" is given by the "Father of all Fatherhood" alone.

37. This looks as if in this system the Fruit of the Pleroma was also the Father of the Fullnesses. The phrase "He made a world and bore it into the Temple" seems to mean that He assumed a body of manifestation.

38. The veil which surrounded the Pleroma or World of Divine Ideas was called "Stauros" (Cross) and Horos (Boundary). Cp. Hippolytus (vi. 3): "Now it is called 'Boundary' because it bounds off the Deficiency from the Fullness [so as to make it] exterior to it. It is called Partaker because it partakes of the Deficiency as well; and it is called 'Cross' because it hath been fixed immovably and unchangeably, so that nothing of the Deficiency should be able to approach the æons within the Fullness."

See also the "Gnostic Crucifixion," 9, 10, 11 (Acts of John): "[The Cross] is the defining (or delimitation) of all things, both the firm necessity of things fixed from things unstable, and the harmony of wisdom. And as it is Wisdom in Harmony, there are those on the Right and those on the Left—powers, authorities, principalities and daemons, energies, threats, powers of wrath, slanderings—and the Lower Root from which hath come forth the things in genesis. This, then, is the Cross which by the Word hath been the means of 'Cross-beaming' all things—at the same time separating off the things that proceed from genesis and those below from those above, and also compacting them all into one."

The "Mantle" in which the Man is clad and which severs and orders all things is evidently another aspect of the same idea. The use of the term "veil" is suggestive, as the term is so often employed in Hellenistic Mysticism in connection with "Initiation." Finally, it is just worth noting that it is possible that what Origen has to say about the self-limitation of God is influenced by the tradition concerning the Horos or "Boundary."

39. This is undoubtedly a reference to the Mystical Crucifixion so often mentioned in previous notes. It is the Master Symbol of the Unitive State, of the reconciliation and union of God and Man, and of the participation of the individual in the Universal. Its presence at this point of the text is most suggestive. The candidate, "the Birth of Matter," stands, mystically at any rate, before the Veil at the Foot of the Cross. To pass the Veil and to enter into the Fullness means being united with the Master in His Passion and Crucifixion.

The Cross is evidently a Tau, and I suggest that the frontispiece may represent this Mystery, the Crucifixion of the Æon, O, upon Staurus, the Cross and the Master being One, A+O+ and A+O+. The meaning of XMI is unknown. It has been suggested that it is (with EIC +THEOS+) a symbol of the Trinity in Unity, or a veil of the Divine Name.

40. The terms I have translated as "Sole Unstainable," "Sole [Foundation]-stone of Adamant" are "Amiantos," "Adamantos." Besides meaning "unstainable," Amiantos was the name of a pale green stone. Readers interested in the legend of the Graal will recall that the Graal is

represented as a green stone in the "Parzival" of Von Eschenbach. "Adamantos" is "diamond." Here and in the account of the Monad as the Metropolis of Monogenes, "filled with men of every race and with all the statues of the king," there is a curious parallel to be found to a happening in the life of Saint Theresa. "Being once in prayer," she says, "the Diamond was represented to me like a flash; although I saw nothing formed, still, it was a representation with all clearness how all things are seen in God, and how all are contained in Him.... Let us say that the Divinity is like a very lustrous Diamond, larger than all the world, or like a mirror—and all that we do is seen in this Diamond, it being so fashioned that it includes everything within itself, because there is nothing but what is contained in this magnitude."

I have ventured to insert [Foundation] because I think that there is a punning allusion to "Adamas." Cp. Naasene Document: "The 'rock' means Adamas. This is the corner-stone ... which I insert in the foundation of Zion. By this he means allegorically the plasm of man. For Adamas, who is inserted in the inner Man, and the foundations of Zion are ... the wall and palisade (sc. Horos) in which is the inner Man."

41. The prayer seems to be for the transmutation of the members of the order by mystical marriages with their archetypal "selves," that the mysteries of the Crucifixion, Resurrection, Ascension, and of the Descent of the Paraclete may be realised after a certain manner.

42. Compare this passage with what has already been said concerning an attempt to form an Ideal Order. "A place of Metanoia" implies here a radical change of the whole being rather than "repentance" as ordinarily understood. The "topos" of Autogenes, the Self-begotten, was the first station of the journey of the Light-Spark without the Pleroma, and is the last station of the return within.

The extant "Gospel of Mary" (Codex Akhmim), which was "reviewed" by Irenaeus, and was therefore composed before 180 A.D., states that from the Light of the Christ and the Incorruptible proceed forth four great Lights to surround Autogenes. Their names are Harmozel, Oroiael, Daveithi, and Èleleth. Irenaeus says, "Charis [Grace] was conjoined with the great and first Luminary, and this they will have to be the Saviour and call him Harmogen"—the Harmes-begotten. The name "Harmes" appears in the present MS., and is evidently a name for Barbelo. These things are important for the date of the Greek original. The allusions to Pistis-Sophia are probably interpolated; there seems to be no room for her adventures in the scheme of the text. But what are we to make of the mysterious "Baptism in the name of Barpharanges"? Does "Barpharanges" (the meaning of which no one seems to know) simply = Harmogenes = the begotten from Barbelo, "the Virginal Spirit," the Image seen in the "pure water of Light"? If so, then we have in all probability an allusion to the Gnostic Baptism with the Holy Spirit or Light. "Harmogenes" will be the Child of the Mystical Marriage with the Virginal Spirit by which the "Spiritual" recover their true manhood, a "blessed æon of æons": that is to say, that the Epopt himself is mystically "Autogenes," the "Self-begotten," having been reborn a god in God. The rest of the text is missing.

43. This Hymn to the Light seems to stand in some close connection with the text we have been discussing. If what has been suggested concerning the contents of the Greek original should prove correct, both the nature and position of the Hymn become plain. It consists of various acts of the will not altogether unlike some of those prescribed in certain Catholic manuals for those in the Unitive way. It is the form of Prayer given by the "Director" or "Master" to his disciple, to be used together with the MS. as part of his preparation for, what I believe to be, the "Baptism of Light." A large part of the Hymn seems to be missing owing to the state of the MS., and the order is uncertain.

Jeremy Puma

Perfect Day Living:
The Political Challenge

"All the comparisons that (Jesus) makes tend to show that the disciples of Jesus are necessarily few in number with little power. The leaven in the dough. The salt in the soup. The sheep in the middle of wolves, and how many other images. Jesus seems to have never had the vision of a triumphant and triumphing Church encircling the globe. He always presents a secret power which changes things on the inside, which works spiritually…"

Jacques Ellul, *The Subversion of Christianity*

———————————

I'd like to issue a challenge to you. Given the current political climate in the West, and the undeniably important events unfolding in the Middle East, I'd like to challenge you to consider your involvement in the Political Machine very carefully. Are gnosis and politics reconcilable? Does the gnostic have a political duty? Can the gnostic depend upon political activism to further social change? Although we don't have any solid answers—and nor should we—there are some considerations which merit discussion, especially given the impending upcoming U.S. election cycle. They present the gnostic with an excellent opportunity to investigate the idea of power, both worldly and otherwise, and scrutinize one's own decision to become involved with both or either.

To me, the ultimate exemplar of the relationship between the gnostic and the powers of the world is Jesus himself. Now, Jesus obviously understood the value of direct action. He turned over the tables of the moneychangers. He healed the sick and lame (a wonderful example of the power of direct action if ever there was one!). He speechified on the Mount (or Plain, depending). he was most certainly a radical, very much concerned with social issues.

But, when we really take a look at the life of Jesus, what kind of activist was he? Every single clue we find when we investigate this question seems to indicate that Jesus was, in essence, unconcerned with matters of the State. One of the more important components of the message of Christ is undeniably a separation between the powers of the world and the power of God.

Remember, Christ denied the Kingdoms of the World when they were offered to him by the Tempter. As Jacques Ellul has noted in the highly recommended Anarchy and Christianity, he counseled us to "render unto Caesar" the coinage that bears his sign, but to God the things that bear his. Most significantly, he counseled his companions, again and again, through both word and deed, to avoid exercising power over others, no matter whether the opportunity presented itself. In fact, he very clearly states that the possession of power is a hindrance for the gnostic, and implores his listeners to give it up:

"I say to you, let him who possesses power renounce it and repent."

The Dialogue of the Saviour

"…[L]et him who possesses power renounce it."

The Gospel of Thomas

We know from pretty much every single Sethian tradition represented in the Nag Hammadi Library that the Archons are responsible for worldly power. This is an essential part of the Gnostic message. Obviously, it's a fool's game to try to pin the Archon label on actual individuals; no person is an Archon. Instead, the mechanisms of worldly power—including and perhaps even most significantly, political power—are manifestations of the Archonic essence, both macro- and microcosmically. Jesus rebels not against the power of the State, or even against the power of Organized Religion, but against the Will to Power behind these things.

Playing with the Political Machine can become a dangerous addiction (something I know from experience). Freedom of Speech is far overrated; Freedom of Thought is more valuable by a wide margin. Becoming embroiled in the gears and wheels of Political Machine leads to impassioned involvement with the systems of the world, and when this happens, our thoughts are no longer our own. We become convinced that those with different views are "others," who have less inherent value. We compromise our positions based on the propaganda employed by all agents of Politics (be they Left or Right, all politicians and those in their employ are propagandists). We concede our right to protest to those who establish "Protest Zones" (when you need to apply for a permit to protest, you've entered into a contract with the Archons).

The ultimate goal of the Political Machine—any political system, be it Democracy, Socialism, Communism, Authoritarianism, etc.—is the domination of opposing Political Viewpoints via the exercise of power. I refer to the "Political Machine" because this system is indeed mechanical; like a wretched robot, it churns and smokes as it moves ever forward towards its own goals.

Even those political systems which are generally understood as "benign" are intended and designed to expand as far as possible through the exercise of power. Power does not need violent expression; power can be the enforcement of law, the granting of social necessities. Even the State that provides health care to all of its citizens does so through the exercise of power, as long as the possibility remains that they can deny that health care "for the good of the State." Any State that maintains the potential for the violent exercise of power, either offensive or defensive—any state that has weapons—is part of the Political Machine, and inherently Archonic. The State inexorably trends towards Totalitarianism, and rebellion against the state invariably results in the establishment of another Totalitarianism.

The modern Western State, and the Archonic powers at its root, have assimilated and humiliated the concept of "Freedom of Speech," and created a society in which one is truly free to say whatever one wants to say, provided it is said within the limited semiotic circle the State provides. It has realized that when one's thoughts are under its power, and when it controls the words, it doesn't matter what one says. The Gnostic, however, understands that Wisdom is equally important to Word, and that freedom to exercise Wisdom is only possible when one has emerged from the blanket of the Political Machine and its propagandists.

The Political Machine also requires one to compromise one's own self-knowledge—to pick the "lesser evil," for example. Whenever you are forced to compromise your self-knowledge, the ideals to which you ascribe, you are not exercising Freedom of Thought. This may be an acceptable bargain in certain cases, but this decision needs to be made with full awareness that one is making a deal with the Archons, so to speak, and that when one makes a Political decision based on a compromise of one's position, one is truly compromising one's own freedom to decide.

None of this is to say that the gnostic shouldn't be involved in social issues, or that one should abstain from voting if one is so inclined; indeed, "shoulds" and "shouldn'ts" create the problems in the first place. If one believes one can initiate positive change through the Political Machine, then one should obviously feel free to do so. And, to be sure, there are politicians who are good, honest people, who desire a better world.

An individual gnostic may choose to support a politician or a political party, or to engage in activism, without fear of straying from the gnostic path, provided that their involvement in the Political Machine results from the intimate self-knowledge that is the mandate of anyone who identifies as a gnostic. Nonetheless, for the gnostic, true change—radical change—can only come about outside of the political sphere. It can only come about through developing an intimate self-knowledge—gnosis.

The gnostic who desires social change must be able to penetrate the illusions of the Political Machine. He or she must understand the language of propaganda and advertising, and the difference between Free Speech and Free Thought. He or she must act based on self-knowledge, as a Secret Missionary, and avoid at all costs becoming embroiled in the cesspool of partisanship. He or she must understand the difference between activism and sentimentalism, and must learn when the Archons are attempting to manipulate the emotions. His or her only allegiance must be to the Christos and Sophia, and those in need of compassion. Only if these preconditions are met can we truly produce any kind of radical change.

So, when deciding the extent to which you will participate in the Political Machine, I challenge you to learn about propaganda, to study the control systems behind your favored candidate. I challenge you to understand why Philip K. Dick said, "To fight the Empire is to be infected by its derangement." But mostly, I challenge you to gnosis, to understand completely why you are involved and with whom because you know yourself, through yourself, that your thoughts are Free no matter what you choose to say.

Andrew Phillip Smith

Into the Bridal Chamber:
Myths and History: A Ramble

Kidnapped by pirates, the god Dionysus caused the mast of the pirate ship to sprout grape-bearing vines, tranformed into a lion and changed the pirates into dolphins. In 1592 Columbus sailed the ocean blue. The former is a myth, expressing the status of Dionysus as the god of wine, the latter historical fact enshrined in a popular rhyme. Branwen, sister of Brân, the king of Britain, was abducted and taken to Ireland by Matholwch, king of Ireland. Brân, a giant, waded over the Irish Sea with his warband to rescue her with the result that Ireland was devastated and had to be repopulated by the five surviving couples. Myth of course, found in Branwen Daughter of Llyr, the Second Branch of the Mabinogi, in its surviving form a produce of twelfth century Wales. However, Celtic scholar John Koch has shown convincingly that the story of Branwen contains folk memories of an historical event that occurred in Greece in the third century BCE. Myths can contain history, or be raw source material for history, but there is no way for historians to decide which elements may contain genuine folk memory without an external historical or archaeological source with which it can be checked and confirmed.

However, history itself—the study of the past using written records, supplemented by archaeology and judicious use of other sources—is itself an ongoing enterprise. The academic critical nature of modern history allows existing consensus views to be revised or overturned in the light of new evidence, new techniques and new insights. Academic history does not follow a straight line of progress and once-acceptable theories may be refuted only to resurface with a new generation of scholars. "History is like a palimpsest, a medieval parchment which, as the inks of one set of writing faded, another document was written on top it, until over the years several layers of writing accumulated, one on top of the other . . . "[1]

Though many enthusiastic historians may say that they want to get at the truth, history is not truth. It is at best a quest for truth, an endless search that can never arrive at its destination. Were an historical subject area to be utterly exhausted of new data and new interpretation, should we be able to state definitively that nothing more could be known about the subject, we would not arrive at a destination, we should merely have to conclude that the trail has gone cold.

Postmodernism revels in this historical relativism and extreme scepticism. We cannot truly know the past, we can only as contemporary people interact with the texts. What we call history is historians interacting with the texts and artefacts from the past. There is no truth. However freeing postmodernism may seem on one's first encounter with it, however playful and full of possibility, its superficiality and lack of absolute value soon become apparent. Surely not all attempts at historical endeavour are equal. Careful research into the awful events at Nazi concentration camps, harrowing personal interviews, lists of prisoners and of the dead are surely superior to rabid holocaust denial tracts, despite both being "narratives". "The emphasis of postmodernists [is] on history as a form of literature, on the individuality of the historian's reading of the past and on the historian as a creator of fictions rather than purveyor of objective knowledge . . . "[2]

Yet every attempt at history does have its bias. Secular rationalism is refreshing and stimulating when applied to religious history. It is a great antidote to the dreary conventional religiosity that can still inform so much of the research into Christian history. Yet what if secular rationalism is not fundamentally our own worldview and conflicts with at least some aspects of it? Should we adopt a methodological atheism, carve out a separate secular-critical personality and keep our spiritual convictions away from it? Many Christian scholars and scientists do this more or less successfully—witness the head of the Human Genome Project, Francis Collins, scientist and evangelist Christian.

Or do we abandon critical standards more or less entirely and allow our worldviews to determine our view of history? There are advantages and limitations to either approach.

E.H. Carr, author of the pre-postmodern classic *What Is History?* believed that history was about exploration and interpretation rather than telling a story.

"A genuine historian will never manipulate or distort the materials which the past has left behind and which form the basis for the historian's work; but within the limits of what the sources allow there is plenty of room for differing emphases and interpretations . . . "[3]

Yet history and story share the same root, the Latin word *historia*. Once the most rigorous and guarded historical analysis has been carried out, one is left with a story. The processes of both mythmaking and history produce stories. Humans need stories. How willing should we be to revise or abandon our favourite stories once their historical foundations have been questioned or refuted? And the progress of history isn't simply a result of arbitrary historical changes but may be based on superior argument and analysis, along with new discoveries.

The reader will surely have guessed, has she made it this far, that I am leading on to the history and interpretation of Gnosticism. The study of the Gnostics is a historical one. If we do not place the Nag Hammadi writings within a historical context we can only interpret them from the point of view of our contemporary culture—something that radical postmodernists would argue is the only possible approach anyway. Most people probably initially approach the Gnostic scriptures in a naïve way, reading into them whatever it is that they wish to find. However, like these uninformed readers, most of us are not primarily interested in the Gnostics and their writings for historical reasons alone. Their writings and their viewpoints appeal to us. We may feel that there is illumination in these texts, that their writers and the thousands of Gnostics who dies unknown and unremembered experienced spiritual illumination and development. We may feel that the Gnostic writings are our scriptures. We look to the Gnostics for truth—spiritual truth— or at least for a representation of truth in an essentialist way.

So here we are, seeking genuine spiritual truths in ancient texts. The truth that we seek may be fundamental to the nature of the universe. Or we may feel that we are approaching the truth, or doing our best to seek for the truth without having any complete certainty that we can know it in any absolute way. Either way, we may feel that the message of the Gnostics, at least as it is expressed in the Nag Hammadi writings is somehow, to a greater or lesser extent, in essence true. Whatever, we probably believe that the Gnostics are conveying some sort of essential truth through the medium of myth. Yet to thoroughly understand those myths we need to know something of their culture. Thus to understand the Gnostic myth we need to do history, or to read the writings of those who are doing history—historians. Particularly important is the background of Platonism and the Hebrew and Christian scriptures.

But—as I have previously noted—historical interpretation moves on and differs from generation to generation. This has been particularly acute in the last twenty years of Gnostic studies. First, the very category of Gnosticism itself has been brought into question.

As an academic category Gnosticism was founded on the writings of the heresiologists—Irenaeus, Tertullian, Hippolytus, Epiphanius—who detested the Gnostics and their ideas. Hence the concept of Gnosticism as a coherent set of ideas and as a social grouping has been deconstructed and found wanting by many scholars. Any list of fundamental Gnostic concepts can be shown to be inconsistent. Few gnostic writings contain the majority of these ideas. The dichotomy of orthodox and heresy was the creation not of the Gnostics but of their enemies. If we read the Gnostic writings through the lens of Gnosticism we may well be misinterpreting them.

The followup to this deconstruction of Gnosticism is a tendency to see Gnostics as primarily part of the diversity of early Christianity. This is typified by David Brakke's recent and interesting book *The Gnostics*.

Many of us who are interested in Gnosticism have based our notion of it on popular books by academics such as Hans Jonas, Kurt Rudolph or Elaine Pagels, or on books by amateur scholars among whom I would count myself, Sean Martin, Stuart Holroyd and Stephan Hoeller. Others base their understanding of the Gnostics on interpretations that are already considerably further from the intrinsic meaning of Gnostic texts, basing their Gnosticism on holistic readings more compatible with esoteric Christianity and other forms of modern spirituality.

Should our understanding of Gnosticism shift as the academic understanding shifts? We can hardly wait for the academics to come to any sort of final understanding—we would be long dead along with our children and grandchildren even if this could be the case. What of opinions that were never based on any reliable historical data in the first place?

I pose this as a question and I can recommend no single answer to it. Personally I don't call myself a Gnostic and I don't consider my own worldview to be truly Gnostic. This isn't an attempt to sidestep the issue or shrug off responsibility. I simply don't consider my own spiritual outlook, as fragmentary as it may currently be, to be close enough to make that leap towards being a self-proclaimed Gnostic, because I feel, rightly or wrongly, that to commit to a genuinely, wholly gnostic spirituality would be to deny something of my own concerns. Yet I certainly view Gnosticism from an aspect that is not primarily historical but personal and spiritual.

Also I am a keen follower of academic developments. If one has a reasonable knowledge of the texts and their interpretations, some knowledge of the structure and vocabulary of ancient languages and the requisite intelligence and interest, one can read and attempt to understand the academic arguments. Then one is free, within the limits of one's knowledge and ability, to assess the arguments and express one's agreement or reservations, or even to remain unconvinced. Certainly the objectives of an amateur (one who pursues a discipline for the love of it) may often seem naïve to professionals. But one doesn't necessarily have to bow down to authority. The academic system isn't perfect and the weight of tradition, respectability and academic politics is a burden which the layman doesn't have to bear.[4] On the other hand professional scholars have the time, training, resources—both libraries and the dialectic with other, more experience scholars that aren't available to those outside the academy. They have a lot of time to devote to the subject and of course they are intelligent. Yet academics make mistakes too.[5]

And of course one interprets the world and its history according to one's own worldview. Most conservative Christians believe in the physical resurrection of Christ, as a more-or-less unique event in history. Yet of course this is unacceptable as secular history. Such scholars either shuffle awkwardly around the methodological naturalism that is so essential to contemporary historicism or allow their faith positions to trump rationalism and determine their conclusions. How many conservative Christian scholars argue for an early date for the

Gospel of Thomas?

The problem with so-called faith history is that one loses the ability to talk to those who don't share one's faith. I find it unbelievable that Jesus should be able to walk on water. It is therefore impossible for me to discuss the historicity of John 6:16-21 with anyone who does believe that Jesus (and probably no one else apart from, briefly, Peter) could do so. Equally, if I believe that altered or higher states of consciousness are essential to self-development or to anything that might resemble salvation someone who doesn't hold this point of view might find me to be a frustrating conversationalist on the matter.[6]

And yet we surely ought, to some degree, to read history in the light of our own spiritual experience Perhaps we are reduced to a pragmatic mixture of let-and-let-live and it's-my-opinion-and-I reserve the right to argue with anyone who doesn't agree with me.

I come back to the issue of history and myth,. Pre-modern people (and many in the world today) believe in their myths, or in the essential points enshrined in those myths. But as moderns we also see the world in a rational or semi-rational way. We want our personal myths to be historically true, to have our cake and eat it. But history has a different method to myth. At this point I throw my arms in the air and abandon my incoherent ramble. Probably we'll all continue doing what we do anyway.

Notes

1 Richard J. Evans in "Prologue: What is History—Now?" in *What Is History Now?* ed. David Cannadine (Palgrave, 2004).

2 Cannadine/Evans p. 14.

3 Ibid. p. 16.

4 Mark Goodacre recently advised young scholars not to take on a well-loved consensus theory too early in their careers as he had in his opposition to Q. http://ntweblog.blogspot.com/2010/11/finding-your-niche-in-biblical-studies.html

5 e.g., As a minor example, Norman Perrin's recent book on the *Gospel of Thomas*, *Thomas, The Other Gospel*, erroneously states that there are six extant copies of the Apocryphon of John. There are in fact four.

6 Actually I flatter myself that I'm capable of briefly putting aside my own opinions in conversations of this sort.

Book Reviews

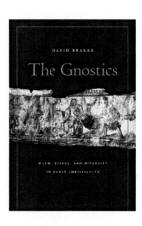

*The Gnostics: Myth,
Ritual and Diversity
in Early Christianity.*
**David Brakke.
Hardcover, Harvard
University Press,
180pp. $29.95.**

In the last couple of decades, Gnosticism, at least as an academic category, has been critiqued and deconstructed. It has been shown—again, specifically in a scholarly context—to be inconsistent and to have developed historically as an outgrowth of the heresiological church fathers' attack on competing groups with whom they disagreed. More recently scholarship has gone beyond critique and is approaching the evidence of the heresiological accounts and the Nag Hammadi library from a different angle. In general scholars are attempting to see the Gnostics primarily as Christians.

David Brakke is part of this new academic vanguard. Following the lead of Bentley Layton, a renowned Coptologist and author of the popular The Gnostic Scriptures, Brakke identifies the Gnostics as the group otherwise known in scholarship as the Sethians. These were the people that Irenaeus specifically referred to as Gnostics or as "the Gnostic school of thought" (Greek *gnostikoi*.) Brakke believes that "the Gnostics" was a proper name for a sect, and that they identified themselves as such. They are characterised by the use of the Gnostic myth

described by Irenaeus which closely mirrors the myth found in the Apocryphon of John. That and seven other texts are reliably considered to belong to the Gnostics (Sethians) and a further three texts, including the Gospel of Judas and Thunder: Perfect Mind are possible. Brakke himself is inclined to include the Gospel of Judas but has some reservations. The Valentinians were not Gnostics, in that they did not refer to themselves as such, and were differentiated from the actual Gnostics. Gnosticism itself disappears as a "bloated and distorted" scholarly category in which historical delineation, typology of religion and other usages overlap awkwardly and inconsistently. In seeking to define Gnosticism as something different to Christianity the similarities between the Gnostics and other second century Christianities are overlooked. Centuries of special pleading—these people are heretics, they are not like us—are therefore washed away.

This new picture that emerges has some attractive features. For instance, the use of a demiurgic figure is by no means distinctive to Gnosticism. Brakke points out that "all Jews and Christians with any philosophical interests ascribed the creation of the world (in full or in part) to a deity lower than the highest God . . . " (p.22) The church father Justin Martyr (counted as a Middle Platonist) equated God's Wisdom (Sophia) with God's Word (Logos) with Christ, and assigned a mediating and formative role to these figures as a variety of the platonic demiurge. Irenaeus too differentiated between the "invisible and accessible" father and the Son and the Spirit, who are lower, more accessible, powers. Irenaeus even specified that seven heavens surrounded the Earth, in line with Gnostic and other ancient beliefs.

Brakke focuses on the state of Christianity in Rome, the area for which we have the most information, in the first half of the second century, arguing that its Christian groups were small and multiple, and that the Gnostics (Sethians) were simply one among the many Christian sects. As the varieties of Christianity differentiated themselves increasingly from one another, we see the heresiological attacks appear but also the Valentinian appropriation of the Gnostic myth, the use of the word Gnostic by Clement of Alexandria to indicate a spiritual elite and the development of the Christian philosophies of Clement and Origen that adapt and compete with Gnostic thought. Thus the Gnostics have in effect contributed to the ongoing development of Christianity rather than been forced out of it as a perverse and heretical exception to the general rule.

The author writes well and clearly and never adopts an attacking stance. While the distinctiveness of "Gnosticism" is diminished, the significance of the Gnostics and Valentinians is not.

However, as a layman I don't have quite such an overwhelming need to keep my categories so neat and tidy. The English noun "Gnostic" resembles and naturally transforms itself into an adjective—the -ic ending is common in English adjectives such as "basic" and "academic". It is therefore natural to describe teachings that resemble those of the Gnostics as "Gnostic". Even if the Valentinians didn't call themselves Gnostic (and no Valentinian text refers to Valentinians or even to Valentinus either) they were Gnostic in the adjectival sense of having adapted many of the distinctive features of the Gnostics and hence—hey presto!—are Gnostic. Moreover, there is something spiritually appealing that I find in the writings of the Sethians and Valentinians that is certainly not present in Irenaeus or Justin Martyr, though it perhaps appears in a diluted form in Origen and Clement of Alexandria.

The lack of Christian reference in some Sethian texts is not well accounted for. Brakke believes that the Gnostics were always Christian (he doesn't permit an early Jewish Gnosticism) but that references to Jesus were perhaps avoided when the earlier parts of the Gnostic myth are described. He doesn't deal with the centrality of Seth rather than Jesus in Sethian myth. Personally I prefer to refer to the Sethians as Christian-related and unlike the Valentinians I'm not sure that they should be described as Christians if Christ was not at the core of their teachings.

I came away from the book having a fresh perspective on the context of the Gnostics, but I am not quite persuaded that his hypothesis is superior to others. Still, this is a stimulating attempt to make something fresh from the evidence.

Andrew Phillip Smith

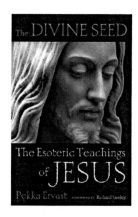

The Divine Seed: The Esoteric Teachings of Jesus. Pekka Ervast, Foreword by Richard Smoley. **Quest Books, Paperback, 128pp, $14.95.**

I'd never heard of Pekka Ervast until I came across this little book. He was a Finnish Theosophist and Rosicrucian, and in his relatively short life^_he died in 1934 aged 58^_ he gave over 800 public lectures and produced an esoteric commentary on the Kalevala, the Finnish national epic.

In The Divine Seed Ervast examines the key teachings of the New Testament—the parables of Jesus, the Lord's Prayer, and the Sermon on the Mount—from an esoteric perspective. He contends that we can read the Scriptures in three ways: "in the light of feeling, of intelligence, and of will". We are all familiar with the first two.

The "light of feeling" is the way of faith: we read as believers, from the standpoint of certain preconceptions. The "light of intelligence" is the way of the critic who is bent on establishing authorship, dates of composition, sources and the like. These two ways are "external and preparatory"; they cleanse the soul and stimulate the intellect but they do not "reveal the wisdom and beauty of the holy book". Only the third way can do this, and the third way is the way of the will—allowing the teachings to become part of our life experience. The book explains clearly how we can do this.

I was particularly impressed by his analysis of the Pater Noster. Ervast considers that we should approach it as a "formula for meditation" rather than a prayer for public or even private recitation. We should also be aware that it is a meditation for the disciple, i.e. the one who can confidently and sincerely pray "thy will be done". Some of Ervast's comments are quite startling. For example, "give us this day our daily bread" is not, as many assume, simply a request that the material needs of the day might be provided. "Daily" is an inadequate translation of the Greek word *epiousios*, which, in Jerome's Vulgate (late fourth century), is translated into Latin as "supersubstantialem", best rendered as "above material". We are not praying for material sustenance but for spiritual insight, which can only come through an acceptance of the sufferings inherent in our mortal existence.

Ervast presents a dimension of Christianity which has been forgotten or even anathematized by orthodoxy. He assumes the reality of reincarnation and uses terms like karma and dharma which have disappeared from Christian vocabulary but which need to be revived if Christians want to present a cogent theodicy to the world.

I liked this book enormously. It is clearly written, with only the occasional reminder that the text is a translation from the original Finnish. It has a good introduction and useful notes by Richard Smoley, the former editor of Gnosis: A Journal of the Western Inner Traditions. You can read it in an afternoon but

its insights will stay with you for a long time. I'm only sorry I came upon the work of Ervast so late in my life, and I wonder just how many other masters of the spiritual life are unknown to us because their works were written in the languages of non-colonial nations.

Bill Darlison

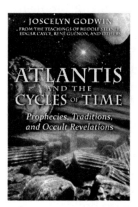

***Atlantis and the Cycles of Time: Prophecies, Traditions, and Occult Revelations.* Joscelyn Godwin. Inner Traditions, Paperback, 448pp. $19.95**

Ever since Plato wrote his account in the *Timaeus* (also the origin of the idea of the demiurge) and Critias, the possibility of a lost, sunken civilization has fascinated the western mind. The appeal of Atlantis is immediately defined by Godwin: "That there was a high culture in prehistoric times." (p.1) He goes on in the first chapter to quickly dispense with what he considers to be the least interesting views of Atlantis. These are not the weakest theories but the most straightforward and rational claims that Atlantis was a relatively recent phenomenon—for instance, the volcanic island of Santorini which erupted in the second millennium BCE. Candidates for Atlantis in this chapter include Thera/Santorini, Crete, Malta, Sicily, Cyprus, the Sahara, Arctica, the Carribbean, Central and South America and the Irish Sea.

But this is a book concerned with the history of extravagant speculation on Atlantis rather than an assessment of the likeliest sources for the legend. Godwin launches straight into his theme without providing a basic description of Plato's Atlantis—surely something of an oversight as not every reader can be expected to be familiar with this ultimate literary origin of the Atlantis myth. Through French esotericism and Theosophy Atlantis and other lost civilizations become linked to the theory of racial origins—according to who you read there are four, five or seven distinct races plus various sub-races. The German Ariosophists prove to be the intermediary between Theosophical racial concepts and full-blown Nazism. The bulk of the book is a collection of bewildering fantasies about Atlantis, the result of medium trance, akashic records, channelling, and plain old good old-fashioned making-stuff-up. Godwin averages 80 footnotes per chapter, in this scholarly and well-annotated book.

The varieties of Atlantises go on and on. Godwin organises them by country (German, French, British, each with their typical qualities). The theosophical Atlantis requires two chapters. There are spiritual dictations of various types, from the obscure Oahspe: A Kasman Bible through to the famous readings of Edgar Cayce. Modern day New Age channellers then pick up the torch, including J.Z. Knight (Godwin comments that she has every right to register Ramtha, the god who speaks through her, as her personal trademark!) (p.291)

Particular themes are repeated through the Atlantean visions. The origins of the pure races. A catastrophe concerning one or more moons. The strange advanced technology of the Atlanteans. The notion of world epochs. Disaster caused by the shifting of the earth's magnetic poles. The corrupting influence of technology.

Several of the repeated themes re-emerge in the channelled material. Some of them don't seem to be dependent on the previously published accounts. Some people may see this as evidence that there is truth behind the various visions of Atlantis—perhaps there are indeed entities communicating prehistoric facts. Godwin seems to feel that this is indicative of some factor in the nature of channelling, and I am inclined to agree with him.

I was a little disappointed not to discover anything about the writings on Atlantis between the time of Plato and the eighteenth century Fabre d'Olivet. Admittedly Godwin has had his

work cut out to research and synthesise bast amounts of often tedious and lengthy material, but it would have been nice to have found out something of the pre-enlightenment history of Atlantology, if indeed there was any.

Of the dozens of accounts of Atlantis two stood out particularly for me. Hugh Clayton Randall-Stephens The Book of Truth, dictated to the Englishman in 1925, contains a form of Gnostic theology in which an initial trinity of father-mother and the Son emanated a series of dual-sexed creative beings. A further demiurgic figure known first as Eranus and then Satanaku, upset the evolution of an entirely spiritual humanity by creating "material" beings independently of the divine plan, who could reproduce without permission of the godhead. These ended up as "a population of monsters, on an Earth that was cut off from communication with other spheres (p.179.) This is an intriguing mishmash of a Sethian-style trinity, emanated syzygies, the anthropos and the evil demiurge.

The other is an account of Atlantis as given in Gurdjieff's Beelzebub's Tales. Godwin laments of Beelzebub's Tales, "Only someone already fascinated by Gurdjieff's teachings would read it through once, let alone the three times prescribed as a minimum for understanding it. I make no such claim."

He adds later, "Whoever rewrites the work in a sensible language and at half its length will being doing a service to humanity and, in my opinion, to Gurdjieff himself." (p.234.)

The preceding chapters make it obvious to me that Gurdjieff's account of the Earth's second moon Anulios was influenced by Theosophy, ditto his delightfully wicked account of the origin of apes—not the ancestors of humans nor descended from humans as per Blavatsky but the product of women and beasts mating. This story of the origin of the apes is, I would hazard a guess, to do with Gurdjieff's idea of triads in which not merely proposition and opposition but three forces are required to produce a phenomenon. Gurdjieff explains that Anulios means "Remorse of Conscience" and hence suggests an unusually explicit (for Gurdjieff0 psychological interpretation of the myth of the second moon. The Atlanteans knew of this second celestial counterweight—conscience— whereas we have forgotten about it.

Should we weary occasionally of tale after tale of extravagant Atlantean fantasy, Godwin salts the pudding with a wry humour and spicy details of the esotericists and eccentrics responsible for the grand theories. All in all this is an amazing work of scholarship and Godwin is to be commended (and sympathised with) for his thorough handling of the subject.

Andrew Phillip Smith

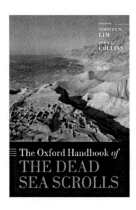

The Oxford Handbook of the Dead Sea Scrolls.
Edited by Timothy H. Lim and John J. Collins. OUP, Hardcover, 785pp. $150/£86.

The Dead Sea Scrolls—occasionally confused with the Nag Hammadi library by the general public—have received a good more attention, both scholarly and popular, than the Gnostic writings. I have always felt that this is unfortunate as the contents of the Nag Hammadi library are, to my mind, both intrinsically more interesting and historically more important. Yet the transition from discovery to publication was for the NHL relatively straightforward, even if it did take thirty years, in comparison to the Dead Sea Scrolls, which suffered and we should be grateful that the Gnostic writings did not suffer quite the same degree of academic wrangling and incompetence that so blighted the Dead Sea Scrolls. The Dead Sea Scrolls have even perhaps cast some light on Gnostic origins, with John Turner suggesting that the Sethians might have originated in a withdrawal from the authority of the Jerusalem Temple, as was the case with

the Dead Sea Scroll community. Interesting comparison has been made between elements of Mandaean purity rituals and those found in the DSS.

The Oxford Handbook of the Dead Sea Scrolls is intended to probe the areas of controversy rather than sum up the state of scholarship as did earlier The Encyclopedia of the Dead Sea Scrolls .

Broken up into easily digestible sections, which is unusual for such an erudite compilation, this volume covers the whole gamut of scholarly investigation. There are few illustrations. The sections examine the archaeology and physical environs of Qumran, where the scrolls were discovered. They are then examined against the background of Jewish history and the sectarian movement that kept the scrolls. Despite some severe critiquing of Qumran as an Essene community associated with the production of the scrolls, most scholars still see this as the case, although every detail is up for questioning. After some essays discussing the languages in the scrolls and the importance of the DSS's early exemplars of biblical texts, the collection moves on to discuss religious themes such as purity, apocalypticism and mysticism and the relationship between the scrolls and early Christianity and later Judaism.

Reading the articles in the anthology gives one the feeling of being involved in the continuing development of the understanding of these writings.

Arthur Craddock

A Complete Guide to the Soul. Patrick Harpur. Rider, Paperback, 240pp. £9.99.

In my 2006 book *Gnostic Writings on the Soul: Annotated & Explained* I examined the *Exegesis on the Soul* and the *Hymn of the Pearl* and in an introduction provided a selective potted history of the soul throughout history. I decided that the Gnostic view of soul and spirit was a particularly complete and elegant approach to the soul.

In *A Complete Guide to the Soul* Patrick Harpur, author of fine novels and two intriguing nonfiction books on the Otherworld of imagination, the supernatural and mysticism, takes us on a winding tour of the soul. As befits an entity which is internal and immaterial, or at least not physical, Harpur declines to straitjacket the soul and rejects any attempt to quantify or analyse it, to weight or measure it. It is the soul which must speak about the soul. He apologies for "the duplicitous title of this book ("did two-faced Hermes have a hand in it? Or was it just the publisher?") (p.210)

Like the soul this book defies analysis and is difficult even to recapitulate. Chapters deal with various contexts of the soul—the soul and world-soul, soul and body, soul and daimon and psyche and the unconscious and myth and spirit and ego and initiation and the Otherworld. Though he briefly mentions Gnosis it is the soul in Neoplatonism that predominates, along with the integrated body-soul worldview of "primitive" peoples. There are some fascinating anthropological insights in here. But beyond either of these is a Jungian aesthetic.

Harpur is particularly hard on the spirit, preferring the soul itself and giving the spirit a secondary character, rather like an archetype within the soul. Spirit is concerned with transcendence, with hierarchy, with utopias, with the abandonment of this world. Spirit is concerned with oneness, soul with an eclectic multitude. Harpur sees the spirit's fascination with the higher as limiting the vast arenas of the soul.

Since the author has firmly pitched his tent in the field of the soul he excels in the things of the soul, particularly myth. He uses familiar myths, particularly the Greek, quite brilliantly. Time after time he applies these well-known old tales with such insight that it is easy to believe that he

comprehends them at the core. Harpur's prose twists and winds with the rhythm of the soul, lapping over the reader like a dream.

This is a book I shall be returning to, though I have not abandoned my ambition to write a full work on the soul myself. I have also ordered Harpur's other books. Though I find myself not quite in sympathy with his overall approach, this is a rare work and highly recommended to anyone with a soul.

Andrew Phillip Smith

The Hidden Passion.
Laurence Caruana.
Recluse Publishing,
Paperback,
431pp. $21.95.

There are many novels that address the life of Jesus, but few that address Gnostic themes, and none that rely so explicitly and heavily on the Nag Hammadi library as this one. *The Hidden Passion* is a retelling of the story of Jesus from what in orthodox circles would be called the beginning of his ministry to his crucifixion, followed by a very Gnostic culmination. Extensive discourses of Gnostic teachings and initiations are included in the text and a wholly different account of the progress of Jesus and his relationships with his disciples emerges.

The author's method is visible throughout. In preparation for the writing of the novel he compiled what he calls a "Gnostic Q", extracting all the sayings of Jesus found in the Nag Hammadi library. Close paraphrases of these are used liberally in the story. Each of these quotations (plus other noncanonical writings) is indicated by angular brackets, with the source cited in the margins. Caruana is an artist and the book is elegantly designed, so the high level of citation isn't intrusive to the eye.

This novel is a fine way to acquaint oneself with lesser-known parts of the Gnostic writings. From the outset Caruana makes it clear that this is a work of fiction, not an attempt at a Gnostic Historical Jesus. "Lest my intentions be misconstrued from the beginning, this is a novel of the Gnostic Christ." (p. ix.)

I have to say that as a novel I found it hard going at times. The extensive use of scriptural quotation (if noncanonical) unavoidably lends the narrative a certain stiffness at times, particularly in dialogue. But there is more than enough interest in the author's unusual take on Jesus, and his explications of Gnostic teaching, to keep the reader going through any longeurs.

In his afterword Caruana provides short discussions on some of the characters and particular Gnostic ideas and rituals. There is also a helpful glossary and a useful diagram of the Gnostic cosmos. This is one of the most unusual novelizations of the life of Jesus and an excellent way to dig deeper into the treasures of the Nag Hammadi library.

Andrew Phillip Smith

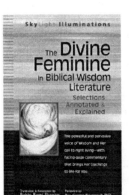

The Divine Feminine in Biblical Wisdom Literature: Selections Annotated and Explained. Rabbi Rami Shapiro with a Foreword by Rev. Dr Cynthia Bourgeault. Skylight Paths, Paperback, 240 pages. $16.99

In the Preface, Rabbi Shapiro tells how he was "pursued" by the Divine Mother and encouraged by her to write this illuminating and uplifting book. The Divine Mother is Wisdom, *Chochma* in Hebrew, *Sophia* in Greek, who appears in the pages of the Bible, but mainly in the *Ketuvim*, ("The Writings'"), those books which the Jewish people relegate to the second rank. Shapiro associates her, no

doubt heretically in the eyes of most of his fellow religionists, with the goddess in Hindu thought, with the Virgin Mary, and with the principle of Wisdom found in the *Tao Te Ching*.

Jewish, Catholic and Protestant orthodoxy will certainly find this idea troubling, but more liberal religionists of all traditions will grasp it as offering genuine point of ecumenical contact. According to Shapiro, orthodoxy generally manifests *mochin d'gadlut*, a Hebrew term he translates as "narrow mind" and which issues in divisive dogmas. By contrast, what is required, he says, is *mochin d'katnut*, "spacious mind", which enables us to see the connections which centuries of religious conflict have obscured.

The rabbi brings his own spacious mind to bear on the biblical books of Job, Ecclesiastes, Psalms, Song of Songs and Proverbs, along with some apocryphal books, notably The Wisdom of Solomon and Ecclesiasticus. He devotes a chapter to an overview of these works, giving a brief account of the origin, content and importance of each one. This is clearly written, free from technical jargon, and very useful indeed, especially for those who are not really familiar with the make-up of the Bible, or who have neglected the apocryphal works on account of their non-canonical status.

The rest of the book comprises a series of meditations on individual passages, which Shapiro gives in his own translation. For example, in chapter 8 (verses 27-29) of the Book of Proverbs we read:

I am. God is my source, and I am his first creation. I before time—I am. Before beginnings—I am. There were as yet no oceans when I was born, no springs deep and overflowing. I am older than the mountains. Elder to the hills, the valleys, and the fields. Before even the first lumps of clay emerged—I am.

Shapiro links this with section 25 of the *Tao Te*

Ching:

> Something mysteriously formed. Born before heaven and earth. In the silence and the void…It is the mother of ten thousand things. I do not know its name. I call it Tao.

This, he says, is echoed in Jesus' claim (John 8:58), "Before Abraham was I am." Shapiro comments:

> All things flow from Her (Wisdom), arise in Her, embody Her as a wave embodies the ocean. You are Her; it is only arrogance that blinds you to that fact. To know Her is to know yourself. To know yourself is to know the world, Her children, as your siblings.

Although Jesus is mentioned in this section, there is nothing much from the New Testament in the whole volume and I was disappointed by this. Nor is there any attempt made to link these Wisdom passages with similar passages in Buddhist, Hindu, or Muslim writings. I sincerely hope that the divine Mother will pursue some other person of spacious mind and inspire them to carry the work this one step further.

But that is a quibble. I heartily recommend this book. After the introductory material it should be taken slowly, maybe at the rate of one passage and its commentary each day. This will give the reader time to think about, meditate upon, inwardly digest—and act upon—the profound teaching that it gives. Rilke told us that the work of the eyes is done and now we should do the heart-work on the images imprisoned within us. This book will help us to do just that.

Bill Darlison

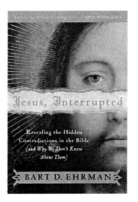

Jesus, Interrupted.
Bart Ehrman.
HarperOne, Paperback,
304pp. $15.99.

Despite its title, this is not principally a book about the gap between the life of Jesus and the traditions that inform the canonical gospels which postdate that life by 30-70 years. Rather it is concerned with the contradictions in the New Testament, known to online pundits as biblical errancy. The book is written chiefly to inform the general public and particularly churchgoers, of the consensus academic opinions on the historicity of the New Testament. Thus Ehrman has sections on basic inconsistencies between the gospels, the quest for the historical Jesus, the formation of the canon and the invention or emergence of Christianity as a distinct religion and a major force in the world.

Ehrman frames the entire book and individual discussions therein with his journey from committed conservative evangelist to liberal evangelist to agnostic. Yet he does not believe that the adoption of historical-critical conclusions about the bible should lead anyone to lose her faith. His own agnosticism is due to his recognition that Christianity could not adequately account for the problem of evil.

Ehrman's insistence on, for the most part, sticking to established majority opinion is both a strength and a weakness. On the one hand, his intention in informing the general reader of the findings of scholarship is not hampered by idiosyncratic views; on the other, the material can be very vanilla-flavoured. This is typical of Ehrman's approach and much in this volume may be found in his other works. With brief sections on early heretical Christianity and apocryphal writings (*Lost Christianities*), an apocalyptic historical Jesus (*Jesus: Apocalyptic Prophet of the New Millennium*), the influence of developing orthodoxy on the text of the

New Testament (*Misquoting Jesus* and *The Orthodox Corruption of Scripture*), and general introductory information on the books of the New Testament (*The New Testament: A Historical Introduction to the Early Christian Writings*), Jesus Interrupted is really an epitome of Ehrman's publishing career thus far. (See Voices of Gnosticism for an extensive interview with Ehrman by Miguel Conner.) I do wonder that he doesn't get bored trotting out the same material over and over again, but as a lecturer I suppose he is used to it.

One notable exception is a passage in which he describes the ancient attitude to forgery and pseudepigraphy—it was definitely frowned upon and was not respectable. Ehrman enumerates ten categories of ancient motivation for forgery, "to provide authority for one's own views" being the principle culprit for Christian forgery. He then runs through the New Testament epistles (excluding the authentic Pauline epistles) showing which are forgeries, in that they present themselves as the work of an earlier writer even though internal evidence shows that they cannot be written by that author. Thus the pastoral epistles, written in the name of Paul, 1 and 2 Peter, etc. are forgeries whereas the epistles of James and Jude may be labelled homonymous, ascribed by later writers to the brothers of Jesus because of a coincidence of name.

It's a brave move, considering his intended audience, and one that he is constantly softening, alternating between calling them forged or pseudonymous in order not to upset the reader.

Since Ehrman's opinions are so standard it is a tragi-comical entertainment to see so many evangelist pseudo-scholars like Craig Evans and Ben Witherington III railing against Ehrman. He must be doing something right.

In short, this is a succinct, well-explained digest of mainstream scholarship expressed in a mildly provocative way. If you are familiar with New Testament historical criticism there is little new here, though it may be an entertaining way of taking a refresher course. If all this is new to you, there aren't many better ways of understanding what Bible scholarship is all about.

Arthur Craddock

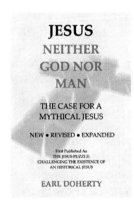

Jesus: Neither Man Nor God by Earl Doherty. Age of Reason Publications, Paperback, 814pp. $39.95.

It is probably unwise for a reviewer to confess that he has not read the entire book under review, but this is what I must admit to here. At a massive 800 pages with a fairly large page size and small type, this volume represents a compendium of all Doherty's thought to date on his hypothesis that Christianity emerged with a mythical Christ at its core. There was never any historical Jesus, not even a shadowy figure about whom little can be known. I have been following Doherty's arguments for over a decade now, through his website (www.jesuspuzzle.com and its various mirrors) and his first, relatively brief book on the subject, also entitled The Jesus Puzzle. While I have never been convinced that there was no human figure behind the admittedly legendary or mythical figure in the gospels I have always been impressed by the depth and tenacity of Doherty's argument and his ability to shed light on otherwise ignored aspects of early Christianity.

This book is incredibly thorough. Doherty's foundation stone is the priority of the Pauline writings. Just about every respectable scholar admits that Paul's view of a transcendent ahistorical crucified Christ precedes the Galilean of the gospels, at least in terms of literary precedence. Most would admit that there is precious little to suggest that Paul reveals any knowledge of a human being named Jesus as the founder of the movement that he joined. Yet the gospels and their putative sources are always given the lead, with scholars preferring sources that depict a Jesus that walked the earth in the 30s of the common era, even if they are later. Not so Earl Doherty. He takes Paul at his word, and apart from the problematic "born of woman, born under the law" of Galatians 4:4 (for which he gives several suggestions to read it otherwise), has little difficulty in showing that the Christ Jesus of Paul may as well be entirely mythical.

Doherty is no conspiracy theorist (at least not by my standards) and in many ways he is simply taking recent New Testament scholarship to its logical conclusion. For instance, he writes extensively on Q, the hypothetical source of the material common to the synoptic gospels of Matthew and Luke but not Mark. Source critic John Kloppenborg examined the reconstruction of Q and argued that it shows signs of being composed in layers, the bottom layer being a collection of wisdom sayings (more exactly, chreia, an ancient genre of sayings which can have short contextual introductions.) Doherty further examines this bottom layer and argues that there is no need to connect it to a character named Jesus. He sees the earliest Christianity as a meeting of disparate traditions and it is only in Mark that we find the recognisable character upon which the historical Jesus is founded.

He has a chapter on Gnosticism, in which he indicates that he sees the Christ of the Sethians as initially an independent development parallel to the heavenly mythical Christ of Paul and some other early Christian writings such as Hebrews, Revelation, Hermas and the Odes of Solomon. There are some interesting ideas in the chapter, but he shows a lack of knowledge of recent scholarship on Gnosticism (and, to be fair, he can't have time to read everything.) There are a few howlers, particularly "There is no higher God in Valentinianism" (p. 294.) This is simply untrue.

I find fault in Doherty's approach in two ways. One is that his insistence on the complete absence of any human figure that might be at the root of the Jesus of the New Testament. This means that any admission of anyone resembling a human Jesus has to be avoided at all costs, whereas a softer approach which might acknowledge a Jesus as a marginal, vague figure who became associated with the mythical Christ allows for more flexibility. One whiff of a human Jesus and the house of cards collapses. The other is his position as a rationalist atheist. I can help feeling that his lack of sympathy for any kind of religion stands in the way of understanding the religious mentality at times. For instance, I find it odd but not impossible that Paul should fail to give much information on a human Jesus if there was indeed one. Doherty however is at times incredulous.

Dohherty delves into the obscure corners of early Christianity—little-read apocrypha and church fathers like Minucius Felix whom most of us have never heard of. Despite my reservations concerning the overall thesis and certain of Doherty's decisions, this is a monumental work, and one that anyone who is interested in arguments for the mythicist case— actual scholarly discussion and reasoning— must purchase. I will be dipping into this book often for Doherty's unconventional insights and careful detail on all aspects of early Christianity.

Andrew Phillip Smith

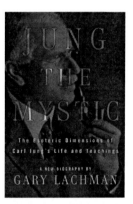

Jung the Mystic.
Gary Lachman.
Tacher, Hardcover,
272pp. $24.95/£21.

Jung has for me always been something of a curiosity. Jungian psychology is not quite a spiritual path nor is most of it (if we are honest) truly a part of scientific psychology. Little of what Jung has proposed is testable in a scientific way. Of course, the same is true of Freudian psychology, but Freud's materialism put him in the mainstream of early twentieth century thought, whereas Jung's influence has been slower to develop, blossoming only in the later twentieth century as the materialistic worldview began to creak and splinter.

Jung considered himself to be primarily a scientist, a self-designation that has perhaps persisted in orthodox and professional Jungian circles, and hence his extensive mystical life has typically been played down or relativized. The publication of the Red Book means that Jung's mystical nature can no longer be shuffled away to one side and, in a very Jungian reconciliation of opposites, we can now see Jung in a more balanced way as mystic and scientist reconciled in the analytical psychologist.

Gary Lachman's *The Mystic Jung* functions both as a study of Jung's spiritual side and as a general biography. Lachman immediately addresses the separation between Jung the Scientist and Jung the Mystic, labelling them personality no. 1 and no. 2 and, particularly in the early years of Jung's adulthood, uses them as a fundamental dichotomy of Jung's character, much as biographers of P.D. Ouspensky (among whom Lachman is to be counted in his very readable *In Search of P.D. Ouspensky*) treat the intellectual Pyotr and emotional Demianovich as contrary sides of Ouspensky's character.

This dichotomy shows up in Jung's private life too. Solitary and patrician he had a number of affairs but maintained a stable family life, relying on his wealthy wife Emma for funds. His powerful interest in Gnosticism, alchemy, parapsychology and the occult was ridiculed by Freud, and his unwillingness to toe Freud's materialistic line and failure to acknowledge the neurotic Freud as the fountainhead and kingpin of psychology, led to their split. I must add that Jung seems a much more admirable person than Freud, and this may well be testimony to the greater benefits of Jung's psychology.

Lachman is right to place Jung alongside Gurdjieff and Steiner as a great spiritual figure of the twentieth century. Yet Jung's scientific veneer placed him in the mainstream of culture. Had Jung been willing to take the leap of faith that would have made him primarily a spiritual figure his general influence would have been diminished and marginalised. Yet, as Lachman comments, Jung was temperamentally unsuited to establishing a set system of thought and this is perhaps to his credit. He wanted others to think too.

In Maurice Nicoll, Jung and Gurdjieff shared a pupil. Nicoll, a promising aspirant in the psychology movement wrote a book based on Jungian principles, Dream Psychology, but defected after meeting Ouspensky and abandoned his practice to live in Gurdjieff's Institute in Fontainbleau until his father died and he returned to Britain. Nicoll continued to use dream interpretation and occasionally referred to Jung in the weekly talks collected in Nicoll's *Psychological Commentaries on the Teachings of Gurdjieff and Ouspensky*. When Jung stayed in a cottage near Aylesbury in England he experienced an unpleasant haunting. In later correspondence with Nicoll in the 1950s he referred to these parapsychological happenings. Nicoll had sent Jung a copy of In Search of the Miraculous. Tellingly Jung declined to read it, explaining that he detested metaphysics. This absence of a spiritual cosmology in Jung's thought and his psychologizing of Gnostic cosmology is again both a strength and a weakness. Jung shied away from the speculative and unverifiable. This protected him from accusations of occultism and mystagoguery but also left a gap in his thought. Jung can offer no greater force in the world than humanity and a vague notion of God. It is an appealing position in the modern world but also limited.

As Lachman makes clear, Jung's mysticism was primarily of the visionary type. Inspired and assailed by difficult and dangerous visionary experiences, it is clear that the most profound of these were beyond his control. Despite the development of the technique of active imagination, Jung was a true mystic. These experiences came to him and he made what he could of them. He was in many ways the vehicle not the summoner, a mystic not a mage.

Aside from the focus on visions, Lachman is excellent on the subject of Jung's supposed anti-semitism. This is no whitewash, but he shows that Jung was always opposed to Nazism and helped the allies by providing psychological profiles of leading Nazis. Certainly he indulged in the sweeping racial generalisations characteristic of the period. But his assessment of Jewish character, while questionable, was not anti-Semitic. He was far harder on the Teutonic character, describing the German peoples as civilized from the waist up only, with a barbaric Teutonic beast waiting to be unleashed.

Lachman also conveys Jung's intense creativity. His mandalas, sculpting, building work and of course the gorgeous and weird illustrations in the Red Book, are genuinely nonrational and persist into Jungian practice today. Overall Lachman depicts Jung as a flawed human being but a genuine seeker and visionary who indeed deserves to be seen not only shoulder to shoulder with Freud and Adler, but alongside Gurdjieff and Steiner too.

Arthur Craddock

Mystery Cults in the Ancient World. Hugh Bowden. Thames & Hudson, Hardcover, 256pp. £28.

The mystery cults were widespread in the ancient world, persisting in Greece and hence Rome and in Mediterranean Hellenistic Asia and Egypt. The experience of powerful ritual and ecstatic union with the god that they offered to initiates was a counterbalance to the more staid religion of household gods and official state religion. As Bowden writes, "It was a basic understanding in most of Greco-Roman religion that the gods could only be indirectly known." (p.14) The mystery religions offered instead direct participation with the god. This heavily illustrated book (189 illustrations, 28 of them in colour) is an excellent and up-to-date introduction to this mysterious and fascinating world.

We know of the mysteries from literature (including the Homeric Hymns, Apuleius' The Golden Ass and commentators such as Plutarch), archeological remains (including those of Pompeii) and art.

The mystery religions include those of Demeter, Dionysus, Isis the late Roman Mithras, and numerous nameless deities referred to as the Great Gods, the Mother, the Mistress and the Maid. The introduction is an excellent synopsis of what is known of the mysteries and the current scholarly approach to this phenomenon. Anthropology views religion as having two modes of expression: the doctrinal and the imagistic. Doctrinal religion, exemplified by Christianity, involves regular repeated ritual with explicitly stated meaning. It is found particularly in large hierarchical societies. Imagistic religion, of which the mystery cults and ancient religion in general may be examples, is the older variety, exists in smaller, less hierarchical communities and uses infrequent ritual presenting startling events, the significance of which usually remains unexplained. It was the experience itself that was important, not any secret knowledge that might have been imparted. The author believes that the notion of arcane knowledge being disclosed during initiation is probably false. The experience itself lingered throughout the lifetime of the initiate. Interpretations of these rites are rare because the initiation was in essence indescribable. Early Christianity has often been included as a form of mystery religion, with its sacred meal and dying and rising God, but Bowden feels that this is inaccurate.

Nor is Bowden convinced that the consumption of drugs such as ergot, or even of alcohol in Bacchic rites played any part. Rather "If we are to look for an external explanation for the power of the Eleusinian experience, the theatre seems a better place to look than the kitchen or brewery." (p.45.)

Each of the chief mysteries is described in the following chapters, along with sections on private initiation (often considered disreputable as they were available to the wealthy for monetary payment, waiving the usual restrictions), on poems and other inscriptions inscribed on gold leaf, on the final disintegration of the mysteries due to the official establishment of Christianity as the religion of the Roman Empire, and plunder by barbarians. Finally there is a glance at those experiences available in the modern world which might resemble those of the mysteries. Pentecostal Christianity, including snake-handling churches, are discussed and there is a nod towards ecstasy-fuelled rave culture. Illustrations of dancing at a Haitian Pentecostal Church and a procession of the holy virgin at Seville are intended to It is surprising that there is no mention of the Naasene Hymn, which imports many of the mystery myths into a Gnostic context.

The writing is clear and accessible, and while the author has his own opinions, this is very much a broad consensus introduction. We are particularly lucky to have extensive sculptural evidence plus the beautiful Roman paintings from Pompeii and other sites. These help to convey something of the non-verbal ritual experience of the mysteries. The Greeks were aesthetic in the religious expression and there is much that is beautiful in the art, myth and literature included here.

Mithraism, the mystery cult that is perhaps most likely to come to mind for the general reader is seen as something of a late outsider, unique in its status as a primarily Roman mystery. Its widespread adoption by soldiers in the Roman Empire has resulted in it being the cult that has the best-preserved temples.

This is well-produces and stimulating book. If you only have a single volume on the ancient mysteries on your shelf, it should be this one.

Arthur Craddock

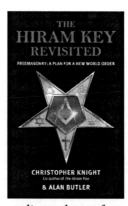

The Hiram Key Revisited: Freemasonry: A Plan for a New World Order. Christopher Knight and Alan Butler. Watkins Publishing, Paperback, 320pp. £8.99

I've got a bit of a soft spot for conspiracy theories, and the wilder they are the better. An earlier volume from Knight and Butler (*Who Built the Moon?*) dealt with what they consider has been the biggest cover-up of all time—the fact that the moon has actually been constructed by an advanced civilisation and placed in the sky to aid the development of life on earth and (no doubt) to provide poets with an endless source of romantic imagery. They make a reasonably good case for it, as they do in the present work for their theory that Freemasonry is the creation of a sinister group called "The Star Families," a secret society descended from the masons who constructed Solomon's Temple and which has been steadily manipulating history for three millennia.

As one might imagine, the story is intricate and convoluted, ingeniously weaving together as it does astrology, the Bible, the Cistercians, the wool industry, architecture, the crusades, the Dead Sea Scrolls, international banking, and (who would have guessed?) good old Rosslyn Chapel. However, it is entertainingly told, well-illustrated, and, as with all good conspiracy theories, the reader is left with the impression that the authors just might be on to something.

Occasionally I was left doubtful about the scholarship. For example, in an attempt to explain the Shekinah ("the divine presence", which the authors consider to be a conjunction of Venus and Mercury) we read:

Every eight years Venus returns to the same point in the sky, but the background stars are now different; astronomically speaking, Venus has moved one fifth of the way through the zodiac. And every 40 years Venus completes one full lap of the zodiac—ending up back where it started.' (Page 8)

Since Venus is never far away from the sun in the sky, it completes one circuit of the zodiac every year or so. The authors are dealing with a complex pattern of relationships and the explanation they give is inadequate and misleading. I have also been unable to trace the source of their contention that "The name 'Jerusalem' in the Canaanite language means "foundation for observing Venus rising". The authors themselves give no indication of where they found this intriguing piece of information.

But by far my biggest problem with the book is the way it is printed and bound. The typeface is quite small and the margins narrow, which means that reading it can be quite a chore. When will publishers learn that the way a book is presented is almost as important as the information it contains?

Bill Darlison

Needles of Stone. Tom Graves. Grey House in the Woods, Paperback, 289pp. £12.95.

Inventing Reality. Tom Graves. Grey House in the Woods, Paperback, 106pp. £7.95.

Leylines—ancient landscape alignments—and mysterious energies associated with ancient monuments such as stone circles have fascinated me since I was a teenager. Fantastic and unlikely extrapolations on these basic themes have in turn dotted the intellectual landscape of New Age, providing wild and unverifiable theories to be exploited commercially. Yet there is a strong body of serious body of research based on on-the-ground, hands-on experience coupled with a capacity for rational, if unconventional, thinking. *Needles of Stone* exhibits the latter character.

It is also a terrific book. Tom Graves brings an engineer's mind to problems that exist not only on the gross physical plane but also in the realms of rarefied energy and even consciousness. The original edition was published in 1978. This Grey House in the Woods edition incorporates all of Graves' subsequent postscripts and additional chapters that have accrued. Over the decades Graves has refined and reconsidered his ideas and even abandoned his interest in ancient mysteries and earth energies, exasperated by the wackiness of many of his fellow pundits, but has returned to them anew.

There is certainly much in this book (if not most of it) that is speculative, but the marriage of experience and constructive critical thinking is exhilarating. Graves is a dowser and uses these techniques to divine the lines of energy, while admitting that the nature of dowsing allows for false positives. My favourite example of the strange phenomena that he encountered is the effect—apparently reproducible—that under certain circumstances causes energy from standing stones to thrust the dowser forcibly backwards. My favourite overall episode is the one where he triggers an energy gate at the Rollright Stones in Oxfordshire, releasing energy that travels to a megalith six miles away and gives Graves an instant migraine. Of course, there is nothing here that is outside of subjective experience (which might be said for energy-dowsing in general) but I love the concept and his careful description of the circumstances.

Along the way he speculates on the nature of

ghosts, weather effects, earth acupuncture, Feng Shui, thought forms and much more. I cannot recommend this book too highly to anyone interested in earth mysteries.

Inventing Reality I found less engaging. Here Graves addresses magic as technology. He offers an insightful critique of the scientific worldview and gives some pointers and practical episodes towards developing an magical alternative. Inventing Reality was first published in 1986, and perhaps some of its ideas have become fairly commonplace. Even so, Graves' exploratory reasoning applied to what is usually considered unreasonable is always a delight and I would be happy to read his entire corpus.

Andrew Phillip Smith

Pistis Sophia: A Coptic Text of Gnosis with Commentary. J.J. Hurtak and Desiree Hurtak. The Academy for Future Science, Hardcover, 908pp (www.pistissophia.org)$50.

The Gnostic Mysteries of Pistis Sophia: Reflections on Book I of Pistis Sophia. Jan Van Rijkenborgh. Rosycross Press, Hardcover, 400pp. $35.

The Path of Light. Christian O'Brien. Dianthus Publishing, Hardcover, 288pp. £18.95.

Pistis Sophia is familiar, if by name only, to many people with an interest in alternative religion. Until the publication of the Nag Hammadi library, it was the best-known Gnostic text, and G.R.S. Mead's translation remains in print in numerous editions. Yet the prominence of the Nag Hammadi library and the shortage of experts in Coptic and Gnostic studies has led to Pistis Sophia being ignored in academia in the last few decades. *The Books of Jeu*, the other major Coptic Gnostic work, has been even more neglected by scholars than *Pistis Sophia*. It is difficult even to find a complete translation. The slack has been taken up instead by esoteric writers. Here we have two relatively recent books on *Pistis Sophia* and one (*The Path of Light*) on the *Pistis Sophia* and the *Books of Jeu*. Each of these books is written from a specific esoteric standpoint.

J.J and Desiree Hurtak provide a translation of commentary of *Pistis Sophia* in a beautiful off-white hardback volume with gold stamping containing a massive 900 pages. Hurtak and Hurtak are the directors of the Academy for Future Science, which researches such subjects as consciousness, alternative archaeology and astrophysics and the like.

The introduction contains a good summary of the cosmology, characters and themes of *Pistis Sophia*. The bulk of the book is an interpretive commentary. It seems that the Hurtaks have indeed gone back to the Coptic, so this constitutes a complete new translation of the *Pistis Sophia* in addition to those of Mead (from a Latin intermediary), George Horner (a literal translation), Violet McDermott and, now, Christian O'Brien. The text is interspersed with the extensive commentary, so there is no easy way to read it continuously. The interpretation is Hurtak's own (J.J. appears to be the cornerstone of the Academy) and quickly extends into metaphysical beliefs that one may or may not agree with. The authors draw particularly from the Kabbalah, but also from Egyptian mythology and Egyptian religion. The result is something of a mish-mash, and the Hurtaks are essentially riffing off the *Pistis Sophia*, but those who like their spirituality eclectic will enjoy it. A useful glossary—the fullest that I recall for the *Pistis Sophia*—rounds off the book.

Jan van Rijkenborgh's *The Gnostic Mysteries of Pistis Sophia* draws on Book I only. The author, a Dutch Rosicrucian, died in 1968 before he could complete his commentary. The translation is that of Mead and this is accompanied by what is very much a modern Rosicrucian interpretation. Hardly any scholarly material is introduced and van Rijkenborgh believes erroneously that *Pistis Sophia* was composed by Valentinus. Whereas the Hurtaks' book, even though it goes off on all sorts of tangents, places the Pistis Sophia at the centre of the discussion, van Rijkenborgh's work has at its core the Rosicrucianism of his "spiritual school" (as the book refers to it) the Lectorium Rosicrucianum. It comes over more as a series of esoteric homilies. As a result it should be of interest to anyone involved in or fascinated by Rosicrucianism, but I find it difficult to recommend it to those who are primarily interested in what it has to say about the *Pistis Sophia*.

Christian O'Brien's *The Path of Light* is intended as a supporting volume for his published research, which included themes of alternative history and astroarcheology. O'Brien, a geologist in his professional life, died in 2001 and this volume was published by a foundation which seeks to further his work. There is actually little in this particular book on his researches into the ancient Near East (Oddly, both O'Brien and J.J. Hurtak have drawn heavily on the *Book of Enoch* in their other writings.) This books contains translations of the *Pistis Sophia* and the *Books of Jeu*. The *Books of Jeu* is otherwise available only in Brill's *The Books of Jeu and the Untitled Text in the Bruce Codex* translated by Violet McDermott, priced at $130 (now the single volume is seemingly back in print) and for several years only in the complete *The Coptic Gnostic Library*, priced at $700. Thus *The Path of Light* contains the only affordable translation of the *Books of Jeu*. It is indeed a fresh translation, along with Pistis Sophia, from Coptic, drawing heavily on Violet McDermott's, to the extent that the publishers obtained the permission of E.J.Brill. O'Brien was also a follower of the Sant Mat teaching, the modern form of which claims descent from Sikhism. He translates a couple of terms into Sant Mat terminology, notable Great Logos and its counterparts as *Shabd*, and the "Archon of the Aeons" as *Kal*. This is a bit intrusive. Although I haven't had time to make an extensive comparison between O'Brien's and McDermott's translations, I would suspect that other interpretive elements have entered. Certainly Christian terminology is minimised or neutered. For instance, where McDermott has "He who has crucified it (the world) is he who has found my word . . . " O'Brien renders this as "He who has overcome the World is he who has found my Shabd. . . " In general the translation runs on parallel lines to McDermott's, making these exceptions all the more conspicuous. The *Books of Jeu* (O'Brien treats the two texts as a piece, reordering part of *Pistis Sophia*) occupies only a sixth of the book, but that might be said to justify the price of the book. There is simply no other translation available.

Each of these books is problematic for a reader who does not share the author's worldview, and they are recognisably the products of small esoteric groups. It is of course wise to check out any small religious group for signs of cult characteristics before any serious involvement with them. Yet I feel quite impressed that these undeniably marginal and small groups have been influenced and affected by these texts—that are now ignored by scholars and seen as second-division by modern Gnostics—enough to write and publish these editions.

Andrew Phillip Smith

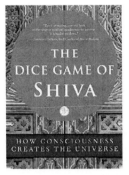

RICHARD SMOLEY

The Dice Game of shiva: How Consciousness Creates the Universe. Richard Smoley. New World Library, Paperback, 240pp. $14.95/£14.50.

What is consciousness, how does it emerge, and what is its significance? Richard Smoley draws on his knowledge and experience of western philosophy, esotericism and Eastern religion in this stimulating discussion. This is very much a discursive work and Smoley doesn't provide any easy answers. Well, that is not quite true, he does give us one easy answer, in reply to the first question, "What is consciousness?" Smoley defines consciousness as the ability to distinguish self and other. This simple solution allows him to delve into all of the world's great traditions, along with modern science, and extract useful material. This distinction between consciousness and experience, or between consciousness and its contents Is found in the Indian myth of shiva and his consort Parvati. Parvati challenges shiva to a game of dice which he perpetually loses, even to the extent of gambling away his own clothes. At a certain point Shiva simply goes happily into seclusion, having lost nothing real. Shiva represents consciousness, Parvati experience. Consciousness continually loses itself in experience yet ultimately nothing is lost. This is essentially the highest form of consciousness, yet Smoley for consciousness in everything, a form of panpsychism although the term is never used. Even atoms have a form of consciousness as they can clearly distinguish between self and other by "knowing" how to combine with other atoms.

Though Smoley is eclectic in his sources he gives none of them an easy ride. Atheism and scientism are found lacking and he places little faith in the ability of quantum mechanics to tell us much about consciousness, at least in

its current state of development. It is probably the western esoteric tradition, including in its broadest sense esoteric Christianity, which receives the greatest respect. Eastern religion and philosophy is well represented here, particularly Advaita Vedanta and older and the lesser known Samkhya philosophy. Yet aspects of these, such as Vedanta's inability to say much about the origin of evil and illusion, the tendency of nondualists to lapse into a kind of dualism (I/illusion), and the philosophical inconsistency and lack of empirical basis that we find in the concept of karma. This is not a debunking. He finds value in all of these ideas but equally finds them lacking once they are examined in depth.

Since consciousness distinguishes between self and other, this leads Smoley to an extraordinarily elegant way of distinguishing between two modes of perceiving God. God as self is the I that is uncovered in meditation or in mystical or transcendent states. God as other is the external God familiar from mainstream Christianity. This is a terrific way of not throwing out the theistic baby with the bathwater. Whatever God may be, it is greater than the little spark of divinity we have within us.

Andrew Phillip Smith

The Thunder: Perfect Mind: A New Translation and Introduction [Hal Taussig, Jared Calaway, Maia Kotrosits, Celene Lillie, Justin Lasser. Palgrave Macmillan, Hardcover, 202pp. $80.

Though it is, after the *Gospel of Thomas* and perhaps the *Gospel of Philip*, the most popular and well-liked of the Nag Hammadi writings, *Thunder: Perfect Mind* has never had an entire volume devoted to it in English, though there has been an academic book in German. The plaintive yet assertive voice of the narrator is familiar in such paradoxical statements as "I am the midwife and she who hasn't given birth . . . I am the bride and the bridegroom, and it is my husband who gave birth to me." This distinct female voice has influenced Umberto Eco, Toni Morrison, the 1991 movie *Daughters of the Dust* and forms the narration of a short film by Jordan and Ridley Scott used as an advert for Pravda. Though they mention some uses of it in music, they omit the album *Thunder: Perfect Mind* by David Tibet's Current 93 (see *The Gnostic* 3 for an interview with David that explores this.)

Written by a team of scholars who studied the text in 2007 at Union Theological Seminary, this new work takes a somewhat postmodern view, analysing *Thunder* principally in terms of gender, power and authority and the general social context of the ancient world. Contemporary reactions to *Thunder* are also featured. The writers reject a Gnostic interpretation, drawing on the work of Karen King, and remain unconvinced by efforts, such as those of Marvin Meyer, to identify the speaker as the Sethian divine mother Barbelo, or as Sophia.

Though they are reluctant to assign any specific background to the text, given the lack of any certain reference points, they are inclined to give it an Egyptian setting. *Thunder* may have originated as a work in Greek, but as we have it is very much at home in Coptic. It contains in verbal devices such as alliteration and occasional rhyme that cannot be translated back into Greek or satisfactorily indicated in English translation. Or at least not in their academic English translation. It would be easy enough to orchestrate similar effects in English but at the cost of other aspects of translation. As a correlation they believe *Thunder* may well have been performed.

One of the most interesting results of the authors' focus on gender is the identity of the "I" who speaks in Thunder. Coptic is a highly gendered language with no neuter. The first person singular, simply "I" in English is also gendered. The female for "I am" is *anok te*,

the male *anok pe*, and a genderless *anok* is sometimes used. Though all other translations give the impression of a consistent speaker, in the Coptic the speaker is usually female (*te*) but sometimes male (*pe*). The translators render these as "I am she who" and "I am he who." Thus it is shocking to go from "I am the whore and the holy woman/I am the wife and the virgin" to "I am he the mother and the daughter." In the last case the subject is suddenly masculine even though the referent figures are obviously feminine. Taussig et al interpret this as a disorienting focus on gender. While one or two of these might plausibly be scribal errors, on the whole the gender-switching must be an intentional feature of the text. Other features of the translation occasionally shock, such as "Do not stare at me in the shit pile, leaving me discarded." The authors emphasise the violence of the text. They also see the last few lines as an ascetic Christian interpretation, though this doesn't mean that *Thunder* couldn't have been a Christian work at inception.

This book gives some unusual insight into a familiar work. The lack of concrete historical investigation can be frustrating, and the repetition and assertive tone can be a little wearying, but anyone who is interested in scraping the surface of *Thunder* is well advised to purchase this. In any case, it has little competition.

Andrew Phillip Smith

Jesus the Sorcerer. Mandrake, Paperback, 320pp. £12.99/$26. *Magic in the New Testament.* Mandrake, Paperback, 356pp. £12.99/$23.

Continuing work begun by Morton Smith and a handful of others, Robert Conner argues convincingly that many of the familiar elements of the actions and sayings of Jesus, and other relevant material, have a strong resemblance to ancient magic. Christians have always asserted, what others do is magic, but what Jesus did was ordained by God, but in these two books Conner seeks to dissolve the arbitrary boundaries between magic and miracle. H explains, "when a term like sorcery is used, it basically means something like 'religion that works.'" p.98.

I found the initial third of *Jesus the Sorcerer* a little unsatisfying. It introduces the reader to the background of historical Jesus research, drawing on fairly recent mainstream attempts such as those of E.P. Sanders, Dominic Crossan and Bart Ehrman. To be sure, Conner pulls out some interesting stuff from these fairly standard works—Crossan, who I hadn't read in several years—is shown to be very perceptive and open-minded. But since I went on an historical Jesus binge about ten years ago, and still haven't quite recovered my appetite, I found the overview a little long and over-familiar. In line with many of these scholars, Conner sees Jesus as apocalyptic.

Jesus' magical practices take many forms. The miracles are shown to often have the step-by-step procedures typical of spells. Jesus' control of demons is typical of a sorcerer and exorcist, even to the use of such technical terms as "binding" and "loosing". The references to various kinds of spirits and to spirit-possession also fit in well with forms of magic in the ancient world. Exorcism is of course practised in charismatic churches today, and of course Christian exorcists will vehemently deny that they are practising anything remotely similar to magic. Conner spends a couple of chapters on the disputed *Secret Gospel of Mark*. He believes it authentic and constructs an ingenious scenario in which the young man is Lazarus.

Conner makes it clear that he dislikes Christianity. Certainly Christianity deserves some bashing—it has bashed, and continues to bash, other religions and perceived competitors enough over the centuries. But Conner's dislike does give the book a slightly sour tone. If Jesus was a failed apocalyptic, then he was just like other failed apocalyptics. A point well made. I would almost have found the book more enjoyable if Conner's opposition to Christianity had been more intense and passionate. As it is, it is a slow-burning antipathy. This is not to suggest that Conner's focus on magic is untended to discredit Christianity. I feel sure that he has simply seen the resemblances and recognised that much of scholarship, which is historically theologically biased, is dishonest in not admitting them and ignoring them.

The second book surveys magic in (and beyond) the New Testament as a whole. Jesus of course still takes pride of place but this broader viewpoint includes Paul and other material. The widespread and intentional ignorance of scholars with regard to magic is highlighted early on, as he mentions two Jewish scholars who covered the manuscripts discovered in the Cairo genizah, a synagogue storeroom. Though their coverage of the other material was thorough, they sifted out the many magical texts, set them aside and treated them as if they didn't exist.

It might be said that Conner never gives Jesus or Christianity the benefit of the doubt—and why should he? Thus familiar aspects of the life of Jesus are seen in a startling new light. The raising of Lazarus is necromancy. The resurrection has much in common with ancient ghost stories. Jesus' prophecy of the destruction of the temple is seen instead as a curse—but didn't Jesus curse the fig tree and cause it to wither?

Such practices as the celibacy of Paul, and perhaps Jesus, he suggests, are in line with techniques of magical purification. Conner remains suspicious of Jesus' sexual orientation, while emphasising that homosexuality is a normal human variation. A chapter is devoted to the magical background of Palestine, including magical practices in the Old testament.

He touches on what I have always considered the worst episode in the New Testament: Peter's striking dead of Ananias and Sapphira, two Christians who have been dipping into the communal pot (Acts 5.) Here I was actually surprised that Conner spent so little time on what, even if magic is forced out of the equation, is clearly an evil miracle.

Among the many fascinating details is the following from Julian the Apostate, the fourth century Roman emperor who briefly restored a synthetic pagan religion to the Empire: "I will point out that Jesus the Nazarene, and Paul also, outdid in every respect all the sorcerers and tricksters." (p.224.) Beyond the first century, the extensive Christian magical papyri and the cult of saints' lives show that magic continued as a Christian practice. He also teases out the extensive resemblances between Christianity and the mystery cults. He concludes, "The New Testament is a book of magic. *Christian* magic, it is true, but magic all the same." (p. 324.)

These are uncomfortable books. The message they convey is not merely that early Christianity was riddled with magic, from which we have been diverted by special pleading, but that it was frequently a nasty form of magic. Those of us who are more or less sympathetic to Christianity may find this distasteful But the evidence should not be ignored.

Andrew Phillip Smith

The Secret of 2012 and a New World Age: Understanding Fractal Time. Greg Braden. Hay House. Paperback. 323pp. £8.99.

I have to confess to being less than thrilled with all the excitement surrounding 2012. I expect Mayan time cycles to have no more—and indeed less-effect on me than did the recent arrival of the western millennium. Possibly the most lasting legacy of the latter is that we all now know that there are two "n"s in millennium. However, the subject of time itself, and its physical, cultural, biological and spiritual components has long fascinated me.

Braden links 2012 and the Mayan time cycles with the concept of fractal time. Fractal geometry exhibits self-similarity on different scales, as shown most clearly by natural phenomena such as fern leaves or, less regularly, clouds, and by those beautiful compouter images, such as the Mandelbrot Set, which can be produced by iterating through relatively simple euations.

The application of fractal theory to time originated with Terrence McKenna. Quiet apart from the theories of Braden and McKenna, our lives are organised culturall, cosmically and biologically on a fractal basis. Our days repeat basic patterns of sleep, meals, work time, leisure time and so on. Our weeks, through their structure has an entirely cultural foundation, are self-similar, and the pattern of the year is determined by the repetition of the seasons accompanied by biological and cultural patterns.

However, this is not quite was is meant by fractal time. It is the more elusive patterns and cycles that concern the author—cycles of war, of the rise of fall of economies and personal cycles of romance, opportunity and prosperity. These, according to Braden, repeat in predictable wave cycles. He provides a "time code calculator" (available online at http://www.gregbraden.com) to identify and predict one's own cycles. In addition to the Mayan calendar, Braden describes the zodiacal precession of the equinoxes, the Bible code and vedantic yuga cycles.

The ideas are in potential fasctinating. The author attempts to buttress his views with scientific argyument and reference. Personally I found the science a bit vague and btroadly painted and over-interpreted. His approach is optimistic, allowing for a spiritual, heart-based transformation of mankind to circumvent natural disaster.

Arthur Craddock

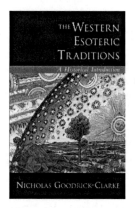

The Western Esoteric Traditions. Nicholas Goodrick-Clarke. Oxford University Press. Hardback. 286pp. $29.95/£19.99

Nicholas Goodrick-Clarke is professor of Western Esotericism at the University of Exeter and as such he is a pioneer in the mainstream academic study of the European and hence North American esoteric and occult streams.

The Western Esoteric Traditions is a broad introduction to and summary of the historical study of a wide variety of spiritual enterprises from Hermetism, Neoplatonism and, briefly, gnosticism up to the varieties of esoterticism on display in the wentieth century. It is quite readable, if necessarily a little dry in places. Each chapter is followed by a list of recommended further reading. Its scholarly nature means that it is thorough, conservative and very well-referenced, but of course there is little commentary on the human or objective value of all these approaches to the world.

As a history of western esotericism it really does deliver the goods. Everything is here: hermetism and Neoplatonism, Renaissance magic, Christian and occult kabbalah, alchemy, Rosicrucianism, Freemasonry, mesmerism, spiritualism, Theosophy, Gurdjieff, esoteric Jungianism and the influence of science (or pseudoscience.) All the major individual figures are well-represented, including Boehme, Paracelsus, Swedenborg (who perhaps disproportionately merits an entire chapter) on to Blavatsky et al.

The introduction reviews attempts to define esotericism. This is a fine epitome of historical esotericsm and a starting point for further research.

Andrew Phillip Smith

Food for Thought

Your head's like mine, like all our heads; big enough to contain every god and devil there ever was. Big enough to hold the weight of oceans and the turning stars. Whole universes fit in there! But what do we choose to keep in this miraculous cabinet? Little broken things, sad trinkets that we play with over and over. The world turns our key and we play the same little tune again and again and we think that tune's all we are.

Grant Morrison

"Choosing the lesser of two evils isn't a bad thing. The cliché makes it sound bad but it's a good thing. You get less evil."

Noam Chomsky

Call the world if you Please "The vale of Soul-making." Then you will find out the use of the world . . . I say "Soul-making" Soul as distinguished from an Intelligence—There may be intelligences or sparks of the divinity in millions—but they are not Souls till they acquire identities, till each one is personally itself. . . . Do you not see how necessary a World of Pains and troubles is to school an Intelligence and make it a Soul? . . . Seriously I think it probable that this System of Soul-making—may have been the Parent of all the more palpable and personal Schemes of Redemption, among the Zoroastrians the Christians and the Hindoos.

John Keats

I distinguish remorse from regret in that remorse is sorrow for what one *did* do whereas regret is misery for what one did *not* do.

Christopher Hitchens

Lucifer tempted the human being and the human being fell into temptation. Lucifer as a black magician wears a bloody colored tunic and covers his head with a red cap like the Bons and the Drukpas from oriental Tibet. The lustful forces of the Luciferians awoke animal passion within human beings; then men and women started to ejaculate their semen. This is the cause for which the Lemurian tribes were expelled from the temples.

Samael Aun Weor

Each of us has a divine counterpart unfallen who can reach a hand down to us to awaken us. This other personality is the authentic waking self; the one we have now is asleep and minor. We are in fact asleep, and in the hands of a dangerous magician disguised as a good god, the deranged creator deity. The bleakness, the evil and pain in this world, the fact that it is a deterministic prison controlled by the demented creator causes us willingly to split with the reality principle early in life, and so to speak willingly fall asleep in delusion.

Philip K. Dick

Biographies

Laurence Caruana graduated from the University of Toronto with a degree in Philosophy, and then studied painting at die Akademie der Bildenden Künste in Vienna. He now lives in France. His paintings are inspired by memories and dreams, experiments with entheogens, and the interplay of different cultural symbols and styles. He is also author of *The Hidden Passion: A Novel of the Gnostic Christ, Based on the Nag Hammadi Texts, Enter Through the Image: The Ancient Image-Language of Myth, Art and Dreams* and *A Manifesto of Visionary Art*.

Miguel Conner is the author of the novel *Stargazer* and host of the Internet radio show *Aeon Byte*, formerly *Coffee, Cigarettes and Gnosis*. Voices of Gnosticism, a selection of his interviews with scholars of Gnosticism is available from Bardic Press.

Arthur Craddock has rehearsed Gnostic sacraments for 15 years but has never carried out a real one. His libertarian Gnostic western novel *Gun Control and the Demiurge* is currently out of print. We apologise for referring to Arthur as Alan Craddock in issue 2, and for not crediting him at all in issue 3.

Bill Darlison has recently retired as the senior minister of Dublin Unitarian Church. He trained in Rome for the Catholic priesthood, but left before ordination and became a Unitarian in 1988. He has been a student of astrology for over forty years and is interested in the influence of astrology on early Christian thought and practice. He is the author of *The Gospel and the Zodiac: The Secret Truth about Jesus*, and *The Shortest Distance: 101 Stories from the World's Spiritual Traditions*.

Michael Grenfell is Professor at Trinity College, Dublin. As an academic, his interests are in language, education and philosophy of education. He was a founder member of the Blake Society at St James in Piccadilly, London and served on their committee for a number of years. He is the author of some twelve books and numerous articles. He has a longstanding interest in Gnosis, Gnosticism, and related arts, literature and philosophies.

Sean Martin is a writer and filmmaker. His books include *The Knights Templar. The Cathars, Andrei Tarkovsky, The Gnostics: The First Christian Heretics, Alchemy and Alchemists* and *The Black Death*. Among his films are *Mystery Play* (2001), *The Notebooks of Cornelius Crow* (2005)

Alan Moore is the author of *Voice of the Fire* and writer of numerous comics and graphics novels including *Watchmen, V for Vendetta, From Hell, A Small Killing, Lost Girls, The League of Extraordinary Gentleman* and *Promethea*,

Petra Mundik currently holds the prestigious Prescott Postgraduate Scholarship in the School of Social and Cultural Studies at the University of Western Australia. She has published extensively on Cormac McCarthy.

Samer Muscati is a documentary photographer, lawyer and former journalist who has worked in Rwanda, Iraq and East Timor in the fields of human rights and development. His photographs have been published in Time Magazine and other publications in North America and Europe. He is currently based out of New York working for Human Rights Watch as a researcher for their Middle East and North Africa division.

Anthony Peake is the author of two internationally acclaimed books, *Is There Life After Death—The Extraordinary Science of What Happens When You Die* and *The Daemon, A Guide To Your Extraordinary Self*. These books have been translated into various foreign languages including Spanish, Russian and Dutch.

In November 2011 his new book Astral Travel: The History and Science of Out-of-The Body Experiences (Watkins Books) will present his new model of consciousness that is suggested within this article. He is also working with a group of Austrian neurologists and psychologists to find a workable way of accessing the "Pleroma" from within the "Black Iron Prison".

He has a very active international Forum where the implications of his Cheating The Ferryman hypothesis is discussed and debated. This can be found at www.anthonypeake.com/forum

Robert M. Price is Professor of Biblical Criticism at the Center for Inquiry Institute as well as the editor of *The Journal of Higher Criticism*. His books include *Beyond Born Again, The Widow Traditions in Luke-Acts: A Feminist-Critical Scrutiny, Deconstructing Jesus,* and *The Incredible Shrinking Son of Man*.

Jeremy Puma has been a student of Gnosticism for over 15 years. He is one of the founding members of the Palm Tree Garden Gnostic community, an online collective of Gnostics from many different traditions, and the Gnostic Order of Allogenes, a collective of independent Gnostic practitioners. Jeremy is the author of a number of books on the theory and practice of Gnosticism in the twenty-first century, all of which can be found online at www.lulu.com/eleleth. He currently maintains two websites at waygnostic.wordpress.com and gnostichealing.wordpress.com. Jeremy lives in Seattle, WA with a lovely lady and two brown dogs.

Andrew Phillip Smith is the editor of *The Gnostic* and author of *A Dictionary of Gnosticism, The Gnostics: History, Tradition, Scriptures, Influence, The Gospel of Philip: Annotated & Explained, The Lost Sayings of Jesus: Annotated & Explained,* and *Gnostic Writings on the Soul: Annotated & Explained*. His skin is as white as a winter moon. He regularly plucks the few grey hairs out of his reddish beard. When his eyes catch the light they sparkle gratuitously. Oh for the days when he had a full head of hair! If you stand close enough you can hear him breathe.

Also Available from Bardic Press

The Gnostic 1 & The Gnostic 2 & The Gnostic 3

Voices of Gnosticism
Miguel Conner

Boyhood With Gurdjieff; Gurdjieff Remembered; Balanced Man
by Fritz Peters (not available in the USA)

New Nightingale, New Rose: Poems From the Divan of Hafiz
translated by Richard Le Gallienne

The Quatrains of Omar Khayyam:
Three Translations of the Rubaiyat
translated by Edward Fitzgerald, Justin McCarthy
and Richard Le Gallienne

Door of the Beloved: Ghazals of Hafiz
translated by Justin McCarthy

The Gospel of Thomas and Christian Wisdom
Stevan Davies

The Four Branches of the Mabinogi
Will Parker

Christ In Islam
James Robson

Don't Forget: P.D. Ouspensky's Life of Self-Remembering
Bob Hunter

Songs of Sorrow and Joy
Ashford Brown

Planetary Types: The Science of Celestial Influence
Tony Cartledge

Visit our website at www.bardic-press.com
email us at info@bardic-press.com

Lightning Source UK Ltd.
Milton Keynes UK
UKOW041837291111

182882UK00008B/73/P

9 781906 834067